Mastering Oracle SQL

Sanjay Mishra and Alan Beaulieu

Beijing · Cambridge · Farnham · Köln · Paris · Sebastopol · Taipei · Tokyo

Mastering Oracle SQL

by Sanjay Mishra and Alan Beaulieu

Published by O'Reilly & Associates, Inc., 1005 Gravenstein Highway North, Sebastopol, CA 95472.

O'Reilly & Associates books may be purchased for educational, business, or sales promotional use. Online editions are also available for most titles (*safari.oreilly.com*). For more information contact our corporate/institutional sales department: (800) 998-9938 or *corporate@oreilly.com*.

Editor:	Jonathan Gennick
Production Editor:	Colleen Gorman
Cover Designers:	Ellie Volckhausen and Emma Colby
Interior Designer:	David Futato

Printing History:

April 2002:   First Edition.

ISBN: 0-596-00129-0
[M]   [7/02]

I dedicate this book to my father.
I wish he were alive to see this book.

—Sanjay Mishra

To my daughters, Michelle and Nicole.

—Alan Beaulieu

Table of Contents

Preface

SQL, which stands for Structured Query Language, is the language for accessing a relational database. SQL provides a set of statements for storing and retrieving data to and from a relational database. It has gained steadily in popularity ever since the first relational database was unleashed upon the world. Other languages have been put forth, but SQL is now accepted as the standard language for almost all relational database implementations, including Oracle.

SQL is different from other programming languages because it is nonprocedural. Unlike programs in other languages, where you specify the sequence of steps to be performed, a SQL program (more appropriately called a SQL statement) only expresses the desired result. The responsibility for determining how the data will be processed in order to generate the desired result is left to the database management system. The nonprocedural nature of SQL makes it easier to access data in application programs.

If you are using an Oracle database, SQL is the interface you use to access the data stored in your database. SQL allows you to create database structures such as tables (to store your data), views, and indexes. SQL allows you to insert data into the database, and to retrieve that stored data in a desired format (for example, you might sort it). Finally, SQL allows you to modify, delete, and otherwise manipulate your stored data. SQL is the key to everything you do with the database. It's important to know how to get the most out of that interface. Mastery over the SQL language is one of the most vital requirements of a database developer or database administrator.

Why We Wrote This Book

Our motivation for writing this book stems from our own experiences learning how to use the Oracle database and Oracle's implementation of the SQL language. Oracle's SQL documentation consists of a reference manual that doesn't go into details about the practical usefulness of the various SQL features that Oracle supports. Nor does the manual present complex, real-life examples.

When we looked for help with SQL in the computer book market, we found that there are really two types of SQL books available. Most are the reference type that describe features and syntax, but that don't tell you how to apply that knowledge to real-life problems. The other type of book, very few in number, discusses the application of SQL in a dry and theoretical style without using any particular vendor's implementation. Since every database vendor implements their own variation of SQL, we find books based on "standard" SQL to be of limited usefulness.

In writing this book, we decided to write a practical book focused squarely on Oracle's version of SQL. Oracle is the market-leading database, and it's also the database on which we've honed our SQL expertise. In this book, we not only cover the most important and useful of Oracle's SQL features, but we show ways to apply them to solve specific problems.

Objectives of This Book

The single most important objective of this book is to help you harness the power of Oracle SQL to the maximum extent possible. You will learn to:

- Understand the features and capabilities of the SQL language, as implemented by Oracle.
- Use complex SQL features such as outer joins, correlated subqueries, hierarchical queries, grouping operations, analytical queries, etc.
- Use DECODE and CASE to implement conditional logic in your SQL queries.
- Write SQL statements that operate against partitions, objects, and collections such as nested tables and variable arrays.
- Use the new SQL features introduced in Oracle9i, such as new date and time features, ANSI-compliant joins, and new grouping and analytical functions.
- Use best practices to write efficient, maintainable SQL queries.

Audience for This Book

This book is for Oracle developers and database administrators. Whether you are new to the world of databases or a seasoned professional, if you use SQL to access an Oracle database, this book is for you. Whether you use simple queries to access data or embed them in PL/SQL or Java programs, SQL is the core of all data access tasks in your application. Knowing the power and flexibility of SQL will improve your productivity, allowing you to get more done in less time, and with increased certainty that the SQL statements you write are indeed correct.

Platform and Version

We used Oracle8*i* (releases 8.1.6 and 8.1.7) and Oracle9*i* (release 9.0.1) in this book. We've covered many of Oracle9*i*'s important new SQL features, including ANSI-standard join syntax, new time/date datatypes, and various analytical functions. Most of the concepts, syntax, and examples apply to earlier releases of Oracle as well. We specifically point out the new Oracle9*i* features.

Structure of This Book

This book is divided into 14 chapters:

- Chapter 1, *Introduction to SQL*, introduces the SQL language and describes its brief history. This chapter is primarily for those readers who have little or no prior SQL experience. You'll find simple examples of the core SQL statements (SELECT, INSERT, UPDATE, and DELETE) and of SQL's basic features.

- Chapter 2, *The WHERE Clause*, describes ways to filter data in your SQL statements. You'll learn to restrict the results of a query to the rows you wish to see, and restrict the results of a data manipulation statement to the rows you wish to modify.

- Chapter 3, *Joins*, describes constructs used to access data from multiple, related tables. The important concepts of inner join and outer join are discussed in this chapter. The new ANSI-compliant join syntax introduced in Oracle9*i* is also discussed.

- Chapter 4, *Group Operations*, shows you how to generate summary information, such as totals and subtotals, from your data. Learn how to define groups of rows, and how to apply various aggregate functions to summarize data in those groups.

- Chapter 5, *Subqueries*, shows you how to use correlated and noncorrelated subqueries and inline views to solve complex problems that would otherwise require procedural code together with more than one query.

- Chapter 6, *Handling Temporal Data*, talks about handling date and time information in an Oracle database. Learn the tricks and traps of querying time-based data. Also learn about Oracle9*i*'s many new date and time datatypes.

- Chapter 7, *Set Operations*, shows you how to use UNION, INTERSECT, and MINUS to combine results from two or more independent component queries into one.

- Chapter 8, *Hierarchical Queries*, shows you how to store and extract hierarchical information (such as in an organizational chart) from a relational table. Oracle provides several features to facilitate working with hierarchical data.

- Chapter 9, *DECODE and CASE*, talks about two very powerful yet simple features of Oracle SQL that enable you to simulate conditional logic in what is otherwise a declarative language. CASE, an ANSI standard construct, was first introduced in Oracle8*i*, and was enhanced in Oracle9*i*.

- Chapter 10, *Partitions, Objects, and Collections*, discusses the issues involved with accessing partitions and collections using SQL. Learn to write SQL statements that operate on specific partitions and subpartitions. Also learn to query object data, nested tables, and variable arrays.

- Chapter 11, *PL/SQL*, explores the integration of SQL and PL/SQL. This chapter describes how to call PL/SQL stored procedures and functions from SQL statements, and how to write efficient SQL statements within PL/SQL programs.

- Chapter 12, *Advanced Group Operations*, deals with complex grouping operations used mostly in decision support systems. We show you how to use Oracle features such as ROLLUP, CUBE, and GROUPING SETS to efficiently generate various levels of summary information required by decision support applications. We also discuss the new Oracle9*i* grouping features that enable composite and concatenated groupings, and the new GROUP_ID and GROUPING_ID functions.

- Chapter 13, *Advanced Analytic SQL*, deals with analytical queries and new analytic functions. Learn how to use ranking, windowing, and reporting functions to generate decision support information. This chapter also covers the new analytic features introduced in Oracle9*i*.

- Chapter 14, *SQL Best Practices*, talks about best practices that you should follow in order to write efficient and maintainable queries. Learn which SQL constructs are the most efficient for a given situation. For example, we describe when it's better to use WHERE instead of HAVING to restrict query results. We also discuss the performance implications of using bind variables vis-à-vis literal SQL.

Conventions Used in This Book

The following typographical conventions are used in this book.

Italic
> Used for filenames, directory names, table names, field names, and URLs. It is also used for emphasis and for the first use of a technical term.

`Constant width`
> Used for examples and to show the contents of files and the output of commands.

`Constant width italic`
> Used in syntax descriptions to indicate user-defined items.

Constant width bold

Indicates user input in examples showing an interaction. Also indicates emphasized code elements to which you should pay particular attention.

Constant width bold italic

Used in code examples to emphasize aspects of the SQL statements, or results, that are under discussion.

UPPERCASE

In syntax descriptions, indicates keywords.

lowercase

In syntax descriptions, indicates user-defined items such as variables.

[ ]

In syntax descriptions, square brackets enclose optional items.

{ }

In syntax descriptions, curly brackets enclose a set of items from which you must choose only one.

|

In syntax descriptions, a vertical bar separates the items enclosed in curly brackets, as in {TRUE | FALSE}.

...

In syntax descriptions, ellipses indicate repeating elements.

Indicates a tip, suggestion, or general note. For example, we use notes to point you to useful new features in Oracle9i.

Indicates a warning or caution. For example, we'll tell you if a certain SQL clause might have unintended consequences if not used carefully.

Comments and Questions

We have tested and verified the information in this book to the best of our ability, but you may find that features have changed or that we have made mistakes. If so, please notify us by writing to:

O'Reilly & Associates
1005 Gravenstein Highway North
Sebastopol, CA 95472
(800) 998-9938 (in the United States or Canada)
(707) 829-0515 (international or local)
(707) 829-0104 (FAX)

You can also send messages electronically. To be put on the mailing list or request a catalog, send email to:

info@oreilly.com

To ask technical questions or comment on the book, send email to:

bookquestions@oreilly.com

We have a web site for this book, where you can find examples and errata (previously reported errors and corrections are available for public view there). You can access this page at:

http://www.oreilly.com/catalog/mastorasql

For more information about this book and others, see the O'Reilly web site:

http://www.oreilly.com

Acknowledgments

We are indebted to a great many people who have contributed in the development and production of this book. We owe a huge debt of gratitude to Jonathan Gennick, the editor of the book. Jonathan's vision for this book, close attention to details, and exceptional editing skills are the reasons this book is here today.

Our sincere thanks to our technical reviewers: Diana Lorentz, Jeff Cox, Stephan Andert, Rich White, Peter Linsley, and Chris Lee, who generously gave their valuable time to read and comment on a draft copy of this book. Their contributions have greatly improved its accuracy, readability, and value.

This book certainly would not have been possible without a lot of hard work and support from the skillful staff at O'Reilly & Associates, including Ellie Volckhausen and Emma Colby, the cover designers, David Futato, the interior designer, Neil Walls, who converted the files, Colleen Gorman, the copyeditor and production editor, Rob Romano and Jessamyn Read, the illustrators, Sheryl Avruch and Ann Schirmer, who provided quality control, and Tom Dinse, the indexer. Also, thanks to Tim O'Reilly for taking time to go through this book and providing valuable feedback.

From Sanjay

My heartfelt thanks to my coauthor Alan for his outstanding technical skills, and for his constant cooperation during the writing of this book. Special thanks to Jonathan for not only editing this book, but also for providing me with remote access to his Oracle9*i* database.

My adventure with Oracle started in the Tribology Workbench project at Tata Steel, Jamshedpur, India. Sincere thanks to my co-workers in the Tribology Workbench project for all the experiments and explorations we did during our learning days with Oracle. Special thanks to Sarosh Muncherji, the Deputy Team Leader, for picking me up for the project and then pushing me into the Oracle world by assigning me the responsibility of being the DBA. Ever since, Oracle database technology has become a way of life for me.

Sincere thanks to my co-workers at i2 Technologies for support and encouragement.

Last, but not the least, I thank my wife, Sudipti, for her support, understanding, and constant encouragement.

From Alan

I would like to thank my coauthor Sanjay and my editor Jonathan Gennick for sharing my vision for this book, and for their technical and editorial prowess. I would never have reached the finish line without your help and encouragement.

Most of all, I would like to thank my wife, Nancy, for her support, patience, and encouragement, and my daughters, Michelle and Nicole, for their love and inspiration.

CHAPTER 1

Introduction to SQL

In this introductory chapter, we explore the origin and utility of the SQL language, demonstrate some of the more useful features of the language, and define a simple database design from which most examples in the book are derived.

What Is SQL?

SQL, which stands for Structured Query Language, is a special-purpose language used to define, access, and manipulate data. SQL is *nonprocedural*, meaning that it describes the necessary components (i.e., tables) and desired results without dictating exactly how results should be computed. Every SQL implementation sits atop a *database engine*, whose job it is to interpret SQL statements and determine how the various data structures in the database should be accessed in order to accurately and efficiently produce the desired outcome.

The SQL language includes two distinct sets of commands: *Data Definition Language* (DDL) is the subset of SQL used to define and modify various data structures, while *Data Manipulation Language* (DML) is the subset of SQL used to access and manipulate data contained within the data structures previously defined via DDL. DDL includes numerous commands for handling such tasks as creating tables, indexes, views, and constraints, while DML is comprised of just four statements:

INSERT
> Adds data to a database.

UPDATE
> Modifies data in a database.

DELETE
> Removes data from a database.

SELECT
> Retrieves data from a database.

Some people feel that DDL is the sole property of database administrators, while database developers are responsible for writing DML statements, but the two are not so easily separated. It is difficult to efficiently access and manipulate data without an understanding of what data structures are available and how they are related; likewise, it is difficult to design appropriate data structures without knowledge of how the data will be accessed. That being said, this book deals almost exclusively with DML, except where DDL is presented in order to set the stage for one or more DML examples. The reasons for focusing on just the DML portion of SQL include:

- DDL is well represented in various books on database design and administration as well as in SQL reference guides.

- Most database performance issues are the result of inefficient DML statements.

- Even with a paltry four statements, DML is a rich enough topic to warrant not just one book, but a whole series of books.*

So why should you care about SQL? In this age of Internet computing and n-tier architectures, does anyone even care about data access anymore? Actually, efficient storage and retrieval of information is more important than ever:

- Many companies now offer services via the Internet. During peak hours, these services may need to handle thousands of concurrent requests, and unacceptable response times equate to lost revenue. For such systems, every SQL statement must be carefully crafted to ensure acceptable performance as data volumes increase.

- We can store a lot more data today than we could five years ago. A single disk array can hold tens of terabytes of data, and the ability to store hundreds of terabytes is just around the corner. Software used to load or analyze data in these environments must harness the full power of SQL in order to process ever-increasing data volumes within constant (or shrinking) time windows.

Hopefully, you now have an appreciation for what SQL is and why it is important. The next section will explore the origins of the SQL language and the support for the SQL standard in Oracle's products.

A Brief History of SQL

In the early 1970s, an IBM research fellow named Dr. E. F. Codd endeavored to apply the rigors of mathematics to the then-untamed world of data storage and retrieval. Codd's work led to the definition of the *relational data model* and a language called

---

* Anyone who writes SQL in an Oracle environment should be armed with the following three books: a reference guide to the SQL language, such as *Oracle SQL: The Essential Reference* (O'Reilly), a performance-tuning guide, such as *Oracle SQL Tuning Pocket Reference* (O'Reilly), and the book you are holding, which shows how to best utilize and combine the various features of Oracle's SQL implementation.

DSL/Alpha for manipulating data in a relational database. IBM liked what they saw, so they commissioned a project called System/R to build a prototype based on Codd's work. Among other things, the System/R team developed a simplified version of DSL called SQUARE, which was later renamed SEQUEL, and finally renamed SQL.

The work done on System/R eventually led to the release of various IBM products based on the relational model. Other companies, such as Oracle, rallied around the relational flag as well. By the mid 1980's, SQL had gathered sufficient momentum in the marketplace to warrant oversight by the American National Standards Institute (ANSI). ANSI released its first SQL standard in 1986, followed by updates in 1989, 1992, and 1999.

Thirty years after the System/R team began prototyping a relational database, SQL is still going strong. While there have been numerous attempts to dethrone relational databases in the marketplace, well-designed relational databases coupled with well-written SQL statements continue to succeed in handling large, complex data sets where other methods fail.

Oracle's SQL Implementation

Given that Oracle was an early adopter of the relational model and SQL, one might think that they would have put a great deal of effort into conforming with the various ANSI standards. For many years, however, the folks at Oracle seemed content that their implementation of SQL was functionally equivalent to the ANSI standards without being overly concerned with true compliance. Beginning with the release of Oracle8*i*, however, Oracle has stepped up its efforts to conform to ANSI standards and has tackled such features as the CASE statement and the left/right/full outer join syntax.

Ironically, the business community seems to be moving in the opposite direction. A few years ago, people were much more concerned with portability and would limit their developers to ANSI-compliant SQL so that they could implement their systems on various database engines. Today, companies tend to pick a database engine to use across the enterprise and allow their developers to use the full range of available options without concern for ANSI-compliance. One reason for this change in attitude is the advent of n-tier architectures, where all database access can be contained within a single tier instead of being scattered throughout an application. Another possible reason might be the emergence of clear leaders in the DBMS market over the last five years, such that managers perceive less risk in which database engine they choose.

Theoretical Versus Practical Terminology

If you were to peruse the various writings on the relational model, you would come across terminology that you will not find used in this book (such as *relations* and *tuples*). Instead, we use practical terms such as tables and rows, and we refer to the various parts of an SQL statement by name rather than by function (i.e., "SELECT clause" instead of *projection*). With all due respect to Dr. Codd, you will never hear the word *tuple* used in a business setting, and, since this book is targeted toward people who use Oracle products to solve business problems, you won't find it here either.

A Simple Database

Because this is a practical book, it contains numerous examples. Rather than fabricating different sets of tables and columns for every chapter or section in the book, we have decided to draw from a single, simple schema for most examples. The subject area that we chose to model is a parts distributor, such as an auto-parts wholesaler or medical device distributor, in which the business fills customer orders for one or more parts that are supplied by external suppliers. Figure 1-1 shows the entity-relationship model for this business.

If you are unfamiliar with entity-relationship models, here is a brief description of how they work. Each box in the model represents an *entity*, which correlates to a database table.* The lines between the entities represents the *relationships* between tables, which correlate to foreign keys. For example, the CUST_ORDER table holds a foreign key to the employee table, which signifies the salesperson responsible for a particular order. Physically, this means that the CUST_ORDER table contains a column holding employee ID numbers, and that, for any given order, the employee ID number indicates the employee who sold that order. If you find this confusing, simply use the diagram as an illustration of the tables and columns found within our database. As you work your way through the SQL examples in this book, return occasionally to the diagram, and you should find that the relationships start making sense.

DML Statements

In this section, we introduce the four statements that comprise the DML portion of SQL. The information presented in this section should be enough to allow you to start writing DML statements. As is discussed at the end of the section, however, DML can look deceptively simple, so keep in mind while reading the section that there are many more facets to DML than are discussed here.

---

* Depending on the purpose of the model, entities may or may not correlate to database tables. For example, a *logical* model depicts business entities and their relationships, whereas a *physical* model illustrates tables and their primary/foreign keys. The model in Figure 1-1 is a physical model.

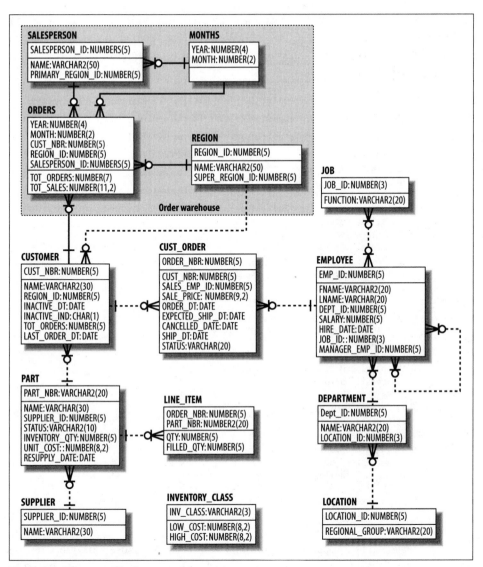

Figure 1-1. The parts distributor model

The SELECT Statement

The SELECT statement is used to retrieve data from a database. The set of data retrieved via a SELECT statement is referred to as a *result set*. Like a table, a result set is comprised of rows and columns, making it possible to populate a table using the result set of a SELECT statement. The SELECT statement can be summarized as follows:

```
SELECT <one or more things>
FROM <one or more places>
WHERE <zero, one, or more conditions apply>
```

While the SELECT and FROM clauses are required, the WHERE clause is optional (although you will seldom see it omitted). We therefore begin with a simple example that retrieves three columns from every row of the customer table:

```
SELECT cust_nbr, name, region_id
FROM customer;
```

```
CUST_NBR NAME                              REGION_ID
-------- -------------------------------- ----------
       1 Cooper Industries                         5
       2 Emblazon Corp.                            5
       3 Ditech Corp.                              5
       4 Flowtech Inc.                             5
       5 Gentech Industries                        5
       6 Spartan Industries                        6
       7 Wallace Labs                              6
       8 Zantech Inc.                              6
       9 Cardinal Technologies                     6
      10 Flowrite Corp.                            6
      11 Glaven Technologies                       7
      12 Johnson Labs                              7
      13 Kimball Corp.                             7
      14 Madden Industries                         7
      15 Turntech Inc.                             7
      16 Paulson Labs                              8
      17 Evans Supply Corp.                        8
      18 Spalding Medical Inc.                     8
      19 Kendall-Taylor Corp.                      8
      20 Malden Labs                               8
      21 Crimson Medical Inc.                      9
      22 Nichols Industries                        9
      23 Owens-Baxter Corp.                        9
      24 Jackson Medical Inc.                      9
      25 Worcester Technologies                    9
      26 Alpha Technologies                       10
      27 Phillips Labs                            10
      28 Jaztech Corp.                            10
      29 Madden-Taylor Inc.                       10
      30 Wallace Industries                       10
```

Since we neglected to impose any conditions via a WHERE clause, our query returns every row from the customer table. If we want to restrict the set of data returned by the query, we could include a WHERE clause with a single condition:

```
SELECT cust_nbr, name, region_id
FROM customer
WHERE region_id = 8;
```

```
CUST_NBR NAME                              REGION_ID
-------- -------------------------------- ----------
      16 Paulson Labs                              8
      17 Evans Supply Corp.                        8
      18 Spalding Medical Inc.                     8
      19 Kendall-Taylor Corp.                      8
      20 Malden Labs                               8
```

Our result set now includes only those customers residing in the region with a region_id of 8. But what if we want to specify a region by name instead of region_id? We could query the region table for a particular name and then query the customer table using the retrieved region_id. Instead of issuing two different queries, however, we could produce the same outcome using a single query by introducing a *join*, as in:

```
SELECT customer.cust_nbr, customer.name, region.name
FROM customer, region
WHERE region.name = 'New England'
  AND region.region_id = customer.region_id;
```

```
CUST_NBR NAME                                  NAME
-------- ------------------------------------  -----------
       1 Cooper Industries                     New England
       2 Emblazon Corp.                        New England
       3 Ditech Corp.                          New England
       4 Flowtech Inc.                         New England
       5 Gentech Industries                    New England
```

Our FROM clause now contains two tables instead of one, and the WHERE clause contains a *join condition* that specifies that the customer and region tables are to be joined using the region_id column found in both tables. Joins and join conditions will be explored in detail in Chapter 3.

Since both the customer and region tables contain a column called *name*, you must specify which table's name column you are interested in. This is done in the previous example by using dot-notation to append the table name in front of each column name. If you would rather not type the full table names, you can assign *table aliases* to each table in the FROM clause and use those aliases instead of the table names in the SELECT and WHERE clauses, as in:

```
SELECT c.cust_nbr, c.name, r.name
FROM customer c, region r
WHERE r.name = `New England'
  AND r.region_id = c.region_id;
```

In this example, we assigned the alias "c" to the customer table and the alias "r" to the region table. Thus, we can use "c." and "r." instead of "customer." and "region." in the SELECT and WHERE clauses.

SELECT clause elements

In the examples thus far, the result sets generated by our queries have contained columns from one or more tables. While most elements in your SELECT clauses will typically be simple column references, a SELECT clause may also include:

- Literal values, such as numbers (1) or strings ('abc')
- Expressions, such as shape.diameter * 3.1415927
- Functions, such as TO_DATE('01-JAN-2002','DD-MON-YYYY')
- Pseudocolumns, such as ROWID, ROWNUM, or LEVEL

While the first three items in this list are fairly straightforward, the last item merits further discussion. Oracle makes available several phantom columns, known as *pseudocolumns*, that do not exist in any tables. Rather, they are values visible during query execution that can be helpful in certain situations.

For example, the pseudocolumn ROWID represents the physical location of a row. This information represents the fastest possible access mechanism. It can be useful if you plan to delete or update a row retrieved via a query. However, you should never store ROWID values in the database, nor should you reference them outside of the transaction in which they are retrieved, since a row's ROWID can change in certain situations, and ROWIDs can be reused after a row has been deleted.

The next example demonstrates each of the different elements from the previous list:

```
SELECT rownum,
  cust_nbr,
  1 multiplier,
  'cust # ' || cust_nbr cust_nbr_str,
  'hello' greeting,
  TO_CHAR(last_order_dt, 'DD-MON-YYYY') last_order
FROM customer;
```

ROWNUM	CUST_NBR	MULTIPLIER	CUST_NBR_STR	GREETING	LAST_ORDER
1	1	1	cust # 1	hello	15-JUN-2000
2	2	1	cust # 2	hello	27-JUN-2000
3	3	1	cust # 3	hello	07-JUL-2000
4	4	1	cust # 4	hello	15-JUL-2000
5	5	1	cust # 5	hello	01-JUN-2000
6	6	1	cust # 6	hello	10-JUN-2000
7	7	1	cust # 7	hello	17-JUN-2000
8	8	1	cust # 8	hello	22-JUN-2000
9	9	1	cust # 9	hello	25-JUN-2000
10	10	1	cust # 10	hello	01-JUN-2000
11	11	1	cust # 11	hello	05-JUN-2000
12	12	1	cust # 12	hello	07-JUN-2000
13	13	1	cust # 13	hello	07-JUN-2000
14	14	1	cust # 14	hello	05-JUN-2000
15	15	1	cust # 15	hello	01-JUN-2000
16	16	1	cust # 16	hello	31-MAY-2000
17	17	1	cust # 17	hello	28-MAY-2000
18	18	1	cust # 18	hello	23-MAY-2000
19	19	1	cust # 19	hello	16-MAY-2000
20	20	1	cust # 20	hello	01-JUN-2000
21	21	1	cust # 21	hello	26-MAY-2000
22	22	1	cust # 22	hello	18-MAY-2000
23	23	1	cust # 23	hello	08-MAY-2000
24	24	1	cust # 24	hello	26-APR-2000
25	25	1	cust # 25	hello	01-JUN-2000
26	26	1	cust # 26	hello	21-MAY-2000
27	27	1	cust # 27	hello	08-MAY-2000
28	28	1	cust # 28	hello	23-APR-2000
29	29	1	cust # 29	hello	06-APR-2000
30	30	1	cust # 30	hello	01-JUN-2000

Interestingly, your SELECT clause is not required to reference columns from any of the tables in the FROM clause. For example, the next query's result set is composed entirely of literals:

```
SELECT 1 num, 'abc' str
FROM customer;
```

```
       NUM STR
---------- ---
         1 abc
         1 abc
         1 abc
         1 abc
         1 abc
         1 abc
         1 abc
         1 abc
         1 abc
         1 abc
         1 abc
         1 abc
         1 abc
         1 abc
         1 abc
         1 abc
         1 abc
         1 abc
         1 abc
         1 abc
         1 abc
         1 abc
         1 abc
         1 abc
         1 abc
         1 abc
         1 abc
         1 abc
         1 abc
         1 abc
```

Since there are 30 rows in the customer table, the query's result set includes 30 identical rows of data.

Ordering your results

In general, there is no guarantee that the result set generated by your query will be in any particular order. If you want your results to be sorted by one or more columns, you can add an ORDER BY clause after the WHERE clause. The following example sorts the results from our New England query by customer name:

```
SELECT c.cust_nbr, c.name, r.name
FROM customer c, region r
WHERE r.name = 'New England'
```

```
        AND r.region_id = c.region_id
ORDER BY c.name;

CUST_NBR NAME                                  NAME
-------- ------------------------------------  -----------
       1 Cooper Industries                     New England
       3 Ditech Corp.                          New England
       2 Emblazon Corp.                        New England
       4 Flowtech Inc.                         New England
       5 Gentech Industries                    New England
```

You may also designate the sort column(s) by their position in the SELECT clause. To sort the previous query by customer number, which is the first column in the SELECT clause, you could issue the following statement:

```
SELECT c.cust_nbr, c.name, r.name
FROM customer c, region r
WHERE r.name = 'New England'
  AND r.region_id = c.region_id
ORDER BY 1;

   CUST_NBR NAME                                 NAME
   -------- ------------------------------------  -----------
          1 Cooper Industries                     New England
          2 Emblazon Corp.                        New England
          3 Ditech Corp.                          New England
          4 Flowtech Inc.                         New England
          5 Gentech Industries                    New England
```

Specifying sort keys by position will certainly save you some typing, but it can often lead to errors if you later change the order of the columns in your SELECT clause.

Removing duplicates

In some cases, your result set may contain duplicate data. For example, if you are compiling a list of parts that were included in last month's orders, the same part number would appear multiple times if more than one order included that part. If you want duplicates removed from your result set, you can include the DISTINCT keyword in your SELECT clause, as in:

```
SELECT DISTINCT li.part_nbr
FROM cust_order co, line_item li
WHERE co.order_dt >= TO_DATE('01-JUL-2001','DD-MON-YYYY')
  AND co.order_dt < TO_DATE('01-AUG-2001','DD-MON-YYYY')
  AND co.order_nbr = li.order_nbr;
```

This query returns the distinct set of parts ordered during July of 2001. Without the DISTINCT keyword, the result set would contain one row for every line-item of every order, and the same part would appear multiple times if it was included in multiple orders. When deciding whether to include DISTINCT in your SELECT clause, keep in mind that finding and removing duplicates necessitates a sort operation, which can add quite a bit of overhead to your query.

The INSERT Statement

The INSERT statement is the mechanism for loading data into your database. Data can be inserted into only one table at a time, although the data being loaded into the table can be pulled from one or more additional tables. When inserting data into a table, you do not need to provide values for every column in the table; however, you need to be aware of the columns that require non-NULL* values and the ones that do not. Let's look at the definition of the employee table:

```
describe employee
```

Name	Null?	Type
EMP_ID	NOT NULL	NUMBER(5)
FNAME		VARCHAR2(20)
LNAME	NOT NULL	VARCHAR2(20)
DEPT_ID	NOT NULL	NUMBER(5)
MANAGER_EMP_ID		NUMBER(5)
SALARY		NUMBER(5)
HIRE_DATE		DATE
JOB_ID		NUMBER(3)

The NOT NULL designation for the emp_id, lname, and dept_id columns indicates that values are required for these three columns. Therefore, we must be sure to provide values for at least these three columns in our INSERT statements, as demonstrated by the following:

```
INSERT INTO employee (emp_id, lname, dept_id)
VALUES (101, 'Smith', 2);
```

The VALUES clause must contain the same number of elements as the column list, and the data types must match the column definitions. In the example, emp_id and dept_id hold numeric values while lname holds character data, so our INSERT statement will execute without error. Oracle always tries to convert data from one type to another automatically, however, so the following statement will also run without errors:

```
INSERT INTO employee (emp_id, lname, dept_id)
VALUES ('101', 'Smith', '2');
```

Sometimes, the data to be inserted needs to be retrieved from one or more tables. Since the SELECT statement generates a result set consisting of rows and columns of data, you can feed the result set from a SELECT statement directly into an INSERT statement, as in:

```
INSERT INTO employee (emp_id, fname, lname, dept_id, hire_date)
SELECT 101, 'Dave', 'Smith', d.dept_id, SYSDATE
FROM department d
WHERE d.name = 'Accounting';
```

---

* NULL indicates the absence of a value. The use of NULL will be studied in Chapter 2.

In this example, the purpose of the SELECT statement is to retrieve the department ID for the Accounting department. The other four columns in the SELECT clause are supplied as literals.

The DELETE Statement

The DELETE statement facilitates the removal of data from the database. Like the SELECT statement, the DELETE statement contains a WHERE clause that specifies the conditions used to identify rows to be deleted. If you neglect to add a WHERE clause to your DELETE statement, all rows will be deleted from the target table. The following statement will delete all employees with the last name of Hooper from the employee table:

```
DELETE FROM employee
WHERE lname = 'Hooper';
```

In some cases, the values needed for one or more of the conditions in your WHERE clause exist in another table. For example, your company may decide to outsource its accounting functions, thereby necessitating the removal of all Accounting personnel from the employee table:

```
DELETE FROM employee
WHERE dept_id =
  (SELECT dept_id
   FROM department
   WHERE name = 'Accounting');
```

The use of the SELECT statement in this example is known as a *subquery* and will be studied in detail in Chapter 5.

The UPDATE Statement

Modifications to existing data are handled by the UPDATE statement. Like the DELETE statement, the UPDATE statement includes a WHERE clause in order to specify which rows should be targeted. The following example shows how you might give a 10% raise to everyone making less than $40,000:

```
UPDATE employee
SET salary = salary * 1.1
WHERE salary < 40000;
```

If you want to modify more than one column in the table, you have two choices: provide a set of column/value pairs separated by commas, or provide a set of columns and a subquery. The following two UPDATE statements modify the inactive_dt and inactive_ind columns in the customer table for any customer who hasn't placed an order in the past year:

```
UPDATE customer
SET inactive_dt = SYSDATE, inactive_ind = 'Y'
WHERE last_order_dt < SYSDATE − 365;
```

```
UPDATE customer
SET (inactive_dt, inactive_ind) =
 (SELECT SYSDATE, 'Y' FROM dual)
WHERE last_order_dt < SYSDATE - 365;
```

The subquery in the second example is a bit forced, since it uses a query against the dual* table to build a result set containing two literals, but it should give you an idea of how you would use a subquery in an UPDATE statement. In later chapters, you will see far more interesting uses for subqueries.

So Why Are There 13 More Chapters?

After reading this chapter, you might think that SQL looks pretty simple (at least the DML portion). At a high level, it is fairly simple, and you now know enough about the language to go write some code. However, you will learn over time that there are numerous ways to arrive at the same end point, and some are more efficient and elegant than others. The true test of SQL mastery is when you no longer have the desire to return to what you were working on the previous year, rip out all the SQL, and recode it. For one of us, it took about nine years to reach that point. Hopefully, this book will help you reach that point in far less time.

While you are reading the rest of the book, you might notice that the majority of examples use SELECT statements, with the remainder somewhat evenly distributed across INSERT, UPDATE, and DELETE statements. This disparity is not indicative of the relative importance of SELECT statements over the other three DML statements; rather, SELECT statements are favored because we can show the query's result set, which should help you to better understand the query, and because many of the points being made using SELECT statements can be applied to UPDATE and DELETE statements as well.

---

* Dual is an Oracle-provided table containing exactly one row with one column. It comes in handy when you need to construct a query that returns exactly one row.

CHAPTER 2

The WHERE Clause

Whether we are querying, modifying, or deleting data, the WHERE clause is the mechanism for identifying the sets of data we want to work with. In this chapter, we explore the role of the WHERE clause in SQL statements, as well as the various options available when building a WHERE clause.

Life Without WHERE

Before we delve into the WHERE clause, let's imagine life without it. Say that you are interested in doing some maintenance on the data in the part table. In order to inspect the data in the table, you issue the following query:

```
SELECT part_nbr, name, supplier_id, status, inventory_qty
FROM part;
```

If the part table contains 10,000 items, the result set returned by the query would consist of 10,000 rows, each with 5 columns. You would then load the 10,000 rows into memory and make your modifications.

Once you have made the required modifications to your data in memory, it is time to apply the changes to the part table. Without the ability to specify the rows to modify, you have no choice but to delete all rows in the table and re-insert all 10,000 rows:

```
DELETE FROM part;

INSERT INTO part (part_nbr, name, supplier_id, status, inventory_qty)
VALUES ('XY5-1002', 'Wonder Widget', 1, 'IN-STOCK', 1);

/* 9,999 more INSERTs on the wall, 9,999 more INSERTS... */
```

While this approach works in theory, it wreaks havoc on performance, concurrency (the ability for more than one user to modify data simultaneously), and scalability.

Now imagine that you want to modify data in the part table only for those parts supplied by Acme Industries. Since the supplier's name is stored in the supplier table, you must include both the part and supplier tables in the FROM clause:

```
SELECT p.part_nbr, p.name, p.supplier_id, p.status, p.inventory_qty,
  s.supplier_id, s.name
FROM part p, supplier s;
```

If 100 companies supply the 10,000 parts in the part table, this query will return 1,000,000 rows. Known as the *Cartesian product*, this number equates to every possible combination of all rows from the two tables. As you sift through the million rows, you would keep only those where the values of p.supplier_id and s.supplier_id are identical and where the s.name column matches 'Acme Industries'. If Acme Industries supplies only 50 of the 10,000 parts in your database, you will end up discarding 999,950 of the 1,000,000 rows returned by your query.

WHERE to the Rescue

Hopefully, these scenarios give you some insight into the utility of the WHERE clause, including the ability to:

1. Filter out unwanted data from a query's result set.
2. Isolate one or more rows of a table for modification.
3. Conditionally join two or more data sets together.

To see how these things are accomplished, let's add a WHERE clause to the previous SELECT statement, which strives to locate all parts supplied by Acme Industries:

```
SELECT p.part_nbr, p.name, p.supplier_id, p.status, p.inventory_qty,
  s.supplier_id, s.name
FROM part p, supplier s
WHERE s.supplier_id = p.supplier_id
  AND s.name = 'Acme Industries';
```

The WHERE clause here is comprised of two parts, known as *conditions*, which are evaluated separately. Conditions always evaluate to either TRUE or FALSE; if there are multiple conditions in a WHERE clause, they all must evaluate to TRUE in order for a given row to be included in the result set.* For this example, a row created by combining data from the part and supplier tables will only be included in the final result set if both tables share a common value for the supplier_id column, and if the value of the name column in the supplier tables matches 'Acme Industries'.† Any other permutation of data from the two tables would evaluate to FALSE and be discarded.

With the addition of the WHERE clause to the previous example, therefore, Oracle will take on the work of discarding undesired rows from the result set, and only 50

---

* This is an oversimplification. As you will see later, using the OR and NOT operators allows the WHERE clause to evaluate to TRUE even if individual conditions evaluate to FALSE.

† Another oversimplification. The Oracle optimizer (the component tasked with finding the most efficient way to execute a query) doesn't first create every possible combination of rows from every table or view in the FROM clause before it begins evaluating conditions. Rather, the optimizer chooses the order in which to evaluate conditions and join data sets so execution time is (hopefully) minimized.

rows will be returned by the query, rather than 1,000,000. Now that you have retrieved the 50 rows of interest from the database, you can begin the process of modifying the data. Keep in mind, however, that with the WHERE clause at your disposal you will no longer need to delete and re-insert your modified data; instead, you can use the UPDATE statement to modify specific rows based on the part_nbr column, which is the unique identifier for the table:

```
UPDATE part
SET status = 'DISCONTINUED'
WHERE part_nbr = 'AI5-4557';
```

While this is certainly an improvement, we can do even better. If your intent is to modify the status for all 50 parts supplied by Acme Industries, there is no need to execute a query at all. Simply execute a single UPDATE statement that finds and modifies all 50 records:

```
UPDATE part
SET status = 'DISCONTINUED'
WHERE supplier_id =
 (SELECT supplier_id
  FROM supplier
  WHERE name = 'Acme Industries');
```

The WHERE clause in this statement consists of a single condition that equates the supplier_id column to the value returned by a query against the supplier table. A query wrapped in parentheses inside another SQL statement is known as a *subquery*; subqueries will be studied extensively in Chapter 5, so don't worry if this looks a bit intimidating. The net result is that the condition will be rewritten to use the value returned by the subquery, as in:

```
UPDATE part
SET status = 'DISCONTINUED'
WHERE supplier_id = 1;
```

When executed, the condition evaluates to TRUE for exactly 50 of the 10,000 rows in the part table, and the status of those 50 rows changes to DISCONTINUED.

WHERE Clause Evaluation

Now that we have seen the WHERE clause in action, let's take a look at how it is evaluated. As we mentioned, the WHERE clause consists of one or more conditions that evaluate independently to TRUE or FALSE. If your WHERE clause consists of multiple conditions, the conditions are separated by the logical operators AND and OR. Depending on the outcome of the individual conditions and the placement of these logical operators, Oracle will assign a final value of TRUE or FALSE to each candidate row, thereby determining whether a row will be included in the final result set.

Let's look at the 'Acme Industries' query again:

```
SELECT p.part_nbr, p.name, p.supplier_id, p.status, p.inventory_qty,
    s.supplier_id, s.name
```

```
FROM part p, supplier s
WHERE s.supplier_id = p.supplier_id
  AND s.name = 'Acme Industries';
```

The WHERE clause consists of two conditions separated by AND. Thus, a row will only be included if both conditions evaluate to TRUE. Table 2-1 shows the possible scenarios when conditions are replaced by their possible outcomes.

Table 2-1. Multiple-condition evaluation using AND

Intermediate result	Final result
WHERE TRUE AND TRUE	TRUE
WHERE FALSE AND FALSE	FALSE
WHERE FALSE AND TRUE	FALSE
WHERE TRUE AND FALSE	FALSE

Using basic logic rules, we can see that the only combination of outcomes that results in a final value of TRUE being assigned to a candidate row is where both conditions evaluate to TRUE. Table 2-2 demonstrates the possible outcomes if our conditions had been separated by OR rather then AND.

Table 2-2. Multiple-condition evaluation using OR

Intermediate result	Final result
WHERE TRUE OR TRUE	TRUE
WHERE FALSE OR FALSE	FALSE
WHERE FALSE OR TRUE	TRUE
WHERE TRUE OR FALSE	TRUE

Next, let's spice our query up a bit by including parts supplied by either Acme Industries or Tilton Enterprises:

```
SELECT p.part_nbr, p.name, p.supplier_id, p.status, p.inventory_qty,
  s.supplier_id, s.name
FROM part p, supplier s
WHERE s.supplier_id = p.supplier_id
  AND (s.name = 'Acme Industries'
    OR s.name = 'Tilton Enterprises');
```

We now have three separate conditions separated by AND and OR with parentheses surrounding two of the conditions. Table 2-3 illustrates the possible outcomes.

Table 2-3. Multiple-condition evaluation using AND and OR

Intermediate result	Final result
WHERE TRUE AND (TRUE OR FALSE)	TRUE
WHERE TRUE AND (FALSE OR TRUE)	TRUE
WHERE TRUE AND (FALSE OR FALSE)	FALSE

Table 2-3. Multiple-condition evaluation using AND and OR (continued)

Intermediate result	Final result
WHERE FALSE AND (TRUE OR FALSE)	FALSE
WHERE FALSE AND (FALSE OR TRUE)	FALSE
WHERE FALSE AND (FALSE OR FALSE)	FALSE

Since a particular part cannot be supplied by both Acme Industries and Tilton Enterprises, the intermediate results TRUE AND (TRUE AND TRUE) and FALSE AND (TRUE AND TRUE) were not included in Table 2-3.

To liven things up even more, we can also throw in the NOT operator. The following query returns data for parts supplied by anyone other than Acme Industries or Tilton Enterprises:

```
SELECT p.part_nbr, p.name, p.supplier_id, p.status, p.inventory_qty,
    s.supplier_id, s.name
FROM part p, supplier s
WHERE s.supplier_id = p.supplier_id
    AND NOT (s.name = 'Acme Industries'
        OR s.name = 'Tilton Enterprises');
```

Table 2-4 demonstrates how the addition of the NOT operator changes the outcome.

Table 2-4. Multiple-condition evaluation using AND, OR, and NOT

Intermediate result	Final result
WHERE TRUE AND NOT (TRUE OR FALSE)	FALSE
WHERE TRUE AND NOT (FALSE OR TRUE)	FALSE
WHERE TRUE AND NOT (FALSE OR FALSE)	TRUE
WHERE FALSE AND NOT (TRUE OR FALSE)	FALSE
WHERE FALSE AND NOT (FALSE OR TRUE)	FALSE
WHERE FALSE AND NOT (FALSE OR FALSE)	FALSE

The use of the NOT operator in the previous example is a bit forced; we will see more natural ways of expressing the same logic in later examples.

Conditions and Expressions

Now that we understand how conditions are grouped together and evaluated, let's look at the different elements that make up a condition. A condition is comprised of one or more *expressions* along with one or more *operators*. Examples of expressions include:

- Numbers
- Columns, such as s.supplier_id

- Literals, such as 'Acme Industries'
- Functions, such as UPPER('abcd')
- Lists of simple expressions, such as (1, 2, 3)
- Subqueries

Examples of operators include:

- Arithmetic operators, such as +, -, *, and /
- Comparison operators, such as =, <, >=, !=, LIKE, and IN

The following sections explore many of the common condition types that use different combinations of the above expression and operator types.

Equality/Inequality Conditions

Most of the conditions that we use when constructing a WHERE clause will be equality conditions used to join data sets together or to isolate specific values. We have already encountered these types of conditions numerous times in previous examples, including:

```
s.supplier_id = p.supplier_id

s.name = 'Acme Industries'

supplier_id = (SELECT supplier_id
    FROM supplier
    WHERE name = 'Acme Industries')
```

In all three cases, we have a column expression followed by a comparison operator (=) followed by another expression. The conditions differ in the type of expression on the right side of the comparison operator. The first example compares one column to another, the second example compares a column to a literal, and the third example compares a column to the value returned by a subquery.

We can also build conditions that use the inequality comparison operator "!=". In a previous example, we used the NOT operator to find information about parts supplied by every supplier other than Acme Industries and Tilton Enterprises. Using the != operator rather than using NOT makes the query easier to understand and removes the need for the OR operator:

```
SELECT p.part_nbr, p.name, p.supplier_id, p.status, p.inventory_qty,
    s.supplier_id, s.name
FROM part p, supplier s
WHERE s.supplier_id = p.supplier_id
    AND s.name != 'Acme Industries'
    AND s.name != 'Tilton Enterprises';
```

While this is an improvement over the previous version, the next section shows an even cleaner way to represent the same logic.

Membership Conditions

Along with determining whether two expressions are identical, it is often useful to determine whether one expression can be found within a set of expressions. Using the IN operator, you can build conditions that will evaluate to TRUE if a given expression exists in a set of expressions:

```
s.name IN ('Acme Industries', 'Tilton Enterprises')
```

You may also add the NOT operator to determine whether an expression does not exist in a set of expressions:

```
s.name NOT IN ('Acme Industries', 'Tilton Enterprises')
```

Most people prefer to use a single condition with IN or NOT IN instead of writing multiple conditions using = or !=, so we will take one last stab at our Acme/Tilton query:

```
SELECT p.part_nbr, p.name, p.supplier_id, p.status, p.inventory_qty,
   s.supplier_id, s.name
FROM part p, supplier s
WHERE s.supplier_id = p.supplier_id
   AND s.name NOT IN ('Acme Industries', 'Tilton Enterprises');
```

Along with prefabricated sets of expressions, subqueries may be employed to generate sets on the fly. If a subquery returns exactly one row, you may use a comparison operator; if a subquery returns more than one row, or if you're not sure whether the subquery might return more than one row, use the IN operator. The following example updates all orders that contain parts supplied by Eastern Importers:

```
UPDATE cust_order
SET sale_price = sale_price *1.1
WHERE cancelled_dt IS NULL
  AND ship_dt IS NULL
  AND order_nbr IN
 (SELECT li.order_nbr
  FROM line_item li,part p, supplier s
  WHERE s.name = 'Eastern Importers'
    AND s.supplier_id = p.supplier_id
    AND p.part_nbr = li.part_nbr);
```

The subquery evaluates to a (potentially empty) set of order numbers. All orders whose order number exists in that set are then modified by the UPDATE statement.

Range Conditions

If you are dealing with dates or numeric data, you may be interested in whether a value falls within a specified range rather than whether it matches a specific value or exists in a finite set. For such cases, you may use the BETWEEN...AND operator, as in:

```
DELETE FROM cust_order
WHERE order_dt BETWEEN '01-JUL-2001' AND '31-JUL-2001';
```

To determine whether a value lies outside a specific range, you can add the NOT operator:

```
SELECT order_nbr, cust_nbr, sale_price
FROM cust_order
WHERE sale_price NOT BETWEEN 1000 AND 10000;
```

When using BETWEEN, make sure the first value is the lowest of the two values provided. While "BETWEEN 1 AND 10" and "BETWEEN 10 AND 1" might seem logically equivalent, specifying the higher value first guarantees that your condition will always evaluate to FALSE.

Ranges may also be specified using the operators <, >, <=, and >=, although doing so requires writing two conditions rather than one. The previous query could also be expressed as:

```
SELECT order_nbr, cust_nbr, sale_price
FROM cust_order
WHERE sale_price < 1000 OR sale_price > 10000;
```

Matching Conditions

When dealing with character data, there are some situations where you are looking for an exact string match, and others where a partial match is sufficient. For the latter case, you can use the LIKE operator along with one or more pattern-matching characters, as in:

```
DELETE FROM part
WHERE part_nbr LIKE 'ABC%';
```

The pattern-matching character "%" matches strings of any length, so all of the following part numbers would be deleted: 'ABC', 'ABC-123', 'ABC9999999'. If you need finer control, you can use the underscore (_) pattern-matching character to match single characters, as in:

```
DELETE FROM part
WHERE part_nbr LIKE '_B_';
```

For this pattern, any part number with exactly 3 characters with a B in the middle would be deleted. Both pattern-matching characters may be utilized in numerous combinations to find the desired data. Additionally, the NOT operator may be employed to find strings that don't match a specified pattern. The following example deletes all parts whose name does not contain a Z in the third position followed later by the string "T1J":

```
DELETE FROM part
WHERE part_nbr NOT LIKE '__Z%T1J%';
```

Oracle provides a slew of built-in functions for handling character data that can be used to build matching conditions. For example, the condition part_nbr LIKE 'ABC%' could be rewritten using the SUBSTR function as SUBSTR(part_nbr, 1, 3) = 'ABC'. For definitions and examples for all of Oracle's built-in functions, see *Oracle SQL: The Essential Reference* (O'Reilly).

Handling NULL

The NULL expression represents the absence of a value. If, when entering an order into the database, you are uncertain when the order will be shipped, it is better to leave the ship date undefined than to fabricate a value. Until the ship date has been determined, therefore, it is best to leave the ship_dt column NULL. NULL is also useful for cases where data is not applicable. For example, a cancelled order's shipping date is no longer applicable and should be set to NULL.

When working with NULL, the concept of equality does not apply; a column may *be* NULL, but it will never *equal* NULL. Therefore, you will need to use the special operator IS when looking for NULL data, as in:

```
UPDATE cust_order
SET expected_ship_dt = SYSDATE + 1
WHERE ship_dt IS NULL;
```

In this example, all orders whose shipping date hasn't been specified will have their expected shipping date bumped forward by one day.

You may also use the NOT operator to locate non-NULL data:

```
UPDATE cust_order
SET expected_ship_dt = NULL
WHERE ship_dt IS NOT NULL;
```

This example sets the expected shipping date to NULL for all orders that have already shipped. Notice that the SET clause uses the equality operator (=) with NULL, whereas the WHERE clause uses the IS and NOT operators. The equality operator is used to set a column to NULL, whereas the IS operator is used to evaluate whether a column is NULL. A great many mistakes might have been avoided had the designers of SQL chosen a special operator to be utilized when setting a column to NULL (i.e., SET expected_ship_dt TO NULL), but this is not the case. To make matters worse, Oracle doesn't complain if you mistakenly use the equality operator when evaluating for NULL. The following query will parse and execute but will never return rows:

```
SELECT order_nbr, cust_nbr, sale_price, order_dt
FROM cust_order
WHERE ship_dt = NULL;
```

Hopefully, you would quickly recognize that the previous query never returns data and replace the equality operator with IS. However, there is a more subtle mistake involving NULL that is harder to spot. Say you are looking for all employees who are not managed by Jeff Blake, whose employee ID is 11. Your first instinct may be to run the following query:

```
SELECT fname, lname, manager_emp_id
FROM employee
WHERE manager_emp_id != 11;
```

```
FNAME                   LNAME                   MANAGER_EMP_ID
--------------------    --------------------    --------------
Alex                    Fox                                 28
Chris                   Anderson                            28
Lynn                    Nichols                             28
Eric                    Iverson                             28
Laura                   Peters                              28
Mark                    Russell                             28
```

While this query returns rows, it leaves out those employees who are top-level managers and, thus, are not managed by anyone. Since NULL is neither equal to 11 nor not equal to 11, this set of employees is absent from the result set. In order to ensure that all employees are considered, you will need to explicitly handle NULL, as in:

```
SELECT fname, lname, manager_emp_id
FROM employee
WHERE manager_emp_id IS NULL OR manager_emp_id != 11;
```

```
FNAME                   LNAME                   MANAGER_EMP_ID
--------------------    --------------------    --------------
Bob                     Brown
John                    Smith
Jeff                    Blake
Alex                    Fox                                 28
Chris                   Anderson                            28
Lynn                    Nichols                             28
Eric                    Iverson                             28
Laura                   Peters                              28
Mark                    Russell                             28
```

Including two conditions for every nullable column in your WHERE clause can get a bit tiresome. Instead, you can use Oracle's built-in function NVL, which substitutes a specified value for columns that are NULL, as in:

```
SELECT fname, lname, manager_emp_id
FROM employee
WHERE NVL(manager_emp_id, -999) != 11;
```

```
FNAME                   LNAME                   MANAGER_EMP_ID
--------------------    --------------------    --------------
Bob                     Brown
John                    Smith
Jeff                    Blake
Alex                    Fox                                 28
Chris                   Anderson                            28
Lynn                    Nichols                             28
Eric                    Iverson                             28
Laura                   Peters                              28
Mark                    Russell                             28
```

In this example, the value -999 is substituted for all NULL values, which, since -999 is never equal to 11, guarantees that all rows whose manager_emp_id column is NULL will be included in the result set. Thus, all employees whose manager_emp_id column is NULL or is *not* NULL and has a value other than 11 will be retrieved by the query.

WHERE to Go from Here

This chapter has introduced the role of the WHERE clause in different types of SQL statements as well as the various components used to build a WHERE clause. Because the WHERE clause plays such an important role in many SQL statements, however, the topic is far from exhausted. Additional coverage of WHERE clause topics may be found in:

- Chapter 3, in which various flavors of join conditions are studied in detail
- Chapter 5, which probes the different types of subqueries along with the appropriate operators for evaluating their results
- Chapter 6, in which various methods of handling date/time data are explored
- Chapter 14, which explores certain aspects of the WHERE clause from the standpoint of performance and efficiency

Additionally, here are a few tips to help you make the most of your WHERE clauses:

1. Check your join conditions carefully. Make sure that each data set in the FROM clause is properly joined. Keep in mind that some joins require multiple conditions. See Chapter 3 for more information.

2. Avoid unnecessary joins. Just because two data sets in your FROM clause contain the same column does not necessitate a join condition be added to your WHERE clause. In some designs, redundant data has been propagated to multiple tables through a process called *denormalization*. Take the time to understand the database design, and ask your DBA or database designer for a current data model.

3. Use parentheses. Oracle maintains both operator precedence and condition precedence, meaning there are clearly defined rules for the order in which things will be evaluated, but the safest route for you and for those who will later maintain your code is to dictate evaluation order using parentheses. For operators, specifying (5 * p.inventory_qty) + 2 rather than 5 * p.inventory_qty + 2 makes the order in which the operations should be performed clear. For conditions, use parentheses any time the OR operator is employed.

4. Use consistent indentation. For example, if the previous line contains a left parenthesis without a matching right parenthesis, indent the current line to show that it is a continuation of the previous line.

5. When using OR, put the condition requiring the least effort to evaluate first. If the first condition evaluates to TRUE, Oracle won't bother evaluating the remaining OR'd conditions, possibly saving significant execution time. This strategy is useful with correlated subqueries, which are generally executed once per candidate row.

6. Handle NULLs properly. After writing your WHERE clause, inspect each condition with respect to its ability to properly handle NULL values. Take the time to understand the table definitions in your database so that you know which columns allow NULLs.

7. Pick up introductory books on logic and set theory at your local library. While understanding these two topics won't necessarily get you invited to more cocktail parties, it will certainly make you a better SQL programmer.

CHAPTER 3
Joins

Most of the things in life are not self-contained. There is not one shop where you will find all your requirements. This is valid for database tables as well. Quite often, you need information from more than one table. The SQL construct that combines data from two or more tables is called a *join*. This chapter takes you into the details of joins, their types, and their usage.

A join is a SQL query that extracts information from two or more tables or views. When you specify multiple tables or views in the FROM clause of a query, Oracle performs a join, linking rows from multiple tables together. There are several types of joins to be aware of:

Inner joins
> Inner joins are the regular joins. An inner join returns the rows that satisfy the join condition. Each row returned by an inner join contains data from all tables involved in the join.

Outer joins
> Outer joins are an extension to the inner joins. An outer join returns the rows that satisfy the join condition and also the rows from one table for which no corresponding rows (i.e., that satisfy the join condition) exist in the other table.

Self joins
> A self join is a join of a table to itself.

The following sections discuss each of these joins with examples.

Inner Joins

An inner join returns the rows that satisfy the join condition. Let's take an example to understand the concept of a join. Say you want to list the name and department name for each employee. To do this, you would use the following SQL statement:

```
SELECT E.LNAME, D.NAME
FROM EMPLOYEE E, DEPARTMENT D
```

```
WHERE E.DEPT_ID = D.DEPT_ID;

LNAME        NAME
----------   --------------
SMITH        RESEARCH
ALLEN        SALES
WARD         SALES
JONES        RESEARCH
MARTIN       SALES
BLAKE        SALES
CLARK        ACCOUNTING
SCOTT        RESEARCH
KING         ACCOUNTING
TURNER       SALES
ADAMS        RESEARCH
JAMES        SALES
FORD         RESEARCH
MILLER       ACCOUNTING

14 rows selected.
```

This example queries two tables, because the employee name is stored in the EMPLOYEE table, whereas the department name is stored in the DEPARTMENT table. Notice that the FROM clause lists two tables EMPLOYEE and DEPARTMENT, separated by a comma (,). If you need to join three or more tables, you have to specify all the tables in the FROM clause separated by commas. The SELECT list may include columns from any of the tables specified in the FROM clause.

Note the use of table aliases in this query. It is common practice to use table aliases while selecting data from multiple tables. Whenever there is an ambiguity in the column names, you must use a table alias (or the table name) to qualify any ambiguous column names. For example, the column name DEPT_ID appears in both the tables. Therefore, the table aliases E and D are used in the WHERE clause to ask Oracle to equate DEPT_ID column from EMPLOYEE table with the DEPT_ID column from the DEPARTMENT table. Note that the table aliases have been used with the columns in the SELECT clause as well, even though the column names are unambiguous. It is good practice to use table aliases everywhere in a query if you are using them at all.

Cartesian Product

If you don't specify the join condition while joining two tables, Oracle combines each row from the first table with each row of the second table. This type of result set is called as a Cartesian product. The number of rows in a Cartesian product is the product of the number of rows in each table. Here's an example of a Cartesian product:

```
SELECT E.LNAME, D.NAME
FROM EMPLOYEE E, DEPARTMENT D;
```

```
LNAME       NAME
----------  --------------
SMITH       ACCOUNTING
ALLEN       ACCOUNTING
WARD        ACCOUNTING
JONES       ACCOUNTING
MARTIN      ACCOUNTING
BLAKE       ACCOUNTING
...
...
...
SCOTT       OPERATIONS
KING        OPERATIONS
TURNER      OPERATIONS
ADAMS       OPERATIONS
JAMES       OPERATIONS
FORD        OPERATIONS
MILLER      OPERATIONS

56 rows selected.
```

Note that since the query didn't specify a join condition, each row from the EMPLOYEE table is combined with each row from the DEPARTMENT table. Needless to say, this result set is of little use. More often than not a Cartesian product produces a result set containing misleading rows. Therefore, unless you are sure that you want a Cartesian product, don't forget to include the join condition when you specify more than one table in the FROM clause.

Join Condition

Usually when you perform a join, you specify a condition in the WHERE clause that relates the tables specified in the FROM clause. This condition is referred to as the join condition. The join condition specifies how the rows from one table will be combined with the rows of another table. Usually, the join condition is applied to the foreign key columns. In the first example in the previous section, the WHERE clause specifies the join condition by which the DEPT_ID column of the EMPLOYEE table is equated with the DEPT_ID column of the DEPARTMENT table:

```
WHERE E.DEPT_ID = D.DEPT_ID
```

To perform the join, Oracle picks up one combination of rows from the two tables, and checks to see whether the join condition is true. If the join condition is true, Oracle includes this combination of rows in the result set. The process is repeated for all combinations of rows from the two tables. Some of the things that you should know about the join condition are discussed in the following list.

- The columns specified in the join condition need not be specified in the SELECT list. In the following example, the join condition involves the DEPT_ID column from the EMPLOYEE and DEPARTMENT tables; however, the DEPT_ID column is not selected:

```
SELECT E.LNAME, D.NAME
FROM EMPLOYEE E, DEPARTMENT D
WHERE E.DEPT_ID = D.DEPT_ID;
```

- Usually the join condition is specified on the foreign key columns of one table and the primary key or unique key columns of another table. However, you can specify other columns as well. Each join condition involves columns that relate two tables.

- A join condition may involve more than one column. This is usually the case when a foreign key constraint consists of multiple columns.

- The total number of join conditions is always equal to the total number of tables less one.

- A join condition must involve columns with compatible datatypes. Note that the datatype of the columns involved in a join condition need to be *compatible*, not *the same*. Oracle performs automatic datatype conversion between the join columns, if required.

- It is not necessary that a join condition involve the equal to (=) operator. A join condition may contain other operators as well. Joins involving other operators are discussed later in this section.

Equi-Join Versus Non-Equi-Join

The join condition determines whether the join is an equi-join or a non-equi-join. When a join condition relates two tables by equating the columns from the tables, it is an *equi-join*. When a join condition relates two tables by an operator other than equality, it is a *non-equi-join*. A query may contain equi-joins as well as non-equi-joins.

Equi-joins are the most common join type. For example, if you want to list all the parts supplied by all the suppliers, you can join the SUPPLIER table with the PART table by equating the SUPPLIER_ID from one table to that of the other:

```
SELECT S.NAME SUPPLIER_NAME, P.NAME PART_NAME
FROM SUPPLIER S, PART P
WHERE S.SUPPLIER_ID = P.SUPPLIER_ID;
```

However, there are situations in which you need non-equi-joins to get the required information. For example, if you want to list the INVENTORY_CLASS of each PART, you need to execute the following query:

```
SELECT P.NAME PART_NAME, C.CLASS INV_CLASS
FROM PART P, INVENTORY_CLASS C
WHERE P.UNIT_COST BETWEEN C.LOW_COST AND C.HIGH_COST;
```

Note the use of the BETWEEN operator while relating the UNIT_COST column from the PART table with the LOW_COST and HIGH_COST columns of the INVENTORY_CLASS table.

Outer Joins

Sometimes while performing a join between two tables, you need to return all the rows from one table even when there are no corresponding rows in the other table. Consider the following two tables, SUPPLIER and PART:

```
SELECT * FROM SUPPLIER;

SUPPLIER_ID NAME
----------- -----------------------------
        101 Pacific Disks, Inc.
        102 Silicon Valley MicroChips
        103 Blue River Electronics

SELECT * FROM PART;

PART_NBR NAME                SUPPLIER_ID STATUS INVENTORY_QTY UNIT_COST RESUPPLY_DATE
-------- ------------------- ----------- ------ ------------- --------- -------------
HD211    20 GB Hard Disk             101 ACTIVE             5      2000 12-DEC-00
P3000    3000 MHz Processor          102 ACTIVE            12       600 03-NOV-00
```

If you want to list all the suppliers and all the parts supplied by them, it is natural to use the following query:

```
SELECT S.SUPPLIER_ID, S.NAME SUPPLIER_NAME, P.PART_NBR, P.NAME PART_NAME
FROM SUPPLIER S, PART P
WHERE S.SUPPLIER_ID = P.SUPPLIER_ID;

SUPPLIER_ID SUPPLIER_NAME                      PART_NBR   PART_NAME
----------- ---------------------------------- ---------- -------------------
        101 Pacific Disks, Inc.                HD211      20 GB Hard Disk
        102 Silicon Valley MicroChips          P3000      3000 MHz Processor
```

Note that even though we have three suppliers, this query lists only two of them, because the third supplier (Blue River Electronics) doesn't currently supply any part. When Oracle performs the join between SUPPLIER table and PART table, it matches the SUPPLIER_ID from these two tables (as specified by the join condition). Since SUPPLIER_ID 103 doesn't have any corresponding record in the PART table, that supplier is not included in the result set. This type of join is the most natural, and is known as an *inner join*.

> The concept of the inner join is easier to understand in terms of the Cartesian product. While performing a join of SUPPLIER and PART tables, a Cartesian product is first formed (conceptually, Oracle doesn't physically materialize this Cartesian product), and then the conditions in the WHERE clause restrict the results to only those rows where the SUPPLIER_ID values match.

However, we want to see all the suppliers even if they don't supply any parts. Oracle provides a special type of join to include rows from one table that don't have matching rows from the other table. This type of join is known as an *outer join*. An outer join allows us to return rows for all suppliers, and also for parts in cases where a supplier currently supplies parts. In cases where a supplier doesn't supply parts, NULLs are returned for the PART table columns in the result set.

The syntax of the outer join is a bit different from that of the inner join, because it includes a special operator called the *outer join operator*. The outer join operator is a plus sign enclosed in parentheses, i.e., (+). This operator is used in the join condition in the WHERE clause following a field name from the table that you wish to be considered the optional table. In our suppliers and parts example, the PART table doesn't have information for one supplier. Therefore, we will simply add a (+) operator to the join condition on the side of the PART table. The query and the result set look as follows:

```
SELECT S.SUPPLIER_ID, S.NAME SUPPLIER_NAME, P.PART_NBR, P.NAME PART_NAME
FROM SUPPLIER S, PART P
WHERE S.SUPPLIER_ID = P.SUPPLIER_ID (+);


SUPPLIER_ID SUPPLIER_NAME                         PART_NBR   PART_NAME
----------- ------------------------------       ---------- --------------------
        101 Pacific Disks, Inc.                   HD211      20 GB Hard Disk
        102 Silicon Valley MicroChips             P3000      3000 MHz Processor
        103 Blue River Electronics
```

Note the (+) operator following P.SUPPLIER_ID. That makes PART the optional table in this join. If a supplier does not currently supply any parts, Oracle will fabricate a PART record with all NULLs for that supplier. Thus, the query results can include all suppliers, regardless of whether they currently supply parts. You can see that the PART columns for supplier 103 in this example all have NULL values.

The outer join operator (+) can appear on either the left or the right side of the join condition. However, make sure you apply this operator to the appropriate table in the context of your query. For example, it makes no difference to the result if you switch the two sides of the equality operator in the previous example:

```
SELECT S.SUPPLIER_ID, S.NAME SUPPLIER_NAME, P.PART_NBR, P.NAME PART_NAME
FROM SUPPLIER S, PART P
WHERE P.SUPPLIER_ID (+) = S.SUPPLIER_ID;


SUPPLIER_ID SUPPLIER_NAME                         PART_NBR   PART_NAME
----------- ------------------------------       ---------- --------------------
        101 Pacific Disks, Inc.                   HD211      20 GB Hard Disk
        102 Silicon Valley MicroChips             P3000      3000 MHz Processor
        103 Blue River Electronics
```

However, if you associate the (+) operator with the wrong table, you may get unexpected results. For example:

```
SELECT S.SUPPLIER_ID, S.NAME SUPPLIER_NAME, P.PART_NBR, P.NAME PART_NAME
FROM SUPPLIER S, PART P
WHERE P.SUPPLIER_ID = S.SUPPLIER_ID (+);
```

```
SUPPLIER_ID SUPPLIER_NAME                      PART_NBR   PART_NAME
----------- ------------------------------    ---------- --------------------
        101 Pacific Disks, Inc.               HD211      20 GB Hard Disk
        102 Silicon Valley MicroChips         P3000      3000 MHz Processor
```

Here, the outer join operator is placed on the side of the SUPPLIER table in the join condition. By doing this, you are asking Oracle to print the parts and their corresponding suppliers, as well as the parts without a supplier. However, in our example data, all the parts have a corresponding supplier. Therefore, the results are the same as if we had done an inner join.

Restrictions on Outer Joins

There are some rules and restrictions on how you can use an outer join query. When you perform an outer join in a query, Oracle doesn't allow you to perform certain other operations in the same query. We discuss these restrictions and some of the work-arounds in this list.

- The outer join operator can appear on only one side of an expression in the join condition. You get an ORA-1468 error if you attempt to use it on both sides. For example:

  ```
  SELECT S.SUPPLIER_ID, S.NAME SUPPLIER_NAME, P.PART_NBR, P.NAME PART_NAME
  FROM SUPPLIER S, PART P
  WHERE S.SUPPLIER_ID (+) = P.SUPPLIER_ID (+);

  WHERE S.SUPPLIER_ID (+) = P.SUPPLIER_ID (+)
                          *
  ERROR at line 3:
  ORA-01468: a predicate may reference only one outer-joined table
  ```

  If you are attempting a two-sided outer join by placing the (+) operator on both sides in the join condition, please refer to the section "Full Outer Joins," which follows this section.

- If a join involves more than two tables, then one table can't be outer joined with more than one other table in the query. Let's look at the following example:

  ```
  DESC EMPLOYEE
   Name                           Null?    Type
   ------------------------------ -------- ----
   EMP_ID                         NOT NULL NUMBER(4)
   LNAME                                   VARCHAR2(15)
   FNAME                                   VARCHAR2(15)
   DEPT_ID                                 NUMBER(2)
   MANAGER_EMP_ID                          NUMBER(4)
   SALARY                                  NUMBER(7,2)
   HIRE_DATE                               DATE
   JOB_ID                                  NUMBER(3)
  ```

```
DESC JOB
Name                             Null?      Type
------------------------------   --------   ----
JOB_ID                           NOT NULL   NUMBER(3)
FUNCTION                                    VARCHAR2(30)
```

```
DESC DEPARTMENT
Name                             Null?      Type
------------------------------   --------   ----
DEPT_ID                          NOT NULL   NUMBER(2)
NAME                                        VARCHAR2(14)
LOCATION_ID                                 NUMBER(3)
```

If you want to list the job function and department name of all the employees, and want to include all the departments and jobs that don't have any corresponding employees, you would probably attempt to join the EMPLOYEE table with the JOB table and the DEPARTMENT table, and make both the joins outer joins. However, since one table can't be outer-joined with more than one table you get the following error:

```
SELECT E.LNAME, J.FUNCTION, D.NAME
FROM EMPLOYEE E, JOB J, DEPARTMENT D
WHERE E.JOB_ID (+) = J.JOB_ID
AND E.DEPT_ID (+) = D.DEPT_ID;

WHERE E.JOB_ID (+) = J.JOB_ID
                *
ERROR at line 3:
ORA-01417: a table may be outer joined to at most one other table
```

As a work around, you can create a view with an outer join between two tables, and then outer join the view with the third table:

```
CREATE VIEW V_EMP_JOB
AS SELECT E.DEPT_ID, E.LNAME, J.FUNCTION
FROM EMPLOYEE E, JOB J
WHERE E.JOB_ID (+) = J.JOB_ID;

SELECT V.LNAME, V.FUNCTION, D.NAME
FROM V_EMP_JOB V, DEPARTMENT D
WHERE V.DEPT_ID (+) = D.DEPT_ID;
```

Instead of creating a view, you can use an inline view to achieve the same result:

```
SELECT V.LNAME, V.FUNCTION, D.NAME
FROM (SELECT E.DEPT_ID, E.LNAME, J.FUNCTION
      FROM EMPLOYEE E, JOB J
      WHERE E.JOB_ID (+) = J.JOB_ID) V, DEPARTMENT D
WHERE V.DEPT_ID (+) = D.DEPT_ID;
```

Inline views are discussed in Chapter 5.

• An outer join condition containing the (+) operator may not use the IN operator. For example:

```
SELECT E.LNAME, J.FUNCTION
FROM EMPLOYEE E, JOB J
```

```
WHERE E.JOB_ID (+) IN (668, 670, 667);
WHERE E.JOB_ID (+) IN (668, 670, 667)
                  *
ERROR at line 3:
ORA-01719: outer join operator (+) not allowed in operand of OR or IN
```

- An outer join condition containing the OR operator may not be combined with another condition using the OR operator. For example:

```
SELECT E.LNAME, D.NAME
FROM EMPLOYEE E, DEPARTMENT D
WHERE E.DEPT_ID = D.DEPT_ID (+)
OR D.DEPT_ID = 10;
WHERE E.DEPT_ID = D.DEPT_ID (+)
              *
ERROR at line 3:
ORA-01719: outer join operator (+) not allowed in operand of OR or IN
```

- A condition containing the (+) operator may not involve a subquery. For example:

```
SELECT E.LNAME
FROM EMPLOYEE E
WHERE E.DEPT_ID (+) =
(SELECT DEPT_ID FROM DEPARTMENT WHERE NAME = 'ACCOUNTING');
(SELECT DEPT_ID FROM DEPARTMENT WHERE NAME = 'ACCOUNTING')
                                                         *
ERROR at line 4:
ORA-01799: a column may not be outer-joined to a subquery
```

As a work around, you can use an inline view to achieve the desired effect:

```
SELECT E.LNAME
FROM EMPLOYEE E,
(SELECT DEPT_ID FROM DEPARTMENT WHERE NAME = 'ACCOUNTING') V
WHERE E.DEPT_ID (+) = V.DEPT_ID;
```

Inline views are discussed in Chapter 5.

Full Outer Joins

An outer join extends the result of an inner join by including rows from one table (table A, for example) that don't have corresponding rows in another table (table B, for example). An important thing to note here is that the outer join operation will not include the rows from table B that don't have corresponding rows in table A. In other words, an outer join is unidirectional. There are situations when you may want a bidirectional outer join, i.e., you want to include all the rows from A and B that are:

- From the result of the inner join.
- From A that don't have corresponding rows in B.
- From B that don't have corresponding rows in A.

Let's take an example to understand this further. Consider the following two tables: LOCATION and DEPARTMENT:

```
DESC LOCATION
Name                              Null?    Type
-------------------------------- -------- ----
LOCATION_ID                       NOT NULL NUMBER(3)
REGIONAL_GROUP                             VARCHAR2(20)

DESC DEPARTMENT
Name                              Null?    Type
-------------------------------- -------- ----
DEPT_ID                           NOT NULL NUMBER(2)
NAME                                       VARCHAR2(14)
LOCATION_ID                                NUMBER(3)
```

Assume there are locations in the LOCATION table that don't have corresponding departments in the DEPARTMENT table, and that at the same time there are departments in the DEPARTMENT table without a LOCATION_ID pointing to corresponding LOCATION rows. If you perform an inner join of these two tables, you will get only the departments and locations that have corresponding rows in both the tables.

```
SELECT D.DEPT_ID, D.NAME, L.REGIONAL_GROUP
FROM DEPARTMENT D, LOCATION L
WHERE D.LOCATION_ID = L.LOCATION_ID;

     DEPT_ID NAME           REGIONAL_GROUP
------------- -------------- --------------------
          10 ACCOUNTING     NEW YORK
          20 RESEARCH       DALLAS
          30 SALES          CHICAGO
          40 OPERATIONS     BOSTON
          12 RESEARCH       NEW YORK
          13 SALES          NEW YORK
          14 OPERATIONS     NEW YORK
          23 SALES          DALLAS
          24 OPERATIONS     DALLAS
          34 OPERATIONS     CHICAGO
          43 SALES          BOSTON

11 rows selected.
```

There are locations that don't have any departments. To include those locations in this list, you have to perform an outer join with the (+) operator on the department side, making the DEPARTMENT table the optional table in the query. Notice that Oracle supplies NULLs for missing DEPARTMENT data.

```
SELECT D.DEPT_ID, D.NAME, L.REGIONAL_GROUP
FROM DEPARTMENT D, LOCATION L
WHERE D.LOCATION_ID (+) = L.LOCATION_ID;

     DEPT_ID NAME           REGIONAL_GROUP
------------- -------------- --------------------
          10 ACCOUNTING     NEW YORK
          12 RESEARCH       NEW YORK
          14 OPERATIONS     NEW YORK
```

```
            13  SALES           NEW YORK
            30  SALES           CHICAGO
            34  OPERATIONS      CHICAGO
            20  RESEARCH        DALLAS
            23  SALES           DALLAS
            24  OPERATIONS      DALLAS
                                SAN FRANCISCO
            40  OPERATIONS      BOSTON
            43  SALES           BOSTON
```

```
12 rows selected.
```

There are departments that don't belong to any location. If you want to include
those departments in the result set, perform an outer join with the (+) operator on
the location side.

```
SELECT D.DEPT_ID, D.NAME, L.REGIONAL_GROUP
FROM DEPARTMENT D, LOCATION L
WHERE D.LOCATION_ID = L.LOCATION_ID (+) ;
```

```
      DEPT_ID NAME             REGIONAL_GROUP
    ------------- --------------- --------------------
           10 ACCOUNTING       NEW YORK
           20 RESEARCH         DALLAS
           30 SALES            CHICAGO
           40 OPERATIONS       BOSTON
           12 RESEARCH         NEW YORK
           13 SALES            NEW YORK
           14 OPERATIONS       NEW YORK
           23 SALES            DALLAS
           24 OPERATIONS       DALLAS
           34 OPERATIONS       CHICAGO
           43 SALES            BOSTON
           50 MARKETING
           60 CONSULTING
```

```
13 rows selected.
```

However, the previous query excluded any location that doesn't have a department.
If you want to include the departments without a location as well as the locations
without a department, you will probably try to use a two-sided outer join, correctly
termed a *full outer join*, like the following:

```
SELECT D.DEPT_ID, D.NAME, L.REGIONAL_GROUP
FROM DEPARTMENT D, LOCATION L
WHERE D.LOCATION_ID (+) = L.LOCATION_ID (+);
WHERE D.LOCATION_ID (+) = L.LOCATION_ID (+)
                       *
ERROR at line 3:
ORA-01468: a predicate may reference only one outer-joined table
```

As you can see, a two-sided outer join is not allowed. A UNION of two SELECT
statements is a work around for this problem. In the following example, the first
SELECT represents an outer join in which DEPARTMENT is the optional table. The

second SELECT has the LOCATION table as the optional table. Between the two SELECTS, you get all locations and all departments. The UNION operation eliminates duplicate rows, and the result is a full outer join:

```
SELECT D.DEPT_ID, D.NAME, L.REGIONAL_GROUP
FROM DEPARTMENT D, LOCATION L
WHERE D.LOCATION_ID (+) = L.LOCATION_ID
UNION
SELECT D.DEPT_ID, D.NAME, L.REGIONAL_GROUP
FROM DEPARTMENT D, LOCATION L
WHERE D.LOCATION_ID = L.LOCATION_ID (+) ;
```

```
    DEPT_ID NAME            REGIONAL_GROUP
------------- --------------- --------------------
         10 ACCOUNTING      NEW YORK
         12 RESEARCH        NEW YORK
         13 SALES           NEW YORK
         14 OPERATIONS      NEW YORK
         20 RESEARCH        DALLAS
         23 SALES           DALLAS
         24 OPERATIONS      DALLAS
         30 SALES           CHICAGO
         34 OPERATIONS      CHICAGO
         40 OPERATIONS      BOSTON
         43 SALES           BOSTON
         50 MARKETING
         60 CONSULTING

                            SAN FRANCISCO
```

```
14 rows selected.
```

As you can see, this UNION query includes all the rows you would expect to see in a full outer join. UNION queries are discussed in more detail in Chapter 7.

 Oracle9*i* introduces new ANSI-compatible join syntax that enables full outer joins in a much more straightforward way than the previous example. The new syntax is discussed at the end of this chapter.

Self Joins

There are situations in which one row of a table is related to another row of the same table. The EMPLOYEE table is a good example. The manager of one employee is also an employee. The rows for both are in the same EMPLOYEE table. This relationship is indicated in the MANAGER_EMP_ID column:

```
CREATE TABLE EMPLOYEE (
EMP_ID          NUMBER (4) NOT NULL PRIMARY KEY,
FNAME           VARCHAR2 (15),
LNAME           VARCHAR2 (15),
DEPT_ID         NUMBER (2),
MANAGER_EMP_ID  NUMBER (4) REFERENCES EMPLOYEE(EMP_ID),
```

```
SALARY        NUMBER (7,2),
HIRE_DATE     DATE,
JOB_ID        NUMBER (3));
```

To get information about an employee and his manager, you have to join the EMPLOYEE table with itself. This is achieved by specifying the EMPLOYEE table twice in the FROM clause and using two different table aliases, thereby treating EMPLOYEE as if it were two separate tables. The following example lists the name of each employee and his manager:

```
SELECT E.NAME EMPLOYEE, M.NAME MANAGER
FROM EMPLOYEE E, EMPLOYEE M
WHERE E.MANAGER_EMP_ID = M.EMP_ID;


EMPLOYEE   MANAGER
---------- ----------
SMITH      FORD
ALLEN      BLAKE
WARD       BLAKE
JONES      KING
MARTIN     BLAKE
BLAKE      KING
CLARK      KING
SCOTT      JONES
TURNER     BLAKE
ADAMS      SCOTT
JAMES      BLAKE
FORD       JONES
MILLER     CLARK

13 rows selected.
```

Notice the use of the EMPLOYEE table twice in the FROM clause with two different aliases. Also notice the join condition that reads as: "Where the employee's MANAGER_EMP_ID is the same as his manager's EMP_ID."

Self Outer Joins

Even though the EMPLOYEE table has 14 rows, the previous query returned only 13 rows. This is because there is an employee without a MANAGER_EMP_ID. Oracle excludes this row from the result set while performing the self inner join. To include the employee(s) without a MANAGER_EMP_ID, you need an outer join:

```
SELECT E.LNAME EMPLOYEE, M.LNAME MANAGER
FROM EMPLOYEE E, EMPLOYEE M
WHERE E.MANAGER_EMP_ID = M.EMP_ID (+);

EMPLOYEE   MANAGER
---------- ----------
SMITH      FORD
ALLEN      BLAKE
WARD       BLAKE
```

```
JONES        KING
MARTIN       BLAKE
BLAKE        KING
CLARK        KING
SCOTT        JONES
KING
TURNER       BLAKE
ADAMS        SCOTT
JAMES        BLAKE
FORD         JONES
MILLER       CLARK

14 rows selected.
```

Be careful when placing the (+) operator in a join condition. If you put the (+) on the wrong side, you will get an absurd result set that makes no sense. In this case, the EMPLOYEE table we need to make optional is the one from which we are drawing manager names.

Self Non-Equi-Joins

The previous example showed self-equi-joins. However, there are situations when you need to perform self-non-equi-joins. We will illustrate this by an example. Let's assume that you are in charge of organizing interdepartmental basket ball competition within your company. It is your responsibility to draw the teams and schedule the competition. You query the DEPARTMENT table and get the following result:

```
SELECT NAME FROM DEPARTMENT;

NAME
--------------
ACCOUNTING
RESEARCH
SALES
OPERATIONS
```

You find that there are four departments, and to make a fair competition, you decide that each department plays against the other three departments once, and at the end the department with the maximum wins is declared the winner. You have been to an Oracle SQL training class recently, and decide to apply the concept of self join. You execute the following query:

```
SELECT D1.NAME TEAM1, D2.NAME TEAM2
FROM DEPARTMENT D1, DEPARTMENT D2;

TEAM1          TEAM2
-------------- --------------
ACCOUNTING     ACCOUNTING
RESEARCH       ACCOUNTING
SALES          ACCOUNTING
OPERATIONS     ACCOUNTING
```

```
ACCOUNTING        RESEARCH
RESEARCH          RESEARCH
SALES             RESEARCH
OPERATIONS        RESEARCH
ACCOUNTING        SALES
RESEARCH          SALES
SALES             SALES
OPERATIONS        SALES
ACCOUNTING        OPERATIONS
RESEARCH          OPERATIONS
SALES             OPERATIONS
OPERATIONS        OPERATIONS
```

```
16 rows selected.
```

Disappointing results. From your knowledge of high school mathematics, you know that four teams each playing once with the other three makes six combinations. However, your SQL query returned 16 rows. Now you realize that since you didn't specify any join condition, you got a Cartesian product from your query. You put in a join condition, and your query and results now look as follows:

```
SELECT D1.NAME TEAM1, D2.NAME TEAM2
FROM DEPARTMENT D1, DEPARTMENT D2
WHERE D1.DEPT_ID = D2.DEPT_ID;

TEAM1             TEAM2
--------------    --------------
ACCOUNTING        ACCOUNTING
RESEARCH          RESEARCH
SALES             SALES
OPERATIONS        OPERATIONS
```

Oops! The equi-join returned a very unwanted result. A team can't play against itself. You realize your mistake, and this sparks the idea that you can use non-equi-joins in this situation. You rewrite the query as a non-equi-join. You don't want a team to play against itself, and therefore replace the "=" operator in the join condition with "!=". Let's look at the results:

```
SELECT D1.NAME TEAM1, D2.NAME TEAM2
FROM DEPARTMENT D1, DEPARTMENT D2
WHERE D1.DEPT_ID != D2.DEPT_ID;

TEAM1             TEAM2
--------------    --------------
RESEARCH          ACCOUNTING
SALES             ACCOUNTING
OPERATIONS        ACCOUNTING
ACCOUNTING        RESEARCH
SALES             RESEARCH
OPERATIONS        RESEARCH
ACCOUNTING        SALES
RESEARCH          SALES
OPERATIONS        SALES
```

```
ACCOUNTING    OPERATIONS
RESEARCH      OPERATIONS
SALES         OPERATIONS
```

12 rows selected.

Still not done. In this result set, you have permutations such as (RESEARCH, ACCOUNTING) and (ACCOUNTING, RESEARCH), and so on. Therefore, each team plays against the others twice. You need to remove these permutations, which you rightly consider to be duplicates. You think about using DISTINCT. DISTINCT will not help here, because the row (RESEARCH, ACCOUNTING) is different from the row (ACCOUNTING, RESEARCH) from the viewpoint of DISTINCT; but not from the viewpoint of your requirement. After some thought, you want to try out an inequality operator other than "!=". You decide to go with the less-than (<) operator. Here are the results you get:

```
SELECT D1.NAME TEAM1, D2.NAME TEAM2
FROM DEPARTMENT D1, DEPARTMENT D2
WHERE D1.DEPT_ID < D2.DEPT_ID;

TEAM1          TEAM2
-------------- --------------
ACCOUNTING     RESEARCH
ACCOUNTING     SALES
RESEARCH       SALES
ACCOUNTING     OPERATIONS
RESEARCH       OPERATIONS
SALES          OPERATIONS
```

6 rows selected.

That's it! Now you have six combinations: each team plays against the other three just once. Let's examine why this version of the query works. Conceptually, when Oracle executes this query, a Cartesian product is first formed with 16 rows. Then the less-than (<) operator in the join condition restricts the result set to those rows in which the DEPT_ID of Team 1 is less than the DEPT_ID of Team 2. The less-than (<) operator eliminates the duplicates, because for any given permutation of two departments this condition is satisfied for only one. Using greater-than (>) instead of less-than (<) will also give you the required result, but the TEAM1 and TEAM2 values will be reversed:

```
SELECT D1.NAME TEAM1, D2.NAME TEAM2
FROM DEPARTMENT D1, DEPARTMENT D2
WHERE D1.DEPT_ID > D2.DEPT_ID;

TEAM1          TEAM2
-------------- --------------
RESEARCH       ACCOUNTING
SALES          ACCOUNTING
OPERATIONS     ACCOUNTING
SALES          RESEARCH
```

```
OPERATIONS      RESEARCH
OPERATIONS      SALES
```

6 rows selected.

Don't be disheartened by the painful process you had to go through to get this result. Sometimes you have to go through an agonizing experience to get simple results such as these. That's life. Now that you have the team combinations right, go a bit further and assign a date for each match. Use "tomorrow" as the starting date:

```
SELECT D1.NAME TEAM1, D2.NAME TEAM2, SYSDATE + ROWNUM MATCH_DATE
FROM DEPARTMENT D1, DEPARTMENT D2
WHERE D1.DEPT_ID < D2.DEPT_ID;
```

```
TEAM1           TEAM2           MATCH_DATE
--------------  --------------  ---------
ACCOUNTING      RESEARCH        30-APR-01
ACCOUNTING      SALES           01-MAY-01
RESEARCH        SALES           02-MAY-01
ACCOUNTING      OPERATIONS      03-MAY-01
RESEARCH        OPERATIONS      04-MAY-01
SALES           OPERATIONS      05-MAY-01
```

6 rows selected.

Now publish these results on the corporate intranet along with the rules and regulations for the competition, and you are done.

Joins and Subqueries

Joins can sometimes be used to good advantage in reformulating SELECT statements that would otherwise contain subqueries. Consider the problem of obtaining a list of suppliers of parts for which your inventory has dropped below ten units. You might begin by writing a query such as the following:

```
SELECT supplier_id, name
FROM supplier s
WHERE EXISTS (SELECT *
             FROM part p
             WHERE p.inventory_qty < 10
               AND p.supplier_id = s.supplier_id);
```

The subquery in this SELECT statement is a correlated subquery, which means that it will be executed once for each row in the supplier table. Assuming that you have no indexes on the INVENTORY_QTY and SUPPLIER_ID columns of the PART table, this query could result in multiple, full-table scans of the PART table. It's possible to restate the query using a join, for example:

```
SELECT s.supplier_id, s.name
FROM supplier s, part p
WHERE p.supplier_id = s.supplier_id
  AND p.inventory_qty < 10;
```

Whether the join version or the subquery version of a query is more efficient depends on the specific situation. It may be worth your while to test both approaches to see which has a lower cost.

DML Statements on a Join View

A join view is a view based on a join. Special considerations apply when you issue a DML (INSERT, UPDATE, or DELETE) statement against a join view. Ever thought about what happens when you insert a row into a join view—which table does the row go into? And what happens when you delete a row from a join view—which table does it gets deleted from? This section deals with these questions.

To be modifiable, a join view must not contain any of the following:

- Hierarchical query clauses, such as START WITH or CONNECT BY
- GROUP BY or HAVING clauses
- Set operations, such as UNION, UNION ALL, INTERSECT, MINUS
- Aggregate functions, such as AVG, COUNT, MAX, MIN, SUM, and so forth
- The DISTINCT operator
- The ROWNUM pseudocolumn

A DML statement on a join view can modify only one base table of the view. Apart from these rules, therefore, a join view must also have one key preserved table to be modified.

Key-Preserved Tables

A key-preserved table is the most important requirement in order for a join view to be modifiable. In a join, a table is called a *key-preserved table* if its keys are preserved through the join—every key of the table can also be a key of the resultant join result set. Every primary key or unique key value in the base table must also be unique in the result set of the join. Let's take an example to understand the concept of key preserved tables better.

```
DESC EMPLOYEE
Name                           Null?    Type
------------------------------ -------- ----
EMP_ID                         NOT NULL NUMBER(4)
LNAME                                   VARCHAR2(15)
FNAME                                   VARCHAR2(15)
DEPT_ID                                 NUMBER(2)
MANAGER_EMP_ID                          NUMBER(4)
SALARY                                  NUMBER(7,2)
HIRE_DATE                               DATE
JOB_ID                                  NUMBER(3)
```

```
DESC RETAILER
Name                              Null?      Type
------------------------------- --------   ----
RTLR_NBR                                    NOT NULL NUMBER(6)
NAME                                        VARCHAR2(45)
ADDRESS                                     VARCHAR2(40)
CITY                                        VARCHAR2(30)
STATE                                       VARCHAR2(2)
ZIP_CODE                                    VARCHAR2(9)
AREA_CODE                                   NUMBER(3)
PHONE_NUMBER                                NUMBER(7)
SALESPERSON_ID                              NUMBER(4)
CREDIT_LIMIT                                NUMBER(9,2)
COMMENTS                                    LONG


CREATE VIEW V_RTLR_EMP AS
SELECT C.RTLR_NBR, C.NAME, C.CITY, E.EMP_ID, E.LNAME SALES_REP
FROM RETAILER C, EMPLOYEE E
WHERE C.SALESPERSON_ID = E.EMP_ID;


View created.


SELECT * FROM V_RTLR_EMP;
```

RTLR_NBR	NAME	CITY	EMP_	SALES_REP
100	JOCKSPORTS	BELMONT	7844	TURNER
101	TKB SPORT SHOP	REDWOOD CITY	7521	WARD
102	VOLLYRITE	BURLINGAME	7654	MARTIN
103	JUST TENNIS	BURLINGAME	7521	WARD
104	EVERY MOUNTAIN	CUPERTINO	7499	ALLEN
105	K + T SPORTS	SANTA CLARA	7844	TURNER
106	SHAPE UP	PALO ALTO	7521	WARD
107	WOMENS SPORTS	SUNNYVALE	7499	ALLEN
201	STADIUM SPORTS	NEW YORK	7557	SHAW
202	HOOPS	LEICESTER	7820	ROSS
203	REBOUND SPORTS	NEW YORK	7557	SHAW
204	THE POWER FORWARD	DALLAS	7560	DUNCAN
205	POINT GUARD	YONKERS	7557	SHAW
206	THE COLISEUM	SCARSDALE	7557	SHAW
207	FAST BREAK	CONCORD	7820	ROSS
208	AL AND BOB'S SPORTS	AUSTIN	7560	DUNCAN
211	AT BAT	BROOKLINE	7820	ROSS
212	ALL SPORT	BROOKLYN	7600	PORTER
213	GOOD SPORT	SUNNYSIDE	7600	PORTER
214	AL'S PRO SHOP	SPRING	7564	LANGE
215	BOB'S FAMILY SPORTS	HOUSTON	7654	MARTIN
216	THE ALL AMERICAN	CHELSEA	7820	ROSS
217	HIT, THROW, AND RUN	GRAPEVINE	7564	LANGE
218	THE OUTFIELD	FLUSHING	7820	ROSS
221	WHEELS AND DEALS	HOUSTON	7789	WEST
222	JUST BIKES	DALLAS	7789	WEST
223	VELO SPORTS	MALDEN	7820	ROSS
224	JOE'S BIKE SHOP	GRAND PRARIE	7789	WEST

```
225 BOB'S SWIM, CYCLE, AND RUN   IRVING           7789 WEST
226 CENTURY SHOP                 HUNTINGTON       7555 PETERS
227 THE TOUR                     SOMERVILLE       7820 ROSS
228 FITNESS FIRST                JACKSON HEIGHTS 7555 PETERS
```

32 rows selected.

The view V_RTLR_EMP is a join of RETAILER and EMPLOYEE tables on the RETAILER.SALESPERSON_ID and EMPLOYEE.EMP_ID columns. Is there a key-preserved table in this join view? Which one—or is it both? If you observe the relationship between the two tables and the join query, you will notice that RTLR_NBR is the key of the RETAILER table, as well as the key of the result of the join. This is because there is only one row in the RETAILER table for every row in the join view V_RTLR_EMP and every row in the view has a unique RTLR_NBR. Therefore, the table RETAILER is a key-preserved table in this join view. How about the EMPLOYEE table? The key of the EMPLOYEE table is not preserved through the join because EMP_ID is not unique in the view, consequently EMP_ID can't be a key for the result of the join. Therefore, the table EMPLOYEE is not a key-preserved table in this view.

You must remember the following important points regarding key-preserved tables:

- Key-preservation is a property of the table inside the join view, not the table itself independently. A table may be key-preserved in one join view, and may not be key-preserved in another join view. For example, if we create a join view by joining the EMPLOYEE table with the DEPARTMENT table on the DEPT_ID column, then in the resulting view the EMPLOYEE table will be key-preserved, but the DEPARTMENT table will not be a key-preserved table.

- It is not necessary for the key column(s) of a table to be SELECTed in the join view for the table to be key-preserved. For example, in the V_RTLR_EMP view discussed previously, the RETAILER table would have been the key-preserved table even if we had not included the RTLR_NBR column in the SELECT list.

- On the other hand, if we select the key column(s) of a table in the view definition, it doesn't make that table key-preserved. In the V_RTLR_EMP view, even though we have included EMP_ID in the SELECT list, the EMPLOYEE table is not key-preserved.

- The key-preserved property of a table in a join view doesn't depend on the data inside the table. It depends on the schema design and the relationship between the tables.

The following sections discuss how you can use INSERT, UPDATE, and DELETE statements on a join view.

INSERT Statements on a Join View

Let's issue an INSERT statement against the join view V_RTLR_EMP that attempts to insert a record into the RETAILER table:

```
INSERT INTO V_RTLR_EMP (RTLR_NBR, NAME, SALESPERSON_ID)
VALUES (345, 'X-MART STORES', 7820);

1 row created.
```

That worked. Now let's try this INSERT statement, which also supplies a value for a column from the EMPLOYEE table:

```
INSERT INTO V_RTLR_EMP (RTLR_NBR, NAME, SALESPERSON_ID, SALES_REP)
VALUES (456, 'LEE PARK RECREATION CENTER', 7599, 'JAMES');
INSERT INTO V_RTLR_EMP (RTLR_NBR, NAME, SALESPERSON_ID, SALES_REP)
                                                         *
ERROR at line 1:
ORA-01776: cannot modify more than one base table through a join view
```

This INSERT statement attempts to insert values into two tables (RETAILER and EMPLOYEE), which is not allowed. You can't refer to the columns of a non-key-preserved table in an INSERT statement. Moreover, INSERT statements are not allowed on a join view if the view is created using the WITH CHECK OPTION clause, even if you are attempting to insert into the key-preserved table only. For example:

```
CREATE VIEW V_RTLR_EMP_WCO AS
SELECT C.RTLR_NBR, C.NAME, C.CITY, C.SALESPERSON_ID, E.LNAME SALES_REP
FROM RETAILER C, EMPLOYEE E
WHERE C.SALESPERSON_ID = E.EMP_ID
WITH CHECK OPTION;

View created.

INSERT INTO V_RTLR_EMP_WCO (RTLR_NBR, NAME, SALESPERSON_ID)
VALUES (345, 'X-MART STORES', 7820);
INSERT INTO V_RTLR_EMP_WCO (RTLR_NBR, NAME, SALESPERSON_ID)
                           *
ERROR at line 1:
ORA-01733: virtual column not allowed here
```

The error message "ORA-01733: virtual column not allowed here" may not be very clear, but it indicates that you are not allowed to insert into this join view.

DELETE Statements on a Join View

DELETE operations can be performed on a join view if the join view has one and only one key-preserved table. The view V_RTLR_EMP discussed previously has only one key-preserved table, RETAILER; therefore, you can delete from this join view as in the following example:

```
DELETE FROM V_RTLR_EMP
WHERE RTLR_NBR = 214;
```

```
1 row deleted.
```

Let's take another example where there is more than one key-preserved table. We will create a view from the self join example we discussed earlier in this chapter and attempt to delete from the view.

```
CREATE VIEW V_DEPT_TEAM AS
SELECT D1.NAME TEAM1, D2.NAME TEAM2
FROM DEPARTMENT D1, DEPARTMENT D2
WHERE D1.DEPT_ID > D2.DEPT_ID;
```

```
View created.
```

```
DELETE FROM V_DEPT_TEAM
WHERE TEAM1 = 'SALES';
DELETE FROM V_DEPT_TEAM
            *
ERROR at line 1:
ORA-01752: cannot delete from view without exactly one key-preserved table
```

UPDATE Statements on a Join View

An UPDATE operation can be performed on a join view if it attempts to update a column in the key-preserved table. For example:

```
UPDATE V_RTLR_EMP
SET NAME = 'PRO SPORTS'
WHERE RTLR_NBR = 214;
```

```
1 row updated.
```

This UPDATE is successful since it updated the NAME column of the RETAILER table, which is key-preserved. However, the following UPDATE statement will fail because it attempts to modify the SALES_REP column that maps to the EMPLOYEE table, which is non-key-preserved:

```
UPDATE V_RTLR_EMP
SET SALES_REP = 'ANDREW'
WHERE RTLR_NBR = 214;
SET SALES_REP = 'ANDREW'
    *
ERROR at line 2:
ORA-01779: cannot modify a column which maps to a non key-preserved table
```

The WITH CHECK OPTION further restricts the ability to modify a join view. If a join view is created using the WITH CHECK OPTION clause, you can't modify any of the join columns, nor any of the columns from the repeated tables:

```
UPDATE V_RTLR_EMP_WCO
SET SALESPERSON_ID = 7784
WHERE RTLR_NBR = 214;
```

```
SET SALESPERSON_ID = 7784
        *
ERROR at line 2:
ORA-01733: virtual column not allowed here
```

The error message "ORA-01733: virtual column not allowed here" indicates that you are not allowed to update the indicated column.

Data Dictionary Views to Find Updateable Columns

Oracle provides the data dictionary view USER_UPDATABLE_COLUMNS that shows all modifiable columns in all tables and views in a user's schema. This can be helpful if you have a view that you wish to update, but aren't sure whether it's updateable. USER_UPDATABLE_COLUMNS has the following definition:

```
DESC USER_UPDATABLE_COLUMNS
 Name            Null?     Type
 -------------- -------- -------------
 OWNER          NOT NULL VARCHAR2(30)
 TABLE_NAME     NOT NULL VARCHAR2(30)
 COLUMN_NAME    NOT NULL VARCHAR2(30)
 UPDATABLE               VARCHAR2(3)
 INSERTABLE              VARCHAR2(3)
 DELETABLE               VARCHAR2(3)
```

 ALL_UPDATABLE_COLUMNS shows all views you can access (as opposed to just those you own), and DBA_UPDATABLE_COL-UMNS (for DBAs only) shows all views in the database.

The following example shows the view being queried for a list of updateable columns in the V_RTLR_EMP_WCO view:

```
SELECT * FROM USER_UPDATABLE_COLUMNS
WHERE TABLE_NAME = 'V_RTLR_EMP_WCO';

OWNER    TABLE_NAME        COLUMN_NAME       UPD INS DEL
-------  ----------------  ----------------  --- --- ---
DEMO     V_RTLR_EMP_WCO    RTLR_NBR          YES YES YES
DEMO     V_RTLR_EMP_WCO    NAME              YES YES YES
DEMO     V_RTLR_EMP_WCO    CITY              YES YES YES
DEMO     V_RTLR_EMP_WCO    SALESPERSON_ID    NO  NO  NO
DEMO     V_RTLR_EMP_WCO    SALES_REP         NO  NO  NO
```

Compare the updateable columns of the view V_RTLR_EMP_WCO with those of the view V_RTLR_EMP:

```
SELECT * FROM USER_UPDATABLE_COLUMNS
WHERE TABLE_NAME = 'V_RTLR_EMP';

OWNER    TABLE_NAME     COLUMN_NAME       UPD INS DEL
-------  -------------  ----------------  --- ---
DEMO     V_RTLR_EMP     RTLR_NBR          YES YES YES
DEMO     V_RTLR_EMP     NAME              YES YES YES
```

```
DEMO    V_RTLR_EMP    CITY              YES YES YES
DEMO    V_RTLR_EMP    SALESPERSON_ID    YES YES YES
DEMO    V_RTLR_EMP    SALES_REP         NO  NO  NO
```

Notice that the column SALESPERSON_ID is modifiable in V_RTLR_EMP, but not in V_RTLR_EMP_WCO.

ANSI-Standard Join Syntax in Oracle9i

Oracle9*i* introduced new join syntax that is compliant to the ANSI SQL standard defined for SQL/92. Prior to Oracle9*i*, Oracle supported the join syntax defined in the SQL/86 standard. In addition, Oracle supported outer joins through the proprietary outer join operator (+), discussed earlier in this chapter. The old join syntax and the proprietary outer join operator are still supported in Oracle9*i*. However, the ANSI standard join syntax introduces several new keywords and new ways to specify joins and join conditions.

New Join Syntax

With the traditional join syntax, you specify multiple tables in the FROM clause separated by commas, as in the following example:

```
SELECT L.LOCATION_ID, D.NAME, L.REGIONAL_GROUP
FROM DEPARTMENT D, LOCATION L
WHERE D.LOCATION_ID = L.LOCATION_ID;
```

With the new syntax in Oracle9*i*, you specify the join type with the JOIN keyword in the FROM clause. For example, to perform an inner join between tables DEPARTMENT and LOCATION, you specify:

```
FROM DEPARTMENT D INNER JOIN LOCATION L
```

In the traditional join syntax, the join condition is specified in the WHERE clause. With the new syntax in Oracle9*i*, the purpose of the WHERE clause is for filtering only. The join condition is separated from the WHERE clause and put in a new ON clause, which appears as part of the FROM clause. The join condition of the previous example will be specified using the new syntax as:

```
ON D.LOCATION_ID = L.LOCATION_ID;
```

The complete join, using the new syntax, will be:

```
SELECT L.LOCATION_ID, D.NAME, L.REGIONAL_GROUP
FROM DEPARTMENT D INNER JOIN LOCATION L
ON D.LOCATION_ID = L.LOCATION_ID;
```

Specifying the join condition is further simplified if:

- You use equi-joins, and
- The column names are identical in both the tables.

If these two conditions are satisfied, you can apply the new USING clause to specify the join condition. In the previous example, we used an equi-join. Also, the column involved in the join condition (LOCATION_ID) is named identically in both the tables. Therefore, this join condition can also be written as:

```
FROM DEPARTMENT D INNER JOIN LOCATION L
USING (LOCATION_ID);
```

The USING clause affects the semantics of the SELECT clause as well. The USING clause tells Oracle that the tables in the join have identical names for the column in the USING clause. Now, Oracle merges those two columns and recognizes only one such column. If you have included the join column in the SELECT list, Oracle doesn't allow you to qualify the column with a table name (or table alias). Our SELECT clause, then, needs to appear as follows:

```
SELECT LOCATION_ID, D.NAME, L.REGIONAL_GROUP
```

The complete syntax with the USING clause will be:

```
SELECT LOCATION_ID, D.NAME, L.REGIONAL_GROUP
FROM DEPARTMENT D INNER JOIN LOCATION L
USING (LOCATION_ID);
```

If you attempt to qualify the join column name in the SELECT list using either an alias or a table name, you will get an error:

```
SELECT L.LOCATION_ID, D.NAME, L.REGIONAL_GROUP
FROM DEPARTMENT D INNER JOIN LOCATION L
USING (LOCATION_ID);
SELECT L.LOCATION_ID, D.NAME, L.REGIONAL_GROUP
       *
ERROR at line 1:
ORA-25154: column part of USING clause cannot have qualifier
```

 The behavior of USING contrasts with the traditional join syntax, in which you must qualify the identical column names with the table name or table alias.

If a join condition consists of multiple columns, you need to specify all the column conditions in the ON clause separated by AND. For example, if tables A and B are joined based on columns c1 and c2, the join condition would be:

```
SELECT ...
FROM A INNER JOIN B
ON A.c1 = B.c1 AND A.c2 = B.c2
```

If the column names are identical in the two tables, you can use the USING clause and specify all the columns in one USING clause, separated by commas. The previous join condition can be rewritten as:

```
SELECT ...
FROM A INNER JOIN B
USING (c1, c2)
```

> The new join syntax doesn't allow you to accidentally forget the join condition while performing a join, and thereby helps prevent you from accidentally generating a Cartesian product. When you specify any of the new join keywords in the FROM clause, you tell Oracle that you are going to perform a JOIN, and Oracle insists that you specify the join condition in an ON or USING clause.

ANSI Outer Join Syntax

We discussed Oracle's traditional outer join syntax earlier in this chapter. The ANSI outer join syntax doesn't use the outer join operator (+) in the join condition; rather, it specifies the join type in the FROM clause. The syntax of ANSI outer join is:

```
FROM table1 { LEFT | RIGHT | FULL } [OUTER] JOIN table2
```

The syntax elements are:

table1, table2
    Specifies the tables on which you are performing the outer join.

LEFT
    Specifies that the results be generated using all rows from table1. For those rows in table1 that don't have corresponding rows in table2, NULLs are returned in the result set for the table2 columns. This is the equivalent of specifying (+) on the table2 side of the join condition in the traditional syntax.

RIGHT

Specifies that the results be generated using all rows from table2. For those rows in table2 that don't have corresponding rows in table1, NULLs are returned in the result set for the table1 columns. This is the equivalent of specifying (+) on the table1 side of the join condition in the traditional syntax.

FULL

Specifies that the results be generated using all rows from table1 and table2. For those rows in table1 that don't have corresponding rows in table2, NULLs are returned in the result set for the table2 columns. Additionally, for those rows in table2 that don't have corresponding rows in table1, NULLs are returned in the result set for the table1 columns. There is no equivalent in the traditional syntax for a FULL OUTER JOIN.

OUTER

Specifies that you are performing an OUTER join. This keyword is optional. If you use LEFT, RIGHT, or FULL, Oracle automatically assumes an outer join. The OUTER is for completeness sake, and complements the INNER keyword.

To perform a LEFT OUTER JOIN between the DEPARTMENT and LOCATION tables, you can use:

```
SELECT D.DEPT_ID, D.NAME, L.REGIONAL_GROUP
FROM DEPARTMENT D LEFT OUTER JOIN LOCATION L
ON D.LOCATION_ID = L.LOCATION_ID;
```

```
  DEPT_ID NAME            REGIONAL_GROUP
--------- --------------  --------------------
       10 ACCOUNTING      NEW YORK
       20 RESEARCH        DALLAS
       30 SALES           CHICAGO
       40 OPERATIONS      BOSTON
       12 RESEARCH        NEW YORK
       13 SALES           NEW YORK
       14 OPERATIONS      NEW YORK
       23 SALES           DALLAS
       24 OPERATIONS      DALLAS
       34 OPERATIONS      CHICAGO
       43 SALES           BOSTON
       50 MARKETING
       60 CONSULTING
```

```
13 rows selected.
```

This query lists all the rows from the DEPARTMENT table and the corresponding locations from the LOCATION table. For the rows from DEPARTMENT with no corresponding rows in LOCATION, NULLs are returned in the L.REGIONAL_GROUP column in the result set. It is equivalent to the following traditional outer join query:

```
SELECT D.DEPT_ID, D.NAME, L.REGIONAL_GROUP
FROM DEPARTMENT D, LOCATION L
WHERE D.LOCATION_ID = L.LOCATION_ID (+);
```

To perform a RIGHT OUTER JOIN between the DEPARTMENT and LOCATION tables, you can use:

```
SELECT D.DEPT_ID, D.NAME, L.REGIONAL_GROUP
FROM DEPARTMENT D RIGHT OUTER JOIN LOCATION L
ON D.LOCATION_ID = L.LOCATION_ID;
```

```
    DEPT_ID NAME            REGIONAL_GROUP
------------- -------------- --------------------
         10 ACCOUNTING      NEW YORK
         12 RESEARCH        NEW YORK
         14 OPERATIONS      NEW YORK
         13 SALES           NEW YORK
         30 SALES           CHICAGO
         34 OPERATIONS      CHICAGO
         20 RESEARCH        DALLAS
         23 SALES           DALLAS
         24 OPERATIONS      DALLAS
                            SAN FRANCISCO
         40 OPERATIONS      BOSTON
         43 SALES           BOSTON

12 rows selected.
```

This query lists all the rows from the LOCATION table, and their corresponding departments from the DEPARTMENT table. For the rows from LOCATION that don't have corresponding rows in DEPARTMENT, NULLs are returned in D.DEPT_ID and D.NAME columns in the result set. This query is equivalent to the following traditional outer join query:

```
SELECT D.DEPT_ID, D.NAME, L.REGIONAL_GROUP
FROM DEPARTMENT D, LOCATION L
WHERE D.LOCATION_ID (+) = L.LOCATION_ID;
```

If you want to include the departments without a location, as well as the locations without a department, you need to do a full outer join:

```
SELECT D.DEPT_ID, D.NAME, L.REGIONAL_GROUP
FROM DEPARTMENT D FULL OUTER JOIN LOCATION L
ON D.LOCATION_ID = L.LOCATION_ID;
```

```
    DEPT_ID NAME            REGIONAL_GROUP
------------- -------------- --------------------
         10 ACCOUNTING      NEW YORK
         12 RESEARCH        NEW YORK
         13 SALES           NEW YORK
         14 OPERATIONS      NEW YORK
         20 RESEARCH        DALLAS
         23 SALES           DALLAS
         24 OPERATIONS      DALLAS
         30 SALES           CHICAGO
         34 OPERATIONS      CHICAGO
         40 OPERATIONS      BOSTON
         43 SALES           BOSTON
```

```
        50 MARKETING
        60 CONSULTING
                        SAN FRANCISCO
    14 rows selected.
```

We have seen earlier in this chapter that you can't perform a full outer join using the (+) operator on both sides in the join condition. In the section titled "Full Outer Joins," we showed how you can circumvent this restriction by using a UNION query. With the new syntax in Oracle9*i*, you no longer need to perform a UNION query to do a full outer join. The new syntax is not only ANSI-compliant, it is elegant and efficient as well.

Advantages of the New Join Syntax

The new join syntax represents a bit of an adjustment to developers who are used to using Oracle's traditional join syntax, including the outer join operator (+). However, there are several advantages of using the new syntax:

- The new join syntax follows the ANSI standard and therefore makes your code more portable.
- The new ON and USING clauses help in separating the join conditions from other filter conditions in the WHERE clause. This enhances development productivity and maintainability of your code.
- The new syntax makes it possible to perform a full outer join without having to perform a UNION of two SELECT queries.

We recommend that while working with Oracle9*i*, you use the new join syntax instead of the traditional join syntax.

CHAPTER 4

Group Operations

Group operations are quite common in the day-to-day life of a SQL programmer. If we use SQL to access a database, it is quite common to expect questions like:

- What is the maximum salary in this department?
- How many managers are there in each department?
- What is the number of customers for each product?
- Can we print the monthly aggregate sales for each region?

We need group operations to answer these questions. Oracle provides a rich set of features to handle group operations. These features include aggregate functions, the GROUP BY clause, the HAVING clause, the GROUPING function, and the extensions to the GROUP BY clause—ROLLUP and CUBE.

 This chapter deals with simple group operations involving the aggregate functions, the GROUP BY and HAVING clauses. Advanced group operations such as GROUPING, ROLLUP, and CUBE are discussed in Chapter 12.

Aggregate Functions

In essence, an aggregate function summarizes the results of an expression over a number of rows, returning a single value. The general syntax for most of the aggregate functions is as follows:

    aggregate_function([DISTINCT | ALL] expression)

The syntax elements are:

aggregate_function
    Gives the name of the function, e.g., SUM, COUNT, AVG, MAX, MIN, etc.

DISTINCT
    Specifies that the aggregate function should consider only distinct values of the argument expression.

ALL

Specifies that the aggregate function should consider all values, including all duplicate values, of the argument expression. The default is ALL.

expression

Specifies a column, or any other expression, on which we want to perform the aggregation.

Let's look at a simple example. The following SQL uses the MAX function to find the maximum salary of all employees:

```
SELECT MAX(SALARY) FROM EMPLOYEE;

MAX(SALARY)
-----------
       5000
```

In subsequent sections, we use a series of slightly more involved examples that illustrate various aspects of aggregate function behavior. For those examples, we use the following CUST_ORDER table:

```
DESC CUST_ORDER
Name                            Null?     Type
------------------------------- --------- --------------
ORDER_NBR                       NOT NULL  NUMBER(7)
CUST_NBR                        NOT NULL  NUMBER(5)
SALES_EMP_ID                    NOT NULL  NUMBER(5)
SALE_PRICE                                NUMBER(9,2)
ORDER_DT                        NOT NULL  DATE
EXPECTED_SHIP_DT                NOT NULL  DATE
CANCELLED_DT                              DATE
SHIP_DT                                   DATE
STATUS                                    VARCHAR2(20)

SELECT ORDER_NBR, CUST_NBR, SALES_EMP_ID, SALE_PRICE,
ORDER_DT, EXPECTED_SHIP_DT
FROM CUST_ORDER;

ORDER_NBR   CUST_NBR SALES_EMP_ID SALE_PRICE ORDER_DT  EXPECTED_
---------- --------- ------------ ---------- --------- ---------
      1001       231         7354         99 22-JUL-01 23-JUL-01
      1000       201         7354            19-JUL-01 24-JUL-01
      1002       255         7368            12-JUL-01 25-JUL-01
      1003       264         7368         56 16-JUL-01 26-JUL-01
      1004       244         7368         34 18-JUL-01 27-JUL-01
      1005       288         7368         99 22-JUL-01 24-JUL-01
      1006       231         7354            22-JUL-01 28-JUL-01
      1007       255         7368         25 20-JUL-01 22-JUL-01
      1008       255         7368         25 21-JUL-01 23-JUL-01
      1009       231         7354         56 18-JUL-01 22-JUL-01
      1012       231         7354         99 22-JUL-01 23-JUL-01
      1011       201         7354            19-JUL-01 24-JUL-01
      1015       255         7368            12-JUL-01 25-JUL-01
      1017       264         7368         56 16-JUL-01 26-JUL-01
```

1019	244	7368	34	18-JUL-01	27-JUL-01
1021	288	7368	99	22-JUL-01	24-JUL-01
1023	231	7354		22-JUL-01	28-JUL-01
1025	255	7368	25	20-JUL-01	22-JUL-01
1027	255	7368	25	21-JUL-01	23-JUL-01
1029	231	7354	56	18-JUL-01	22-JUL-01

20 rows selected.

NULLs and Aggregate Functions

Notice that the column SALE_PRICE in the CUST_ORDER table is nullable, and that it contains NULL values for some rows. To examine the effect of NULLs in an aggregate function, we execute the following SQL:

```
SELECT COUNT(*), COUNT(SALE_PRICE) FROM CUST_ORDER;

COUNT(*) COUNT(SALE_PRICE)
-------- -----------------
      20                14
```

Notice the difference in the output of COUNT(*) and COUNT(SALE_PRICE). This is because COUNT(SALE_PRICE) ignores NULLs, whereas COUNT(*) doesn't. The reason COUNT(*) doesn't ignore NULLs is because it counts rows, not COLUMN values. The concept of NULL doesn't apply to a row as a whole. Other than COUNT(*), there is only one other aggregate function that doesn't ignore NULLs, and that is GROUPING. All other aggregate functions ignore NULLs. We will discuss GROUPING in Chapter 12. For now, let's examine the effect of NULLs when they are ignored.

SUM, MAX, MIN, AVG, etc. all ignore NULLs. Therefore, if we are trying to find a value such as the average sale price in the CUST_ORDER table, the average will be of the 14 rows that have a value for that column. The following example shows the count of all rows, the total of all sale prices, and the average of all sale prices:

```
SELECT COUNT(*), SUM(SALE_PRICE), AVG(SALE_PRICE)
FROM CUST_ORDER;

COUNT(*) SUM(SALE_PRICE) AVG(SALE_PRICE)
--------------- --------------- ---------------
             20             788       56.2857143
```

Note that AVG(SALE_PRICE) is not equal to SUM(SALE_PRICE) / COUNT(*). If it were, the result of AVG(SALE_PRICE) would have been 788 / 20 = 39.4. But, since the AVG function ignores NULLS, it divides the total sale price by 14, and not by 20 (788 / 14 = 56.2857143).

There may be situations where we want an average to be taken over all the rows in a table, not just the rows with non-NULL values for the column in question. In these situations we have to use the NVL function within the AVG function call to assign 0 (or some other useful value) to the column in place of any NULL values. (DECODE or the new COALESCE function can be used in place of NVL. See Chapter 9 for details.) Here's an example:

```
SELECT AVG(NVL(SALE_PRICE,0)) FROM CUST_ORDER;

AVG(NVL(SALE_PRICE,0))
----------------------
                  39.4
```

Notice that the use of NVL causes all 20 rows to be considered for average computation, and the rows with NULL values for SALE_PRICE are assumed to have a 0 value for that column.

Use of DISTINCT and ALL

Most aggregate functions allow the use of DISTINCT or ALL along with the expression argument. DISTINCT allows us to disregard duplicate expression values, while ALL causes duplicate expression values to be included in the result. Notice that the column CUST_NBR has duplicate values. Observe the result of the following SQL:

```
SELECT COUNT(CUST_NBR), COUNT(DISTINCT CUST_NBR), COUNT(ALL CUST_NBR)
FROM CUST_ORDER;

COUNT(CUST_NBR) COUNT(DISTINCTCUST_NBR) COUNT(ALLCUST_NBR)
--------------- ----------------------- ------------------
             20                       6                 20
```

There are six distinct values in the CUST_NBR column. Therefore, COUNT(DISTINCT CUST_NBR) returns 6, whereas COUNT(CUST_NBR) and COUNT(ALL CUST_NBR) both return 20. ALL is the default, which means that if we don't specify either DISTINCT or ALL before the expression argument in an aggregate function, the function will consider all the rows that have a non-NULL value for the expression.

An important thing to note here is that ALL doesn't cause an aggregate function to consider NULL values. For example, COUNT(ALL SALE_PRICE) in the following example still returns 14, and not 20.

```
SELECT COUNT(ALL SALE_PRICE) FROM CUST_ORDER;

COUNT(ALLSALE_PRICE)
--------------------
                  14
```

Since ALL is the default, we can explicitly use ALL with every aggregate function. However, the aggregate functions that take more than one argument as input don't allow the use of DISTINCT. These include CORR, COVAR_POP, COVAR_SAMP, and all the linear regression functions.

In addition, some functions that take only one argument as input don't allow the use of DISTINCT. This category includes STTDEV_POP, STDDEV_SAMP, VAR_POP, VAR_SAMP, and GROUPING.

If we try to use DISTINCT with an aggregate function that doesn't allow it, we will get an error. For example:

```
SELECT STDDEV_POP(DISTINCT SALE_PRICE)
FROM CUST_ORDER;
SELECT STDDEV_POP(DISTINCT SALE_PRICE)
       *
ERROR at line 1:
ORA-30482: DISTINCT option not allowed for this function
```

However, using ALL with such a function doesn't cause any error. For example:

```
SELECT STDDEV_POP(ALL SALE_PRICE)
FROM CUST_ORDER;

STDDEV_POP(ALLSALE_PRICE)
-------------------------
               29.5282639
```

The GROUP BY Clause

The GROUP BY clause, along with the aggregate functions, groups a result set into multiple groups, and then produces a single row of summary information for each group. For example, if we want to find the total number of orders for each customer, execute the following query:

```
SELECT CUST_NBR, COUNT(ORDER_NBR)
FROM CUST_ORDER
GROUP BY CUST_NBR;

  CUST_NBR COUNT(ORDER_NBR)
---------- ----------------
       201                2
       231                6
       244                2
       255                6
       264                2
       288                2

6 rows selected.
```

The query produces one summary line of output for each customer. This is the essence of a GROUP BY query. We asked Oracle to GROUP the results BY CUST_NBR; therefore, it produced one output row for each distinct value of CUST_NBR. Each data value for a given customer represents a summary based on all rows for that customer.

The nonaggregate expression CUST_NBR in the SELECT list also appears in the GROUP BY clause. If we have a mix of aggregate and nonaggregate expressions in the SELECT list, SQL expects that we are trying to perform a GROUP BY operation, and we must also specify all nonaggregate expressions in the GROUP BY clause.

SQL returns an error if we fail to do so. For example, if we omit the GROUP BY clause, the following error is returned:

```
SELECT CUST_NBR, SALES_EMP_ID, COUNT(ORDER_NBR)
FROM CUST_ORDER;
SELECT CUST_NBR, SALES_EMP_ID, COUNT(ORDER_NBR)
       *
ERROR at line 1:
ORA-00937: not a single-group group function
```

Similarly, if we forget to include all nonaggregate expressions from the SELECT list in the GROUP BY clause, SQL returns the following error:

```
SELECT CUST_NBR, SALES_EMP_ID, COUNT(ORDER_NBR)
FROM CUST_ORDER
GROUP BY CUST_NBR;
SELECT CUST_NBR, SALES_EMP_ID, COUNT(ORDER_NBR)
                 *
ERROR at line 1:
ORA-00979: not a GROUP BY expression
```

Finally, we can't use a group function (aggregate function) in the GROUP BY clause. We will get an error if we attempt to do so, as in the following example:

```
SELECT CUST_NBR, COUNT(ORDER_NBR)
FROM CUST_ORDER
GROUP BY CUST_NBR, COUNT(ORDER_NBR);
GROUP BY CUST_NBR, COUNT(ORDER_NBR)
                         *
ERROR at line 3:
ORA-00934: group function is not allowed here
```

If we have a constant in our SELECT list, we don't need to include it in the GROUP BY clause. However, including the constant in the GROUP BY clause doesn't alter the result. Therefore, both the following statements will produce the same output:

```
SELECT 'CUSTOMER', CUST_NBR, COUNT(ORDER_NBR)
FROM CUST_ORDER
GROUP BY CUST_NBR;

SELECT 'CUSTOMER', CUST_NBR, COUNT(ORDER_NBR)
FROM CUST_ORDER
GROUP BY 'CUSTOMER', CUST_NBR;

'CUSTOME   CUST_NBR COUNT(ORDER_NBR)
--------   -------- ----------------
CUSTOMER        201                2
CUSTOMER        231                6
CUSTOMER        244                2
CUSTOMER        255                6
CUSTOMER        264                2
CUSTOMER        288                2

6 rows selected.
```

There are certain situations when we want an expression in the select list, but don't want to group by the same. For example, we might want to display a line number along with the summary information for each customer. Attempt to do so using the following query, and we will get an error:

```
SELECT ROWNUM, CUST_NBR, COUNT(ORDER_NBR)
FROM CUST_ORDER
GROUP BY CUST_NBR;
SELECT ROWNUM, CUST_NBR, COUNT(ORDER_NBR)
       *
ERROR at line 1:
ORA-00979: not a GROUP BY expression
```

If we include ROWNUM in the GROUP BY clause, we'll get the following, unexpected result:

```
SELECT ROWNUM, CUST_NBR, COUNT(ORDER_NBR)
FROM CUST_ORDER
GROUP BY ROWNUM, CUST_NBR;
```

ROWNUM	CUST_NBR	COUNT(ORDER_NBR)
1	231	1
2	201	1
3	255	1
4	264	1
5	244	1
6	288	1
7	231	1
8	255	1
9	255	1
10	231	1
11	231	1
12	201	1
13	255	1
14	264	1
15	244	1
16	288	1
17	231	1
18	255	1
19	255	1
20	231	1

```
20 rows selected.
```

We certainly didn't want this result, did we? We wanted to receive one summary row for each customer, and then to display ROWNUM for those lines. But when we include ROWNUM in the GROUP BY clause, it produces one summary row for each row selected from the table CUST_ORDER. To get the expected result, we should use the following SQL:

```
SELECT ROWNUM, V.*
FROM (SELECT CUST_NBR, COUNT(ORDER_NBR)
```

```
       FROM CUST_ORDER GROUP BY CUST_NBR) V;

    ROWNUM   CUST_NBR COUNT(ORDER_NBR)
---------- ---------- ----------------
         1        201                2
         2        231                6
         3        244                2
         4        255                6
         5        264                2
         6        288                2
```

    6 rows selected.

The construct in the FROM clause is called an inline view. Read more about inline views in Chapter 5.

Syntactically, it is not mandatory to include all the expressions of the GROUP BY clause in the SELECT list. However, those expressions not in the SELECT list will not be represented in the output; therefore, the output may not make much sense. For example:

```
SELECT COUNT(ORDER_NBR)
FROM CUST_ORDER
GROUP BY CUST_NBR;

COUNT(ORDER_NBR)
----------------
               2
               6
               2
               6
               2
               2
```

    6 rows selected.

This query produces a count of orders for each customer (by grouping based on CUST_NBR), but without the CUST_NBR in the output we can't associate the counts with the customers. Extending the previous example, we can see that without a consistent SELECT list and GROUP BY clause, the output may be a bit confusing. The following example produces output that at first glance seems useful:

```
SELECT CUST_NBR, COUNT(ORDER_NBR)
FROM CUST_ORDER
GROUP BY CUST_NBR, ORDER_DT;

  CUST_NBR COUNT(ORDER_NBR)
---------- ----------------
       201                2
       231                2
       231                4
       244                2
```

```
255                 2
255                 2
255                 2
264                 2
288                 2
```

9 rows selected.

From the output, it appears that we are trying to obtain a count of orders for each customer. However, there are multiple rows in the output for some CUST_NBR values. The fact that we have included ORDER_DT in the GROUP BY clause, and therefore generated a summary result for each combination of CUST_NBR and ORDER_DT, is missing from the output. We can't make sense of the output unless the output and the SQL statement are looked at together. We can't expect all readers of SQL output to understand SQL syntax, can we? Therefore, we always recommend maintaining consistency between the nonaggregate expressions in the SELECT list and the expressions in the GROUP BY clause. A more meaningful version of the previous SQL statement would be as follows:

```
SELECT CUST_NBR, ORDER_DT, COUNT(ORDER_NBR)
FROM CUST_ORDER
GROUP BY CUST_NBR, ORDER_DT;


  CUST_NBR ORDER_DT  COUNT(ORDER_NBR)
---------- --------- ----------------
       201 19-JUL-01                2
       231 18-JUL-01                2
       231 22-JUL-01                4
       244 18-JUL-01                2
       255 12-JUL-01                2
       255 20-JUL-01                2
       255 21-JUL-01                2
       264 16-JUL-01                2
       288 22-JUL-01                2
```

9 rows selected.

This output is consistent with the GROUP BY clause in the query. We're more likely to make the correct assumption about what this output represents.

GROUP BY Clause and NULL Values

When we GROUP BY a column that contains NULL values for some rows, all the rows with NULL values are placed into a single group and presented as one summary row in the output. For example:

```
SELECT SALE_PRICE, COUNT(ORDER_NBR)
FROM CUST_ORDER
GROUP BY SALE_PRICE;
```

```
SALE_PRICE COUNT(ORDER_NBR)
---------- ----------------
        25                4
        34                2
        56                4
        99                4
                          6
```

Notice that the last row in the output consists of a NULL value for the column SALE_PRICE. Since the GROUP BY clause inherently performs an ORDER BY on the group by columns, the row containing the NULL value is put at the end. If we want this row to be the first row in the output, we can perform an ORDER BY on SALE_PRICE in descending order:

```
SELECT SALE_PRICE, COUNT(ORDER_NBR)
FROM CUST_ORDER
GROUP BY SALE_PRICE
ORDER BY SALE_PRICE DESC;

SALE_PRICE COUNT(ORDER_NBR)
---------- ----------------
                          6
        99                4
        56                4
        34                2
        25                4
```

GROUP BY Clause with WHERE Clause

While producing summary results using the GROUP BY clause, we can filter records from the table based on a WHERE clause, as in the following example, which produces a count of orders in which the sale price exceeds $25.00 for each customer:

```
SELECT CUST_NBR, COUNT(ORDER_NBR)
FROM CUST_ORDER
WHERE SALE_PRICE > 25
GROUP BY CUST_NBR;

CUST_NBR COUNT(ORDER_NBR)
---------- ----------------
       231                4
       244                2
       264                2
       288                2
```

While executing a SQL statement with a WHERE clause and a GROUP BY clause, Oracle first applies the WHERE clause and filters out the rows that don't satisfy the WHERE condition. The rows that satisfy the WHERE clause are then grouped using the GROUP BY clause.

The SQL syntax requires that the WHERE clause must come before the GROUP BY clause. Otherwise, the following error is returned:

```
SELECT CUST_NBR, COUNT(ORDER_NBR)
FROM CUST_ORDER
GROUP BY CUST_NBR
WHERE SALE_PRICE > 25;
WHERE SALE_PRICE > 25
      *
ERROR at line 4:
ORA-00933: SQL command not properly ended
```

The HAVING Clause

The HAVING clause is closely associated with the GROUP BY clause. The HAV-
ING clause is used to put a filter on the groups created by the GROUP BY clause. If a
query has a HAVING clause along with a GROUP BY clause, the result set will
include only the groups that satisfy the condition specified in the HAVING clause.
Let's look at some examples that illustrate this. The following query returns the
number of orders per customer:

```
SELECT CUST_NBR, COUNT(ORDER_NBR)
FROM CUST_ORDER
GROUP BY CUST_NBR
HAVING CUST_NBR < 260;

  CUST_NBR COUNT(ORDER_NBR)
---------- ----------------
       201                2
       231                6
       244                2
       255                6
```

Notice that the output only includes customers with numbers below 260. That's
because the HAVING clause specified CUST_NBR < 260 as a condition. Orders for
all customers were counted, but only those groups that matched the specified HAV-
ING condition were returned as the result.

The previous example is a poor use of the HAVING clause, because that clause only
references unsummarized data. It's more efficient to use WHERE CUST_NBR < 260
instead of HAVING CUST_NBR < 260, because the WHERE clause eliminates rows
prior to summarization, whereas HAVING eliminates groups post-summarization. A
better version of the previous query would be:

```
SELECT CUST_NBR, COUNT(ORDER_NBR)
FROM CUST_ORDER
WHERE CUST_NBR < 260;
```

The next example shows a more appropriate use of the HAVING clause:

```
SELECT CUST_NBR, COUNT(ORDER_NBR)
FROM CUST_ORDER
GROUP BY CUST_NBR
HAVING COUNT(ORDER_NBR) > 2;
```

```
CUST_NBR COUNT(ORDER_NBR)
---------- ----------------
       231                6
       255                6
```

Note the use of an aggregate function in the HAVING clause. This is an appropriate use for HAVING, because the results of the aggregate function cannot be determined until after the grouping takes place.

The syntax for the HAVING clause is similar to that of the WHERE clause. However, there is one restriction on the condition in the HAVING clause. The condition can only refer to expressions in the SELECT list or the GROUP BY clause. If we specify an expression in the HAVING clause that isn't in the SELECT list or the GROUP BY clause, we will get an error. For example:

```
SELECT CUST_NBR, COUNT(ORDER_NBR)
FROM CUST_ORDER
GROUP BY CUST_NBR
HAVING ORDER_DT < SYSDATE;
HAVING ORDER_DT < SYSDATE
       *
ERROR at line 4:
ORA-00979: not a GROUP BY expression
```

The order of the GROUP BY clause and the HAVING clause in a SELECT statement is not important. We can specify the GROUP BY clause before the HAVING clause, or vice versa. Therefore the following two queries are the same and produce the same result:

```
SELECT CUST_NBR, COUNT(ORDER_NBR)
FROM CUST_ORDER
GROUP BY CUST_NBR
HAVING COUNT(ORDER_NBR) > 1;

SELECT CUST_NBR, COUNT(ORDER_NBR)
FROM CUST_ORDER
HAVING COUNT(ORDER_NBR) > 1
GROUP BY CUST_NBR;

CUST_NBR COUNT(ORDER_NBR)
---------- ----------------
       231                6
       255                6
```

We can use a WHERE clause and a HAVING clause together in a query. When we do, it is important to understand the impact of the two clauses. Note that the WHERE clause is executed first, and the rows that don't satisfy the WHERE condition are not passed to the GROUP BY clause. The GROUP BY clause summarizes the filtered data into groups, and then the HAVING clause is applied to the groups to eliminate the groups that don't satisfy the HAVING condition. The following example illustrates this:

```
SELECT CUST_NBR, COUNT(ORDER_NBR)
FROM CUST_ORDER
WHERE SALE_PRICE > 25
GROUP BY CUST_NBR
HAVING COUNT(ORDER_NBR) > 1;
```

```
CUST_NBR COUNT(ORDER_NBR)
---------- ----------------
       231                4
       244                2
       264                2
       288                2
```

In this example, the WHERE clause first eliminates all the orders that don't satisfy the condition SALE_PRICE > 25. The rest of the rows are grouped on CUST_NBR. The HAVING clause eliminates the customers that don't have more than one order.

CHAPTER 5
Subqueries

Some endeavors require a certain level of preparation before the main activity can commence. Cooking, for example, often involves pre-mixing sets of ingredients before they are combined. Similarly, certain types of SQL statements benefit from the creation of intermediate result sets to aid in statement execution. The structure responsible for generating intermediate result sets is the subquery. This chapter will define and illustrate the use of subqueries in SQL statements.

What Is a Subquery?

A *subquery* is a SELECT statement that is nested within another SQL statement. For the purpose of this discussion, we will call the SQL statement that contains a subquery the *containing statement*. Subqueries are executed prior to execution of the containing SQL statement (see "Correlated Subqueries" later in this chapter for the exception to this rule), and the result set generated by the subquery is discarded after the containing SQL statement has finished execution. Thus, a subquery can be thought of as a temporary table with statement scope.

Syntactically, subqueries are enclosed within parentheses. For example, the following SELECT statement contains a simple subquery in its WHERE clause:

```
SELECT * FROM customer
WHERE cust_nbr = (SELECT 123 FROM dual);
```

The subquery in this statement is absurdly simple, and completely unnecessary, but it does serve to illustrate a point. When this statement is executed, the subquery is evaluated first. The result of that subquery then becomes a value in the WHERE clause expression:

```
SELECT * FROM customer
WHERE cust_nbr = 123;
```

With the subquery out of the way, the containing query can now be evaluated. In this case, it would bring back information about customer number 123.

Subqueries are most often found in the WHERE clause of a SELECT, UPDATE, or DELETE statement. A subquery may either be *correlated* with its containing SQL statement, meaning that it references one or more columns from the containing statement, or it might reference nothing outside itself, in which case it is called a *noncorrelated* subquery. A less-commonly-used but powerful variety of subquery, called the *inline view*, occurs in the FROM clause of a select statement. Inline views are always noncorrelated; they are evaluated first and behave like unindexed tables cached in memory for the remainder of the query.

Subqueries are useful because they allow comparisons to be made without changing the size of the result set. For example, we might want to find all customers that placed orders last month, but we might not want any given customer to be included more than once, regardless of the number of orders placed by that customer. Whereas joining the customer and orders tables would expand the result set by the number of orders placed by each customer, a subquery against the orders table using the IN or EXISTS operator would determine whether each customer placed an order, without regard for the number of orders placed.

Noncorrelated Subqueries

Noncorrelated subqueries allow each row from the containing SQL statement to be compared to a set of values. Divide noncorrelated subqueries into the following three categories, depending on the number of rows and columns returned in their result set:

- Single-row, single-column subqueries
- Multiple-row, single-column subqueries
- Multiple-column subqueries

Depending on the category, different sets of operators may be employed by the containing SQL statement to interact with the subquery.

Single-Row, Single-Column Subqueries

A subquery that returns a single row with a single column is treated like a scalar by the containing statement; not surprisingly, these types of subqueries are known as *scalar subqueries*. The subquery may appear on either side of a condition, and the usual comparison operators (=, <, >, !=, <=, >=) are employed. The following query illustrates the utility of single-row, single-column subqueries by finding all employees earning an above-average salary. The subquery returns the average salary, and the containing query then returns all employees who earn more than that amount.

```
SELECT lname
FROM employee
WHERE salary > (SELECT AVG(salary)
                FROM EMPLOYEE);
```

```
LNAME
--------------------
Brown
Smith
Blake
Isaacs
Jacobs
King
Fox
Anderson
Nichols
Iverson
Peters
Russell
```

As this query demonstrates, it can be perfectly reasonable for a subquery to reference the same tables as the containing query. In fact, subqueries are frequently used to isolate a subset of records within a table. For example, many applications include maintenance routines that clean up operational data, such as exception or load logs. Every week, a script might delete all but the latest day's activity. For example:

```
DELETE FROM load_log
WHERE load_dt < (SELECT MAX(TRUNC(load_dt))
                 FROM load_log);
```

Noncorrelated subqueries are also commonly found outside the WHERE clause, as illustrated by the following query, which identifies the salesperson responsible for the most orders:

```
SELECT sales_emp_id, COUNT(*)
FROM cust_order
GROUP BY sales_emp_id
HAVING COUNT(*) = (SELECT MAX(COUNT(*))
                   FROM cust_order
                   GROUP BY sales_emp_id);
```

```
SALES_EMP_ID   COUNT(*)
------------ ----------
          30        121
```

This subquery calculates the number of orders attributable to each salesperson, and then applies the MAX function to return only the highest number of orders. The containing query performs the same aggregation as the subquery and then keeps only those salespeople whose total sales count matches the maximum value returned by the subquery. Interestingly, the containing query can return more than one row if multiple salespeople tie for the maximum sales count, while the subquery is guaranteed to return a single row and column. If it seems wasteful that the subquery and containing query both perform the same aggregation, it is; see Chapter 13 for more efficient ways to handle these types of queries.

So far, we have seen scalar subqueries in the WHERE and HAVING clauses of SELECT statements, along with the WHERE clause of a DELETE statement. Before we delve deeper into the different types of subqueries, let's explore where else sub-queries can and can't be utilized in SQL statements:

- The FROM clause may contain any type of noncorrelated subquery.
- The SELECT and ORDER BY clauses may contain scalar subqueries.
- The GROUP BY clause may not contain subqueries.
- The START WITH and CONNECT BY clauses, used for querying hierarchical data, may contain subqueries and will be examined in detail in Chapter 8.

Multiple-Row Subqueries

Now that we know how to use single-row, single-column subqueries, let's explore how to use subqueries that return multiple rows. When a subquery returns more than one row, it is not possible to use only comparison operators, since a single value cannot be directly compared to a set of values. However, a single value *can* be compared to each value in a set. To accomplish this, the special keywords ANY and ALL may be used with comparison operators to determine if a value is equal to (or less than, greater than, etc.) *any* members of the set or *all* members of the set. Consider the following query:

```
SELECT fname, lname
FROM employee
WHERE dept_id = 3 AND salary >= ALL
  (SELECT salary
   FROM employee
   WHERE dept_id = 3);


FNAME                LNAME
-------------------- --------------------
Mark                 Russell
```

The subquery returns the set of salaries for department 3, and the containing query checks each employee in the department to see if her salary is greater or equal to every salary returned by the subquery. Thus, this query retrieves the name of the highest paid person in department 3. While everyone except the lowest paid employee has a salary >= *some* of the salaries in the departement, only the highest paid employee has a salary >= *all* of the salaries in the department. If multiple employees tie for the highest salary in the department, multiple names will be returned.

Another way to phrase the previous query is to find the employee whose salary is not less than any other salary in the department. We can do this using the ANY operator:

```
SELECT fname, lname
FROM employee
WHERE dept_id = 3 AND NOT salary < ANY
  (SELECT salary
   FROM employee
   WHERE dept_id = 3);
```

There are almost always multiple ways to phrase the same query. One of the challenges of writing SQL is striking the right balance between efficiency and readability. In this case, I might prefer using AND salary >= ALL over AND NOT salary < ANY because the first variation is easier to understand; however, the latter form might prove more efficient, since each evaluation of the subquery results requires from 1 to N comparisons when using ANY versus exactly N comparisons when using ALL.*

The next query uses the ANY operator to find all employees whose salary exceeds that of any top-level manager:

```
SELECT fname, lname
FROM employee
WHERE manager_emp_id IS NOT NULL
  AND salary > ANY
  (SELECT salary
   FROM employee
   WHERE manager_emp_id IS NULL);
```

```
FNAME                LNAME
-------------------- --------------------
Laura                Peters
Mark                 Russell
```

The subquery returns the set of salaries for all top-level managers, and the containing query returns the names of non-top-level managers whose salary exceeds any of the salaries returned by the subquery. Any time this query returns one or more rows, rest assured that top-level management will vote themselves a pay increase.

For the previous three queries, failure to include either the ANY or ALL operators will result in the following error:

```
ORA-01427: single-row subquery returns more than one row
```

The wording of this error message is a bit confusing. After all, how can a single-row subquery return multiple rows? What the error message is trying to convey is that a multiple-row subquery has been identified where only a single-row subquery is allowed. If we are not absolutely certain that our subquery will return exactly one row, we must include ANY or ALL to ensure our code doesn't fail in the future.

Along with ANY and ALL, we may also use the IN operator for working with multi-row subqueries. Using IN with a subquery is functionally equivalent to using = ANY, and returns TRUE if a match is found in the set returned by the subquery. The following query uses IN to postpone shipment of all orders containing parts which are not currently in stock:

```
UPDATE cust_order
SET expected_ship_dt = TRUNC(SYSDATE) + 1
```

---

* If there are 100 people in the department, each of the 100 salaries needs to be compared to the entire set of 100. When using ANY, the comparison can be suspended as soon as a larger salary is identified in the set, whereas using ALL requires 100 comparisons to ensure that there are no smaller salaries in the set.

```
WHERE ship_dt IS NULL AND order_nbr IN
  (SELECT l.order_nbr
   FROM line_item l, part p
   WHERE l.part_nbr = p.part_nbr AND p.inventory_qty = 0);
```

The subquery returns the set of orders requesting out-of-stock parts, and the containing UPDATE statement modifies the expected ship date of all orders in the set. We think you will agree that IN is more intuitive than = ANY, which is why IN is almost always used in such situations. Similarly, we can use NOT IN instead of using != ANY as demonstrated by the next query, which deletes all customers who haven't placed an order in the past five years:

```
DELETE FROM customer
WHERE cust_nbr NOT IN
  (SELECT cust_nbr
   FROM cust_order
   WHERE order_dt >= TRUNC(SYSDATE) - (365 * 5));
```

The subquery returns the set of customers that *have* placed an order in the past five years, and the containing DELETE statement removes all customers that are not in the set returned by the subquery.

Finding members of one set that do *not* exist in another set is referred to as an *anti-join*. As the name implies, an anti-join is the opposite of a join; rows from table A are returned if the specified data is *not* found in table B. The Oracle optimizer can employ multiple strategies for executing such queries, including a *merge anti-join* or a *hash anti-join*.[*]

Multiple-Column Subqueries

While all of the previous examples compare a single column from the containing SQL statement to the result set returned by the subquery, it is also possible to issue a subquery against multiple columns. Consider the following UPDATE statement, which rolls up data from an operational table into an aggregate table:

```
UPDATE monthly_orders SET
  tot_orders = (SELECT COUNT(*)
    FROM cust_order
    WHERE order_dt >= TO_DATE('01-NOV-2001','DD-MON-YYYY')
      AND order_dt < TO_DATE('01-DEC-2001','DD-MON-YYYY')
      AND cancelled_dt IS NULL),
  max_order_amt = (SELECT MAX(sale_price)
    FROM cust_order
    WHERE order_dt >= TO_DATE('01-NOV-2001','DD-MON-YYYY')
      AND order_dt < TO_DATE('01-DEC-2001','DD-MON-YYYY')
      AND cancelled_dt IS NULL),
```

---

[*] Since this is not a tuning book, I will refrain from delving into the inner workings of the Oracle optimizer and how the optimizer can be influenced via hints. For more information, please see the *Oracle SQL Tuning Pocket Reference* by Mark Gurry (O'Reilly).

```
          min_order_amt = (SELECT MIN(sale_price)
            FROM cust_order
            WHERE order_dt >= TO_DATE('01-NOV-2001','DD-MON-YYYY')
              AND order_dt < TO_DATE('01-DEC-2001','DD-MON-YYYY')
              AND cancelled_dt IS NULL),
          tot_amt = (SELECT SUM(sale_price)
            FROM cust_order
            WHERE order_dt >= TO_DATE('01-NOV-2001','DD-MON-YYYY')
              AND order_dt < TO_DATE('01-DEC-2001','DD-MON-YYYY')
              AND cancelled_dt IS NULL)
      WHERE month = 11 and year = 2001;
```

The UPDATE statement modifies four columns in the monthly_orders table, and values for each of the four columns are calculated by aggregating data in the cust_order table. Looking closely, we see that the WHERE clauses for all four subqueries are identical; only the aggregation type differs in the four queries. The next query demonstrates how all four columns can be populated with a single trip through the cust_order table:

```
UPDATE monthly_orders
SET (tot_orders, max_order_amt, min_order_amt, tot_amt) =
  (SELECT COUNT(*), MAX(sale_price), MIN(sale_price), SUM(sale_price)
   FROM cust_order
   WHERE order_dt >= TO_DATE('01-NOV-2001','DD-MON-YYYY')
     AND order_dt < TO_DATE('01-DEC-2001','DD-MON-YYYY')
     AND cancelled_dt IS NULL)
WHERE month = 11 and year = 2001;
```

The second statement achieves the same result more efficiently than the first by performing four aggregations during one trip through the cust_order table, rather than one aggregation during each of four separate trips.

Whereas the previous example demonstrates the use of a multiple-column subquery in the SET clause of an UPDATE statement, such subqueries may also be utilized in the WHERE clause of a SELECT, UPDATE, or DELETE statement. The next statement deletes all items from open orders that include discontinued parts:

```
DELETE FROM line_item
WHERE (order_nbr, part_nbr) IN
 (SELECT c.order_nbr, p.part_nbr
  FROM cust_order c, line_item li, part p
  WHERE c.ship_dt IS NULL AND c.cancelled_dt IS NULL
    AND c.order_nbr = li.order_nbr
    AND li.part_nbr = p.part_nbr
    AND p.status = 'DISCONTINUED');
```

Note the use of the IN operator in the WHERE clause. Two columns are listed together in parentheses prior to the IN keyword. Values in these two columns are compared to the set of two values returned by each row of the subquery. If a match is found, the row is removed from the line_item table.

Correlated Subqueries

A subquery that references one or more columns from its containing SQL statement is called a *correlated subquery*. Unlike noncorrelated subqueries, which are executed exactly once prior to execution of the containing statement, a correlated subquery is executed once for each candidate row in the intermediate result set of the containing query. For example, consider the following query, which locates all parts supplied by Acme Industries that have been purchased ten or more times since December:

```
SELECT p.part_nbr, p.name
FROM supplier s, part p
WHERE s.name = 'Acme Industries'
  AND s.supplier_id = p.supplier_id
  AND 10 <=
   (SELECT COUNT(*)
    FROM cust_order co, line_item li
    WHERE li.part_nbr = p.part_nbr
      AND li.order_nbr = co.order_nbr
      AND co.order_dt >= TO_DATE('01-DEC-2001','DD-MON-YYYY'));
```

The reference to p.part_nbr is what makes the subquery correlated; values for p. part_nbr must be supplied by the containing query before the subquery can execute. If there are 10,000 parts in the part table, but only 100 are supplied by Acme Industries, the subquery will be executed once for each of the 100 rows in the intermediate result set created by joining the part and supplier tables.[*]

Correlated subqueries are often used to test whether relationships exist without regard to cardinality. We might, for example, want to find all parts that have shipped at least once in 2002. The EXISTS operator is used for these types of queries, as illustrated by the following query:

```
SELECT p.part_nbr, p.name, p.unit_cost
FROM part p
WHERE EXISTS
 (SELECT 1 FROM line_item li, cust_order co
  WHERE li.part_nbr = p.part_nbr
    AND li.order_nbr = co.order_nbr
    AND co.ship_dt >= TO_DATE('01-JAN-2002','DD-MON-YYYY'));
```

As long as the subquery returns one or more rows, the EXISTS condition is satisfied without regard for how many rows were actually returned by the subquery. Since the EXISTS operator returns TRUE or FALSE depending on the number of rows returned by the subquery, the actual columns returned by the subquery are irrelevant. The SELECT clause requires at least one column, however, so it is common practice to use either the literal "1" or the wildcard "*".

---

[*] It is possible to ask for the subquery to be evaluated earlier in the execution plan using the PUSH_SUBQ hint; once again, we suggest you pick up a good book on Oracle tuning if you are interested in learning more.

Conversely, we can test whether a relationship does not exist:

```
UPDATE customer c
SET c.inactive_ind = 'Y', c.inactive_dt = TRUNC(SYSDATE)
WHERE c.inactive_dt IS NULL
  AND NOT EXISTS (SELECT 1 FROM cust_order co
    WHERE co.cust_nbr = c.cust_nbr
      AND co.order_dt > TRUNC(SYSDATE) - 365);
```

This statement makes all customer records inactive for those customers who haven't placed an order in the past year. Such queries are commonly found in maintenance routines. For example, foreign key constraints might prevent child records from referring to a nonexistent parent, but it is possible to have parent records without children. If business rules prohibit this situation, we might run a utility each week that removes these records, as in:

```
DELETE FROM cust_order co
WHERE co.order_dt > TRUNC(SYSDATE) - 7
  AND co.cancelled_dt IS NULL
  AND NOT EXISTS
    (SELECT 1 FROM line_item li
    WHERE li.order_nbr = co.order_nbr);
```

A query that includes a correlated subquery using the EXISTS operator is referred to as a *semi-join*. A semi-join includes rows in table A for which corresponding data is found one or more times in table B. Thus, the size of the final result set is unaffected by the number of matches found in table B. Similar to the anti-join discussed earlier, the Oracle optimizer can employ multiple strategies for executing such queries, including a *merge semi-join* or a *hash semi-join*.

While they are very often used together, the use of correlated subqueries does not require the EXISTS operator. If our database design includes denormalized columns, for example, we might run nightly routines to recalculate the denormalized data, as in:

```
UPDATE customer c
SET (c.tot_orders, c.last_order_dt) =
 (SELECT COUNT(*), MAX(co.order_dt)
  FROM cust_order co
  WHERE co.cust_nbr = c.cust_nbr
    AND co.cancelled_dt IS NULL);
```

Because a SET clause assigns values to columns in the table, the only operator allowed is "=". The subquery returns exactly one row (thanks to the aggregation functions), so the results may be safely assigned to the target columns. Rather than recalculating the entire sum each day, a more efficient method might be to update only those customers who placed orders today:

```
UPDATE customer c SET (c.tot_orders, c.last_order_dt) =
 (SELECT c.tot_orders + COUNT(*), MAX(co.order_dt)
  FROM cust_order co
  WHERE co.cust_nbr = c.cust_nbr
    AND co.cancelled_dt IS NULL
    AND co.order_dt >= TRUNC(SYSDATE))
```

```
WHERE c.cust_nbr IN
  (SELECT co.cust_nbr FROM cust_order co
   WHERE co.order_dt >= TRUNC(SYSDATE)
     AND co.cancelled_dt IS NULL);
```

As the previous statement shows, data from the containing query can be used for other purposes in the correlated subquery than just join conditions in the WHERE clause. In this example, the SELECT clause of the correlated subquery adds today's sales totals to the previous value of tot_orders in the customer table to arrive at the new value.

Inline Views

Most texts covering SQL define the FROM clause of a SELECT statement as containing a list of tables and/or views. Please abandon this definition and replace it with the following: the FROM clause contains a list of data sets. In this light, it is easy to see how the FROM clause can contain tables (permanent data sets), views (virtual data sets), and SELECT statements (temporary data sets). A SELECT statement in the FROM clause of a containing SELECT statement is referred to as an *inline view*:[*] it is one of the most powerful, underutilized features of Oracle SQL. Here's a simple example:

```
SELECT d.dept_id, d.name, emp_cnt.tot
FROM department d,
  (SELECT dept_id, COUNT(*) tot
   FROM employee
   GROUP BY dept_id) emp_cnt
WHERE d.dept_id = emp_cnt.dept_id;

   DEPT_ID NAME                       TOT
---------- -------------------- ----------
         1 Human Resources              1
         2 Accounting                   1
         3 Sales                       24
```

In this example, the FROM clause references the department table and an inline view called emp_cnt, which calculates the number of employees in each department. The two sets are joined using dept_id and the ID, name, and employee count are returned for each department. While this example is fairly simple, inline views allow us to do things in a single query that might otherwise require multiple select statements or a procedural language to accomplish.

Inline View Basics

Because the result set from an inline view is referenced by other elements of the containing query, we must give our inline view a name and provide aliases for all ambiguous

---

[*] In the authors' opinion, the name "inline view" is confusing and tends to intimidate people. Since it is a subquery that executes prior to the containing query, a more palatable name might have been a "pre-query."

columns. In the previous example, the inline view was given the name "emp_cnt", and the alias "tot" was assigned to the COUNT(*) column. Similar to other types of subqueries, inline views may join multiple tables, call built-in and user-defined functions, specify optimizer hints, and include GROUP BY, HAVING, and CONNECT BY clauses. Unlike other types of subqueries, an inline view may also contain an ORDER BY clause, which opens several interesting possibilities (see "Subquery Case Study: The Top N Performers" later in the chapter for an example using ORDER BY in a subquery).

Inline views are particularly useful when we need to combine data at different levels of aggregation. In the previous example, we needed to retrieve all rows from the department table and include aggregated data from the employee table, so I chose to do the aggregation within an inline view and join the results to the department table. Anyone involved in report generation or data warehouse extraction, transformation, and load (ETL) applications has doubtless encountered situations where data from various levels of aggregation needs to be combined; with inline views, we should be able to produce the desired results in a single SQL statement rather than having to break the logic into multiple pieces or write code in a procedural language.

When considering using an inline view, ask the following questions:

1. What value does the inline view add to the readability and, more importantly, the performance of the containing query?

2. How large will the result set generated by the inline view be?

3. How often, if ever, will I have need of this particular data set?

In general, using an inline view should enhance the readability and performance of the query, and it should generate a manageable data set that is of no value to other statements or sessions; otherwise, we may want to consider building a permanent or temporary table so that we can share the data between sessions and build additional indexes as needed.

Query Execution

Inline views are always executed prior to the containing query and, thus, may not reference columns from other tables or inline views from the same query. After execution, the containing query interacts with the inline view as if it were an unindexed, in-memory table. If inline views are nested, the innermost inline view is executed first, followed by the next-innermost inline view, and so on. Consider the following query:

```
SELECT d.dept_id dept_id, d.name dept_name,
  dept_orders.tot_orders tot_orders
FROM department d,
   (SELECT e.dept_id dept_id, SUM(emp_orders.tot_orders) tot_orders
    FROM employee e,
     (SELECT sales_emp_id, COUNT(*) tot_orders
      FROM cust_order
      WHERE order_dt >= TRUNC(SYSDATE) - 365
```

```
      AND cancelled_dt IS NULL
    GROUP BY sales_emp_id
  ) emp_orders
  WHERE e.emp_id = emp_orders.sales_emp_id
  GROUP BY e.dept_id
  ) dept_orders
WHERE d.dept_id = dept_orders.dept_id;


DEPT_ID DEPT_NAME            TOT_ORDERS
---------- -------------------- ----------
      3 Sales                      2760
```

If you're new to inline views, this query might be intimidating. Start with the innermost query, understand the result set generated by that query, and move outward to the next level. Since inline views must be noncorrelated, you can run each inline view's SELECT statement individually and look at the results.[*] For the previous query, executing the emp_orders inline view generates the following result set:

```
SELECT sales_emp_id, COUNT(*) tot_orders
FROM cust_order
WHERE order_dt >= TRUNC(SYSDATE) - 365
  AND cancelled_dt IS NULL
GROUP BY sales_emp_id

SALES_EMP_ID TOT_ORDERS
------------ ----------
          11        115
          12        115
          13        115
          14        115
          15        115
          16        115
          17        115
          18        115
          19        115
          20        114
          21        115
          22        115
          23        115
          24        115
          25        115
          26        115
          27        115
          28        115
          29        115
          30        116
          31        115
          32        115
          33        115
          34        115
```

[*] From the standpoint of the inline view, this would constitute an "out-of-query experience."

The emp_orders set contains all salespeople who booked orders in the last year, along with the total number of orders booked. The next level up is the dept_orders inline view, which joins the emp_orders data set to the employee table and aggregates the number of orders up to the department level. The resulting data set looks as follows:

```
SELECT e.dept_id dept_id, SUM(emp_orders.tot_orders) tot_orders
FROM employee e,
  (SELECT sales_emp_id, COUNT(*) tot_orders
   FROM cust_order
   WHERE order_dt >= TRUNC(SYSDATE) - 365
     AND cancelled_dt IS NULL
   GROUP BY sales_emp_id
  ) emp_orders
WHERE e.emp_id = emp_orders.sales_emp_id
GROUP BY e.dept_id

   DEPT_ID TOT_ORDERS
---------- ----------
         3       2185
         4        575
```

Finally, the dept_orders set is joined to the department table, and the final result set is:

```
DEPT_ID DEPT_NAME            TOT_ORDERS
------- -------------------- ----------
      3 Domestic Sales             2185
      4 International Sales          575
```

After query execution completes, the emp_orders and dept_orders result sets are discarded.

Data Set Fabrication

Along with querying existing tables, inline views may be used to fabricate special-purpose data sets that don't exist in the database. For example, we might want to aggregate orders over the last year by small, medium, and large orders, but the concept of order sizes may not have been defined in our database. We could build a table with three records to define the different sizes and their boundaries, but we only need this information for a single query, and we don't want to clutter our database with dozens of small, special-purpose tables. One solution is to use set operators like UNION* to construct a custom-built data set, as in:

```
SELECT 'SMALL' name, 0 lower_bound, 999 upper_bound from dual
UNION ALL
SELECT 'MEDIUM' name, 1000 lower_bound, 24999 upper_bound from dual
UNION ALL
SELECT 'LARGE' name, 25000 lower_bound, 9999999 upper_bound from dual;
```

---

* Set operators will be covered in detail in Chapter 7. The UNION operator is used to combine individual sets of data into a single set.

```
NAME    LOWER_BOUND UPPER_BOUND
------  ----------- -----------
SMALL             0         999
MEDIUM         1000       24999
LARGE         25000     9999999
```

We can then wrap this query in an inline view and use it to do our aggregations:

```
SELECT sizes.name order_size, SUM(co.sale_price) tot_dollars
FROM cust_order co,
 (SELECT 'SMALL' name, 0 lower_bound, 999 upper_bound from dual
  UNION ALL
  SELECT 'MEDIUM' name, 1000 lower_bound, 24999 upper_bound from dual
  UNION ALL
  SELECT 'LARGE' name, 25000 lower_bound, 9999999 upper_bound from dual
 ) sizes
WHERE co.cancelled_dt IS NULL
  AND co.order_dt >= TO_DATE('01-JAN-2001','DD-MON-YYYY')
  AND co.order_dt < TO_DATE('01-JAN-2002','DD-MON-YYYY')
  AND co.sale_price BETWEEN sizes.lower_bound AND sizes.upper_bound
GROUP BY sizes.name;
```

```
ORDER_  TOT_DOLLARS
------  -----------
LARGE       7136214
MEDIUM     32395018
SMALL         63676
```

One word of caution: when constructing a set of ranges, make sure there are no gaps through which data may slip. For example, an order totaling $999.50 would not appear in either the small or medium categories, since $999.50 is neither between $0 and $999 nor between $1,000 and $24,999. One solution is to overlap the region boundaries so that there is no gap through which data can slip. Note that we can no longer use BETWEEN with this approach.

```
SELECT sizes.name order_size, SUM(co.sale_price) tot_dollars
FROM cust_order co,
 (SELECT 'SMALL' name, 0 lower_bound, 1000 upper_bound from dual
  UNION ALL
  SELECT 'MEDIUM' name, 1000 lower_bound, 25000 upper_bound from dual
  UNION ALL
  SELECT 'LARGE' name, 25000 lower_bound, 9999999 upper_bound from dual
 ) sizes
WHERE co.cancelled_dt IS NULL
  AND co.order_dt >= TO_DATE('01-JAN-2001', 'DD-MON-YYYY')
  AND co.order_dt < TO_DATE('01-JAN-2002', 'DD-MON-YYYY')
  AND co.sale_price >= sizes.lower_bound
    AND co.sale_price < sizes.upper_bound
GROUP BY sizes.name;
```

Now that we have neither an overlap or gap between our buckets, we can be sure that no data will be left out of the aggregations.

Fabricated data sets can also be useful for determining what data is *not* stored in our database. For example, our manager might ask for a report listing the aggregate sales for each day of the year 2000, including days with no sales. While our cust_order table contains records for every day that had orders, there is no table in the database containing a record for every day of the year. In order to provide our manager with an answer, we will need to fabricate a driving table containing a record for every day in 2000, and then outer join it to the set of aggregated sales for the same period.

Since a year contains either 365 or 366 days, we will build the set {0, 1, 2, ..., 399}, add each member of the set to the start date of 01/01/2000, and let Oracle throw away the rows that don't belong in 2000. To build the set {0, 1, 2, ..., 399}, we will create the sets {0, 1, 2, ..., 10}, {0, 10, 20, 30, ..., 90}, and {0, 100, 200, 300} and add members of the three sets across the Cartesian product:

```
SELECT ones.x + tens.x + hundreds.x tot
FROM
 (SELECT 0 x FROM dual UNION ALL
  SELECT 1 x FROM dual UNION ALL
  SELECT 2 x FROM dual UNION ALL
  SELECT 3 x FROM dual UNION ALL
  SELECT 4 x FROM dual UNION ALL
  SELECT 5 x FROM dual UNION ALL
  SELECT 6 x FROM dual UNION ALL
  SELECT 7 x FROM dual UNION ALL
  SELECT 8 x FROM dual UNION ALL
  SELECT 9 x FROM dual) ones,
 (SELECT 0 x FROM dual UNION ALL
  SELECT 10 x FROM dual UNION ALL
  SELECT 20 x FROM dual UNION ALL
  SELECT 30 x FROM dual UNION ALL
  SELECT 40 x FROM dual UNION ALL
  SELECT 50 x FROM dual UNION ALL
  SELECT 60 x FROM dual UNION ALL
  SELECT 70 x FROM dual UNION ALL
  SELECT 80 x FROM dual UNION ALL
  SELECT 90 x FROM dual) tens,
 (SELECT 0 x FROM dual UNION ALL
  SELECT 100 x FROM dual UNION ALL
  SELECT 200 x FROM dual UNION ALL
  SELECT 300 x FROM dual) hundreds
```

Since this query has no WHERE clause, every combination of the rows in the ones, tens, and hundreds sets will be generated, and the sum of the three numbers in each row will produce the set {0, 1, 2, ..., 399}. The next query generates the set of days in 2000 by adding each number in the set to the base date and then discarding days that fall in 2001:

```
SELECT days.dt
FROM
 (SELECT TO_DATE('01-JAN-2000', 'DD-MON-YYYY') +
    ones.x + tens.x + hundreds.x dt
  FROM
```

```
    (SELECT 0 x FROM dual UNION ALL
     SELECT 1 x FROM dual UNION ALL
     SELECT 2 x FROM dual UNION ALL
     SELECT 3 x FROM dual UNION ALL
     SELECT 4 x FROM dual UNION ALL
     SELECT 5 x FROM dual UNION ALL
     SELECT 6 x FROM dual UNION ALL
     SELECT 7 x FROM dual UNION ALL
     SELECT 8 x FROM dual UNION ALL
     SELECT 9 x FROM dual) ones,
    (SELECT 0 x FROM dual UNION ALL
     SELECT 10 x FROM dual UNION ALL
     SELECT 20 x FROM dual UNION ALL
     SELECT 30 x FROM dual UNION ALL
     SELECT 40 x FROM dual UNION ALL
     SELECT 50 x FROM dual UNION ALL
     SELECT 60 x FROM dual UNION ALL
     SELECT 70 x FROM dual UNION ALL
     SELECT 80 x FROM dual UNION ALL
     SELECT 90 x FROM dual) tens,
    (SELECT 0 x FROM dual UNION ALL
     SELECT 100 x FROM dual UNION ALL
     SELECT 200 x FROM dual UNION ALL
     SELECT 300 x FROM dual) hundreds) days
  WHERE days.dt < TO_DATE('01-JAN-2001', 'DD-MON-YYYY');
```

Since 2000 happens to be a leap year, the result set will contain 366 rows, one for each day of 2000. This query can then be wrapped in another inline view and used as the driving table for generating the report. Whether you would actually want to use such a strategy in your code is up to you; the main purpose of this example is to help get the creative juices flowing.

Overcoming SQL Restrictions

The use of certain features of Oracle SQL can impose restrictions on our SQL statements. When these features are isolated from the rest of the query inside an inline view, however, these restrictions can be sidestepped. In this section, we explore how inline views can overcome limitations with hierarchical and aggregation queries.

Hierarchical queries

Hierarchical queries allow recursive relationships to be traversed. As an example of a recursive relationship, consider a table called "region" that holds data about sales territories. Regions are arranged in a hierarchy, and each record in the region table references the region in which it is contained, as illustrated by the following data:

```
SELECT * FROM region;
```

REGION_ID	REGION_NAME	SUPER_REGION_ID
1	North America	
2	Canada	1

```
 3  United States          1
 4  Mexico                 1
 5  New England            3
 6  Mid-Atlantic           3
 7  SouthEast US           3
 8  SouthWest US           3
 9  NorthWest US           3
10  Central US             3
11  Europe
12  France                11
13  Germany               11
14  Spain                 11
```

Each record in the customer table references the smallest of its applicable regions. Given a particular region, it is possible to construct a query that traverses up or down the hierarchy by utilizing the START WITH and CONNECT BY clauses:

```
SELECT region_id, name, super_region_id
  FROM region
  START WITH name = `North America'
  CONNECT BY PRIOR region_id = super_region_id;

REGION_ID NAME                 SUPER_REGION_ID
---------- -------------------- ---------------
        1 North America
        2 Canada                             1
        3 United States                      1
        5 New England                        3
        6 Mid-Atlantic                       3
        7 SouthEast US                       3
        8 SouthWest US                       3
        9 NorthWest US                       3
       10 Central US                         3
        4 Mexico                             1
```

The query just shown traverses the region hierarchy starting with the North America region and working down the tree. Looking carefully at the results, we see that the Canada, United States, and Mexico regions all point to the North America region via the super_region_id field. The remainder of the rows all point to the United States region. Thus, we have identified a three-level hierarchy with one node at the top, three nodes in the second level, and six nodes in the third level underneath the United States node. For a detailed look at hierarchical queries, see Chapter 8.

Imagine that we have been asked to generate a report showing total sales in 2001 for each sub-region of North America. However, hierarchical queries have the restriction that the table being traversed cannot be joined to other tables within the same query, so it might seem impossible to generate the report from a single query. Using an inline view, however, we can isolate the hierarchical query on the region table from the customer and cust_order tables, as in:

```
SELECT na_regions.name region_name,
  SUM(co.sale_price) total_sales
```

```
FROM cust_order co, customer c,
 (SELECT region_id, name
  FROM region
  START WITH name = 'North America'
  CONNECT BY PRIOR region_id = super_region_id) na_regions
WHERE co.cancelled_dt IS NULL
  AND co.order_dt >= TO_DATE('01-JAN-2001','DD-MON-YYYY')
  AND co.order_dt < TO_DATE('01-JAN-2002','DD-MON-YYYY')
  AND co.cust_nbr = c.cust_nbr
  AND c.region_id = na_regions.region_id
GROUP BY na_regions.name;

REGION_NAME             TOTAL_SALES
--------------------    -----------
Central US                 6238901
Mid-Atlantic               6307766
New England                6585641
NorthWest US               6739374
SouthEast US               6868495
SouthWest US               6854731
```

Even though the na_regions set includes the North America and United States regions, customer records always point to the smallest applicable region, which is why these particular regions do not show up in the final result set.

By placing the hierarchical query within an inline view, we are able to temporarily flatten the region hierarchy to suit the purposes of the query, which allows us to bypass the restriction on hierarchical queries without resorting to splitting the logic into multiple pieces. The next section will demonstrate a similar strategy for working with aggregation queries.

Aggregate queries

Queries that perform aggregations have the following restriction: all nonaggregate columns in the SELECT clause must be included in the GROUP BY clause. Consider the following query, which aggregates sales data by customer and salesperson, and then adds supporting data from the customer, region, employee, and department tables:

```
SELECT c.name customer, r.name region,
   e.fname || ' ' || e.lname salesperson, d.name department,
   SUM(co.sale_price) total_sales
FROM cust_order co, customer c, region r, employee e, department d
WHERE co.cust_nbr = c.cust_nbr
  AND c.region_id = r.region_id
  AND co.sales_emp_id = e.emp_id
  AND e.dept_id = d.dept_id
  AND co.cancelled_dt IS NULL
  AND co.order_dt >= TO_DATE('01-JAN-2001','DD-MON-YYYY')
GROUP BY c.name, r.name, e.fname || ' ' || e.lname, d.name;
```

Since every nonaggregate in the SELECT clause must be included in the GROUP BY clause, we are forced to sort on five columns, since a sort is needed to generate the groupings. Because every customer is in one and only one region and every employee is in one and only one department, we really only need to sort on the customer and employee fields in order to produce the desired results. Thus, the Oracle engine is wasting its time sorting on the region and department names.

By isolating the aggregation from the supporting tables, however, we can create a more efficient and more understandable query:

```
SELECT c.name customer, r.name region,
  e.fname || ' ' || e.lname salesperson, d.name department,
  cust_emp_orders.total total_sales
FROM customer c, region r, employee e, department d,
  (SELECT cust_nbr, sales_emp_id, SUM(sale_price) total
   FROM cust_order
   WHERE cancelled_dt IS NULL
     AND order_dt >= TO_DATE('01-JAN-2001','DD-MON-YYYY')
   GROUP BY cust_nbr, sales_emp_id) cust_emp_orders
WHERE cust_emp_orders.cust_nbr = c.cust_nbr
  AND c.region_id = r.region_id
  AND cust_emp_orders.sales_emp_id = e.emp_id
  AND e.dept_id = d.dept_id;
```

Since the cust_order table includes the customer number and salesperson ID, we can perform the aggregation against these two columns without the need to include the other four tables. Not only are we sorting on fewer columns, we are sorting on numeric fields (customer number and employee ID) rather than potentially lengthy strings (customer name, region name, employee name, and department name). The containing query uses the cust_nbr and sales_emp_id columns from the inline view to join to the customer and employee tables, which in turn are used to join to the region and department tables.

By performing the aggregation within an inline view, we have sidestepped the restriction that all nonaggregates be included in the GROUP BY clause. We have also shortened execution time by eliminating unnecessary sorts, and we have minimized the number of joins to the customer, region, employee, and department tables. Depending on the amount of data in the tables, these improvements could yield significant performance gains.

Inline Views in DML Statements

Now that we are comfortable with inline views, it's time to add another wrinkle: inline views may also be used in INSERT, UPDATE, and DELETE statements. In most cases, using an inline view in a DML statement improves readability but otherwise adds little value to statement execution. To illustrate, we'll begin with a fairly simple UPDATE statement and then show the equivalent statement using an inline view:

```
UPDATE cust_order co SET co.expected_ship_dt = co.expected_ship_dt + 7
WHERE co.cancelled_dt IS NULL AND co.ship_dt IS NULL
  AND EXISTS (SELECT 1 FROM line_item li, part p
```

```
WHERE li.order_nbr = co.order_nbr
  AND li.part_nbr = p.part_nbr
  AND p.inventory_qty = 0);
```

This statement uses an EXISTS condition to locate orders that include out-of-stock parts. The next version uses an inline view called suspended_orders to identify the same set of orders:

```
UPDATE (SELECT co.expected_ship_dt exp_ship_dt
  FROM cust_order co
  WHERE co.cancelled_dt IS NULL AND co.ship_dt IS NULL
    AND EXISTS (SELECT 1 FROM line_item li, part p
      WHERE li.order_nbr = co.order_nbr
        AND li.part_nbr = p.part_nbr
        AND p.inventory_qty = 0)) suspended_orders
SET suspended_orders.exp_ship_dt = suspended_orders.exp_ship_dt + 7;
```

In the first statement, the WHERE clause of the UPDATE statement determines the set of rows to be updated, whereas in the second statement, the result set returned by the SELECT statement determines the target rows. Otherwise, they are identical. In order for the inline view to add extra value to the statement, it must be able to do something that the simple update statement can not do: join multiple tables. The following version attempts to do just that by replacing the subquery with a three-table join:

```
UPDATE (SELECT co.expected_ship_dt exp_ship_dt
  FROM cust_order co, line_item li, part p
  WHERE co.cancelled_dt IS NULL AND co.ship_dt IS NULL
    AND co.order_nbr = li.order_nbr AND li.part_nbr = p.part_nbr
    AND p.inventory_qty = 0) suspended_orders
SET suspended_orders.exp_ship_dt = suspended_orders.exp_ship_dt + 7;
```

However, statement execution results in the following error:

```
ORA-01779: cannot modify a column which maps to a non key-preserved table
```

As is often the case in life, we can't get something for nothing. In order to take advantage of the ability to join multiple tables within a DML statement, we must abide by the following rules:

- Only one of the joined tables in an inline view may be modified by the containing DML statement.

- In order to be modifiable, the target table's key must be preserved in the result set of the inline view.

While the previous update statement attempts to modify only one table (cust_order), the key (order_nbr) is not preserved in the result set, since an order has multiple line items. In other words, rows in the result set generated by the three-table join cannot be uniquely identified using just the order_nbr field, so it is not possible to update the cust_order table via this particular three table join. However, it is possible to update or delete from the line_item table using the same join, since the key of the line_item table matches the key of the result set returned from the inline view (order_nbr and part_nbr). The next statement deletes rows from the line_item table using an inline view nearly identical to the one that failed for the previous UPDATE attempt:

```
DELETE FROM (SELECT li.order_nbr order_nbr, li.part_nbr part_nbr
  FROM cust_order co, line_item li, part p
  WHERE co.cancelled_dt IS NULL AND co.ship_dt IS NULL
    AND co.order_nbr = li.order_nbr AND li.part_nbr = p.part_nbr
    AND p.inventory_qty = 0) suspended_orders;
```

The column(s) referenced in the SELECT clause of the inline view are actually irrelevant. Since the line_item table is the only key-preserved table of the three tables listed in the FROM clause, this is the table on which the DELETE statement operates. While utilizing an inline view in a DELETE statement can be more efficient, it's somewhat disturbing that it is not immediately obvious which table is the focus of the DELETE statement. A reasonable convention when writing such statements would be to always select the key columns from the target table.

Restricting Access Using WITH CHECK OPTION

Another way in which inline views can add value to DML statements is by restricting both the rows and columns that may be modified. For example, most companies only allow members of Human Resources to see or modify salary information. By restricting the columns visible to the DML statement, we can effectively hide the salary column:

```
UPDATE (SELECT emp_id, fname, lname, dept_id, manager_emp_id
  FROM employee) emp
SET emp.manager_emp_id = 11
WHERE emp.dept_id = 4;
```

While the previous statement executes cleanly, attempting to add the salary column to the SET clause would yield the following error:

```
UPDATE (SELECT emp_id, fname, lname, dept_id, manager_emp_id
  FROM employee) emp
SET emp.manager_emp_id = 11, emp.salary = 1000000000
WHERE emp.dept_id = 4;
```

```
ORA-00904: invalid column name
```

Of course, the person writing the UPDATE statement has full access to the table; the intent here is to protect against unauthorized modifications by the users. This might prove useful in an n-tier environment, where the interface layer interacts with a business-logic layer.

While this mechanism is useful for restricting access to particular columns, it does not limit access to particular rows in the target table. In order to restrict the rows that may be modified using a DML statement, we can add a WHERE clause to the inline view and specify WITH CHECK OPTION. For example, we may want to restrict the users from modifying data for any employee in the HR department:

```
UPDATE (SELECT emp_id, fname, lname, dept_id, manager_emp_id
   FROM employee
   WHERE dept_id !=
    (SELECT dept_id FROM department WHERE name = 'Human Resources')
   WITH CHECK OPTION) emp
SET emp.manager_emp_id = 11
WHERE emp.dept_id = 4;
```

The addition of WITH CHECK OPTION to the inline view constrains the DML statement to comply with the WHERE clause of the inline view. An attempt to update or delete data for an employee in the HR department will not succeed but will not raise an exception (updates/deletes 0 rows). However, an attempt to add a new employee to the HR department will yield the following error:

```
ORA-01402: view WITH CHECK OPTION where-clause violation
```

Thus, the following statement will fail with ORA-01402 because it attempts to add an employee to the Human Resources department:

```
INSERT INTO (SELECT emp_id, fname, lname, dept_id, manager_emp_id
   FROM employee
   WHERE dept_id !=
    (SELECT dept_id FROM department
      WHERE name = 'Human Resources')
   WITH CHECK OPTION) emp
SELECT 99, 'Charles', 'Brown', d.dept_id, NULL
FROM department d
WHERE d.name = 'Human Resources';
```

Subquery Case Study: The Top N Performers

Certain queries that are easily described in English have traditionally been difficult to formulate in SQL. One common example is the "Find the top five salespeople" query. The complexity stems from the fact that data from a table must first be aggregated, and then the aggregated values must be sorted and compared to one another in order to identify the top or bottom performers. In this section, you will see how subqueries may be used to answer such questions. At the end of the section, we introduce ranking functions, a new feature of Oracle SQL that was specifically designed for these types of queries.

A Look at the Data

Consider the problem of finding the top five sales people. Let's assume that we are basing our evaluation on the amount of revenue each salesperson brought in during the previous year. Our first task, then, would be to sum the dollar amount of all orders booked by each saleperson during the year in question. The following query does this for the year 2001:

```
SELECT e.lname employee, SUM(co.sale_price) total_sales
FROM cust_order co, employee e
```

```
WHERE co.order_dt >= TO_DATE('01-JAN-2001','DD-MON-YYYY')
  AND co.order_dt < TO_DATE('01-JAN-2002','DD-MON-YYYY')
  AND co.ship_dt IS NOT NULL AND co.cancelled_dt IS NULL
  AND co.sales_emp_id = e.emp_id
GROUP BY e.lname
ORDER BY 2 DESC;
```

```
EMPLOYEE              TOTAL_SALES
--------------------  -----------
Blake                     1927580
Houseman                  1814327
Russell                   1784596
Boorman                   1768813
Isaacs                    1761814
McGowan                   1761814
Anderson                  1757883
Evans                     1737093
Fletcher                  1735575
Dunn                      1723305
Jacobs                    1710831
Thomas                    1695124
Powers                    1688252
Walters                   1672522
Fox                       1645204
King                      1625456
Nichols                   1542152
Young                     1516776
Grossman                  1501039
Iverson                   1468316
Freeman                   1461898
Levitz                    1458053
Peters                    1443837
Jones                     1392648
```

It appears that Isaacs and McGowan have tied for fifth place, which, as you will see,
adds an interesting wrinkle to the problem.

Your Assignment

It seems that the boss was so tickled with this year's sales that she has asked you, the
IT manager, to see that each of the top five salespeople receive a bonus equal to 1%
of their yearly sales. No problem, you say. You quickly throw together the following
report using your favorite feature, the inline view, and send it off to the boss:

```
SELECT e.lname employee, top5_emp_orders.tot_sales total_sales,
  ROUND(top5_emp_orders.tot_sales * 0.01) bonus
FROM
  (SELECT all_emp_orders.sales_emp_id emp_id,
    all_emp_orders.tot_sales tot_sales
  FROM
    (SELECT sales_emp_id, SUM(sale_price) tot_sales
    FROM cust_order
    WHERE order_dt >= TO_DATE('01-JAN-2001','DD-MON-YYYY')
```

```
      AND order_dt < TO_DATE('01-JAN-2002','DD-MON-YYYY')
      AND ship_dt IS NOT NULL AND cancelled_dt IS NULL
    GROUP BY sales_emp_id
    ORDER BY 2 DESC
  ) all_emp_orders
 WHERE ROWNUM <= 5
 ) top5_emp_orders, employee e
WHERE top5_emp_orders.emp_id = e.emp_id;
```

```
EMPLOYEE              TOTAL_SALES      BONUS
--------------------  -----------  ----------
Blake                     1927580       19276
Houseman                  1814327       18143
Russell                   1784596       17846
Boorman                   1768813       17688
McGowan                   1761814       17618
```

The howl emitted by Isaacs can be heard for five square blocks. The boss, looking a bit harried, asks you to take another stab at it. Upon reviewing your query, the problem becomes immediately evident; the inline view aggregates the sales data and sorts the results, and the containing query grabs the first five sorted rows and discards the rest. Although it could easily have been McGowan, since there is no second sort column, Isaacs was arbitrarily omitted from the result set.

Second Attempt

You console yourself with the fact that you gave the boss exactly what she asked for: the top five salespeople. However, you realize that part of your job as IT manager is to give people what they need, not necessarily what they ask for, so you rephrase the boss's request as follows: give a bonus to all salespeople whose total sales ranked in the top five last year. This will require two steps: find the fifth highest sales total last year, and then find all salespeople whose total sales meet or exceed that figure.

```
SELECT e.lname employee, top5_emp_orders.tot_sales total_sales,
  ROUND(top5_emp_orders.tot_sales * 0.01) bonus
FROM employee e,
 (SELECT sales_emp_id, SUM(sale_price) tot_sales
  FROM cust_order
  WHERE order_dt >= TO_DATE('01-JAN-2001','DD-MON-YYYY')
    AND order_dt < TO_DATE('01-JAN-2002','DD-MON-YYYY')
    AND ship_dt IS NOT NULL AND cancelled_dt IS NULL
  GROUP BY sales_emp_id
  HAVING SUM(sale_price) IN
   (SELECT all_emp_orders.tot_sales
    FROM
     (SELECT SUM(sale_price) tot_sales
      FROM cust_order
      WHERE order_dt >= TO_DATE('01-JAN-2001','DD-MON-YYYY')
        AND order_dt < TO_DATE('01-JAN-2002','DD-MON-YYYY')
        AND ship_dt IS NOT NULL AND cancelled_dt IS NULL
      GROUP BY sales_emp_id
```

```
      ORDER BY 1 DESC
      ) all_emp_orders
    WHERE ROWNUM <= 5)
  ) top5_emp_orders
WHERE top5_emp_orders.sales_emp_id = e.emp_id
ORDER BY 2 DESC;


EMPLOYEE              TOTAL_SALES     BONUS
--------------------  -----------   ----------
Blake                   1927580       19276
Houseman                1814327       18143
Russell                 1784596       17846
Boorman                 1768813       17688
McGowan                 1761814       17618
Isaacs                  1761814       17618
```

Thus, there are actually six top five salespeople. The main difference between your first attempt and the second is the addition of the HAVING clause in the inline view. The subquery in the HAVING clause returns the five highest sales totals, and the inline view then returns all salespeople (potentially more than five) whose total sales exist in the set returned by the subquery.

While you are confident in your latest results, there are several aspects of the query that bother you:

- The aggregation of sales data is performed twice.
- The query will never contend for Most Elegant Query of the Year.
- You could've sworn you read about a new feature for handling these types of queries. . . .

In fact, there is a new feature for performing ranking queries that is available in release 8.1.6 and later. That feature is the RANK function.

Final Answer

New in 8.1.6, the RANK function is specifically designed to help you write queries to answer questions like the one posed in this case study. Part of a set of analytic functions (all of which will be explored in Chapter 13), the RANK function may be used to assign a ranking to each element of a set. The RANK function understands that there may be ties in the set of values being ranked and leaves gaps in the ranking to compensate. The following query illustrates how rankings would be assigned to the entire set of salespeople; notice how the RANK function leaves a gap between the fifth and seventh rankings to compensate for the fact that two rows share the fifth spot in the ranking:

```
SELECT sales_emp_id, SUM(sale_price) tot_sales,
  RANK( ) OVER (ORDER BY SUM(sale_price) DESC) sales_rank
FROM cust_order
WHERE order_dt >= TO_DATE('01-JAN-2001','DD-MON-YYYY')
  AND order_dt < TO_DATE('01-JAN-2002','DD-MON-YYYY')
```

```
    AND ship_dt IS NOT NULL AND cancelled_dt IS NULL
GROUP BY sales_emp_id;

SALES_EMP_ID  TOT_SALES SALES_RANK
------------ ---------- ----------
          11    1927580          1
          24    1814327          2
          34    1784596          3
          18    1768813          4
          25    1761814          5
          26    1761814          5
          30    1757883          7
          21    1737093          8
          19    1735575          9
          20    1723305         10
          27    1710831         11
          14    1695124         12
          15    1688252         13
          22    1672522         14
          29    1645204         15
          28    1625456         16
          31    1542152         17
          23    1516776         18
          13    1501039         19
          32    1468316         20
          12    1461898         21
          17    1458053         22
          33    1443837         23
          16    1392648         24
```

Leaving gaps in the rankings whenever ties are encountered is critical for properly handling these types of queries.[*] Table 5-1 shows the number of rows that would be returned for this data set for various top-N queries.

Table 5-1. Rows returned for N = {1,2,3,…,9}

Top-N salespeople	Rows returned
1	1
2	2
3	3
4	4
5	6
6	6
7	7
8	8
9	9

[*] If we do not wish to have gaps in the ranking, we can use the DENSE_RANK function intead.

As you can see, the result sets would be identical for both the "top five" and "top six" versions of this query for this particular data set.

By wrapping the previous RANK query in an inline view, we can retrieve the salespeople with a ranking of five or less and join the results to the employee table to generate the final result set:

```
SELECT e.lname employee, top5_emp_orders.tot_sales total_sales,
  ROUND(top5_emp_orders.tot_sales * 0.01) bonus
FROM
 (SELECT all_emp_orders.sales_emp_id emp_id,
   all_emp_orders.tot_sales tot_sales
  FROM
   (SELECT sales_emp_id, SUM(sale_price) tot_sales,
     RANK( ) OVER (ORDER BY SUM(sale_price) DESC) sales_rank
    FROM cust_order
    WHERE order_dt >= TO_DATE('01-JAN-2001','DD-MON-YYYY')
      AND order_dt < TO_DATE('01-JAN-2002','DD-MON-YYYY')
      AND ship_dt IS NOT NULL AND cancelled_dt IS NULL
    GROUP BY sales_emp_id
   ) all_emp_orders
  WHERE all_emp_orders.sales_rank <= 5
 ) top5_emp_orders, employee e
WHERE top5_emp_orders.emp_id = e.emp_id
ORDER BY 2 DESC;
```

EMPLOYEE	TOTAL_SALES	BONUS
Blake	1927580	19276
Houseman	1814327	18143
Russell	1784596	17846
Boorman	1768813	17688
McGowan	1761814	17618
Isaacs	1761814	17618

If this query is familiar, that's because it's almost identical to the first attempt, except that the RANK function is used instead of the pseudocolumn ROWNUM to determine where to draw the line between the top five salespeople and the rest of the pack.

Now that you are happy with your query and confident in your results, you show your findings to your boss. "Nice work," she says. "Why don't you give yourself a bonus as well? In fact, you can have Isaacs's bonus, since he quit this morning." Salespeople can be so touchy.

CHAPTER 6

Handling Temporal Data

"Time and tide wait for none," goes the wise saying. As database developers, we may not deal with tide-related information every day, but we need to deal with time-related information every day. The hire date of an employee, your pay day, the rent or mortgage payment date, the time duration required for a financial investment to mature, and the start date and time of your new car insurance are all examples of temporal data that we deal with every single day.

The need for effective management of temporal information became critical at the turn of the century, when most of us had to devise ways to handle the two-digit year correctly as it increased from 99 to 00, and then to 01. In this age of global e-business, the concepts of time are even more involved than ever before, because businesses are carried out around the clock across time zone boundaries.

A database needs to effectively and efficiently handle the storage, retrieval, and manipulation of the following types of temporal data:

- Dates
- Times
- Date and time intervals
- Time zones

Oracle's support for temporal data is mature and efficient. Oracle8*i* supports convenient manipulation of date and time data. Oracle9*i* enhanced this support by introducing a new set of features including the support for fractional seconds, date and time intervals, and time zones.

Internal DATE Storage Format

Oracle's DATE datatype holds date as well as time information. Regardless of the date format we use, Oracle stores dates internally in one standard format. Internal to the database a date is a fixed-length, seven-byte field. The seven bytes represent the following pieces of information:

1. The Century
2. The Year
3. The Month
4. The Day
5. The Hour
6. The Minute
7. The Second

Note that even though the datatype is called a DATE, it also stores the time. We choose the components to display (the date, the time, the date and the time, etc.) when we retrieve a DATE value from the database. Or, if we are fetching a DATE value into a program (e.g., a Java program) we might choose to extract the date elements of interest after transferring the entire date/time value to that program.

Getting Dates In and Out of a Database

In the real world, dates are not always represented using Oracle's DATE datatype. At various times, we'll need to convert DATEs to other datatypes and vice versa. This is particularly true when we interface an Oracle database with an external system, for example when we are accepting date input from an external system in which dates are represented as strings of characters (or even as numbers), or when we are sending output from an Oracle database to another application that doesn't understand Oracle's DATE datatype. We also need to convert DATE values to text when we display dates on a screen or generate a printed report.

Oracle provides two extremely useful functions to convert dates:

- TO_DATE
- TO_CHAR

As their names suggest, TO_DATE is used to convert character data, or numeric data, into a DATE value, and TO_CHAR is used to convert a DATE value into a string of characters. Date formats, discussed later in this section, come in particularly handy for such conversions.

TO_DATE

TO_DATE is a built-in SQL function that converts a character string into a date. Input to the TO_DATE function can be a string literal, a PL/SQL variable, or a database column of the CHAR or VARCHAR2 datatype.

Call TO_DATE as follows:

```
TO_DATE(string [,format])
```

The syntax elements are:

string

> Specifies a string literal, a PL/SQL variable, or a database column containing character data (or even numeric data) convertible to a date.

format

> Specifies the format of the input string. The format must be a valid combination of format codes shown later in this chapter in the "Date Formats" section.

Specifying a date format is optional. When we don't specify a format, the input string is assumed to be in the default date format (specified by the NLS_DATE_FORMAT parameter setting).

> We can convert a number to a DATE using TO_DATE. When we supply a number to the TO_DATE function, Oracle implicitly converts the input number into a string, and then the resulting string gets passed as input to TO_DATE.

Using the default date format

Every Oracle database has a default date format. If our DBA has not specified anything different, the default date format is as follows:

```
DD-MON-YY
```

When we invoke TO_DATE without explicitly specifying a date format, Oracle expects our input string to be in the default date format. The following INSERT statement converts a string in the default date format into a date, which is then inserted into the EMPLOYEE table:

```
INSERT INTO EMPLOYEE
(EMP_ID, FNAME, LNAME, DEPT_ID, MANAGER_EMP_ID, SALARY, HIRE_DATE)
VALUES
(2304, 'John', 'Smith', 20, 1258, 20000, TO_DATE('22-OCT-99'));

1 row created.

SELECT * FROM EMPLOYEE;

  EMP_ID FNAME      LNAME      DEPT_ID MANAGER_EMP_ID    SALARY HIRE_DATE
------- ---------- ------- ---------- --------------- ---------- ---------
    2304 John       Smith           20            1258      20000 22-OCT-99
```

Note the HIRE_DATE column is a DATE field, and the character string '22-OCT-99' was converted to a date by the TO_DATE function. We don't need the format in this case, because the supplied string is in the default date format. In fact, since the supplied string is in the default date format, we don't even need the TO_DATE function. Oracle automatically performs an implicit type conversion, as in this example:

```
INSERT INTO EMPLOYEE
(EMP_ID, FNAME, LNAME, DEPT_ID, MANAGER_EMP_ID, SALARY, HIRE_DATE)
VALUES
(2304, 'John', 'Smith', 20, 1258, 20000, '22-OCT-99');

1 row created.
```

Even though Oracle provides means for implicit datatype conversions, we recommend always using explicit conversions, because implicit conversions are not obvious and may lead to confusion. They may also suddenly fail should a DBA change the database's default date format.

Specifying a date format

If we wish to specify a date format, there are at least two approaches we can take:

- Specify the format at the session level, in which case it applies to all implicit conversions, and to all TO_DATE conversions for which we do not explicitly specify some other format.
- Specify the format as a parameter to a TO_DATE call.

The following example changes the default date format for the session, and then uses TO_DATE to convert a number to date.

```
ALTER SESSION SET NLS_DATE_FORMAT = 'MMDDYY';

Session altered.

INSERT INTO EMPLOYEE
(EMP_ID, FNAME, LNAME, DEPT_ID, MANAGER_EMP_ID, SALARY, HIRE_DATE)
VALUES
(2304, 'John', 'Smith', 20, 1258, 20000, TO_DATE(102299));

1 row created.
```

Since the default date format has been changed prior to the conversion, the conversion function TO_DATE doesn't need the date format as an input parameter.

 While it is possible to pass a number such as 102299 to the TO_DATE function, relying on Oracle's implicit conversion to change the number to a string, and then into a date, it's probably best to pass a string as input to the TO_DATE function.

If we attempt this insert without setting the default date format to match the format of the date in the input string, we get an error when Oracle tries to convert the date:

```
ALTER SESSION SET NLS_DATE_FORMAT = 'DD-MON-YY';

Session altered.
```

```
INSERT INTO EMPLOYEE
(EMP_ID, FNAME, LNAME, DEPT_ID, MANAGER_EMP_ID, SALARY, HIRE_DATE)
VALUES
(2304, 'John', 'Smith', 20, 1258, 20000, TO_DATE('102299'));
(2304, 'John', 'Smith', 20, 1258, 20000, TO_DATE('102299'))
                                                          *
ERROR at line 4:
ORA-01861: literal does not match format string
```

In such situations, if we do not wish to change our session's default date format, we must specify the date format as the second input parameter to the TO_DATE function:

```
ALTER SESSION SET NLS_DATE_FORMAT = 'DD-MON-YY';

Session altered.

INSERT INTO EMPLOYEE
(EMP_ID, FNAME, LNAME, DEPT_ID, MANAGER_EMP_ID, SALARY, HIRE_DATE)
VALUES
(2304, 'John', 'Smith', 20, 1258, 20000, TO_DATE('102299','MMDDYY'));

1 row created.

SELECT * FROM EMPLOYEE;

  EMP_ID FNAME   LNAME      DEPT_ID MANAGER_EMP_ID   SALARY HIRE_DATE
 ------- ------- ------- ---------- -------------- ---------- ---------
    2304 John    Smith           20           1258      20000 22-OCT-99
```

Note how TO_DATE interprets the string '102299' as being in the format 'MMD-DYY'. Also note that in the result of the SELECT, the date is displayed using the default date format of the session, not the format in which it was inserted.

Let's look at one more example to see how a database character column can be converted to a DATE. Let's assume that the REPORT_ID column in the REPORT table actually stores the date on which the report was generated, and that the date is in the format 'MMDDYYYY'. Now, we can use TO_DATE on that column to display the date on which the report was generated:

```
SELECT SENT_TO, REPORT_ID, TO_DATE(REPORT_ID,'MMDDYYYY') DATE_GENERATED
FROM REPORT;

SENT_TO                    REPORT_I  DATE_GENE
-------------------------- --------- ---------
Manager                    01011999  01-JAN-99
Director                   01121999  12-JAN-99
Vice President             01231999  23-JAN-99
```

In this example, the TO_DATE function converts the MMDDYYYY data in the column to a date. That date is then implicitly converted into a character string for display purposes, using the default date format.

TO_CHAR

The TO_CHAR function is the opposite of the TO_DATE function, and converts a date into a string of characters. Call TO_CHAR as follows:

```
TO_CHAR(date [,format])
```

The syntax elements are:

date

Specifies a PL/SQL variable or a database column of the DATE datatype.

format

Specifies the desired format of the output string. The format must be a valid combination of date format elements as described later in the section "Date Formats."

The format is optional. When the format is not specified, the date is output in the default date format (as specified by NLS_DATE_FORMAT).

The following example uses TO_CHAR to convert an input date into a string using the default date format:

```
SELECT FNAME, TO_CHAR(HIRE_DATE) FROM EMPLOYEE;

FNAME                TO_CHAR(H
-------------------- ---------
John                 22-OCT-99
```

The following example uses TO_CHAR to convert a date into a string, and explicitly specifies a date format:

```
SELECT FNAME, TO_CHAR(HIRE_DATE,'MM/DD/YY') FROM EMPLOYEE;

FNAME                TO_CHAR(
-------------------- --------
John                 10/22/99
```

There are situations when we may need to combine TO_CHAR with TO_DATE. For example, if we want to know on what day of the week January 1, 2000 fell, we can use the following query:

```
SELECT TO_CHAR(TO_DATE('01-JAN-2000','DD-MON-YYYY'),'Day') FROM DUAL;

TO_CHAR(T
---------
Saturday
```

In this example, the input string '01-JAN-2000' is first converted into a date and then the TO_CHAR function is used to convert this date into a string representing the day of the week.

Date Formats

We can display dates in a number of ways. Every country, every industry has its own standard of displaying dates. Oracle provides us with date format codes so that we can interpret and display dates in a wide variety of date formats.

A simple example of displaying a date is:

```
SELECT SYSDATE FROM DUAL;

SYSDATE
---------
03-OCT-01
```

By default, the date is displayed using the DD-MON-YY format. This format uses two digits for the date (zero padded on the left), three characters for the month (the first three characters of the English name of the month in uppercase), and two digits for the year of the century (zero padded on the left). The default date format for the database is controlled by the NLS_DATE_FORMAT initialization parameter. We can use ALTER SYSTEM or ALTER SESSION commands to change the default date format for the instance or the session respectively. Let's take another example to see how we can display a date in a format other than the default format:

```
SELECT TO_CHAR(SYSDATE,'MM/DD/YYYY') FROM DUAL;

TO_CHAR(SY
----------
10/03/2001
```

The example converts the date into the format 'MM/DD/YYYY' with the TO_CHAR function. There are many ways to represent a date. These vary from country to country, from industry to industry, and from application to application. Table 6-1 describes the various date formats. Most of the examples in Table 6-1 are based on 03-OCT-2001 03:34:48 PM. Those that involve B.C. dates use the year 2105 B.C. Those that specifically demonstrate A.M. times are based on 03-OCT-2001 11:00:00 AM.

Table 6-1. Oracle date format codes

Component	Options	Example	
		Format	Date
Punctuation	-/,;:.*	DD-MON-YY	03-OCT-01
	Space	DD MM YYYY	03 10 2001
	"Text"	DD "of" Month	03 of October
Day	DD (Day of the month)	MM/DD/YY	10/03/01
	DDD (Day of the year)	DDD/YY	276/01
	D (Day of the week)	D MM/YY	4 10/01

Table 6-1. Oracle date format codes (continued)

Component	Options	Example	
		Format	**Date**
	DAY (Name of the day)	DAY MM/YY	WEDNESDAY 10/01
	day (Name of the day, in lower case)	day MM/YY	wednesday 10/01
	Day (Name of the day, in mixed case)	Day MM/YY	Wednesday 10/01
	DY (Abbreviated name of the day)	DY MM/YY	WED 10/01
	Dy (Abbreviated name of the day)	Dy MM/YY	Wed 10/01
Month	MM (Two digit month)	MM/DD/YY	10/03/01
	MONTH (Name of the month, in upper case)	MONTH YY	OCTOBER 01
	Month (Name of the month, in mixed case)	Month YY	October 01
	MON (Abbreviated name of the month)	MON YY	OCT 01
	Mon (Name of the month, in mixed case)	Mon YY	Oct 01
	RM (Roman Numeral Month)	DD-RM-YY	03-X-01
Year	Y (Last one digit of year)	MM Y	10 1
	YY (Last two digit of year)	MM YY	10 01
	YYY (Last three digits of year)	MM YYY	10 001
	YYYY (Four digits of year)	MM YYYY	10 2001
	Y,YYY (Year with comma)	MM Y,YYY	10 2,001
	YEAR (Year spelled out)	MM YEAR	10 TWO THOUSAND ONE
	Year (Year spelled out, in mixed case)	MM Year	10 Two Thousand One
	SYYYY (Four digits of year with '-' sign for BC)	SYYYY	-2105
	Y,YYY (Year with comma)	MM Y,YYY	10 2,001

Table 6-1. Oracle date format codes (continued)

Component	Options	Example	
		Format	Date
	RR (Round Year depending upon the current year)	DD-MON-RR	03-OCT-01
	RRRR (Round Year depending upon the current year)	DD-MON-RRRR	03-OCT-2001
	I (Last one digit of the ISO Standard year)	MM I	10 1
	IY (Last two digit of the ISO Standard year)	MM IY	10 01
	IYY (Last three digits of the ISO Standard year)	MM IYY	10 001
	IYYY (Four digits of the ISO Standard year)	MM IYYY	10 2001
Century	CC (Century)	CC	21
	SCC (Century with '-' sign for BC)	SCC	-22
Week	W (Week of the month)	W	1
	WW (Week of the year)	WW	40
	IW (Week of the year in ISO standard)	IW	40
Quarter	Q (Quarter of the year)	Q	4
Hour	HH (Hour of the day 1–12)	HH	03
	HH12 (Hour of the day 1–12)	HH	03
	HH24 (Hour of the day 0–23)	HH24	15
Minute	MI (Minute of hour 0–59)	MI	34
Second	SS (Second of minute 0–59)	SS	48
	SSSSS (Seconds past midnight)	SSSSS	42098
AM/PM	AM (Meridian indicator)	HH:MI AM	11:00 AM
	A.M. (Meridian indicator with dots)	HH:MI A.M.	11:00 A.M.

Table 6-1. Oracle date format codes (continued)

Component	Options	Example		
		Format	**Date**	
	PM (Meridian indicator)	HH:MI PM	03:34 PM	
	P.M. (Meridian indicator with dots)	HH:MI P.M.	03:34 P.M.	
AD/BC	AD (AD indicator)	YY AD	01 AD	
	A.D. (AD indicator with dots)	YY A.D.	01 A.D.	
	BC (BC indicator)	YY BC	05 BC	
	B.C. (BC indicator with dots)	YY B.C.	05 B.C.	
Julian Day	J (Number of days since January 1, 4712 BC)	J	2452186	
Suffix	TH (Ordinal Number)	DDTH	03RD	
	SP (Spelled Number)	MMSP	TEN	
	SPTH (Spelled Ordinal Number)	DDSPTH	THIRD	
	THSP (Spelled Ordinal Number)	DDTHSP	THIRD	

AD/BC indicators

Oracle provides two formats, AD and BC, to characterize a year (two more with dots—A.D., B.C.). However, they both serve the same purpose, and we can use either of them with equivalent results. If we have used the format BC in our query, and the date we are applying this format to comes out to be an AD year, Oracle is intelligent enough to print AD instead of BC, and vice versa. For example:

```
SELECT TO_CHAR(SYSDATE, 'YYYY AD'),
       TO_CHAR(SYSDATE, 'YYYY BC') FROM DUAL;

TO_CHAR( TO_CHAR(
-------- --------
 2001 AD  2001 AD

SELECT TO_CHAR(ADD_MONTHS(SYSDATE,-50000), 'YYYY AD'),
       TO_CHAR(ADD_MONTHS(SYSDATE,-50000), 'YYYY BC') FROM DUAL;

TO_CHAR( TO_CHAR(
-------- --------
 2165 BC  2165 BC
```

In the first example, even though we supplied the BC format with the SYSDATE, it printed 2001 AD in the output, and in the second example, even though we supplied AD with a date 50,000 months earlier (in the BC), it printed BC in the output.

AM/PM indicators

The AM/PM indicators (as well as A.M. and P.M.) behave exactly the same as the AD/BC indicators. If we have used the AM format in our query, and the time we are applying this format to comes out to be a PM time, Oracle is intelligent enough to print PM instead of AM, and vice versa. For example:

```
SELECT TO_CHAR(SYSDATE, 'HH:MI:SS AM'),
       TO_CHAR(SYSDATE, 'HH:MI:SS PM'),
       TO_CHAR(SYSDATE - 8/24, 'HH:MI:SS AM'),
       TO_CHAR(SYSDATE - 8/24, 'HH:MI:SS PM')
FROM DUAL;

TO_CHAR(SYS TO_CHAR(SYS TO_CHAR(SYS TO_CHAR(SYS
----------- ----------- ----------- -----------
06:58:07 PM 06:58:07 PM 10:58:07 AM 10:58:07 AM
```

MINUTES: MI or MM

Many SQL beginners assume that since HH represents hours and SS represents seconds, MM would represent minutes, and try to write the following SQL queries to print the current time:

```
SELECT TO_CHAR(SYSDATE, 'HH:MM:SS') FROM DUAL;

TO_CHAR(
--------
02:10:32
```

However, this is wrong. MM represents months and not minutes. The format for minutes is MI. Therefore, remember to use MI instead of MM when attempting to get the minutes part of the date. The correct query is:

```
SELECT TO_CHAR(SYSDATE, 'HH:MI:SS') FROM DUAL;

TO_CHAR(
--------
02:57:21
```

It becomes extremely difficult to debug an application if the MM format is embedded in the code instead of MI.

Case-sensitivity of formats

Some date formats are case-sensitive while others aren't. The formats that represent numbers are not case-sensitive. For example:

```
SELECT TO_CHAR(SYSDATE, 'HH:MI') UPPER,
TO_CHAR(SYSDATE, 'hh:mi') LOWER,
TO_CHAR(SYSDATE, 'Hh:mI') MIXED
FROM DUAL;

UPPER LOWER MIXED
----- ----- -----
03:17 03:17 03:17
```

Note that the format HH:MI is case-insensitive—no matter which case we use for the format, the output is the same. The same applies to all other formats that represent numbers, for example, DD, MM, YY, etc.

Date formats that represent textual date components are case sensitive. For example, the format "DAY" is different from "day." The following rules apply for determining the case of the output when a textual date format is used:

- If the first character of the format is lowercase, then the output will be lowercase, regardless of the case of the other characters in the format.

  ```
  SELECT TO_CHAR(SYSDATE, 'month'),
         TO_CHAR(SYSDATE, 'mONTH'),
         TO_CHAR(SYSDATE, 'moNTh')
  FROM DUAL;

  TO_CHAR(S TO_CHAR(S TO_CHAR(S
  --------- --------- ---------
  october   october   october
  ```

- If the first character of the format mask is uppercase and the second character is also uppercase, then the output will be uppercase, regardless of the case of the other characters in the format.

  ```
  SELECT TO_CHAR(SYSDATE, 'MOnth'),
         TO_CHAR(SYSDATE, 'MONTH')
  FROM DUAL;

  TO_CHAR(S TO_CHAR(S
  --------- ---------
  OCTOBER   OCTOBER
  ```

- If the first character of the format mask is uppercase and the second character is lowercase, then the output will have an uppercase first character and all other characters lowercase, regardless of the case of the other characters in the format.

  ```
  SELECT TO_CHAR(SYSDATE, 'MoNTH'), TO_CHAR(SYSDATE, 'Month')
  FROM DUAL;

  TO_CHAR(S TO_CHAR(S
  --------- ---------
  October   October
  ```

These rules apply to all text elements, such as those used to represent month names, day names, and so forth.

Two-digit years

Even though Oracle stores the century of the year internally, it allows us to use two-digit years. Therefore, it is important to know how the century is handled when we use a two-digit year. Oracle provides two two-digit year formats that we can use: YY and RR.

With the YY year format, the first two digits are assumed to be the current date:

```
ALTER SESSION SET NLS_DATE_FORMAT = 'DD-MON-YY';

Session altered.

SELECT SYSDATE, TO_CHAR(SYSDATE,'DD-MON-YYYY') FROM DUAL;

SYSDATE    TO_CHAR(SYS
---------  -----------
06-OCT-01 06-OCT-2001

SELECT TO_CHAR(TO_DATE('10-DEC-99'),'DD-MON-YYYY'),
       TO_CHAR(TO_DATE('10-DEC-01'),'DD-MON-YYYY') FROM DUAL;

TO_CHAR(TO_ TO_CHAR(TO_
----------- -----------
10-DEC-2099 10-DEC-2001
```

Since the current date was 06-OCT-2001 when this was written, the first two digits of the years in this example are assumed to be 20.

With the RR year format, the first two digits of the specified year are determined based upon the last two digits of the current year and the last two digits of year specified. The following rules apply:

- If the specified year is less than 50, and the last two digits of the current year are less than 50, then the first two digits of the return date are the same as the first two digits of the current date.
- If the specified year is less than 50, and the last two digits of the current year are greater than or equal to 50, then first two digits of the return date are 1 greater than the first two digits of the current date.
- If the specified year is greater than 50, and the last two digits of the current year are less than 50, then first two digits of the return date are 1 less than the first two digits of the current date.
- If the specified year is greater than 50, and the last two digits of the current year are greater than or equal to 50, then the first two digits of the return date are the same as the first two digits of the current date.

The following example demonstrates these rules:

```
ALTER SESSION SET NLS_DATE_FORMAT = 'DD-MON-RR';

Session altered.
```

```
SELECT SYSDATE, TO_CHAR(SYSDATE,'DD-MON-YYYY') FROM DUAL;

SYSDATE    TO_CHAR(SYS
---------  -----------
06-OCT-01  06-OCT-2001

SELECT TO_CHAR(TO_DATE('10-DEC-99'),'DD-MON-YYYY'),
       TO_CHAR(TO_DATE('10-DEC-01'),'DD-MON-YYYY') FROM DUAL;

TO_CHAR(TO_  TO_CHAR(TO_
-----------  -----------
10-DEC-1999  10-DEC-2001
```

The ALTER SESSION command sets the default date format to DD-MON-RR. The next SELECT uses SYSDATE to show the current date at the time the example was executed. The final SELECT demonstrates the use of the RR date format (both TO_DATE calls rely on the default format set earlier). Note that the DD-MON-RR date format treats 10-DEC-99 as 10-DEC-1999, whereas treats 10-DEC-01 as 10-DEC-2001. Compare this output to the rules we just listed.

The year format RRRR (four Rs) allows us to enter either a two-digit year or a four-digit year. If we enter a four-digit year, Oracle behaves as if the year format was YYYY. If we enter a two-digit year, Oracle behaves as if the year format is RR. The RRRR format is rarely used. Most SQL programmers prefer to use either YYYY, or to explicitly specify RR.

Date Literals

DATE literals are specified in the ANSI standard as a way of representing date constants, and take the following form:

```
DATE 'YYYY-MM-DD'
```

Note that the ANSI date literal doesn't contain the time information. We also can't specify a format. If we want to specify a date literal using this ANSI syntax, we must always use the YYYY-MM-DD date format. The following example illustrates the use of a DATE literal in a SQL statement:

```
INSERT INTO EMPLOYEE
(EMP_ID, FNAME, LNAME, DEPT_ID, MANAGER_EMP_ID, SALARY, HIRE_DATE)
VALUES
(2304, 'John', 'Smith', 20, 1258, 20000, DATE '1999-10-22');

1 row created.

SELECT * FROM EMPLOYEE;

EMP_ID FNAME    LNAME   DEPT_ID MANAGER_EMP_ID   SALARY HIRE_DATE
------- -------- ------- --------- --------------- ---------- ---------
   2304 John     Smith        20            1258    20000 22-OCT-99
```

In this example, the date literal DATE '1999-10-22' is interpreted as 22-OCT-99.

ISO Standard Issues

The ISO standard determines the start date of the first week of the year based upon whether most of the days in the week belong to the new year or to the previous year. If January 1st is a Monday, Tuesday, Wednesday, or a Thursday, then January 1st belongs to the first week of the new ISO year. The first day of the ISO year is either January 1st (if it is a Monday) or the previous Monday (which actually goes back to the last calendar year). For example, if January 1st is a Tuesday, then the first day of the ISO year is Monday, December 31, of the prior calendar year.

If January 1st is a Friday, Saturday, or a Sunday, then January 1st belongs to the last week of the previous ISO year. The first day of the first week of the new ISO year is then considered to be the Monday following January 1st. For example, if January 1 falls on a Saturday, then the first day of the ISO year is considered to be Monday, January 3.

If we need to work with ISO dates, Oracle provides date formats that treat ISO years differently from calendar years. These ISO formats are:

IW
> Represents the week of the year in ISO standard.

I, IY, IYY and IYYY
> Represents the ISO year.

The following sections describe ISO weeks and years with examples.

ISO standard weeks

In the ISO standard, weeks of the year are counted differently than regular calendar weeks. In a regular calendar, the first week of the year starts on January 1st. 01-JAN is the first date of the first week. However, in the ISO standard, a week always starts on a Monday and ends on a Sunday. Therefore, the first date of the first week is considered to be the date of the nearest Monday. This date could be a couple of days later than 01-JAN, or it could be a couple of days earlier (in the previous year).

The format WW returns the week of the year in terms of the regular calendar, and the format IW returns the week of the year in terms of the ISO standard. Since 01-JAN-2001 was a Monday, it was considered the start date of the first week in terms of the regular calendar as well as in terms of the ISO standard. Therefore, if we compute the week number of any date in the year 2001, the results will be the same whether we use the regular calendar or the ISO calendar. For example:

```
SELECT TO_CHAR(TO_DATE('10-DEC-01'),'WW'),
       TO_CHAR(TO_DATE('10-DEC-01'),'IW')
FROM DUAL;

TO TO
-- --
50 50
```

However, the year 1999 didn't start on a Monday. Therefore, for some dates, the week number in the ISO standard could be different from that of the regular calendar. For example:

```
SELECT TO_CHAR(TO_DATE('10-DEC-99'),'WW'),
       TO_CHAR(TO_DATE('10-DEC-99'),'IW')
FROM DUAL;

TO TO
-- --
50 49
```

The ISO Standard can cause a year to have 53 weeks. Here's an example:

```
SELECT TO_CHAR(TO_DATE('01-JAN-99'),'IW'), TO_CHAR(TO_DATE('01-JAN-99'),'Day')
FROM DUAL;

TO TO_CHAR(T
-- ---------
53 Friday
```

Note that the ISO standard treats 1st January of 1999 to be in the 53rd week of 1998, because it falls on a Friday. The first week of 1999 starts on the subsequent Monday, which is 4th January, as per the ISO standard.

ISO standard year

The year formats I, IY, IYY, and IYYY represent the ISO year. IYYY represents the four digit ISO year, IYY represents the last three digits of the ISO year, IY represents the last two digits of the ISO year, and I represents the last digit of the ISO year. Remember that the start date of an ISO year is not necessarily January 1. The following example returns the ISO and calendar years for January 1, 1999:

```
SELECT TO_CHAR(TO_DATE('01-JAN-99'),'IYYY'),
       TO_CHAR(TO_DATE('01-JAN-99'),'YYYY') FROM DUAL;

TO_C TO_C
---- ----
1998 1999
```

Notice that even though the calendar year is 1999, the ISO year is considered to be 1998. That's because 01-Jan-1999 fell on a Friday—late in the week, which causes the week to be considered part of the previous ISO year. The following example demonstrates the opposite situation:

```
SELECT TO_CHAR(TO_DATE('31-DEC-90'),'IYYY'),
       TO_CHAR(TO_DATE('31-DEC-90'),'YYYY') FROM DUAL;

TO_C TO_C
---- ----
1991 1990
```

This time, the calendar year is 1990, but the date 31-Dec-1990 is considered to be in ISO year 1991. This is because 01-Jan-1991 fell on a Tuesday, early enough in the week for the entire week to be considered part of the next ISO year.

Date Manipulation

Date arithmetic is an important aspect of our day-to-day life. We find the age of a person by subtracting his date of birth from today's date. We compute the date a warranty expires by adding the warranty period to the purchase date. Drivers' license expirations, bank interest calculation, and a host of other things all depend on date arithmetic. It is extremely important for any database to support such common date arithmetic operations.

Oracle provides some very good date arithmetic features. Not only can we add and subtract dates, but Oracle also provides a number of other helpful functions for manipulating date values. We discuss these features in detail in this section. Table 6-2 lists various date manipulation functions provided by Oracle SQL.

Table 6-2. Date functions

Function	Use
ADD_MONTHS	Adds months to a date
LAST_DAY	Computes the last day of the month
MONTHS_BETWEEN	Determines the number of months between two dates
NEW_TIME	Translates a time to a new time zone
NEXT_DAY	Returns the date of the next specified weekday
ROUND	Rounds a date/time value to a specified element
SYSDATE	Returns the current date and time
TO_CHAR	Converts dates to strings
TO_DATE	Converts strings and numbers to dates
TRUNC	Truncates a date/time value to a specific element

Addition

Adding two dates doesn't make sense. However, we can add days, months, years, hours, minutes, and seconds to a date to generate a future date and time. The "+" operator allows us to add numbers to a date. The unit of a number added to a date is assumed to be days. Therefore, to find tomorrow's date, we can add 1 to SYSDATE:

```
SELECT SYSDATE, SYSDATE+1 FROM DUAL;

SYSDATE   SYSDATE+1
--------- ---------
05-OCT-01 06-OCT-01
```

Any time we add a number to a date, Oracle assumes that the number represents a number of days. Therefore, if we want to add multiples of a day (week, month, year, etc.) to a date, we first need to multiply by a conversion factor. For example, to add one week to today's date, we add 7 (7 days in a week times 1 day) to SYSDATE:

```
SELECT SYSDATE+7 FROM DUAL;


SYSDATE+7
---------
12-OCT-01
```

Similarly, if we want to add fractions of a day (hour, minute, second) to a date, we first need to convert such fractions into a fractional number of days. Do this by dividing by a conversion factor. For example, to add 20 minutes to the current date and time, we need to add (20 minutes/1,440 minutes in a day) to SYSDATE:

```
SELECT TO_CHAR(SYSDATE,'DD-MON-YY HH:MI:SS'),
TO_CHAR(SYSDATE+(20/1440),'DD-MON-YY HH:MI:SS')
FROM DUAL;


TO_CHAR(SYSDATE,'D TO_CHAR(SYSDATE+(2
------------------ ------------------
05-OCT-01 01:22:03 05-OCT-01 01:42:03
```

Adding months to a date is not as easy as adding weeks, because all months don't have the same number of days—some have 30, some 31, some 28, and at times even 29. To add one month to a date, we need to know how many days that calendar month will have. Therefore, adding months to a date by converting those months to a number of days involves lots of homework, which is error-prone. Fortunately, Oracle does all the homework for us, and provides a built-in SQL function to add months to dates. This function is called ADD_MONTHS, and we call it as follows:

```
ADD_MONTHS (date, number)
```

The syntax elements are:

date

Specifies a database column defined as type DATE or a string with a date in the default date format.

number

Specifies the number of months to add to the input date.

The following example shows the computation of an employee's biannual review date by using ADD_MONTHS to add six months to the employee's HIRE_DATE:

```
SELECT FNAME, HIRE_DATE, ADD_MONTHS(HIRE_DATE, 6) REVIEW_DATE FROM EMPLOYEE;


FNAME              HIRE_DATE REVIEW_DA
------------------ --------- ---------
John               22-OCT-99 22-APR-00
```

Notice that in this example the input date and the result date both fall on the 22nd of the month. This would not have happened if we had added 180 days to the input date. ADD_MONTHS is "smart" in one other way too. The following example adds 6 months to 31st December, 1999:

```
SELECT ADD_MONTHS('31-DEC-99',6) FROM DUAL;

ADD_MONTH
---------
30-JUN-00
```

The ADD_MONTHS function is intelligent enough to know that adding 6 months to 31st December should result in the last day of June. And since the last of June is 30th (not 31st), it returns 30th June, 2000.

Subtraction

Even though no other arithmetic operation (addition, multiplication, division) between two dates makes any sense, subtracting one date from another date is a very common and useful operation. The "-"operator allows us to subtract a date from a date, or a number from a date.

Subtracting one date from another date returns the number of days between those two dates. Subtracting a number from a date returns a date that number of days in the past.

The following example displays the lead time of a set of orders by subtracting the date on which the order was placed (ORDER_DT) from the expected ship date (EXPECTED_SHIP_DT):

```
SELECT ORDER_NBR, EXPECTED_SHIP_DT - ORDER_DT LEAD_TIME
FROM CUST_ORDER;

ORDER_NBR   LEAD_TIME
---------- ----------
      1001           1
      1000           5
      1002          13
      1003          10
      1004           9
      1005           2
      1006           6
      1007           2
      1008           2
      1009           4
      1012           1
      1011           5
      1015          13
      1017          10
      1019           9
      1021           2
```

```
1023      6
1025      2
1027      2
1029      4
```

Along with subtracting one date from another, we can also subtract a number from a date. For example, subtracting 1 from SYSDATE gives yesterday, and subtracting 7 from SYSDATE yields the same day last week:

```
SELECT SYSDATE, SYSDATE - 1, SYSDATE - 7 FROM DUAL;

SYSDATE    SYSDATE-1 SYSDATE-7
---------  --------- ---------
05-OCT-01 04-OCT-01 28-SEP-01
```

Unlike ADD_MONTHS, Oracle doesn't provide a SUBTRACT_MONTHS function. To subtract months from a date, use the ADD_MONTHS function, and pass a negative number as the second parameter:

```
SELECT SYSDATE, ADD_MONTHS(SYSDATE, -6) FROM DUAL;

SYSDATE    ADD_MONTH
---------  ---------
05-OCT-01 05-APR-01
```

Earlier in this section we saw that subtracting a date from another date returns the number of days between the two dates. There are times when we may want to know the number of months between two dates. Consider that subtracting an employee's HIRE_DATE from SYSDATE yields the number of days of experience the employee has with her employer:

```
SELECT SYSDATE-HIRE_DATE FROM EMPLOYEE;

SYSDATE-HIRE_DATE
-----------------
         714.0786
```

It's better, in most cases, to find the number of months of experience rather than the number of days. We know that dividing the number of days between two dates by 30 won't accurately calculate the number of months between those two dates. Therefore, Oracle provides the built-in SQL function MONTHS_BETWEEN for finding the number of months between two dates. MONTHS_BETWEEN is called as follows:

```
MONTHS_BETWEEN (date1, date2)
```

The syntax elements are:

date1

Specifies the end of the time period in question. This should be either a DATE value or a string in the default date format.

date2

Specifies the beginning of the time period in question. Like date1, this should also be a DATE value or a string in the default date format.

MONTHS_BETWEEN subtracts date2 from date1. So, if date2 comes later than date1 in the chronology, then MONTHS_BETWEEN will return a negative value. The following example demonstrates two calls to MONTHS_BETWEEN. Both calls use the same two dates, but in different orders.

```
SELECT MONTHS_BETWEEN(SYSDATE,HIRE_DATE)
       MONTHS_BETWEEN(HIRE_DATE, SYSDATE)
FROM EMPLOYEE;

MONTHS_BETWEEN(SYSDATE,HIRE_DATE) MONTHS_BETWEEN(HIRE_DATE,SYSDATE)
--------------------------------- ---------------------------------
                       23.4542111                       -23.454218
```

There is no YEARS_BETWEEN function. To find the number of years between two dates, we can either subtract the two dates to find the number of days and then divide by 365, or use MONTHS_BETWEEN to find the number of months and then divide by 12. Years don't have the same number of days—some have 365 days and others have 366 days. Therefore, it is not accurate to divide the number of days by 365 to get the number of years. On the other hand, all years have 12 months, whether a leap year or not. Therefore, the most accurate way to calculate the number of years between two dates is to use the MONTHS_BETWEEN function to find the number of months and then divide by 12 to get the number of years.

Last Day of the Month

Oracle provides a built-in function to get the last day of a month. The function is LAST_DAY, and it's called as follows:

```
LAST_DAY (date)
```

The syntax element is:

date
    Specifies a DATE value, or a string with a date in the default date format.

LAST_DAY returns the last day of the month containing the input date. For example, to find the last date of the current month, we can use the following SQL statement:

```
SELECT LAST_DAY(SYSDATE) "Next Payment Date" FROM DUAL;

Next Paym
---------
31-OCT-01
```

Sometimes it's useful to be able to determine the first day of a given month; it would be nice if Oracle would provide a FIRST_DAY function. One approach to getting the first day of the month for a given date is to use the following expression:

```
ADD_MONTHS((LAST_DAY(date)+1), -1)
```

This expression finds the last day of the month represented by date. It then adds 1 to get to the first day of the subsequent month, and finally uses ADD_MONTHS with an argument of −1 to go back to the beginning of the month in which we started. The result is the first day of the month in which the given date falls. Other approaches to this problem are possible; this is just one that works well for us. This approach has the advantage of preserving the time component of the date in question.

Next Day

Oracle provides a built-in function to get the date of the next occurrence of a specified day of the week. The function is NEXT_DAY, and it's called as follows:

```
NEXT_DAY (date, string)
```

The syntax elements are:

date
> Specifies a DATE value, or a string with a date in the default date format.

string
> Specifies the name of a weekday.

To find the date of the next Friday, we can use the following SQL statement:

```
SELECT NEXT_DAY(SYSDATE, 'Friday') "Vacation Start Date" FROM DUAL;

Vacation
---------
12-OCT-01
```

If the specified string is not a valid day of the week, we will get an error:

```
SELECT NEXT_DAY(SYSDATE, 'ABCD') FROM DUAL;
SELECT NEXT_DAY(SYSDATE, 'ABCD') FROM DUAL
                         *
ERROR at line 1:
ORA-01846: not a valid day of the week
```

Rounding and Truncating Dates

Rounding and truncating dates is similar in concept to the rounding and truncating of numbers, but more involved because an Oracle DATE contains date as well as time information. Use the ROUND function to round a date/time value to a specific element; use the TRUNC function to truncate a date/time value to a specific element. Following is the syntax for invoking these two functions:

```
ROUND(date [, format])
TRUNC(date [, format])
```

The syntax elements are:

date
> Specifies a DATE value.

format
> Specifies the date element to round or truncate to.

The return value depends upon the specified format, which is an optional parameter. If we don't specify a format in the call to ROUND, the function returns a date by rounding the input to the nearest day. If we don't specify a format in the call to TRUNC, that function returns a date by removing the fractional part of the day.

When using ROUND and TRUNC to round to the nearest day, or to truncate a date, the functions set the time fields of the return value to the beginning of the returned day, i.e., 12:00:00 AM (00:00:00 in HH24 format). For example:

```
SELECT TO_CHAR(SYSDATE, 'DD-MON-YY HH:MI:SS AM'),
       TO_CHAR(ROUND(SYSDATE), 'DD-MON-YY HH:MI:SS AM'),
       TO_CHAR(TRUNC(SYSDATE), 'DD-MON-YY HH:MI:SS AM')
FROM DUAL;

TO_CHAR(SYSDATE,'DD-M TO_CHAR(ROUND(SYSDATE TO_CHAR(TRUNC(SYSDATE
-------------------- ---------------------- ----------------------
06-OCT-01 07:35:48 AM 06-OCT-01 12:00:00 AM 06-OCT-01 12:00:00 AM
```

Notice that since the input time (SYSDATE) is before 12 noon, the output of ROUND and TRUNC are the same. However, if the input time were after 12 noon, the output of ROUND and TRUNC would be different, as in the following example.

```
SELECT TO_CHAR(SYSDATE, 'DD-MON-YY HH:MI:SS AM'),
       TO_CHAR(ROUND(SYSDATE), 'DD-MON-YY HH:MI:SS AM'),
       TO_CHAR(TRUNC(SYSDATE), 'DD-MON-YY HH:MI:SS AM')
FROM DUAL;

TO_CHAR(SYSDATE,'DD-M TO_CHAR(ROUND(SYSDATE TO_CHAR(TRUNC(SYSDATE
-------------------- ---------------------- ----------------------
06-OCT-01 05:35:48 PM 07-OCT-01 12:00:00 AM 06-OCT-01 12:00:00 AM
```

Since the input time is past 12 noon, ROUND returns the beginning of the next day. However, TRUNC still returns the beginning of the input date. This is similar to the rounding and truncating of numbers.

When we specify a format as an input to the ROUND and TRUNC functions, things become a bit more involved, but the concepts of rounding and truncating still remain the same. The difference is that the rounding and truncating are now based on the format we specify. For example, if we specify the format as YYYY, the input date will be truncated based on the year, which means that if the input date is before the middle of the year (July 1st), both ROUND and TRUNC will return the first day of the year. If the input date is after July 1st, ROUND will return the first day of the next year, whereas TRUNC will return the first day of the input year. For example:

```
SELECT TO_CHAR(SYSDATE-180, 'DD-MON-YYYY HH24:MI:SS'),
       TO_CHAR(ROUND(SYSDATE-180,'YYYY'),'DD-MON-YYYY HH24:MI:SS'),
       TO_CHAR(TRUNC(SYSDATE-180,'YYYY'),'DD-MON-YYYY HH24:MI:SS')
FROM DUAL;

TO_CHAR(SYSDATE-180, TO_CHAR(ROUND(SYSDAT TO_CHAR(TRUNC(SYSDAT
-------------------- ---------------------- ----------------------
09-APR-2001 20:58:33 01-JAN-2001 00:00:00 01-JAN-2001 00:00:00
```

```
SELECT TO_CHAR(SYSDATE, 'DD-MON-YYYY HH24:MI:SS'),
       TO_CHAR(ROUND(SYSDATE,'YYYY'),'DD-MON-YYYY HH24:MI:SS'),
       TO_CHAR(TRUNC(SYSDATE,'YYYY'),'DD-MON-YYYY HH24:MI:SS')
FROM DUAL;

TO_CHAR(SYSDATE,'DD-  TO_CHAR(ROUND(SYSDAT  TO_CHAR(TRUNC(SYSDAT
--------------------  --------------------  --------------------
06-OCT-2001 20:58:49  01-JAN-2002 00:00:00  01-JAN-2001 00:00:00
```

Similarly, we can round or truncate a date to a specific month, quarter, week, century, hour, minute, and so forth by using the appropriate format. Table 6-3 lists the formats (and their meanings) that can be used with the ROUND and TRUNC functions.

Table 6-3. Date formats for use with ROUND and TRUNC

Rounding unit	Format	Remarks
Century	CC	TRUNC returns the first date of the century.
	SCC	If the input date is before the middle of the century (01-JAN-xx51), ROUND returns the first date of the century; otherwise, ROUND returns the first date of the next century.
Year	SYYYY	TRUNC returns the first date of the year.
	YYYY	If the input date is before the middle of the year (01-JUL), ROUND returns the first
	YEAR	date of the year; otherwise, ROUND returns the first date of the next year.
	SYEAR	
	YYY	
	YY	
	Y	
ISO	IYYY	TRUNC returns the first date of the ISO year.
	IYY	If the input date is before the middle of the ISO year, ROUND returns the first date of
	IY	the ISO year; otherwise, ROUND returns the first date of the next ISO year.
	I	
Quarter	Q	TRUNC returns the first date of the quarter.
		If the input date is before the middle of the quarter (the 16th day of the second month of the quarter), ROUND returns the first date of the year; otherwise, ROUND returns the first date of the next quarter.
Month	MONTH	TRUNC returns the first date of the month.
	MON	If the input date is before the middle of the month (the 16th day of the month),
	MM	ROUND returns the first date of the year; otherwise, ROUND returns the first date of
	RM	the next month.
Week	WW	TRUNC returns the first date of the week.
		If the input date is before the middle of the week (based on the first day of the year), ROUND returns the first date of the week; otherwise, the first date of the next week.
ISO Week	IW	TRUNC returns the first date of the ISO week.
		If the input date is before the middle of the week (based on the first day of the ISO year), ROUND returns the first date of the week; otherwise, ROUND returns the first date of the next week.

Table 6-3. Date formats for use with ROUND and TRUNC (continued)

Rounding unit	Format	Remarks
Week	W	TRUNC returns the first date of the week.
		If the input date is before the middle of the week (based on the first day of the month), ROUND returns the first date of the week; otherwise, ROUND returns the first date of the next week.
Day	DDD	TRUNC returns the beginning of the day.
	DD	If the input time is before the middle of the day (12:00 noon), ROUND returns the
	J	beginning of the day, otherwise the beginning of the next day.
Day of the week	DAY	TRUNC returns the first date of the week.
	DY	If the input date is before the middle of the week (based on the first day of the
	D	month), ROUND returns the first date of the week, otherwise the first date of the next week.
Hour	HH	TRUNC returns the beginning of the hour.
	HH12	If the input time is before the middle of the hour (00:30), ROUND returns the begin-
	HH24	ning of the hour; otherwise, ROUND returns the beginning of the next hour.
Minute	MI	TRUNC returns the beginning of the minute.
		If the input time is before the middle of the minute (00:00:30), ROUND returns the beginning of the minute; otherwise, ROUND returns the beginning of the next minute.

NEW_TIME

Let's say you work in an office in the New York City and want to schedule a video conference with a customer in Los Angeles. If you aren't careful about the time difference between the two cities, you might end up scheduling the meeting at 9:00 A.M. your time. Hopefully, you know that this is not the proper time to call your customer if you really want to make the deal, because it is too early to expect him to be in the office (9:00 A.M. in New York is 6:00 A.M. in Los Angeles). If you need to deal with time zones in the database, Oracle's built-in NEW_TIME function comes to your rescue. It converts a date and time in a given time zone into a date and time in another time zone. Call NEW_TIME as follows:

```
NEW_TIME (date, input_time_zone, output_time_zone)
```

The syntax elements are:

date

Specifies a literal, PL/SQL DATE variable, or a database column of DATE datatype.

input_time_zone

Specifies the name of the input time zone (as a string).

output_time_zone

Specifies the name of the output time zone (as a string).

As an example, to find out the time in Los Angeles when it is 9:00 A.M. at New York, you can use the following SQL:

```
ALTER SESSION SET NLS_DATE_FORMAT = 'DD-MON-YY HH:MI:SS AM';

Session altered.

SELECT NEW_TIME('11-NOV-01 09:00:00 AM','EST','PST') FROM DUAL;

NEW_TIME('11-NOV-0109
----------------------
11-NOV-01 06:00:00 AM
```

In this example, EST and PST correspond to Eastern Standard Time and Pacific Standard Time, respectively.

SELECTing Data Based on Date Ranges

There are times when we need to SELECT data from a table based on a given date range. Let's say you have been asked to print all orders placed on a given date, say 22-MAY-01. Probably, your immediate response would be a query such as the following:

```
SELECT * FROM CUST_ORDER
WHERE ORDER_DT = '22-MAY-01';

no rows selected
```

There's no output. Surprised? Although you know there are orders on 22-MAY-01, this query didn't return any rows. The reason is that ORDER_DT is a DATE column, and contains time as well as date information. On the other hand, the date literal '22-MAY-01' doesn't contain any time information. When you don't specify the time portion in a date literal, the time portion is assumed to be beginning of the day, i.e., 12:00:00 A.M. (or 00:00:00 in 24 hour format). In the CUST_ORDER table, the time components in the ORDER_DT column are other than 12:00:00 A.M. In this case, the correct query to print orders placed on 22-MAY-01 is:

```
SELECT * FROM CUST_ORDER
WHERE ORDER_DT BETWEEN TO_DATE('22-MAY-01 00:00:00','DD-MON-YY HH24:MI:SS')
AND TO_DATE('22-MAY-01 23:59:59','DD-MON-YY HH24:MI:SS');

ORDER_NBR CUST SALES_EMP SALE_PRICE ORDER_DT  EXPECTED_ CANCELLED SHIP STATUS
--------- ---- --------- ---------- --------- --------- --------- ---- ---------
     1001    1         3         99 22-MAY-01 23-MAY-01                 DELIVERED
     1005    8         3         99 22-MAY-01 24-MAY-01                 DELIVERED
     1021    8         7         99 22-MAY-01 24-MAY-01                 DELIVERED
```

The query treats the one day as a range: 22-MAY-01 00:00:00 to 22-MAY-01 23:59:59. Thus, the query returns any order placed at any time during 22-MAY-01.

Another way to solve this problem of needing to ignore the time components in a DATE column would be to truncate the date, and then compare the truncated result with the input literal:

```
SELECT * FROM CUST_ORDER
WHERE TRUNC(ORDER_DT) = '22-MAY-01';
```

ORDER_NBR	CUST	SALES_EMP	SALE_PRICE	ORDER_DT	EXPECTED_	CANCELLED	SHIP	STATUS
1001	1	3	99	22-MAY-01	23-MAY-01			DELIVERED
1005	8	3	99	22-MAY-01	24-MAY-01			DELIVERED
1021	8	7	99	22-MAY-01	24-MAY-01			DELIVERED

The TRUNC function sets the time portion to the beginning of the day. Therefore, the equality comparison with the date literal '22-MAY-01' returns the expected output. The same result can be achieved by converting ORDER_DT to a character string in a format matching that of the input data.

```
SELECT * FROM CUST_ORDER
WHERE TO_CHAR(ORDER_DT,'DD-MON-YY') = '22-MAY-01';
```

The downside to the approach of using the TRUNC and TO_CHAR functions is that the resulting query cannot make use of any index that happens to be on the ORDER_DT column. This can have significant performance implications. On the other hand, the date range solution, while more complex to code, does not preclude the use of any index on the column in question.

 Oracle8i and higher support the use of function-based indexes, which, if created correctly, allow for the use of indexes even when functions are applied to columns.

You can use the same techniques shown in this section to SELECT data based on any given date range, even if that range spans more than just one day.

Creating a Date Pivot Table

For certain types of queries, it's helpful to have a table with one row for each date over a period of time. For example, you might wish to have one row for each date in the current year. You can use the TRUNC function in conjunction with some PL/SQL code to create such a table:

```
CREATE TABLE DATES_OF_YEAR (ONE_DAY DATE);

Table created.

DECLARE
  I NUMBER;
  START_DAY DATE := TRUNC(SYSDATE,'YY');
BEGIN
```

```
   FOR I IN 0 .. (TRUNC(ADD_MONTHS(SYSDATE,12),'YY') - 1) - (TRUNC(SYSDATE,'YY'))
   LOOP
     INSERT INTO DATES_OF_YEAR VALUES (START_DAY+I);
   END LOOP;
END;
/

PL/SQL procedure successfully completed.

SELECT COUNT(*) FROM DATES_OF_YEAR;

  COUNT(*)
----------
       365
```

The DATES_OF_YEAR table is now populated with the 365 days of the year 2001. We can now play with this table to generate various useful lists of dates.

Let's say there are two paydays where you work—the 15th of each month and the last day of each month. Use the following query against the DATES_OF_YEAR table to generate a list of all paydays in the year 2001.

```
SELECT ONE_DAY PAYDAY FROM DATES_OF_YEAR
WHERE TO_CHAR(ONE_DAY,'DD') = '15'
OR ONE_DAY = LAST_DAY(ONE_DAY);

PAYDAY
---------
15-JAN-01
31-JAN-01
15-FEB-01
28-FEB-01
15-MAR-01
31-MAR-01
15-APR-01
30-APR-01
15-MAY-01
31-MAY-01
15-JUN-01
30-JUN-01
15-JUL-01
31-JUL-01
15-AUG-01
31-AUG-01
15-SEP-01
30-SEP-01
15-OCT-01
31-OCT-01
15-NOV-01
30-NOV-01
15-DEC-01
31-DEC-01

24 rows selected.
```

Quite often you are told by a government organization that the processing of a document will take "x" number of days. When they say something like that, they usually mean "x" number of working days. Thus, in order to calculate the expected completion date, you need to count "x" days from the current date, skipping Saturdays and Sundays. Obviously, you can't use simple date arithmetic, because simple date subtraction doesn't exclude weekend days. What you can do is use the DATES_OF_YEAR table. For example:

```
SELECT COUNT(*) FROM DATES_OF_YEAR
WHERE RTRIM(TO_CHAR(ONE_DAY,'DAY')) NOT IN ('SATURDAY', 'SUNDAY')
AND ONE_DAY BETWEEN '&d1' AND '&d2';

Enter value for d1: 18-FEB-01
Enter value for d2: 15-MAR-01
old   3: AND ONE_DAY BETWEEN '&d1' AND '&d2'
new   3: AND ONE_DAY BETWEEN '18-FEB-01' AND '15-MAR-01'

  COUNT(*)
----------
        19
```

This query counts the number of days between the two dates you enter, excluding Saturdays and the Sundays. The TO_CHAR function with the 'DAY' format converts each candidate date (from the DATES_OF_YEAR table) to a day of the week, and the NOT IN operator excludes the days that are Saturdays and Sundays. Notice the use of the RTRIM function with TO_CHAR. We used RTRIM because TO_CHAR produces the DAY as a nine-character string, with blank padded to the right. RTRIM eliminates those extra spaces.

There could be holidays between two dates, and the queries shown in this section don't deal with that possibility. To take holidays into account, you need another table (perhaps named HOLIDAYS) that lists all the holidays in the year. You can then modify the previous query to exclude days listed in the HOLIDAYS table.

Summarizing by a DATE/Time Element

Let's say you want to print a quarterly summary of all your orders. You want to print the total number of orders and total sale price for each quarter. The order table is as follows:

```
SELECT * FROM CUST_ORDER;
```

ORDER_NBR	CUST	SALES	PRICE	ORDER_DT	EXPECTED_	CANCELLED	SHIP	STATUS
1001	1	3	99	22-MAY-01	23-MAY-01			DELIVERED
1000	1	4		19-JAN-01	24-JAN-01	21-JAN-01		CANCELLED
1002	5	6		12-JUL-01	25-JUL-01	14-JUL-01		CANCELLED
1003	4	5	56	16-NOV-01	26-NOV-01			DELIVERED
1004	4	4	34	18-JAN-01	27-JAN-01			PENDING
1005	8	3	99	22-MAY-01	24-MAY-01			DELIVERED

```
1006   1   8       22-JUL-01 28-JUL-01 24-JUL-01   CANCELLED
1007   5   1   25 20-NOV-01 22-NOV-01             PENDING
1008   5   1   25 21-JAN-01 23-JAN-01             PENDING
1009   1   5   56 18-MAY-01 22-MAY-01             DELIVERED
1012   1   2   99 22-JAN-01 23-JAN-01             DELIVERED
1011   1   3       19-NOV-01 24-NOV-01 21-NOV-01   CANCELLED
1015   5   3       12-NOV-01 25-NOV-01 14-NOV-01   CANCELLED
1017   4   1   56 16-MAY-01 26-MAY-01             DELIVERED
1019   4   9   34 18-NOV-01 27-NOV-01             PENDING
1021   8   7   99 22-MAY-01 24-MAY-01             DELIVERED
1023   1   1       22-NOV-01 28-NOV-01 24-NOV-01   CANCELLED
1025   5   3   25 20-MAY-01 22-MAY-01             PENDING
1027   5   1   25 21-NOV-01 23-NOV-01             PENDING
1029   1   5   56 18-MAY-01 22-MAY-01             DELIVERED
```

```
20 rows selected.
```

There is no quarter column in the CUST_ORDER table. You have to manipulate the ORDER_DT column to generate the quarter. The following SQL statement does this using the TO_CHAR function along with a date format. In addition to being used in the SELECT list, notice that TO_CHAR is used in the GROUP BY clause to group the results by quarter.

```
SELECT 'Q'||TO_CHAR(ORDER_DT, 'Q') QUARTER, COUNT(*), SUM(NVL(SALE_PRICE,0))
FROM CUST_ORDER
GROUP BY 'Q'||TO_CHAR(ORDER_DT, 'Q');

QU   COUNT(*) SUM(NVL(SALE_PRICE,0))
--   -------- ---------------------
Q1       4                     158
Q2       7                     490
Q3       2                       0
Q4       7                     140
```

Using this same technique, you can summarize data by week, month, year, hour, minute, or any other date/time unit that you choose.

Oracle9i New DATETIME Features

With Oracle9*i*, Oracle introduced features to enhance support for temporal data. These new features form the basis of Oracle's support for:

- Time zones
- Date and time data with fractional seconds
- Date and time intervals

In this section we discuss these enhancements and their uses.

Time Zones

In the Internet economy, business is carried out across geographical boundaries and time zones. Oracle facilitates global e-business through its support for time zones. With Oracle9i, a database and a session can now be associated with time zones. Having database and session time zones enables users in geographically distant regions to exchange temporal data with the database without having to bother about the time differences between their location and the server's location.

Database time zone

We can set the time zone of a database when we create the database. After creating the database, we can change the time zone using the ALTER DATABASE command. Both CREATE DATABASE and ALTER DATABASE take an optional SET TIME_ ZONE clause. Specify a time zone in one of the two ways:

- By specifying a displacement from the Coordinated Universal Time (UTC).
- By specifying a time zone region.

The displacement from the UTC is specified in hours and minutes with a + or – sign. Every time zone region is given a region name. For example, EST is the region name for Eastern Standard Time. We can also use such a region name to set the time zone of a database.

 UTC was formerly known as Greenwich Mean Time (GMT).

The syntax of SET TIME_ZONE clause is:

```
SET TIME_ZONE = '+ | - HH:MI' | 'time_zone_region'
```

The following examples use this clause to set the time zone of a database:

```
CREATE DATABASE ... SET TIME_ZONE = '-05:00';

ALTER DATABASE ... SET TIME_ZONE = 'EST';
```

Both of the previous examples set the time zone to Eastern Standard Time. The first example uses a displacement (–05:00) from the UTC. The second example uses the region name (EST).

 If we do not explicitly set the database time zone, Oracle defaults to the operating system time zone. If the operating system time zone is not a valid Oracle time zone, UTC is used as the default time zone.

Session time zone

Each session can have a time zone as well. The time zone of a session can be set by using the ALTER SESSION SET TIME_ZONE clause. The syntax for the SET TIME_ZONE clause in the ALTER SESSION statement is the same as that in the CREATE DATABASE and ALTER DATABASE statements.

The following example shows two ways to set the time zone of a session to Pacific Standard Time:

```
ALTER SESSION SET TIME_ZONE = '-08:00';
```

```
ALTER SESSION SET TIME_ZONE = 'PST';
```

To set the session time zone to the local operating system time zone (e.g., the time zone of a PC initiating a remote user session), we can use the LOCAL keyword in the SET TIME_ZONE clause, as in the following example:

```
ALTER SESSION SET TIME_ZONE = LOCAL;
```

To set the session time zone to the database time zone, use the DBTIMEZONE keyword in the SET TIME_ZONE clause, as in the following example:

```
ALTER SESSION SET TIME_ZONE = DBTIMEZONE;
```

We will talk more about the DBTIMEZONE keyword later.

 If the session time zone has not been explicitly set, Oracle defaults to the local operating system time zone. If the operating system time zone is not a valid Oracle time zone, UTC is used as the default time zone.

Date and Time Data with Fractional Seconds

To provide support for the fractional seconds along with date and time data, Oracle9*i* introduced the following new temporal datatypes:

- TIMESTAMP
- TIMESTAMP WITH TIMEZONE
- TIMESTAMP WITH LOCAL TIMEZONE

These datatypes provide ways to handle time values resolved down to the fraction of a second, and in different time zones. The following sections discuss these datatypes.

TIMESTAMP

The TIMESTAMP datatype extends the DATE type to support more precise time values. A TIMESTAMP includes all the components of the DATE datatype (century, year, month, day, hour, minute, second) plus fractional seconds. A TIMESTAMP datatype is specified as:

```
TIMESTAMP [ (precision for fractional seconds) ]
```

The precision for the fractional seconds is specified in the parentheses. We can specify integer values between 0 and 9 for fractional precision. A precision of 9 means that we can have 9 digits to the right of the decimal. As you can see from the syntax notation, the precision field is optional. If we don't specify the precision, it defaults to 6; i.e., TIMESTAMP is the same as TIMESTAMP(6).

The following example creates a table with a TIMESTAMP column:

```
CREATE TABLE TRANSACTION (
TRANSACTION_ID NUMBER(10),
TRANSACTION_TIMESTAMP TIMESTAMP,
STATUS VARCHAR2(12));

Table created.

DESC TRANSACTION
Name                            Null?     Type
------------------------------- --------- ---------------
TRANSACTION_ID                            NUMBER(10)
TRANSACTION_TIMESTAMP                     TIMESTAMP(6)
STATUS                                    VARCHAR2(12)
```

Note that even though we specified just TIMESTAMP as the datatype of the column TRANSACTION_TIMESTAMP, it appears as TIMESTAMP(6) when we describe the table. To insert data into this column, we can use a TIMESTAMP literal in the following format:

```
TIMESTAMP 'YYYY-MM-DD HH:MI:SS.xxxxxxxxx'
```

A TIMESTAMP literal can have up to 9 digits of fractional seconds. The fractional part is optional, but the date and time elements are mandatory and must be provided in the specified format. Here's an example in which data is inserted into a table with a TIMESTAMP column:

```
INSERT INTO TRANSACTION
VALUES (1001, TIMESTAMP '1998-12-31 08:23:46.368', 'OPEN');

1 row created.

SELECT * FROM TRANSACTION;

TRANSACTION_ID TRANSACTION_TIMESTAMP                STATUS
-------------- ------------------------------------ ---------
          1001 31-DEC-98 08.23.46.368000 AM         OPEN
```

TIMESTAMP WITH TIME ZONE

The TIMESTAMP WITH TIME ZONE datatype further extends the TIMESTAMP type to include a time zone displacement. A TIMESTAMP WITH TIME ZONE datatype is specified as:

```
TIMESTAMP [ (precision for fractional seconds) ] WITH TIME ZONE
```

The precision for fractional seconds is the same as that for the TIMESTAMP datatype. The time zone displacement is the time difference in hours and minutes, between the local time and GMT (Greenwich Mean Time, also known as Coordinated Universal Time or UTC). We supply such displacements when we store values in the column, and the database retains the displacements so that those values can later be translated into any target time zone desired by the user.

The following example creates a table with a TIMESTAMP column:

```
CREATE TABLE TRANSACTION_TIME_ZONE (
TRANSACTION_ID NUMBER(10),
TRANSACTION_TIMESTAMP TIMESTAMP(3) WITH TIME ZONE,
STATUS VARCHAR2(12));

Table created.

DESC TRANSACTION_TIME_ZONE
Name                             Null?    Type
-------------------------------- -------- -------------------------
TRANSACTION_ID                            NUMBER(10)
TRANSACTION_TIMESTAMP                     TIMESTAMP(3) WITH TIME ZONE
STATUS                                    VARCHAR2(12)
```

To insert data into the TRANSACTION_TIMESTAMP column, we can use a TIMESTAMP literal with a time zone displacement, which takes the following form:

```
TIMESTAMP 'YYYY-MM-DD HH:MI:SS.xxxxxxxxx {+|-} HH:MI'
```

Here is an example showing how to insert data into a table with a TIMESTAMP WITH TIME ZONE column:

```
INSERT INTO TRANSACTION_TIME_ZONE
VALUES (1002, TIMESTAMP '1998-12-31 08:23:46.368 -10:30', 'NEW');

1 row created.

SELECT * FROM TRANSACTION_TIME_ZONE;

TRANSACTION_ID TRANSACTION_TIMESTAMP                 STATUS
-------------- ------------------------------------- -------
          1002 31-DEC-98 08.23.46.368 AM -10:30      NEW
```

Note that even though the datatype is called TIMESTAMP WITH TIME ZONE, the literal still uses just the TIMESTAMP keyword. Also note that the literal specifies a date/time displacement using the {+|−}hour:minute notation.

If we are specifying a time zone displacement with a TIMESTAMP literal, we must specify the sign of the displacement (i.e., + or −). The range of the hour in a time zone displacement is −12 through +13, and the range of a minute is 0 through 59. A displacement outside these ranges will generate an error.

When we don't specify a time zone displacement, the displacement is not assumed to be zero; instead, the timestamp is assumed to be in the local time zone, and the value of the displacement defaults to the displacement of the local time zone. In the following example, the input data doesn't specify any time zone. Therefore, Oracle assumes the timestamp to be in the local time zone, and stores the local time zone along with the timestamp in the database column.

```
INSERT INTO TRANSACTION_TIME_ZONE
VALUES (1003, TIMESTAMP '1999-12-31 08:23:46.368', 'NEW');

1 row created.

SELECT * FROM TRANSACTION_TIME_ZONE;

TRANSACTION_ID TRANSACTION_TIMESTAMP                STATUS
-------------- ------------------------------------ -------
          1003 31-DEC-99 08.23.46.368 AM -05:00     NEW
```

TIMESTAMP WITH LOCAL TIME ZONE

The TIMESTAMP WITH LOCAL TIME ZONE datatype is a variant of the TIMESTAMP WITH TIME ZONE datatype. A TIMESTAMP WITH LOCAL TIME ZONE datatype is specified as:

```
TIMESTAMP [ (precision for fractional seconds) ] WITH LOCAL TIME ZONE
```

The precision for the fractional seconds is the same as that in the TIMESTAMP datatype. TIMESTAMP WITH LOCAL TIME ZONE differs from TIMESTAMP WITH TIME ZONE in the following ways:

- The time zone displacement is not stored as part of the column data.
- The data stored in the database is normalized to the time zone of the database. To normalize an input date to the database time zone, the input time is converted to a time in the database time zone.
- When the data is retrieved, Oracle returns the data in the time zone of the user session.

The following example creates a table with a TIMESTAMP column:

```
CREATE TABLE TRANSACTION_LOCAL_TIME_ZONE (
TRANSACTION_ID NUMBER(10),
TRANSACTION_TIMESTAMP TIMESTAMP(3) WITH LOCAL TIME ZONE,
STATUS VARCHAR2(12));

Table created.

DESC TRANSACTION_LOCAL_TIME_ZONE
 Name                     Null?    Type
 ------------------------ -------- ------------------------
 TRANSACTION_ID                    NUMBER(10)
 TRANSACTION_TIMESTAMP             TIMESTAMP(3) WITH LOCAL TIME ZONE
 STATUS                            VARCHAR2(12)
```

There is no literal for the TIMESTAMP WITH LOCAL TIME ZONE datatype. To insert data into this column, we use a TIMESTAMP literal. For example:

```
INSERT INTO TRANSACTION_LOCAL_TIME_ZONE VALUES (
2001, TIMESTAMP '1998-12-31 10:00:00 -3:00', 'NEW');

1 row created.

SELECT * FROM TRANSACTION_LOCAL_TIME_ZONE;

TRANSACTION_ID TRANSACTION_TIMESTAMP     STATUS
-------------- ------------------------- -------
          2001 31-DEC-98 08.00.00 AM     NEW
```

Note that the time zone displacement is not stored in the database. The data is stored in the database in the normalized form with respect to the database time zone. What this means is that the input time is converted into a time in the database time zone before being storing in the database. The database time zone is −5:00. Therefore, −3:00 is 2 hours ahead of the database time zone, and 10:00:00 − 3:00 is the same as 08:00:00 − 5:00. Since the time is normalized with respect to the database time zone, the displacement does not need to be stored in the database.

Date and Time Intervals

Date and time interval data are an integral part of our day-to-day life. Common examples of interval data are the age of a person, the maturity period of a bond or certificate of deposit, and the warranty period of your car. Prior to Oracle9*i*, we all used the NUMBER datatype to represent such data, and the logic needed to deal with interval data had to be coded at the application level. Oracle9*i* provides two new datatypes to handle interval data:

- INTERVAL YEAR TO MONTH
- INTERVAL DAY TO SECOND

The following sections discuss the use of these datatypes.

INTERVAL YEAR TO MONTH

The INTERVAL YEAR TO MONTH type stores a period of time expressed as a number of years and months. An INTERVAL YEAR TO MONTH datatype is specified as:

```
INTERVAL YEAR [ (precision for year) ] TO MONTH
```

The precision specifies the number of digits in the year field. The precision can range from 0 to 9, and the default value is 2. The default precision of two allows for a maximum interval of 99 years, 11 months.

The following example creates a table with INTERVAL YEAR TO MONTH datatype:

```
CREATE TABLE EVENT_HISTORY (
EVENT_ID NUMBER(10),
```

```
EVENT_DURATION INTERVAL YEAR TO MONTH);
```

Table created.

```
DESC EVENT_HISTORY
 Name                            Null?    Type
 ---------------------------     -------- -----------------------
 EVENT_ID                                 NUMBER(10)
 EVENT_DURATION                           INTERVAL YEAR(2) TO MONTH
```

The next example uses the NUMTOYMINTERVAL (NUM-TO-YM-INTERVAL) function to insert data into a database column of type INTERVAL YEAR TO MONTH. This function converts a NUMBER value into a value of type INTERVAL YEAR TO MONTH, and is discussed later in this chapter in the section "Manipulating Timestamps and Intervals."

```
INSERT INTO EVENT_HISTORY VALUES (5001, NUMTOYMINTERVAL(2,'YEAR'));
```

1 row created.

```
INSERT INTO EVENT_HISTORY VALUES (5002, NUMTOYMINTERVAL(2.5,'MONTH'));
```

1 row created.

```
SELECT * FROM EVENT_HISTORY;

  EVENT_ID EVENT_DURATION
---------- ------------------
      5001 +02-00
      5002 +00-02
```

The second argument to the NUMTOYMINTERVAL function specifies the unit of the first argument. Therefore, in the first example, the number 2 is treated as 2 years, and in the second example, the number 2.5 is treated as 2 months. Note that the fractional part of a month is ignored. An INTERVAL YEAR TO MONTH value is only in terms of years and months, not fractional months. Any fractional values of a month are truncated.

INTERVAL DAY TO SECOND

The INTERVAL DAY TO SECOND type stores a period of time expressed as a number of days, hours, minutes, seconds, and fractions of a second. An INTERVAL DAY TO SECOND datatype is specified as:

```
INTERVAL DAY [(precision for day)]
TO SECOND [(precision for fractional seconds)]
```

The precision for day specifies the number of digits in the day field. This precision can range from 0 to 9, and the default value is 2. The precision for fractional seconds is the number of digits in the fractional part of second. It can range from 0 to 9, and the default value is 6.

The following example creates a table with INTERVAL DAY TO SECOND datatype:

```
CREATE TABLE BATCH_JOB_HISTORY (
JOB_ID NUMBER(6),
JOB_DURATION INTERVAL DAY(3) TO SECOND(6));

Table created.

DESC BATCH_JOB_HISTORY
 Name                    Null?    Type
 ---------------------- -------- -----------------------------
 JOB_ID                           NUMBER(6)
 JOB_DURATION                     INTERVAL DAY(3) TO SECOND(6)
```

Here's how to insert data into a table with an INTERVAL DAY TO SECOND column:

```
INSERT INTO BATCH_JOB_HISTORY VALUES
(6001, NUMTODSINTERVAL(5369.2589,'SECOND'));

1 row created.

SELECT * FROM BATCH_JOB_HISTORY;

    JOB_ID JOB_DURATION
---------- ----------------------------------------
      6001 +00 01:29:29.258900
```

To insert into a database column of type INTERVAL DAY TO SECOND, we used a function NUMTODSINTERVAL (NUM-TO-DS-INTERVAL). This function converts a NUMBER value into a value of type INTERVAL DAY TO SECOND, and is discussed in the section "Manipulating Timestamps and Intervals" later in this chapter.

INTERVAL Literals

Just as Oracle supports DATE and TIMESTAMP literals, it supports INTERVAL literals too. There are two interval datatypes, and two types of corresponding interval literals: YEAR TO MONTH interval literals and DAY TO SECOND interval literals.

YEAR TO MONTH Interval Literals

A YEAR TO MONTH interval literal represents a time period in terms of years and months. A YEAR TO MONTH interval literal takes on the following form:

```
INTERVAL 'y [- m]' YEAR[(precision_for_year)] [TO MONTH]
```

The syntax elements are:

y

An integer value specifying the years.

m

An optional integer value specifying the months. You must include the TO MONTH keywords if you specify a month value.

precision_for_year

   Specifies the number of digits to allow for the year. The default is 2. The valid range is from 0 to 9.

The default precision for the year value is 2. If the literal represents a time period greater than 99 years, then we must specify a high-enough precision for the year. The integer value for the month, as well as the MONTH keyword, are optional. If you specify a month value, it must be between 0 and 11. You also need to use the TO MONTH keywords when you specify a month value.

The following example inserts a YEAR TO MONTH interval literal into an INTERVAL YEAR TO MONTH column:

```
INSERT INTO EVENT_HISTORY
VALUES (6001, INTERVAL '5-2' YEAR TO MONTH);

1 row created.

SELECT * FROM EVENT_HISTORY;

  EVENT_ID EVENT_DURATION
---------- -----------------------------------------
      6001 +05-02
```

The following example uses a YEAR TO MONTH interval literal to specify a time period of exactly four years. Note that no value for months is included:

```
SELECT INTERVAL '4' YEAR FROM DUAL;

INTERVAL'4'YEAR
---------------------------------------------
+04-00
```

A YEAR TO MONTH interval literal can also be used to represent months only.

```
SELECT INTERVAL '3' MONTH FROM DUAL;

INTERVAL'3'MONTH
-------------------------------------------------
+00-03

SELECT INTERVAL '30' MONTH FROM DUAL;

INTERVAL'30'MONTH
-------------------------------------------------
+02-06
```

Notice that when we use a YEAR TO MONTH interval literal to represent only months, we can actually specify a month value larger than 11. In such a situation, Oracle normalizes the value into an appropriate number of years and months. This is the only situation where the month can be greater than 11.

DAY TO SECOND Interval Literals

A DAY TO SECOND interval literal represents a time period in terms of days, hours, minutes, and seconds. DAY TO SECOND interval literals take on the following form:

```
INTERVAL 'd [h [:m[:s]]]' DAY[(day_prec)] [TO {HOUR | MINUTE | SECOND[(frac_prec)]}]
```

The syntax elements are:

d

An integer value specifying the days.

h

An optional integer value specifying the hours.

m

An optional integer value specifying the minutes.

s

An optional number value specifying the seconds and fractional seconds.

day_prec
The number of digits to allow for the days. The default is 2. The valid range is from 0 to 9.

frac_prec
The number of digits to allow for fractional seconds.

By default, two digits are allowed for the number of days. If the literal represents a time period of greater than 99 days, then we must specify a precision high enough to accommodate the number of digits we need. There's no need to specify the precision for the hour and minute values. The value for the hours can be between 0 and 23, and the value for the minutes can be between 0 and 59. If you specify fractional seconds, you need to specify a precision for the fractional seconds as well. The precision for the fractional seconds can be between 1 and 9, and the seconds value can be between 0 and 59.999999999.

The following example inserts a DAY TO SECOND interval literal into a column of data type INTERVAL DAY TO SECOND. The time period being represented is 0 days, 3 hours, 16 minutes, 23.45 seconds.

```
INSERT INTO BATCH_JOB_HISTORY
VALUES (2001, INTERVAL '0 3:16:23.45' DAY TO SECOND);

1 row created.

SELECT * FROM BATCH_JOB_HISTORY;

    JOB_ID JOB_DURATION
---------- -------------------------------------------------
      2001 +00 03:16:23.450000
```

The previous example uses all elements of the DAY TO SECOND interval literal. However, you can use fewer elements if that's all you need. For example, the following examples show several valid permutations:

```
SELECT INTERVAL '400' DAY(3) FROM DUAL;

INTERVAL'400'DAY(3)
-----------------------------------------------------------------
+400 00:00:00

SELECT INTERVAL '11:23' HOUR TO MINUTE FROM DUAL;

INTERVAL'11:23'HOURTOMINUTE
-----------------------------------------------------------------
+00 11:23:00

SELECT INTERVAL '11:23' MINUTE TO SECOND FROM DUAL;

INTERVAL'11:23'MINUTETOSECOND
-----------------------------------------------------------------
+00 00:11:23.000000

SELECT INTERVAL '20' MINUTE FROM DUAL;

INTERVAL'20'MINUTE
-----------------------------------------------------------------
+00 00:20:00
```

The only requirement is that you must use a range of contiguous elements. You cannot, for example, specify an interval in terms of only hours and seconds, because you can't omit the intervening minutes value. An interval of 4 hours, 36 seconds would need to be expressed as 4 hours, 0 minutes, 36 seconds.

Manipulating Timestamps and Intervals

To manipulate values of the new datetime and interval datatypes discussed in this chapter, Oracle9i introduced several new built-in SQL functions. Table 6-4 summarizes these functions.

Table 6-4. New DATETIME and INTERVAL functions in Oracle9i

Function	Description	Return datatype
DBTIMEZONE	Returns the database timezone.	Character
SESSIONTIMEZONE	Returns the session timezone.	Character
SYSTIMESTAMP	Returns the system date and timestamp in the session timezone.	TIMESTAMP WITH TIME ZONE
CURRENT_DATE	Returns the current date in the session timezone.	DATE
CURRENT_TIMESTAMP	Returns the current date and timestamp in the session timezone.	TIMESTAMP WITH TIME ZONE
LOCALTIMESTAMP	Returns the current date and timestamp in the session timezone.	TIMESTAMP
TO_TIMESTAMP	Converts character string into TIMESTAMP.	TIMESTAMP

Table 6-4. New DATETIME and INTERVAL functions in Oracle9i (continued)

Function	Description	Return datatype
TO_TIMESTAMP_TZ	Converts character string into TIMESTAMP WITH TIME ZONE.	TIMESTAMP WITH TIME ZONE
FROM_TZ	Converts TIMPSTAMP into TIMESTAMP WITH TIME ZONE.	TIMESTAMP WITH TIME ZONE
NUMTOYMINTERVAL	Converts number into INTERVAL YEAR TO MONTH.	INTERVAL YEAR TO MONTH
NUMTODSINTERVAL	Converts number into INTERVAL DAY TO SECOND.	INTERVAL DAY TO SECOND
TO_YMINTERVAL	Converts character string into INTERVAL YEAR TO MONTH.	TIMESTAMP WITH TIME ZONE
TO_DSINTERVAL	Converts character string into INTERVAL DAY TO SECOND.	INTERVAL DAY TO SECOND
TZ_OFFSET	Returns the time zone offset with respect to UTC.	Character

The time zone is returned as a displacement with respect to UTC, and is displayed with a + or − sign together with an hours:minutes value. These functions are discussed with examples in the following sections.

DBTIMEZONE

The DBTIMEZONE function returns the value of the database time zone. We can use this function as we use SYSDATE:

```
SELECT DBTIMEZONE FROM  DUAL;

DBTIME
------
-07:00
```

SESSIONTIMEZONE

The SESSIONTIMEZONE function returns the value of the session time zone. We can use this function as we use SYSDATE:

```
SELECT SESSIONTIMEZONE FROM  DUAL;

SESSIONTIMEZONE
----------------
-06:00
```

SYSTIMESTAMP

The SYSTIMESTAMP function returns the value of the system date and time, including the fractional parts of a second and the time zone. This is the same as SYSDATE, but with additional information about fractional seconds and the time zone.

```
SELECT SYSTIMESTAMP FROM  DUAL;

SYSTIMESTAMP
------------------------------------
11-NOV-01 01.00.10.040438 AM -05:00
```

SYSTIMESTAMP returns a value in the TIMESTAMP WITH TIMEZONE datatype, and the precision of fractional seconds is always 6.

CURRENT_DATE

The CURRENT_DATE function returns the current date and time in the session time zone. The difference between SYSDATE and CURRENT_DATE is that while SYSDATE is based on the DBTIMEZONE, CURRENT_DATE is based on the SESSIONTIMEZONE.

```
SELECT SYSDATE, CURRENT_DATE FROM DUAL;

SYSDATE                 CURRENT_DATE
----------------------- -----------------------
11-NOV-2001 01:15:40 AM 11-NOV-2001 12:15:41 AM
```

Note that the CURRENT_DATE is behind the SYSDATE by one hour in this example. This is because the session time zone is one hour behind the database time zone.

CURRENT_TIMESTAMP

The CURRENT_TIMESTAMP function returns the current date, the time, the fractional parts of a second, and a time zone displacement. The value returned will be in the session time zone. Note that the difference between SYSTIMESTAMP and CURRENT_TIMESTAMP is that while SYSTIMESTAMP is based on the DBTIMEZONE, CURRENT_TIMESTAMP is based on the SESSIONTIMEZONE.

The function header of CURRENT_TIMESTAMP is:

```
CURRENT_TIMESTAMP [(precision)]
```

The precision argument specifies the precision of the fractional seconds, and is optional. The default precision is 6. The return value is of datatype TIMESTAMP WITH TIME ZONE.

```
SELECT CURRENT_TIMESTAMP FROM DUAL;

CURRENT_TIMESTAMP
------------------------------------------
11-NOV-01 01.42.40.099518 PM -06:00
```

LOCALTIMESTAMP

The LOCALTIMESTAMP function returns the current date, time, and the fractional parts of a second in the session time zone. The function header of LOCALTIMESTAMP is:

```
LOCALTIMESTAMP [(precision)]
```

The precision argument specifies the precision of the fractional seconds, and is optional. The default value is 6. The return value is of datatype TIMESTAMP.

```
SELECT LOCALTIMESTAMP FROM DUAL;

LOCALTIMESTAMP
------------------------------------
11-NOV-01 01.42.55.852724 PM
```

Note that the only difference between LOCALTIMESTAMP and CURRENT_TIME-STAMP is the return type. LOCALTIMESTAMP returns a TIMESTAMP, whereas CURRENT_TIMESTAMP returns a TIMESTAMP WITH TIME ZONE.

TO_TIMESTAMP

The TO_TIMESTAMP function is similar to the TO_DATE function. It converts a character string into a TIMESTAMP. The input to the TO_TIMESTAMP function can be a literal, a PL/SQL variable, or a database column of CHAR or VARCHAR2 datatype.

 The TIMESTAMP keyword can also be used to generate a TIME-STAMP value, but the keyword can only be used with a literal value. TO_TIMESTAMP can operate on PL/SQL variables and database column values.

The function header of TO_TIMESTAMP function is:

```
TO_TIMESTAMP (string [,format])
```

The syntax elements are:

string
> Specifies a character string or a numeric value that is convertible to a TIMES-TAMP. The string or numeric value can be a literal, a value in a PL/SQL variable, or a value in a database column.

format
> Specifies the format of the input string.

The format is optional. When the format is not specified, the input string is assumed to be in the default timestamp format. The default timestamp format is the default date format plus time in the format HH.MI.SS.xxxxxxxxx, where xxxxxxxxx represents fractional seconds. The following example converts a string in the default timestamp format into a timestamp:

```
SELECT TO_TIMESTAMP('11-NOV-01 10.32.22.765488123') FROM DUAL;

TO_TIMESTAMP('11-NOV-0110.32.22.765488123')
-------------------------------------------------------------------
11-NOV-01 10.32.22.765488123 AM
```

The following example specifies the format as the second input parameter to the TO_TIMESTAMP function:

```
SELECT TO_TIMESTAMP('12/10/01','MM/DD/YY') FROM DUAL;

TO_TIMESTAMP('12/10/01','MM/DD/YY')
-------------------------------------------------------------------
10-DEC-01 12.00.00 AM
```

Notice in this second example that since the time portion wasn't provided in the input string, the time is assumed to be the beginning of the day, i.e., 12:00:00 A.M.

TO_TIMESTAMP_TZ

The TO_TIMESTAMP_TZ function is similar to the TO_TIMESTAMP function. The only difference is the return datatype. The return type of TO_TIMESTAMP_TZ is TIMESTAMP WITH TIME ZONE. The input to the TO_TIMESTAMP_TZ function can be a literal, a PL/SQL variable, or a database column of CHAR or VARCHAR2 datatype.

The function header of TO_TIMESTAMP_TZ function is:

```
TO_TIMESTAMP_TZ (string [,format])
```

The syntax elements are:

string
> Specifies a character string or a numeric value that is convertible to a TIMESTAMP WITH TIME ZONE. The string or numeric value can be a literal, a value in a PL/SQL variable, or a value in a database column.

format
> Specifies the format of the input string.

The format is optional. When the format is not specified, the input string is assumed to be in the default format of the TIMESTAMP WITH TIME ZONE datatype. The following example converts a string in the default format into a TIMESTAMP WITH TIME ZONE:

```
SELECT TO_TIMESTAMP_TZ('11-NOV-01 10.32.22.765488123 AM -06:00') FROM DUAL;

TO_TIMESTAMP_TZ('11-NOV-0110.32.22.765488123')
--------------------------------------------------------------------
11-NOV-01 10.32.22.765488123 AM -06:00
```

The following example specifies the format as the second input parameter to the TO_TIMESTAMP_TZ function:

```
SELECT TO_TIMESTAMP_TZ('12/10/01','MM/DD/YY') FROM DUAL;

TO_TIMESTAMP_TZ('12/10/01','MM/DD/YY')
----------------------------------------------------------
10-DEC-01 12.00.00.000000000 AM -06:00
```

Note that since the time portion wasn't provided in the input string, the time is assumed to be the beginning of the day, i.e., 12:00:00 A.M.

The TO_TIMESTAMP_TZ function doesn't convert the input string into a TIMESTAMP WITH LOCAL TIME ZONE datatype. Oracle doesn't provide any function for this purpose. To convert a value to TIMESTAMP WITH LOCAL TIME ZONE, we must use the CAST function, as in the following examples:

```
SELECT CAST('10-DEC-01' AS TIMESTAMP WITH LOCAL TIME ZONE) FROM DUAL;

CAST('10-DEC-01'ASTIMESTAMPWITHLOCALTIMEZONE)
--------------------------------------------------------------------------------
10-DEC-01 12.00.00 AM

SELECT CAST(TO_TIMESTAMP_TZ('12/10/01','MM/DD/YY')
            AS TIMESTAMP WITH LOCAL TIME ZONE)
FROM DUAL;

CAST(TO_TIMESTAMP_TZ('12/10/01','MM/DD/YY')ASTIMESTAMPWITHLOCALTIMEZONE)
--------------------------------------------------------------------------------
10-DEC-01 12.00.00 AM
```

In the first example, the input string is in the default date format. Therefore, no date format is required for conversion. However, in the second example the input string is in a different format than the default; therefore, we must use a conversion function along with a format to convert the string into a value (e.g., TIMESTAMP WITH TIME ZONE) that can then be cast to a TIMESTAMP WITH LOCAL TIME ZONE. We can use either TO_DATE, TO_TIMESTAMP, or TO_TIMESTAMP_TZ, depending upon our input data.

> The CAST function used in these examples is not a SQL function in the truest sense. CAST is actually a SQL expression like DECODE and CASE. The CAST expression converts a value in one datatype to a value in another datatype. In the first example, the CAST expression converts a CHAR literal into a value in the TIMESTAMP WITH LOCAL TIME ZONE datatype. In the second example, the CAST expression converts a value in the TIMESTAMP WITH TIME ZONE datatype into a value in the TIMESTAMP WITH LOCAL TIME ZONE datatype.

FROM_TZ

The FROM_TZ function takes separate TIMESTAMP and time zone values as input, and converts the inputs into a TIMESTAMP WITH TIME ZONE. The function header of the FROM_TZ function is:

```
FROM_TZ (timestamp, time_zone)
```

The syntax elements are:

timestamp
> Specifies a literal string, a PL/SQL variable, or a database column. The input must contain a timestamp value.

time_zone
> Specifies a string containing a time zone in the format [+|-]hh:mi.

The following example illustrates conversion of a timestamp and a time zone into a TIMESTAMP WITH TIME ZONE value:

```
SELECT FROM_TZ(TIMESTAMP '2001-12-10 08:30:00', '-5:00') FROM DUAL;

FROM_TZ(TIMESTAMP'2001-12-1008:30:00','-5:00')
------------------------------------------------------------------------
10-DEC-01 08.30.00.000000000 AM -05:00
```

NUMTOYMINTERVAL

The NUMTOYMINTERVAL (NUM-TO-YM-INTERVAL) function converts a number input into an INTERVAL YEAR TO MONTH literal. The function header of NUMTOYMINTERVAL function is:

```
NUMTOYMINTERVAL (n, unit)
```

The syntax elements are:

n

Specifies a numeric literal or an expression convertible to a number.

unit

Specifies a character string containing the unit of n, and can be either 'YEAR' or 'MONTH'. This is case-insensitive.

The following example inserts a row into a table with a column of type INTERVAL YEAR TO MONTH. The NUMTOYMINTERVAL is used to convert a number into type INTERVAL YEAR TO MONTH.

```
INSERT INTO EVENT_HISTORY VALUES (5001, NUMTOYMINTERVAL(2,'YEAR'));
```

NUMTODSINTERVAL

The NUMTODSINTERVAL (NUM-TO-DS-INTERVAL) function converts a number input into an INTERVAL DAY TO SECOND literal. The function header of NUMTODSINTERVAL function is:

```
NUMTODSINTERVAL (n, unit)
```

The syntax elements are:

n

Specifies a numeric literal or an expression convertible to a number.

unit

Specifies a character string containing the unit of n, and can be either 'DAY', 'HOUR', 'MINUTE' or 'SECOND'. This is case-insensitive.

The following example inserts a row into a table with a column of type INTERVAL DAY TO SECOND. The NUMTODSINTERVAL is used to convert a number into type INTERVAL DAY TO SECOND.

```
INSERT INTO BATCH_JOB_HISTORY VALUES
(6001, NUMTODSINTERVAL(5369.2589,'SECOND'));
```

TO_YMINTERVAL

The TO_YMINTERVAL function is very similar to the TO_DATE function. It converts a character string into an INTERVAL YEAR TO MONTH. The input to the TO_YMINTERVAL function can be a literal, a PL/SQL variable, or a database column of CHAR or VARCHAR2 datatype.

The function header of TO_YMINTERVAL function is:

```
TO_YMINTERVAL (string)
```

The syntax element is:

string

> Specifies a literal string, a PL/SQL variable, or a database column. The input string must contain character or numeric data convertible to an INTERVAL YEAR TO MONTH value. The input string must be in Y-M format, i.e., the year and month values must be separated by a dash (-). All components (year, month and -) must be present in the string.

The following example inserts a row into a table with a column of type INTERVAL YEAR TO MONTH. The TO_YMINTERVAL is used to convert a string into a type INTERVAL YEAR TO MONTH value.

```
INSERT INTO EVENT_HISTORY VALUES (5001, TO_YMINTERVAL('02-04'));
```

In this example, the string '02-04' represents an interval of 2 years and 4 months.

TO_DSINTERVAL

The TO_DSINTERVAL function is similar to the TO_DATE function. It converts a character string into an INTERVAL DAY TO SECOND. The input to the TO_DSINTERVAL function can be a literal, a PL/SQL variable, or a database column of CHAR or VARCHAR2 datatype.

The function header of TO_DSINTERVAL function is:

```
TO_DSINTERVAL (string)
```

The syntax element is:

string

> Specifies a literal string, a PL/SQL variable, or a database column containing character numeric data convertible to an INTERVAL DAY TO SECOND value. The input string must be in D HH:MI:SS format. The day value of the interval is separated by a space from the time value, which is expressed in hours, minutes, and seconds, and is delimited by ":". All components must be present in the string in order for it to be converted to an INTERVAL DAY TO SECOND value.

The following example inserts a row into a table with a column of type INTERVAL DAY TO SECOND. The TO_DSINTERVAL is used to convert a string into type INTERVAL DAY TO SECOND.

```
INSERT INTO BATCH_JOB_HISTORY VALUES (6001, TO_DSINTERVAL('0 2:30:43'));
```

In this example, the string '0 2:30:43' represents an interval of 0 days, 2 hours, 30 minutes, and 43 seconds.

TZ_OFFSET

The TZ_OFFSET function returns the time zone offset of its input. The function header of TZ_OFFSET function is:

```
TZ_OFFSET (time_zone_name | time_zone_offset | DBTIMEZONE | SESSIONTIMEZONE)
```

The syntax elements are:

time_zone_name
> Specifies a string containing a time zone name. A time zone name is given to all the time zones in the world, and we can query the V$TIMEZONE_NAMES dynamic view for a list of valid time zone names.

time_zone_offset
> Specifies a string containing a time zone offset. A time zone offset takes the form of "{+ | −} hh:mi", i.e., hours and minutes preceded by a + or − sign.

DBTIMEZONE
> DBTIMEZONE is a build-in function that returns the time zone of the database.

SESSIONTIMEZONE
> SESSIONTIMEZONE is a build-in function that returns the time zone of the session.

The following example illustrates the use of the TZ_OFFSET function:

```
SELECT TZ_OFFSET('US/Pacific'), TZ_OFFSET('EST'), TZ_OFFSET('+6:30') FROM DUAL;

TZ_OFFS TZ_OFFS TZ_OFFS
------- ------- -------
-08:00  -05:00  +06:30
```

Note that time zone names such as 'US/Eastern' and 'US/Pacific' can be used as well as standard abbreviations such as 'EST', 'PST', and so on. The following example illustrates the use of DBTIMEZONE and SESSIONTIMEZONE with the TZ_OFF-SET function:

```
SELECT TZ_OFFSET(DBTIMEZONE), TZ_OFFSET(SESSIONTIMEZONE) FROM DUAL;

TZ_OFFS TZ_OFFS
------- -------
-07:00  -06:00
```

CHAPTER 7

Set Operations

There are situations when we need to combine the results from two or more SELECT statements. SQL enables us to handle these requirements by using set operations. The result of each SELECT statement can be treated as a set, and SQL set operations can be applied on those sets to arrive at a final result. Oracle SQL supports the following four set operations:

- UNION ALL
- UNION
- MINUS
- INTERSECT

SQL statements containing these set operators are referred to as *compound queries*, and each SELECT statement in a compound query is referred to as a *component query*. Two SELECTs can be combined into a compound query by a set operation only if they satisfy the following two conditions:

1. The result sets of both the queries must have the same number of columns.
2. The datatype of each column in the second result set must match the datatype of its corresponding column in the first result set.

 The datatypes do not need to be the same if those in the second result set can be automatically converted by Oracle (using implicit casting) to types compatible with those in the first result set.

These conditions are also referred to as *union compatibility* conditions. The term union compatibility is used even though these conditions apply to other set operations as well. Set operations are often called *vertical joins*, because the result combines data from two or more SELECTS based on columns instead of rows. The generic syntax of a query involving a set operation is:

```
<component query>
{UNION | UNION ALL | MINUS | INTERSECT}
<component query>
```

The keywords UNION, UNION ALL, MINUS, and INTERSECT are set operators. We can have more than two component queries in a composite query; we will always use one less set operator than the number of component queries.

The following sections discuss syntax, examples, rules, and restrictions for the four set operations.

Set Operators

The following list briefly describes the four set operations supported by Oracle SQL:

UNION ALL
> Combines the results of two SELECT statements into one result set.

UNION
> Combines the results of two SELECT statements into one result set, and then eliminates any duplicate rows from that result set.

MINUS
> Takes the result set of one SELECT statement, and removes those rows that are also returned by a second SELECT statement.

INTERSECT
> Returns only those rows that are returned by each of two SELECT statements.

Before moving on to the details on these set operators, let's look at the following two queries, which we'll use as component queries in our subsequent examples. The first query retrieves all the customers in region 5.

```
SELECT CUST_NBR, NAME
FROM CUSTOMER
WHERE REGION_ID = 5;

  CUST_NBR NAME
---------- -----------------------------
         1 Cooper Industries
         2 Emblazon Corp.
         3 Ditech Corp.
         4 Flowtech Inc.
         5 Gentech Industries
```

The second query retrieves all the customers with the sales representative is 'MARTIN'.

```
SELECT C.CUST_NBR, C.NAME
FROM CUSTOMER C
WHERE C.CUST_NBR IN (SELECT O.CUST_NBR
                     FROM CUST_ORDER O, EMPLOYEE E
                     WHERE O.SALES_EMP_ID = E.EMP_ID
                     AND E.LNAME = 'MARTIN');

  CUST_NBR NAME
---------- -----------------------------
         4 Flowtech Inc.
         8 Zantech Inc.
```

If we look at the results returned by these two queries, we will notice that there is one common row (for Flowtech Inc.). The following sections discuss the effects of the various set operations between these two result sets.

UNION ALL

The UNION ALL operator merges the result sets of two component queries. This operation returns rows retrieved by either of the component queries. The following example illustrates the UNION ALL operation:

```
SELECT CUST_NBR, NAME
FROM CUSTOMER
WHERE REGION_ID = 5
UNION ALL
SELECT C.CUST_NBR, C.NAME
FROM CUSTOMER C
WHERE C.CUST_NBR IN (SELECT O.CUST_NBR
                     FROM CUST_ORDER O, EMPLOYEE E
                     WHERE O.SALES_EMP_ID = E.EMP_ID
                     AND E.LNAME = 'MARTIN');


  CUST_NBR NAME
---------- ------------------------------
         1 Cooper Industries
         2 Emblazon Corp.
         3 Ditech Corp.
         4 Flowtech Inc.
         5 Gentech Industries
         4 Flowtech Inc.
         8 Zantech Inc.

7 rows selected.
```

As we can see from the result set, there is one customer, which is retrieved by both the SELECTs, and therefore appears twice in the result set. The UNION ALL operator simply merges the output of its component queries, without caring about any duplicates in the final result set.

UNION

The UNION operator returns all distinct rows retrieved by two component queries. The UNION operation eliminates duplicates while merging rows retrieved by either of the component queries. The following example illustrates the UNION operation:

```
SELECT CUST_NBR, NAME
FROM CUSTOMER
WHERE REGION_ID = 5
UNION
SELECT C.CUST_NBR, C.NAME
FROM CUSTOMER C
WHERE C.CUST_NBR IN (SELECT O.CUST_NBR
```

```
FROM CUST_ORDER O, EMPLOYEE E
WHERE O.SALES_EMP_ID = E.EMP_ID
AND E.LNAME = 'MARTIN');
```

```
CUST_NBR NAME
---------- ------------------------------
         1 Cooper Industries
         2 Emblazon Corp.
         3 Ditech Corp.
         4 Flowtech Inc.
         5 Gentech Industries
         8 Zantech Inc.
```

6 rows selected.

This query is a modification of the previous query; the keywords UNION ALL have been replaced with UNION. Notice that the result set contains only distinct rows (no duplicates). To eliminate duplicate rows, a UNION operation needs to do some extra tasks as compared to the UNION ALL operation. These extra tasks include sorting and filtering the result set. If we observe carefully, we will notice that the result set of the UNION ALL operation is not sorted, whereas the result set of the UNION operation is sorted. These extra tasks introduce a performance overhead to the UNION operation. A query involving UNION will take extra time compared to the same query with UNION ALL, even if there are no duplicates to remove. Therefore, unless we have a valid need to retrieve only distinct rows, we should use UNION ALL instead of UNION for better performance.

INTERSECT

INTERSECT returns only the rows retrieved by both component queries. Compare this with UNION, which returns the rows retrieved by any of the component queries. If UNION acts like 'OR', INTERSECT acts like 'AND'. For example:

```
SELECT CUST_NBR, NAME
FROM CUSTOMER
WHERE REGION_ID = 5
INTERSECT
SELECT C.CUST_NBR, C.NAME
FROM CUSTOMER C
WHERE C.CUST_NBR IN (SELECT O.CUST_NBR
                     FROM CUST_ORDER O, EMPLOYEE E
                     WHERE O.SALES_EMP_ID = E.EMP_ID
                     AND E.LNAME = 'MARTIN');
```

```
CUST_NBR NAME
---------- ------------------------------
         4 Flowtech Inc.
```

As we saw earlier, "Flowtech Inc." was the only customer retrieved by both SELECT statements. Therefore, the INTERSECT operator returns just that one row.

MINUS

MINUS returns all rows from the first SELECT that are not also returned by the second SELECT. For example:

```
SELECT CUST_NBR, NAME
FROM CUSTOMER
WHERE REGION_ID = 5
MINUS
SELECT C.CUST_NBR, C.NAME
FROM CUSTOMER C
WHERE C.CUST_NBR IN (SELECT O.CUST_NBR
                     FROM CUST_ORDER O, EMPLOYEE E
                     WHERE O.SALES_EMP_ID = E.EMP_ID
                     AND E.LNAME = 'MARTIN');
```

```
  CUST_NBR NAME
---------- ------------------------------
         1 Cooper Industries
         2 Emblazon Corp.
         3 Ditech Corp.
         5 Gentech Industries
```

You might wonder why we don't see "Zantech Inc." in the output. An important thing to note here is that the execution order of component queries in a set operation is from top to bottom. The results of UNION, UNION ALL, and INTERSECT will not change if we alter the ordering of component queries. However, the result of MINUS will be different if we alter the order of the component queries. If we rewrite the previous query by switching the positions of the two SELECTs, we get a completely different result:

```
SELECT C.CUST_NBR, C.NAME
FROM CUSTOMER C
WHERE C.CUST_NBR IN (SELECT O.CUST_NBR
                     FROM CUST_ORDER O, EMPLOYEE E
                     WHERE O.SALES_EMP_ID = E.EMP_ID
                     AND E.LNAME = 'MARTIN')
MINUS
SELECT CUST_NBR, NAME
FROM CUSTOMER
WHERE REGION_ID = 5;
```

```
  CUST_NBR NAME
---------- ------------------------------
         8 Zantech Inc.
```

The row for "Flowtech Inc." is returned by both queries, so in our first MINUS example the first component query adds "Flowtech Inc." to the result set while the second component query removes it. The second example turns the MINUS operation around. The first component query adds "Flowtech Inc." and "Zantech Inc." to the result set. The second component query specifies rows to subtract. One of the rows to subtract is "Flowtech Inc.", leaving "Zantech Inc." as the sole remaining row.

In a MINUS operation, rows may be returned by the second SELECT that are not also returned by the first. These rows are not included in the output.

Using Set Operations to Compare Two Tables

Developers, and even DBAs, occasionally need to compare the contents of two tables to determine whether the tables contain the same data. The need to do this is especially common in test environments, as developers may want to compare a set of data generated by a program under test with a set of "known good" data. Comparison of tables is also useful for automated testing purposes, when we have to compare actual results with a given set of expected results. SQL's set operations provide an interesting solution to this problem of comparing two tables.

The following query uses both MINUS and UNION ALL to compare two tables for equality. The query depends on each table having either a primary key or at least one unique index.

```
(SELECT * FROM CUSTOMER_KNOWN_GOOD
MINUS
SELECT * FROM CUSTOMER_TEST)
UNION ALL
(SELECT * FROM CUSTOMER_TEST
MINUS
SELECT * FROM CUSTOMER_KNOWN_GOOD);
```

Let's talk a bit about how this query works. We can look at it as the union of two compound queries. The parentheses ensure that both MINUS operations take place first before the UNION ALL operation is performed. The result of the first MINUS query will be those rows in CUSTOMER_KNOWN_GOOD that are not also in CUSTOMER_TEST. The result of the second MINUS query will be those rows in CUSTOMER_TEST that are not also in CUSTOMER_KNOWN_GOOD. The UNION ALL operator simply combines these two result sets for convenience. If no rows are returned by this query, then we know that both tables have identical rows. Any rows returned by this query represent differences between the CUSTOMER_TEST and CUSTOMER_KNOWN_GOOD tables.

If the possibility exists for one or both tables to contain duplicate rows, we must use a more general form of this query in order to test two tables for equality. This more general form uses row counts to detect duplicates:

```
(SELECT C1.*,COUNT(*)
 FROM CUSTOMER_KNOWN_GOOD
 GROUP BY C1.CUST_NBR, C1.NAME...
MINUS
 SELECT C2.*, COUNT(*)
 FROM CUSTOMER_TEST C2
 GROUP BY C2.CUST_NBR, C2.NAME...)
```

```
UNION ALL
(SELECT C3.*,COUNT(*)
 FROM CUSTOMER_TEST C3
 GROUP BY C3.CUST_NBR, C3.NAME...
MINUS
 SELECT C4.*, COUNT(*)
 FROM CUSTOMER_KNOWN_GOOD C4
 GROUP BY C4.CUST_NBR, C4.NAME...)
```

This query is getting complex! The GROUP BY clause (see Chapter 4) for each SELECT must list *all* columns for the table being selected. Any duplicate rows will be grouped together, and the count will reflect the number of duplicates. If the number of duplicates is the same in both tables, the MINUS operations will cancel those rows out. If any rows are different, or if any occurrence counts are different, the resulting rows will be reported by the query.

Let's look at an example to illustrate how this query works. We'll start with the following tables and data:

```
DESC CUSTOMER_KNOWN_GOOD
Name                          Null?      Type
----------------------------- --------   ----------------
CUST_NBR                      NOT NULL   NUMBER(5)
NAME                          NOT NULL   VARCHAR2(30)

SELECT * FROM CUSTOMER_KNOWN_GOOD;

  CUST_NBR NAME
---------- ------------------------------
         1 Sony
         1 Sony
         2 Samsung
         3 Panasonic
         3 Panasonic
         3 Panasonic

6 rows selected.

DESC CUSTOMER_TEST
Name                          Null?      Type
----------------------------- --------   ----------------
CUST_NBR                      NOT NULL   NUMBER(5)
NAME                          NOT NULL   VARCHAR2(30)

SELECT * FROM CUSTOMER_TEST;
  CUST_NBR NAME
---------- ------------------------------
         1 Sony
         1 Sony
         2 Samsung
         2 Samsung
         3 Panasonic
```

As we can see the CUSTOMER_KNOWN_GOOD and CUSTOMER_TEST tables have the same structure, but different data. Also notice that none of these tables has a primary or unique key; there are duplicate records in both. The following SQL will compare these two tables effectively:

```
(SELECT C1.*, COUNT(*)
FROM CUSTOMER_KNOWN_GOOD C1
GROUP BY C1.CUST_NBR, C1.NAME
MINUS
SELECT C2.*, COUNT(*)
FROM CUSTOMER_TEST C2
GROUP BY C2.CUST_NBR, C2.NAME)
UNION ALL
(SELECT C3.*, COUNT(*)
FROM CUSTOMER_TEST C3
GROUP BY C3.CUST_NBR, C3.NAME
MINUS
SELECT C4.*, COUNT(*)
FROM CUSTOMER_KNOWN_GOOD C4
GROUP BY C4.CUST_NBR, C4.NAME);
```

```
  CUST_NBR NAME                                  COUNT(*)
---------- ------------------------------------ ----------
         2 Samsung                                       1
         3 Panasonic                                     3
         2 Samsung                                       2
         3 Panasonic                                     1
```

These results indicate that one table (CUSTOMER_KNOWN_GOOD) has one record for "Samsung", whereas the second table (CUSTOMER_TEST) has two records for the same customer. Also, one table (CUSTOMER_KNOWN_GOOD) has three records for "Panasonic", whereas the second table (CUSTOMER_TEST) has one record for the same customer. Both the tables have the same number of rows (two) for "Sony", and therefore "Sony" doesn't appear in the output.

 Duplicate rows are not possible in tables that have a primary key or at least one unique index. Use the short form of the table comparison query for such tables.

Using NULLs in Compound Queries

We discussed union compatibility conditions at the beginning of this chapter. The union compatibility issue gets interesting when NULLs are involved. As we know, NULL doesn't have a datatype, and NULL can be used in place of a value of any datatype. If we purposely select NULL as a column value in a component query, Oracle no longer has two datatypes to compare in order to see whether the two component queries are compatible. For character columns, this is no problem. For example:

```
SELECT 1 NUM, 'DEFINITE' STRING FROM DUAL
UNION
```

```
SELECT 2 NUM, NULL STRING FROM DUAL;

      NUM STRING
---------- --------
        1 DEFINITE
        2
```

Notice that Oracle considers the character string 'DEFINITE' from the first component query to be compatible with the NULL value supplied for the corresponding column in the second component qery. However, if a NUMBER or a DATE column of a component query is set to NULL, we must explicitly tell Oracle what "flavor" of NULL to use. Otherwise, we'll encounter errors. For example:

```
SELECT 1 NUM, 'DEFINITE' STRING FROM DUAL
UNION
SELECT NULL NUM, 'UNKNOWN' STRING FROM DUAL;

SELECT 1 NUM, 'DEFINITE' STRING FROM DUAL
         *
ERROR at line 1:
ORA-01790: expression must have same datatype as corresponding expression
```

Note that the use of NULL in the second component query causes a datatype mismatch between the first column of the first component query, and the first column of the second component query. Using NULL for a DATE column causes the same problem, as in the following example:

```
SELECT 1 NUM, SYSDATE DATES FROM DUAL
UNION
SELECT 2 NUM, NULL DATES FROM DUAL;
SELECT 1 NUM, SYSDATE DATES FROM DUAL
         *
ERROR at line 1:
ORA-01790: expression must have same datatype as corresponding expression
```

In these cases, we need to cast the NULL to a suitable datatype to fix the problem, as in the following examples:

```
SELECT 1 NUM, 'DEFINITE' STRING FROM DUAL
UNION
SELECT TO_NUMBER(NULL) NUM, 'UNKNOWN' STRING FROM DUAL;

      NUM STRING
---------- --------
        1 DEFINITE
          UNKNOWN

SELECT 1 NUM, SYSDATE DATES FROM DUAL
UNION
SELECT 2 NUM, TO_DATE(NULL) DATES FROM DUAL;

      NUM DATES
---------- ---------
        1 06-JAN-02
        2
```

This problem of union compatibility when using NULLs is encountered in Oracle8*i*. However, there is no such problem in Oracle9*i*, as we can see in the following examples generated from an Oracle9*i* database:

```
SELECT 1 NUM, 'DEFINITE' STRING FROM DUAL
UNION
SELECT NULL NUM, 'UNKNOWN' STRING FROM DUAL;

       NUM STRING
---------- --------
         1 DEFINITE
           UNKNOWN

SELECT 1 NUM, SYSDATE DATES FROM DUAL
UNION
SELECT 2 NUM, NULL DATES FROM DUAL;

       NUM DATES
---------- ---------
         1 06-JAN-02
         2
```

Oracle9*i* is smart enough to know which flavor of NULL to use in a compound query.

Rules and Restrictions on Set Operations

Other than the union compatibility conditions discussed at the beginning of the chapter, there are some other rules and restrictions that apply to the set operations. These rules and restrictions are as follows:

Column names for the result set are derived from the first SELECT:

```
SELECT CUST_NBR "Customer ID", NAME "Customer Name"
FROM CUSTOMER
WHERE REGION_ID = 5
UNION
SELECT C.CUST_NBR, C.NAME
FROM CUSTOMER C
WHERE C.CUST_NBR IN (SELECT O.CUST_NBR
                     FROM CUST_ORDER O, EMPLOYEE E
                     WHERE O.SALES_EMP_ID = E.EMP_ID
                     AND E.LNAME = 'MARTIN');

Customer ID Customer Name
----------- ---------------------
          1 Cooper Industries
          2 Emblazon Corp.
          3 Ditech Corp.
          4 Flowtech Inc.
          5 Gentech Industries
          8 Zantech Inc.

6 rows selected.
```

Although both SELECTs use column aliases, the result set takes the column names from the first SELECT. The same thing happens when we create a view based on a set operation. The column names in the view are taken from the first SELECT:

```
CREATE VIEW V_TEST_CUST AS
SELECT CUST_NBR "Customer ID", NAME "Customer Name"
FROM CUSTOMER
WHERE REGION_ID = 5
UNION
SELECT C.CUST_NBR, C.NAME
FROM CUSTOMER C
WHERE C.CUST_NBR IN (SELECT O.CUST_NBR
                     FROM CUST_ORDER O, EMPLOYEE E
                     WHERE O.SALES_EMP_ID = E.EMP_ID
                     AND E.LNAME = 'MARTIN');

View created.

DESC V_TEST_CUST
 Name                             Null?     Type
 ------------------------------   --------  ----
 Customer_ID                                NUMBER
 Customer_Name                              VARCHAR2(45)
```

If we want to use ORDER BY in a query involving set operations, we must place the ORDER BY at the end of the entire statement. The ORDER BY clause can appear only once at the end of the compound query. The component queries can't have individual ORDER BY clauses. For example:

```
SELECT CUST_NBR, NAME
FROM CUSTOMER
WHERE REGION_ID = 5
UNION
SELECT EMP_ID, LNAME
FROM EMPLOYEE
WHERE LNAME = 'MARTIN'
ORDER BY CUST_NBR;

  CUST_NBR NAME
---------- --------------------
         1 Cooper Industries
         2 Emblazon Corp.
         3 Ditech Corp.
         4 Flowtech Inc.
         5 Gentech Industries
      7654 MARTIN

6 rows selected.
```

Note that the column name used in the ORDER BY clause of this query is taken from the first SELECT. We couldn't order these results by EMP_ID. If we attempt to ORDER BY EMP_ID, we will get an error, as in the following example:

```
SELECT CUST_NBR, NAME
FROM CUSTOMER
```

```
WHERE REGION_ID = 5
UNION
SELECT EMP_ID, LNAME
FROM EMPLOYEE
WHERE LNAME = 'MARTIN'ORDER BY EMP_ID;
ORDER BY EMP_ID
              *
ERROR at line 8:
ORA-00904: invalid column name
```

The ORDER BY clause doesn't recognize the column names of the second SELECT. To avoid confusion over column names, it is a common practice to ORDER BY column positions:

```
SELECT CUST_NBR, NAME
FROM CUSTOMER
WHERE REGION_ID = 5
UNION
SELECT EMP_ID, LNAME
FROM EMPLOYEE
WHERE LNAME = 'MARTIN'
ORDER BY 1;

  CUST_NBR NAME
---------- --------------------
         1 Cooper Industries
         2 Emblazon Corp.
         3 Ditech Corp.
         4 Flowtech Inc.
         5 Gentech Industries
      7654 MARTIN

6 rows selected.
```

 Unlike ORDER BY, we can use GROUP BY and HAVING clauses in component queries.

Component queries are executed from top to bottom. If we want to alter the sequence of execution, use parentheses appropriately. For example:

```
SELECT * FROM SUPPLIER_GOOD
UNION
SELECT * FROM SUPPLIER_TEST
MINUS
SELECT * FROM SUPPLIER;

SUPPLIER_ID NAME
----------- --------------------------
          4 Toshiba
```

Oracle performs the UNION between SUPPLIER_GOOD and SUPPLIER_TEST first, and then performs the MINUS between the result of the UNION and the SUPPLIER table. If we want the MINUS between SUPPLIER_TEST and SUPPLIER to be per-formed first, and then the UNION between SUPPLIER_GOOD and the result of MINUS, we must use parentheses to indicate so:

```
SELECT * FROM SUPPLIER_GOOD
UNION
(SELECT * FROM SUPPLIER_TEST
MINUS
SELECT * FROM SUPPLIER);

SUPPLIER_ID NAME
----------- ------------------------
          1 Sony
          2 Samsung
          3 Panasonic
          4 Toshiba
```

The parentheses in this query forces the MINUS to be performed before the UNION. Notice the difference in the result as compared to the previous example.

The following list summarizes some simple rules, restrictions, and notes that don't require examples:

- Set operations are not permitted on columns of type BLOB, CLOB, BFILE, and VARRAY, nor are set operations permitted on nested table columns.

- Since UNION, INTERSECT, and MINUS operators involve sort operations, they are not allowed on LONG columns. However, UNION ALL is allowed on LONG columns.

- Set operations are not allowed on SELECT statements containing TABLE collection expressions.

- SELECT statements involved in set operations can't use the FOR UPDATE clause.

- The number and size of columns in the SELECT list of component queries are limited by the block size of the database. The total bytes of the columns SELECTed can't exceed one database block.

CHAPTER 8

Hierarchical Queries

A relational database is based upon sets, with each table representing a set. However, there are some types of information that are not directly amenable to the set data structure. Think, for example, of an organization chart, a bill of material in a manufacturing and assembly plant, or a family tree. These types of information are hierarchical in nature, and most conveniently represented in a tree structure. In this chapter we discuss how we can represent such hierarchical information in a relational table. We also discuss in detail various SQL constructs that we need to use to extract hierarchical information from a relational table.

Representing Hierarchical Information

Let's look at an example to understand how we can represent hierarchical information in a relational database. As a basis for the example, we'll use an organization chart showing how one employee reports to another within a large organization, as shown in Figure 8-1.

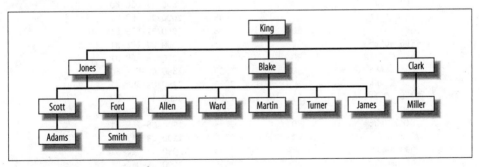

Figure 8-1. An organization chart

Figure 8-1 represents a hierarchy of employees. The information regarding an employee, his manager, and the reporting relationship need to be represented in one table, EMPLOYEE, as shown in the Entity Relationship Diagram in Figure 8-2.

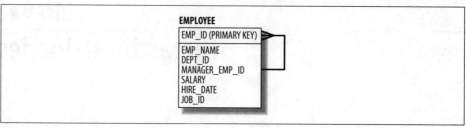

Figure 8-2. Entity Relationship Diagram of the EMPLOYEE table

In Figure 8-2, the EMPLOYEE table refers to itself. The column MANAGER_EMP_ID refers to the EMP_ID column of the same table. To represent hierarchical data, we need to make use of a relationship such as when one column of a table references another column of the same table. When such a relationship is implemented using a database constraint, it is known as *self-referential integrity constraint*. The corresponding CREATE TABLE statement will look as follows:

```
CREATE TABLE EMPLOYEE (
EMP_ID          NUMBER (4) CONSTRAINT EMP_PK PRIMARY KEY,
FNAME           VARCHAR2 (15)NOT NULL,
LNAME           VARCHAR2 (15)NOT NULL,
DEPT_ID         NUMBER (2)NOT NULL,
MANAGER_EMP_ID  NUMBER (4) CONSTRAINT EMP_FK REFERENCES EMPLOYEE(EMP_ID),
SALARY          NUMBER (7,2)NOT NULL,
HIRE_DATE       DATENOT NULL,
JOB_ID          NUMBER (3));
```

As a basis for the examples in this chapter, we'll use the following sample data:

```
SELECT EMP_ID, LNAME, DEPT_ID, MANAGER_EMP_ID, SALARY, HIRE_DATE
FROM EMPLOYEE;
```

EMP_ID	LNAME	DEPT_ID	MANAGER_EMP_ID	SALARY	HIRE_DATE
7369	SMITH	20	7902	800	17-DEC-80
7499	ALLEN	30	7698	1600	20-FEB-81
7521	WARD	30	7698	1250	22-FEB-81
7566	JONES	20	7839	2000	02-APR-81
7654	MARTIN	30	7698	1250	28-SEP-81
7698	BLAKE	30	7839	2850	01-MAY-80
7782	CLARK	10	7839	2450	09-JUN-81
7788	SCOTT	20	7566	3000	19-APR-87
7839	KING	10		5000	17-NOV-81
7844	TURNER	30	7698	1500	08-SEP-81
7876	ADAMS	20	7788	1100	23-MAY-87
7900	JAMES	30	7698	950	03-DEC-81
7902	FORD	20	7566	3000	03-DEC-81
7934	MILLER	10	7782	1300	23-JAN-82

The EMPLOYEE table has two important aspects to be aware of:

- The column MANAGER_EMP_ID
- The EMP_FK constraint

The column MANAGER_EMP_ID stores the EMP_ID of the employee's manager. For example, The MANAGER_EMP_ID for Smith is 7902, which means that Ford is Smith's manager. The employee King doesn't have a MANAGER_EMP_ID, which indicates that King is the uppermost employee. To be able to represent the uppermost employee, the MANAGER_EMP_ID column must be NULLABLE.

There is a foreign key constraint on the MANAGER_EMP_ID column. This enforces the rule that any value we put in the MANAGER_EMP_ID column must be the EMP_ID of a valid employee. Such a constraint is not mandatory when representing hierarchical information. However, it is a good practice to define database constraints to enforce such business rules.

Before moving on to the following sections on manipulating hierarchies, we will introduce some hierarchy terminology. The following list defines terms that we'll use often when working with hierarchical data:

Node
A row in a table that represents a specific entry in a hierarchical tree structure. For example, in Figure 8-1 each employee is considered to be a node.

Parent
A node that is one level up in a tree. In Figure 8-1, King is the parent of Blake, and Blake is the parent of Martin. The term *parent node* is sometimes used in place of just *parent*.

Child
A node that is one level down in a tree. In Figure 8-1, Blake is a child of King. King, in turn, has five children: Allen, Ward, Martin, Turner, and James. The term *child node* is sometimes used in place of just *child*.

Root
The uppermost node in a hierarchical structure. The definition of a root is that it has no parent. In Figure 8-1, King is the root. We can only have one root in any given tree, but it's worth noting that we can have multiple trees in a hierarchical table. If our employee table stored information on employees for multiple companies, we would have one root per company. The term *root node* is sometimes used in place of *root*.

Leaf
A node with no children. Leaf nodes (the term *leaf node* is often used) are the antitheses of root nodes, and represent the lowest levels of a tree structure. The leaf nodes in Figure 8-1 are Adams, Smith, Allen, Ward, Martin, Turner, James, and Miller. Leaf nodes do not all need to be at the same level, but they do need to be without children.

Level
A layer of nodes. In Figure 8-1, King constitutes one level. Jones, Blake, and Clark constitute the next level down, and so forth.

Simple Hierarchy Operations

The processes for extracting some types of information from a table storing hierarchical data are relatively simple, and can be performed using the techniques that we have discussed so far in this book. Extracting more complex information requires using some new SQL constructs, which we'll discuss in the later section titled "Oracle SQL Extensions." In this section, we'll discuss the hierarchy operations that can be performed using what we've learned so far.

Finding the Root Node

Finding the root of a hierarchy tree is easy; we look for the one node with no parent. In the EMPLOYEE table we discussed earlier, the value for MANAGER_EMP_ID is NULL for the uppermost employee, and only for the uppermost employee. The following query searches for cases where MANAGER_EMP_ID is NULL, thereby returning the root node:

```
SELECT EMP_ID, LNAME, DEPT_ID, MANAGER_EMP_ID, SALARY, HIRE_DATE
FROM EMPLOYEE
WHERE MANAGER_EMP_ID IS NULL;
```

```
    EMP_ID LNAME       DEPT_ID MANAGER_EMP_ID   SALARY HIRE_DATE
--------- ---------  --------- -------------- --------- ---------
     7839 KING            10                     5000 17-NOV-81
```

Because the MANAGER_EMP_ID column defines the hierarchy, it's important that it always contain correct data. While populating data in this table, we must make sure to specify a MANAGER_EMP_ID for every row other than the row for the uppermost employee. The uppermost employee doesn't report to anyone (doesn't have a manager), and hence MANAGER_EMP_ID is not applicable for him. If we leave out MANAGER_EMP_ID values for employees that do have managers, those employees will erroneously show up as root nodes.

Finding a Node's Immediate Parent

We may wish to link nodes to their immediate parents. For example, we might want to print a report showing each employee's manager. The name of each employee's manager can be derived by joining the EMPLOYEE table to itself. This type of join is a self join (discussed in Chapter 3). The following query returns the desired result:

```
SELECT E.LNAME "Employee", M.LNAME "Manager"
FROM EMPLOYEE E, EMPLOYEE M
WHERE E.MANAGER_EMP_ID = M.EMP_ID;
```

```
Employee   Manager
---------- ----------
SMITH      FORD
ALLEN      BLAKE
WARD       BLAKE
```

```
JONES      KING
MARTIN     BLAKE
BLAKE      KING
CLARK      KING
SCOTT      JONES
TURNER     BLAKE
ADAMS      SCOTT
JAMES      BLAKE
FORD       JONES
MILLER     CLARK
```

13 rows selected.

Note this query results in only 13 rows, although the EMPLOYEE table has 14 rows.

```
SELECT COUNT(*) FROM EMPLOYEE;
```

```
  COUNT(*)
----------
        14
```

The reason that only 13 rows are returned from the self join is simple. This query lists employees and their managers. But since the uppermost employee KING doesn't have any manager, that row is not produced in the output. If we want all the employees to be produced in the result, we need an outer join, as in the following example:

```
SELECT E.LNAME "Employee", M.LNAME "Manager"
FROM EMPLOYEE E, EMPLOYEE M
WHERE E.MANAGER_EMP_ID = M.EMP_ID (+);
```

```
Employee             Manager
-------------------- --------------------
SMITH                FORD
ALLEN                BLAKE
WARD                 BLAKE
JONES                KING
MARTIN               BLAKE
BLAKE                KING
CLARK                KING
SCOTT                JONES
KING
TURNER               BLAKE
ADAMS                SCOTT
JAMES                BLAKE
FORD                 JONES
MILLER               CLARK
```

14 rows selected.

Outer joins are discussed in detail in Chapter 3.

Finding Leaf Nodes

The opposite problem from finding the root node, which has no parent, is to find leaf nodes, which have no children. Employees who do not manage anyone are the leaf nodes in the hierarchy tree shown in Figure 8-1. At first glance, the following query seems like it should list all employees from the EMPLOYEE table who are not managers of any other employee:

```
SELECT * FROM EMPLOYEE
WHERE EMP_ID NOT IN (SELECT MANAGER_EMP_ID FROM EMPLOYEE);
```

However, when we execute this statement, we will see "No rows selected." Why? It is because the MANAGER_EMP_ID column contains a NULL value in one row (for the uppermost employee), and NULLs can't be compared to any data value. Therefore, to get the employees who don't manage anyone, we need to rewrite the query as follows:

```
SELECT EMP_ID, LNAME, DEPT_ID, MANAGER_EMP_ID, SALARY, HIRE_DATE
FROM EMPLOYEE E
WHERE EMP_ID NOT IN
(SELECT MANAGER_EMP_ID FROM EMPLOYEE
WHERE MANAGER_EMP_ID IS NOT NULL);
```

EMP_ID	LNAME	DEPT_ID	MANAGER_EMP_ID	SALARY	HIRE_DATE
7369	SMITH	20	7902	800	17-DEC-80
7499	ALLEN	30	7698	1600	20-FEB-81
7521	WARD	30	7698	1250	22-FEB-81
7654	MARTIN	30	7698	1250	28-SEP-81
7844	TURNER	30	7698	1500	08-SEP-81
7876	ADAMS	20	7788	1100	23-MAY-87
7900	JAMES	30	7698	950	03-DEC-81
7934	MILLER	10	7782	1300	23-JAN-82

```
8 rows selected.
```

In this example, the subquery returns the EMP_IDs of all the managers. The outer query then returns all the employees, except the ones returned by the subquery. This query can also be written as a correlated subquery using EXISTS instead of IN:

```
SELECT EMP_ID, LNAME, DEPT_ID, MANAGER_EMP_ID, SALARY, HIRE_DATE
FROM EMPLOYEE E
WHERE NOT EXISTS
(SELECT EMP_ID FROM EMPLOYEE E1 WHERE E.EMP_ID = E1.MANAGER_EMP_ID);
```

EMP_ID	LNAME	DEPT_ID	MANAGER_EMP_ID	SALARY	HIRE_DATE
7369	SMITH	20	7902	800	17-DEC-80
7499	ALLEN	30	7698	1600	20-FEB-81
7521	WARD	30	7698	1250	22-FEB-81
7654	MARTIN	30	7698	1250	28-SEP-81
7844	TURNER	30	7698	1500	08-SEP-81
7876	ADAMS	20	7788	1100	23-MAY-87
7900	JAMES	30	7698	950	03-DEC-81
7934	MILLER	10	7782	1300	23-JAN-82

```
8 rows selected.
```

In this example, the correlated subquery checks each employee to see whether he is the manager of any other employee. If NOT, then that particular employee is included in the result set.

Oracle SQL Extensions

In the last few examples, we saw how we can perform some operations on the hierarchical tree by using simple SQL techniques. Operations such as traversing a tree, finding levels, etc., require more complex SQL statements, and also require the use of features designed specifically for working with hierarchical data. Oracle provides some extensions to ANSI SQL to facilitate these operations. But before moving to the Oracle SQL extensions, let's look at how we can traverse a tree using ANSI SQL, and at the problems we'll encounter when doing that.

For example, let's say we want to list each employee with his manager. Using regular Oracle SQL, we can perform self outer joins on the EMPLOYEE table, as shown here:

```
SELECT E_TOP.LNAME, E_2.LNAME, E_3.LNAME, E_4.LNAME
FROM EMPLOYEE E_TOP, EMPLOYEE E_2, EMPLOYEE E_3, EMPLOYEE E_4
WHERE E_TOP.MANAGER_EMP_ID IS NULL
AND E_TOP.EMP_ID = E_2.MANAGER_EMP_ID (+)
AND E_2.EMP_ID = E_3.MANAGER_EMP_ID (+)
AND E_3.EMP_ID = E_4.MANAGER_EMP_ID (+);

LNAME       LNAME       LNAME       LNAME
----------  ----------  ----------  ----------
KING        BLAKE       ALLEN
KING        BLAKE       WARD
KING        BLAKE       MARTIN
KING        JONES       SCOTT       ADAMS
KING        BLAKE       TURNER
KING        BLAKE       JAMES
KING        JONES       FORD        SMITH
KING        CLARK       MILLER

8 rows selected.
```

The query returns eight rows, corresponding to the eight branches of the tree. To get those results, the query performs a self join on four instances of the EMPLOYEE table. Four EMPLOYEE table instances are needed in this statement because there are four levels to the hierarchy. Each level is represented by one copy of the EMPLOYEE table. The outer join is required because one employee (KING) has a NULL value in the MANAGER_EMP_ID column.

This type query has several drawbacks. First of all, we need to know the number of levels in an organization chart when we write the query, and it's not realistic to assume that we will know that information. It's even less realistic to think that the number of levels will remain stable over time. Moreover, we need to join four instances of the EMPLOYEE table together for a four level hierarchy. Imagine an organization with 20 levels—we'd need to join 20 tables. This would cause a huge performance problem.

To circumvent problems such as these, Oracle has provided some extensions to ANSI SQL. Oracle provides the following three constructs to effectively and efficiently perform hierarchical queries:

- The START WITH...CONNECT BY clause
- The PRIOR operator
- The LEVEL pseudocolumn

The following sections discuss these three Oracle extensions in detail.

START WITH...CONNECT BY and PRIOR

We can extract information in hierarchical form from a table containing hierarchical data by using the SELECT statement's START WITH...CONNECT BY clause. The syntax for this clause is:

```
[[START WITH condition1]  CONNECT BY condition2]
```

The syntax elements are:

START WITH condition1
> Specifies the root row(s) of the hierarchy. All rows that satisfy *condition1* are considered root rows. If we don't specify the START WITH clause, all rows are considered root rows, which is usually not desirable. We can include a subquery in *condition1*.

CONNECT BY condition2
> Specifies the relationship between parent rows and child rows in the hierarchy. The relationship is expressed as a comparison expression, where columns from the current row are compared to corresponding parent columns. *condition2* must contain the PRIOR operator, which is used to identify columns from the parent row. *condition2* cannot contain a subquery.

PRIOR is a built-in Oracle SQL operator that is used with hierarchical queries only. In a hierarchical query, the CONNECT BY clause specifies the relationship between parent and child rows. When we use the PRIOR operator in an expression in the CONNECT BY condition, the expression following the PRIOR keyword is evaluated for the parent row of the current row in the query. In the following example, PRIOR is used to connect each row to its parent by connecting MANAGER_EMP_ID in the child to EMP_ID in the parent:

```
SELECT LNAME, EMP_ID, MANAGER_EMP_ID
FROM EMPLOYEE
START WITH MANAGER_EMP_ID IS NULL
CONNECT BY PRIOR EMP_ID = MANAGER_EMP_ID;
```

```
LNAME              EMP_ID MANAGER_EMP_ID
------------------ ------ --------------
KING                 7839
JONES                7566           7839
SCOTT                7788           7566
ADAMS                7876           7788
FORD                 7902           7566
SMITH                7369           7902
BLAKE                7698           7839
ALLEN                7499           7698
WARD                 7521           7698
MARTIN               7654           7698
TURNER               7844           7698
JAMES                7900           7698
CLARK                7782           7839
MILLER               7934           7782

14 rows selected.
```

The PRIOR column does not need to be listed first. The previous query could be restated as:

```
SELECT LNAME, EMP_ID, MANAGER_EMP_ID
FROM EMPLOYEE
START WITH MANAGER_EMP_ID IS NULL
CONNECT BY MANAGER_EMP_ID = PRIOR EMP_ID;
```

Since the CONNECT BY condition specifies the parent-child relationship, it cannot contain a loop. If a row is both parent (direct ancestor) and child (direct descendent) of another row, then we have a loop. For example, if the EMPLOYEE table had the following two rows, they would represent a loop:

```
EMP_ID LNAME      DEPT_ID MANAGER_EMP_ID   SALARY HIRE_DATE
------ ---------- ------- --------------   ------ ---------
  9001 SMITH           20           9002     1800 15-NOV-61
  9002 ALLEN           30           9001    11600 16-NOV-61
```

When a parent-child relationship involves two or more columns, we need to use the PRIOR operator before each parent column. Let's take as an example an assembly in a manufacturing plant. An assembly may consist of several subassemblies, and a given subassembly may further contain one or more subassemblies. All of these are stored in a table, ASSEMBLY:

```
DESC ASSEMBLY
Name                       Null?     Type
-------------------------- --------- -------------
ASSEMBLY_TYPE              NOT NULL  VARCHAR2(4)
ASSEMBLY_ID                NOT NULL  NUMBER(6)
DESCRIPTION                NOT NULL  VARCHAR2(20)
PARENT_ASSEMBLY_TYPE                 VARCHAR2(4)
PARENT_ASSEMBLY_ID                   NUMBER(6)
```

ASSEMBLY_TYPE and ASSEMBLY_ID constitute the primary key of this table, and the columns PARENT_ASSEMBLY_TYPE and PARENT_ASSEMBLY_ID together constitute the self-referential foreign key. Therefore, if we want to perform a hierarchical query on this table, we need to include both columns in the START WITH and the CONNECT BY clauses. Also, we need to use the PRIOR operator before each parent column, as shown in the following example:

```
SELECT * FROM ASSEMBLY
START WITH PARENT_ASSEMBLY_TYPE IS NULL
AND PARENT_ASSEMBLY_ID IS NULL
CONNECT BY PARENT_ASSEMBLY_TYPE = PRIOR ASSEMBLY_TYPE
AND PARENT_ASSEMBLY_ID = PRIOR ASSEMBLY_ID;


ASSE ASSEMBLY_ID DESCRIPTION          PARE PARENT_ASSEMBLY_ID
---- ----------- -------------------- ---- ------------------
A           1234 Assembly A#1234
A           1256 Assembly A#1256      A                  1234
B           6543 Part Unit#6543       A                  1234
A           1675 Part Unit#1675       B                  6543
X           9943 Repair Zone 1
X           5438 Repair Unit #5438    X                  9943
X           1675 Readymade Unit #1675 X                  5438

7 rows selected.
```

The LEVEL Pseudocolumn

In a hierarchy tree, the term *level* refers to one layer of nodes. For example, in Figure 8-1, the root node (consisting of employee KING) is level 1. The next layer (employees JONES, BLAKE, CLARK) is at level 2, and so forth. Oracle provides a pseudocolumn, LEVEL, to represent these levels in a hierarchy tree. Whenever we use the START WITH...CONNECT BY clauses in a hierarchical query, we can use the pseudocolumn LEVEL to return the level number for each row returned by the query. The following example illustrates the use of the LEVEL pseudocolumn:

```
SELECT LEVEL, LNAME, EMP_ID, MANAGER_EMP_ID
FROM EMPLOYEE
START WITH MANAGER_EMP_ID IS NULL
CONNECT BY MANAGER_EMP_ID = PRIOR EMP_ID;


     LEVEL LNAME                    EMP_ID MANAGER_EMP_ID
---------- -------------------- ---------- --------------
         1 KING                       7839
         2 JONES                      7566           7839
         3 SCOTT                      7788           7566
         4 ADAMS                      7876           7788
         3 FORD                       7902           7566
         4 SMITH                      7369           7902
         2 BLAKE                      7698           7839
```

```
3 ALLEN                     7499            7698
3 WARD                      7521            7698
3 MARTIN                    7654            7698
3 TURNER                    7844            7698
3 JAMES                     7900            7698
2 CLARK                     7782            7839
3 MILLER                    7934            7782
```

```
14 rows selected.
```

Note that each employee is now associated with a number, represented by the pseudocolumn LEVEL, that corresponds to its level in the organization chart (see Figure 8-1).

Complex Hierarchy Operations

In this section, we discuss how we can use Oracle SQL's hierarchical extensions to perform complex hierarchical queries.

Finding the Number of Levels

Previously we showed how the LEVEL pseudocolumn generates a level number for each record when we use the START WITH...CONNECT BY clause. We can use the following query to determine the number of levels in the hierarchy by counting the number of distinct level numbers returned by the LEVEL pseudocolumn:

```
SELECT COUNT(DISTINCT LEVEL)
FROM EMPLOYEE
START WITH MANAGER_EMP_ID IS NULL
CONNECT BY PRIOR EMP_ID = MANAGER_EMP_ID;
```

```
COUNT(DISTINCTLEVEL)
--------------------
                   4
```

To determine the number of employees at each level, group the results by LEVEL and count the number of employees in each distinct group. For example:

```
SELECT LEVEL, COUNT(EMP_ID)
FROM EMPLOYEE
START WITH MANAGER_EMP_ID IS NULL
CONNECT BY PRIOR EMP_ID = MANAGER_EMP_ID
GROUP BY LEVEL;
```

```
    LEVEL COUNT(EMP_ID)
--------- -------------
        1             1
        2             3
        3             8
        4             2
```

Listing Records in Hierarchical Order

One of the very common programming challenges SQL programmers face is to list records in a hierarchy in their proper hierarchical order. For example, we might wish to list employees with their subordinates underneath them, as is in the following query:

```
SELECT LEVEL, LPAD(' ',2*(LEVEL - 1)) || LNAME "EMPLOYEE",
       EMP_ID, MANAGER_EMP_ID
FROM EMPLOYEE
START WITH MANAGER_EMP_ID IS NULL
CONNECT BY PRIOR EMP_ID = MANAGER_EMP_ID;
```

LEVEL	Employee	EMP_ID	MANAGER_EMP_ID
1	KING	7839	
2	JONES	7566	7839
3	SCOTT	7788	7566
4	ADAMS	7876	7788
3	FORD	7902	7566
4	SMITH	7369	7902
2	BLAKE	7698	7839
3	ALLEN	7499	7698
3	WARD	7521	7698
3	MARTIN	7654	7698
3	TURNER	7844	7698
3	JAMES	7900	7698
2	CLARK	7782	7839
3	MILLER	7934	7782

```
14 rows selected.
```

Notice that by using the expression LPAD(' ',2*(LEVEL − 1)), we are able to align employee names in a manner that corresponds to their level. As the level number increases, the number of spaces returned by the expression increases, and the employee name is further indented.

The previous query lists all the employees in the EMPLOYEE table. If we want to filter out certain employees based on some condition, then we can use a WHERE clause in our hierarchical query. Here is an example:

```
SELECT LEVEL, LPAD('    ',2*(LEVEL - 1)) || LNAME "EMPLOYEE",
       EMP_ID, MANAGER_EMP_ID, SALARY
FROM EMPLOYEE
WHERE SALARY > 2000
START WITH MANAGER_EMP_ID IS NULL
CONNECT BY MANAGER_EMP_ID = PRIOR EMP_ID;
```

LEVEL	Employee	EMP_ID	MANAGER_EMP_ID	SALARY
1	KING	7839		5000
3	SCOTT	7788	7566	3000
3	FORD	7902	7566	3000

| 2 | BLAKE | 7698 | 7839 | 2850 |
| 2 | CLARK | 7782 | 7839 | 2450 |

This query lists records with salary > 2000. Notice that the WHERE clause restricts the rows returned by the query without affecting other rows in the hierarchy. In our example, the WHERE condition filtered JONES out of the result, but the employees below JONES in the hierarchy (SCOTT and FORD) are not filtered out, and are still indented as they were when JONES was present. The WHERE clause must come before the START WITH...CONNECT BY clause in a hierarchical query, otherwise it will result in a syntax error.

Instead of reporting out the whole organization chart, we may want to list only the subtree under a given employee, JONES for example. To do this, we can modify the START WITH condition so that it specifies JONES as the root of the query. For example:

```
SELECT LEVEL, LPAD('    ',2*(LEVEL - 1)) || LNAME "EMPLOYEE",
       EMP_ID, MANAGER_EMP_ID, SALARY
FROM EMPLOYEE
START WITH LNAME = 'JONES'
CONNECT BY MANAGER_EMP_ID = PRIOR EMP_ID;
```

LEVEL	Employee	EMP_ID	MANAGER_EMP_ID	SALARY
1	JONES	7566	7839	2000
2	SCOTT	7788	7566	3000
3	ADAMS	7876	7788	1100
2	FORD	7902	7566	3000
3	SMITH	7369	7902	800

Notice that since we asked the query to consider JONES as the root of the hierarchy, it assigned level 1 to JONES, level 2 to employees directly reporting to him, and so forth. Be careful while using conditions such as LNAME = 'JONES' in hierarchical queries. In this case, if we have two JONES in our organization, the result returned by the hierarchy may be wrong. It is better to use primary or unique key columns, such as EMP_ID, as the condition in such situations.

In this example, we listed the portion of the organization chart headed by a specific employee. There could be situations when we may need to print the organization chart headed by any employee that meets a specific condition. For example, we may want to list all employees under the employee who has been working in the company for the longest time. In this case, the starting point of the query (the root) is dependent on a condition. Therefore, we have to use a subquery to generate this information and pass it to the main query, as in the following example:

```
SELECT LEVEL, LPAD('    ',2*(LEVEL - 1)) || LNAME "EMPLOYEE",
       EMP_ID, MANAGER_EMP_ID, SALARY
FROM EMPLOYEE
START WITH HIRE_DATE = (SELECT MIN(HIRE_DATE) FROM EMPLOYEE)
CONNECT BY MANAGER_EMP_ID = PRIOR EMP_ID;
```

```
LEVEL EMPLOYEE        EMP_ID MANAGER_EMP_ID    SALARY
----- ------------ ---------- --------------- ----------
    1  BLAKE            7698            7839       2850
    2  ALLEN            7499            7698       1600
    2  WARD             7521            7698       1250
    2  MARTIN           7654            7698       1250
    2  TURNER           7844            7698       1500
    2  JAMES            7900            7698        950

6 rows selected.
```

Note the START WITH clause in this example. The subquery in the START WITH clause returns the minimum HIRE_DATE in the table, which represents the HIRE_DATE of the oldest employee. The main query uses this information as the starting point of the hierarchy and lists the organization structure under this employee.

While using a subquery in the START WITH clause, be aware of how many rows will be returned by the subquery. If more than one row is returned when we are expecting just one row (indicated by the = sign), the query will generate an error. We can get around this by replacing = with the IN operator, but be warned that the hierarchical query may then end up dealing with multiple roots.

Checking for Ascendancy

Another common operation on hierarchical data is to check for ascendancy. In an organization chart, we may ask whether one employee has authority over another. For example: "Does JONES have any authority over BLAKE?" To find out, we need to search for BLAKE in the subtree headed by JONES. If we find BLAKE in the subtree, then we know that BLAKE either directly or indirectly reports to JONES. If we don't find BLAKE in the subtree, then we know that JONES doesn't have any authority over BLAKE. The following query searches for BLAKE in the subtree headed by JONES:

```
SELECT *
FROM EMPLOYEE
WHERE LNAME = 'BLAKE'
START WITH LNAME = 'JONES'
CONNECT BY MANAGER_EMP_ID = PRIOR EMP_ID;

no rows selected
```

The START WITH...CONNECT BY clause in this example generates the subtree headed by JONES, and the WHERE clause filters this subtree to find BLAKE. As we can see, no rows were returned. This means that BLAKE was not found in JONES' subtree, so we know that JONES has no authority over BLAKE. Let's take a look at another example that produces positive results. This time we'll check to see whether JONES has any authority over SMITH:

```
SELECT EMP_ID, LNAME, DEPT_ID, MANAGER_EMP_ID, SALARY, HIRE_DATE
FROM EMPLOYEE
```

```
WHERE LNAME = 'SMITH'
START WITH LNAME = 'JONES'
CONNECT BY MANAGER_EMP_ID = PRIOR EMP_ID;
```

```
    EMP_ID LNAME          DEPT_ID MANAGER_EMP_ID     SALARY HIRE_DATE
---------- ---------- ---------- -------------- ---------- ---------
      7369 SMITH              20           7902        800 17-DEC-80
```

This time, SMITH was found in the list of employees in JONES' subtree, so we know
that at some level JONES has management authority over SMITH.

Deleting a Subtree

Let's assume that the organization we are dealing with splits, and JONES and all his
subordinates form a new company. Therefore, we don't need to maintain JONES
and his subordinates in our EMPLOYEE table. Furthermore, we need to delete the
entire subtree headed by JONES, as shown in Figure 8-1, from our table. We can do
this by using a subquery as in the following example:

```
DELETE FROM EMPLOYEE
WHERE EMP_ID IN
(SELECT EMP_ID FROM EMPLOYEE
START WITH LNAME = 'JONES'
CONNECT BY MANAGER_EMP_ID = PRIOR EMP_ID);
```

```
5 rows deleted.
```

In this example, the subquery generates the subtree headed by JONES, and returns
the EMP_IDs of the employees in that subtree, including JONES'. The outer query
then deletes the records with these EMP_ID values from the EMPLOYEE table.

Listing Multiple Root Nodes

An interesting variation on the problem of listing the root node of a hierarchy is to
find and list the root nodes from several hierarchies that are all stored in the same
table. For example, we might consider department manager's to represent root
nodes, and we might further wish to list all department managers found in the
EMPLOYEE table.

There are no constraints on the employees belonging to any department. However,
we can assume that if A reports to B and B reports to C, and A and C belong to the
same department, then B also belongs to the same department. If an employee's
manager belongs to another department, then that employee is the uppermost
employee, or manager, of his department.

Therefore, to find the uppermost employee in each department, we need to search
the tree for those employees whose managers belong to a different department then
their own. We do that using the following query:

```
SELECT EMP_ID, LNAME, DEPT_ID, MANAGER_EMP_ID, SALARY, HIRE_DATE
FROM EMPLOYEE
```

```
START WITH MANAGER_EMP_ID IS NULL
CONNECT BY MANAGER_EMP_ID = PRIOR EMP_ID
AND DEPT_ID != PRIOR DEPT_ID;
```

```
EMP_ID LNAME     DEPT_ID MANAGER_EMP_ID SALARY HIRE_DATE
------ --------  -------- -------------- ------ ---------
  7839 KING         10                    5000 17-NOV-81
  7566 JONES        20            7839    2975 02-APR-81
  7698 BLAKE        30            7839    2850 01-MAY-81
```

In this example, the extra condition (DEPT_ID != PRIOR DEPT_ID) added to the CONNECT BY clause restricts the output to only those employees whose managers belong to a different department then their own.

Listing the Top Few Levels of a Hierarchy

Another common task in dealing with hierarchical data is listing the top few levels of a hierarchy tree. For example, we may want to list top management employees in an organization. Let's assume that the top two levels in our organization chart constitute top management. We can then use the LEVEL pseudocolumn to identify those employees, as in the following example:

```
SELECT EMP_ID, LNAME, DEPT_ID, MANAGER_EMP_ID, SALARY, HIRE_DATE
FROM EMPLOYEE
WHERE LEVEL <= 2
START WITH MANAGER_EMP_ID IS NULL
CONNECT BY MANAGER_EMP_ID = PRIOR EMP_ID;
```

```
EMP_ID LNAME     DEPT_ID MANAGER_EMP_ID SALARY HIRE_DATE
------ --------  -------- -------------- ------ ---------
  7839 KING         10                    5000 17-NOV-81
  7566 JONES        20            7839    2975 02-APR-81
  7698 BLAKE        30            7839    2850 01-MAY-81
  7782 CLARK        10            7839    2450 09-JUN-81
```

In this example, the LEVEL <= 2 condition in the WHERE clause restricts the results to only those employees in the top two levels of the organization chart.

Aggregating a Hierarchy

Another challenging requirement on hierarchical data is to aggregate a hierarchy. For example, we may want to sum the salaries of all employees reporting to a specific employee. Or, we may want to consider each employee as a root, and for each employee report out the sum of the salaries of all subordinate employees.

The first problem is relatively simple. Earlier we described how to select a subtree headed by an employee. We can easily sum the salaries of all employees in such a subtree. For example:

```
SELECT SUM(SALARY)
FROM EMPLOYEE
START WITH LNAME = 'JONES'
```

```
CONNECT BY MANAGER_EMP_ID = PRIOR EMP_ID;

SUM(SALARY)
-----------
      10875
```

The START WITH LNAME = 'JONES' clause generates the subtree headed by JONES, and the SUM(SALARY) expression sums the salary of employees in this subtree.

The second problem, a seemingly simple extension of the first, is relatively complex. We want to consider each employee as a root, and for each employee we want to sum the salaries of all employees in its subtree. In essence, we want to repeat the previous query for each employee in the table. The following SQL uses an inline view to achieve this:

```
SELECT LNAME, SALARY,
(SELECT SUM(SALARY) FROM EMPLOYEE T1
START WITH LNAME = T2.LNAME
CONNECT BY MANAGER_EMP_ID = PRIOR EMP_ID) SUM_SALARY
FROM EMPLOYEE T2;

LNAME                 SALARY SUM_SALARY
-------------------- ---------- ----------
SMITH                    800        800
ALLEN                   1600       1600
WARD                    1250       1250
JONES                   2975      10875
MARTIN                  1250       1250
BLAKE                   2850       9400
CLARK                   2450       3750
SCOTT                   3000       4100
KING                    5000      29025
TURNER                  1500       1500
ADAMS                   1100       1100
JAMES                    950        950
FORD                    3000       3800
MILLER                  1300       1300

14 rows selected.
```

In this example, the START WITH...CONNECT BY clause in the inline view generates a subtree for each employee. The inline view executes once for every row in the outer EMPLOYEE employee. For each row in the outer EMPLOYEE table, the inline view generates a subtree headed by this employee, and returns the sum of salaries for all the employees in this subtree to the main query.

The result set displays two numbers for each employee. The first number, SALARY, is the employee's own salary. The second number, SUM_SALARY, is the sum of the salaries of all employees under him (including himself). Often programmers resort to PL/SQL to solve this type of problem. However, this query, which combines the power of hierarchical queries with that of inline views, solves this problem in a much more concise and elegant way.

Restrictions on Hierarchical Queries

The following restrictions apply to hierarchical queries that use START WITH... CONNECT BY:

1. A hierarchical query can't use a join.

> There are ways to overcome this restriction. Chapter 5 discusses one such example under the section "Oracle SQL Extensions."

2. A hierarchical query cannot select data from a view that involves a join.

3. We can use an ORDER BY clause within a hierarchical query; however, the ORDER BY clause takes precedence over the hierarchical ordering performed by the START WITH...CONNECT BY clause. Therefore, unless all we care about is the level number, it doesn't make sense to use ORDER BY in a hierarchical query.

The third issue deserves some additional explanation. Let's look at an example to see what happens when we use ORDER BY in a hierarchical query:

```
SELECT LEVEL, LPAD('     ',2*(LEVEL - 1)) || LNAME "EMPLOYEE",
       EMP_ID, MANAGER_EMP_ID, SALARY
FROM EMPLOYEE
START WITH MANAGER_EMP_ID IS NULL
CONNECT BY MANAGER_EMP_ID = PRIOR EMP_ID
ORDER BY SALARY;
```

LEVEL	Employee	EMP_ID	MANAGER_EMP_ID	SALARY
4	SMITH	7369	7902	800
3	JAMES	7900	7698	950
4	ADAMS	7876	7788	1100
3	WARD	7521	7698	1250
3	MARTIN	7654	7698	1250
3	MILLER	7934	7782	1300
3	TURNER	7844	7698	1500
3	ALLEN	7499	7698	1600
2	JONES	7566	7839	2000
2	CLARK	7782	7839	2450
2	BLAKE	7698	7839	2850
3	SCOTT	7788	7566	3000
3	FORD	7902	7566	3000
1	KING	7839		5000

```
14 rows selected.
```

The START WITH...CONNECT BY clause arranges the employees in proper hierarchical order; however, since we also specified an ORDER BY clause in this example, that ORDER BY clause takes precedence and arranges the employees in order of salary, thus distorting the hierarchy representation.

CHAPTER 9

DECODE and CASE

Whether it is for user presentation, report formatting, or data feed extraction, data is seldom presented exactly as it is stored in the database. Instead, data is generally combined, translated, or formatted in some way. While procedural languages such as PL/SQL and Java provide many tools for manipulating data, it is often desirable to perform these manipulations as the data is extracted from the database. Similarly, when updating data, it is far easier to modify the data in place rather than to extract it, modify it, and apply the modified data back to the database. This chapter will focus on two powerful features of Oracle SQL that facilitate various data manipulations: the CASE expression and the DECODE function. Along the way we'll also demonstrate the use of several other functions (such as NVL and NVL2).

DECODE, NVL, and NVL2

Most of Oracle's built-in functions are designed to solve a specific problem. If you need to find the last day of the month containing a particular date, for example, the LAST_DAY function is just the ticket. The DECODE, NVL, and NVL2 functions, however, do not solve a specific problem; rather, they are best described as inline if-then-else statements. These functions are used to make decisions based on data values within an SQL statement without resorting to a procedural language like PL/SQL. Table 9-1 shows the syntax and logic equivalent for each of the three functions.

Table 9-1. If-then-else function logic

Function syntax	Logic equivalent
DECODE(E1, E2, E3, E4)	IF E1 = E2 THEN E3 ELSE E4
NVL(E1, E2)	IF E1 IS NULL THEN E2 ELSE E1
NVL2(E1, E2, E3)	IF E1 IS NULL THEN E3 ELSE E2

The following two sections go into detail about the functions listed in Table 9-1.

DECODE

The DECODE function can be thought of as an inline IF statement. DECODE takes four or more expressions as arguments. Each expression can be a column, a literal, a function, or even a subquery. Let's look at a simple example using DECODE:

```
SELECT lname,
    DECODE(manager_emp_id, NULL, 'MANAGER', 'NON-MANAGER') emp_type
FROM employee;
```

```
LNAME                   EMP_TYPE
--------------------    -----------
Brown                   MANAGER
Smith                   MANAGER
Blake                   MANAGER
Freeman                 NON-MANAGER
Grossman                NON-MANAGER
Thomas                  NON-MANAGER
Powers                  NON-MANAGER
Jones                   NON-MANAGER
Levitz                  NON-MANAGER
Boorman                 NON-MANAGER
Fletcher                NON-MANAGER
Dunn                    NON-MANAGER
Evans                   NON-MANAGER
Walters                 NON-MANAGER
Young                   NON-MANAGER
Houseman                NON-MANAGER
McGowan                 NON-MANAGER
Isaacs                  NON-MANAGER
Jacobs                  NON-MANAGER
King                    NON-MANAGER
Fox                     NON-MANAGER
Anderson                NON-MANAGER
Nichols                 NON-MANAGER
Iverson                 NON-MANAGER
Peters                  NON-MANAGER
Russell                 NON-MANAGER
```

In this example, the first expression is a column, the second is NULL, and the third and fourth expressions are character literals. The intent is to determine whether each employee is a manager by checking whether an employee's manager_emp_id column is NULL. The DECODE function in this example compares each row's manager_emp_id column (the first expression) to NULL (the second expression). If the result of the comparison is true, DECODE returns 'MANAGER' (the third expression), otherwise 'NON-MANAGER' (the last expression) is returned.

Since the DECODE function compares two expressions and returns one of two expressions to the caller, it is important that the expression types are identical or that they can at least be translated to be the same type. This example works because E1 can be compared to E2, and E3 and E4 have the same type. If this were not the case, Oracle would raise an exception, as illustrated by the following example:

```
SELECT lname,
   DECODE(manager_emp_id, SYSDATE, 'MANAGER', 'NON-MANAGER') emp_type
FROM employee;

ERROR at line 1:
ORA-00932: inconsistent datatypes
```

Since the manager_emp_id column, which is numeric, cannot be converted to a DATE type, the Oracle server cannot perform the comparison and must throw an exception. The same exception would be thrown if the two return expressions (E3 and E4) did not have comparable types.

The previous example demonstrates the use of a DECODE function with the minimum number of parameters (four). The next example demonstrates how additional sets of parameters may be utilized for more complex logic:

```
SELECT p.part_nbr part_nbr, p.name part_name, s.name supplier,
   DECODE(p.status, 'INSTOCK', 'In Stock',
      'DISC', 'Discontinued',
      'BACKORD', 'Backordered',
      'ENROUTE', 'Arriving Shortly',
      'UNAVAIL', 'No Shipment Scheduled',
      'Unknown') part_status
FROM part p, supplier s
WHERE p.supplier_id = s.supplier_id;
```

This example compares the value of a part's status column to each of five values, and, if a match is found, returns the corresponding string. If a match is not found, then the string 'Unknown' is returned.

NVL and NVL2

The NVL and NVL2 functions allow you to test an expression to see whether it is NULL. If an expression is NULL, you can return an alternate, non-NULL value, to use in its place. Since any of the expressions in a DECODE statement can be NULL, the NVL and NVL2 functions are actually specialized versions of DECODE. The following example uses NVL2 to produce the same results as the DECODE example shown in the previous section:

```
SELECT lname,
   NVL2(manager_emp_id, 'NON-MANAGER', 'MANAGER') emp_type
FROM employee;

LNAME                EMP_TYPE
-------------------- -----------
Brown                MANAGER
Smith                MANAGER
Blake                MANAGER
Freeman              NON-MANAGER
Grossman             NON-MANAGER
Thomas               NON-MANAGER
Powers               NON-MANAGER
```

```
Jones          NON-MANAGER
Levitz         NON-MANAGER
Boorman        NON-MANAGER
Fletcher       NON-MANAGER
Dunn           NON-MANAGER
Evans          NON-MANAGER
Walters        NON-MANAGER
Young          NON-MANAGER
Houseman       NON-MANAGER
McGowan        NON-MANAGER
Isaacs         NON-MANAGER
Jacobs         NON-MANAGER
King           NON-MANAGER
Fox            NON-MANAGER
Anderson       NON-MANAGER
Nichols        NON-MANAGER
Iverson        NON-MANAGER
Peters         NON-MANAGER
Russell        NON-MANAGER
```

NVL2 looks at the first expression, manager_emp_id in this case. If that expression evaluates to NULL, NVL2 returns the third expression. If the first expression is not NULL, NVL2 returns the second expression. Use NVL2 when you wish to specify alternate values to be returned for the case when an expression is NULL, and also for the case when an expression is not NULL.

The NVL function is most commonly used to substitute a default value when a column is NULL. Otherwise, the column value itself is returned. The next example shows the ID of each employee's manager, but substitutes the word 'NONE' when no manager has been assigned (i.e., when manager_emp_id is NULL):

```
SELECT emp.lname employee, NVL(mgr.lname, 'NONE') manager
FROM employee emp, employee mgr
WHERE emp.manager_emp_id = mgr.emp_id (+);

EMPLOYEE                MANAG
--------------------    -----
Brown                   NONE
Smith                   NONE
Blake                   NONE
Freeman                 Blake
Grossman                Blake
Thomas                  Blake
Powers                  Blake
Jones                   Blake
Levitz                  Blake
Boorman                 Blake
Fletcher                Blake
Dunn                    Blake
Evans                   Blake
Walters                 Blake
Young                   Blake
Houseman                Blake
```

```
McGowan      Blake
Isaacs       Blake
Jacobs       Blake
King         Blake
Fox          King
Anderson     King
Nichols      King
Iverson      King
Peters       King
Russell      King
```

Even though DECODE may be substituted for any NVL or NVL2 function, most people prefer to use NVL or NVL2 when checking to see if an expresssion is NULL, presumably because the intent is clearer. Hopefully, the next section will convince you to use CASE expressions whenever you are in need of if-then-else functionality. Then you won't need to worry about which built-in function to use.

The Case for CASE

The CASE expression made its SQL debut in the SQL-92 specification in 1992. Eight years later, Oracle included the CASE expression in the 8.1.6 release. Like the DECODE function, the CASE expression enables conditional logic within an SQL statement, which might explain why Oracle took so much time implementing this particular feature. If you have been using Oracle for a number of years, you might wonder why you should care about the CASE expression, since DECODE does the job nicely. Here are several reasons why you should make the switch:

- CASE expressions can be used everywhere that DECODE functions are permitted.
- CASE expressions are more readable than DECODE expressions.
- CASE expressions execute faster than DECODE expressions.*
- CASE expressions handle complex logic more gracefully than DECODE expressions.
- CASE is ANSI-compliant, whereas DECODE is proprietary.

The only downside to using CASE over DECODE is that CASE expressions are not supported in Oracle8i's PL/SQL language. If you are using Oracle9i, however, any SQL statements executed from PL/SQL may include CASE expressions.

The SQL-92 specification defines two distinct flavors of the CASE expression: *searched* and *simple*. Searched CASE expressions are the only type supported in the Oracle8i release. If you are using Oracle9i, you may also use simple CASE expressions.

---

* Since CASE is built into Oracle's SQL grammar, there is no need to call a function in order to evaluate the if-then-else logic. While the difference in execution time is miniscule for a single call, the aggregate time savings from not calling a function should become noticeable when working with large result sets.

Searched CASE Expressions

A searched CASE expression evaluates a number of conditions and returns a result determined by which condition is true. The syntax for the SEARCHED CASE expression is as follows:

```
CASE
  WHEN C1 THEN R1
  WHEN C2 THEN R2
  ...
  WHEN CN THEN RN
  ELSE RD
END
```

In the syntax definition, the "C"s represent conditions, and the "R"s represent results. You can use up to 127 WHEN clauses in each CASE expression, so the logic can be quite robust. Conditions are evaluated in order. When a condition is found that evaluates to TRUE, the corresponding result is returned, and execution of the CASE logic ends. Therefore, carefully order WHEN clauses to ensure that the desired results are achieved. The next example illustrates the use of the CASE statement by determining the proper string to show on an order status report:

```
SELECT co.order_nbr, co.cust_nbr,
  CASE WHEN co.expected_ship_dt IS NULL THEN 'NOT YET SCHEDULED'
    WHEN co.expected_ship_dt <= SYSDATE THEN 'SHIPPING DELAYED'
    WHEN co.expected_ship_dt <= SYSDATE + 2 THEN 'SHIPPING SOON'
    ELSE 'BACKORDERED'
  END ship_status
FROM cust_order co
WHERE co.ship_dt IS NULL AND co.cancelled_dt IS NULL;
```

Similar to DECODE, all results in the CASE expression must have comparable types; otherwise, ORA-932 will be thrown. Each condition in each WHEN clause is independent of the others, however, so your conditions can include various data types, as demonstrated in the next example:

```
SELECT co.order_nbr, co.cust_nbr,
  CASE
    WHEN co.sale_price > 10000 THEN 'BIG ORDER'
    WHEN co.cust_nbr IN
      (SELECT cust_nbr FROM customer WHERE tot_orders > 100)
      THEN 'ORDER FROM FREQUENT CUSTOMER'
    WHEN co.order_dt < TRUNC(SYSDATE) - 7 THEN 'OLD ORDER'
    ELSE 'UNINTERESTING ORDER'
  END
FROM cust_order co
WHERE co.ship_dt IS NULL AND co.cancelled_dt IS NULL;
```

Simple CASE Expressions

Simple CASE expressions are structured differently than searched CASE expressions in that the WHEN clauses contain expressions instead of conditions, and a single expression to be compared to the expressions in each WHEN clause is placed in the CASE clause. Here's the syntax:

```
CASE E0
   WHEN E1 THEN R1
   WHEN E2 THEN R2
   ...
   WHEN EN THEN RN
   ELSE RD
END
```

Therefore, each of the expressions E1...EN are compared to expression E0. If a match is found, the corresponding result is returned; otherwise, the default result (RD) is returned. As a result, all of the expressions must be of the same type, since they all must be compared to E0, making simple CASE expressions less flexible than searched CASE expressions. The next example illustrates the use of a simple CASE expression to translate the status code stored in the part table:

```
SELECT p.part_nbr part_nbr, p.name part_name, s.name supplier,
   CASE p.status
      WHEN 'INSTOCK' THEN 'In Stock'
      WHEN 'DISC' THEN 'Discontinued'
      WHEN 'BACKORD' THEN 'Backordered'
      WHEN 'ENROUTE' THEN 'Arriving Shortly'
      WHEN 'UNAVAIL' THEN 'No Shipment Scheduled'
      ELSE 'Unknown'
   END part_status
FROM part p, supplier s
WHERE p.supplier_id = s.supplier_id;
```

A searched CASE can do everything that a simple CASE can do, which is probably the reason Oracle only implemented searched CASE expressions the first time around. For certain uses, such as translating values for a column, simple expressions may prove more efficient if the expression being evaluated is computed via a function call.

DECODE and CASE Examples

The following sections present a variety of examples illustrating the uses of conditional logic in SQL statements. While we recommend that you use the CASE expression rather than the DECODE function, where feasible we provide both DECODE and CASE versions of each example to help illustrate the differences between the two approaches.

Result Set Transformations

You may have run into a situation where you are performing aggregations over a finite set of values, such as days of the week or months of the year, but you want the result set to contain one row with N columns rather than N rows with two columns. Consider the following query, which aggregates sales data for each quarter of 2001:

```
SELECT TO_CHAR(order_dt, 'Q') sales_quarter,
   SUM(sale_price) tot_sales
FROM cust_order
WHERE order_dt >= TO_DATE('01-JAN-2001','DD-MON-YYYY')
   AND order_dt < TO_DATE('01-JAN-2002','DD-MON-YYYY')
GROUP BY TO_CHAR(order_dt, 'Q')
ORDER BY 1;

S TOT_SALES
- ----------
1     9739328
2    10379833
3     9703114
4     9772633
```

In order to transform this result set into a single row with four columns, we need to fabricate a column for each quarter of the year and, within each column, sum only those records whose order date falls in the desired quarter. We can do that with DECODE:

```
SELECT
   SUM(DECODE(TO_CHAR(order_dt, 'Q'), '1', sale_price, 0)) Q_1,
   SUM(DECODE(TO_CHAR (order_dt, 'Q'), '2', sale_price, 0)) Q_2,
   SUM(DECODE(TO_CHAR (order_dt, 'Q'), '3', sale_price, 0)) Q_3,
   SUM(DECODE(TO_CHAR (order_dt, 'Q'), '4', sale_price, 0)) Q_4
FROM cust_order
WHERE order_dt >= TO_DATE('01-JAN-2001','DD-MON-YYYY')
   AND order_dt < TO_DATE('01-JAN-2002','DD-MON-YYYY');

      Q_1         Q_2         Q_3         Q_4
---------- ---------- ---------- ----------
   9739328    10379833    9703114    9772633
```

Each of the four columns in the previous query are identical, except for the quarter being checked by the DECODE function. For the Q_1 column, for example, a value of 0 is returned unless the order falls in the first quarter, in which case the sale_price column is returned. When the values from all orders in 2001 are summed, only the first quarter orders are added to the total (for Q_1), which has the effect of summing all first quarter orders while ignoring orders for quarters 2, 3, and 4. The same logic is used for Q_2, Q_3, and Q_4 to sum orders for quarters 2, 3, and 4 respectively.

The CASE version of this query is as follows:

```
SELECT
   SUM(CASE WHEN TO_CHAR(order_dt, 'Q') = '1' THEN sale_price ELSE 0 END) Q_1,
   SUM(CASE WHEN TO_CHAR(order_dt, 'Q') = '2' THEN sale_price ELSE 0 END) Q_2,
   SUM(CASE WHEN TO_CHAR(order_dt, 'Q') = '3' THEN sale_price ELSE 0 END) Q_3,
   SUM(CASE WHEN TO_CHAR(order_dt, 'Q') = '4' THEN sale_price ELSE 0 END) Q_4
FROM cust_order
WHERE order_dt >= TO_DATE('01-JAN-2001','DD-MON-YYYY')
   AND order_dt < TO_DATE('01-JAN-2002','DD-MON-YYYY');
```

```
    Q_1         Q_2         Q_3         Q_4
---------- ---------- ---------- ----------
   9739328   10379833    9703114    9772633
```

Obviously, such transformations are only practical when the number of values is relatively small. Aggregating sales for each quarter or month works fine, but expanding the query to aggregate sales for each week, with a column for each week, would quickly become tedious.

Selective Function Execution

Imagine you're generating an inventory report. Most of the information resides in your local database, but a trip across a gateway to an external, non-Oracle database is required to gather information for parts supplied by Acme Industries. The round trip from your database through the gateway to the external server and back takes 1.5 seconds on average. There are 10,000 parts in your database, but only 100 require information via the gateway. You create a user-defined function called get_resupply_date to retrieve the resupply date for parts supplied by ACME, and include it in your query:

```
SELECT s.name supplier_name, p.name part_name, p.part_nbr part_number
  p.inventory_qty in_stock, p.resupply_date resupply_date,
  my_pkg.get_resupply_date(p.part_nbr) acme_resupply_date
FROM part p, supplier s
WHERE p.supplier_id = s.supplier_id;
```

You then include logic in your reporting tool to use the acme_resupply_date instead of the resupply_date column if the supplier's name is Acme Industries. You kick off the report, sit back, and wait for the results. And wait. And wait...

Unfortunately, the server is forced to make 10,000 trips across the gateway when only 100 are required. In these types of situations, it is far more efficient to call the function only when necessary, instead of always calling the function and discarding the results when not needed:

```
SELECT s.name supplier_name, p.name part_name, p.part_nbr part_number,
  p.inventory_qty in_stock,
  DECODE(s.name, 'Acme Industries',
    my_pkg.get_resupply_date(p.part_nbr),
    p.resupply_date) resupply_date
FROM part p, supplier s
WHERE p.supplier_id = s.supplier_id;
```

The DECODE function checks if the supplier name is 'Acme Industries'. If so, it calls the function to retrieve the resupply date via the gateway; otherwise, it returns the resupply date from the local part table. The CASE version of this query is as follows:

```
SELECT s.name supplier_name, p.name part_name, p.part_nbr part_number,
  p.inventory_qty in_stock,
  CASE WHEN s.name = 'Acme Industries'
    THEN my_pkg.get_resupply_date(p.part_nbr)
    ELSE p.resupply_date
```

```
        END resupply_date
    FROM part p, supplier s
    WHERE p.supplier_id = s.supplier_id;
```

Now the user-defined function is only executed if the supplier is Acme, reducing the query's execution time drastically. For more information on calling user-defined functions from SQL, see Chapter 11.

Conditional Update

If your database design includes denormalizations, you may run nightly routines to populate the denormalized columns. For example, the part table contains the denormalized column status, the value for which is derived from the inventory_qty and resupply_date columns. To update the status column, you could run four separate UPDATE statements each night, one for each of the four possible values for the status column For example:

```
UPDATE part SET status = 'INSTOCK'
WHERE inventory_qty > 0;

UPDATE part SET status = 'ENROUTE'
WHERE inventory_qty = 0 AND resupply_date < SYSDATE + 5;

UPDATE part SET status = 'BACKORD'
WHERE inventory_qty = 0 AND resupply_date > SYSDATE + 5;

UPDATE part SET status = 'UNAVAIL'
WHERE inventory_qty = 0 and resupply_date IS NULL;
```

Given that columns such as inventory_qty and resupply_date are unlikely to be indexed, each of the four UPDATE statements would require a full table-scan of the part table. By adding conditional expressions to the statement, however, the four UPDATE statements can be combined, resulting in a single scan of the part table:

```
UPDATE part SET status =
  DECODE(inventory_qty, 0,
    DECODE(resupply_date, NULL, 'UNAVAIL',
      DECODE(LEAST(resupply_date, SYSDATE + 5), resupply_date,
        'ENROUTE', 'BACKORD')),
    'INSTOCK');
```

The CASE version of this UPDATE is as follows:

```
UPDATE part SET status =
  CASE WHEN inventory_qty > 0 THEN 'INSTOCK'
    WHEN resupply_date IS NULL THEN 'UNAVAIL'
    WHEN resupply_date < SYSDATE + 5 THEN 'ENROUTE'
    WHEN resupply_date > SYSDATE + 5 THEN 'BACKORD'
    ELSE 'UNKNOWN' END;
```

The readability advantage of the CASE expression is especially apparent here, since the DECODE version requires three nested levels to implement the same conditional logic handled by a single CASE expression.

Optional Update

In some situations, you may need to modify data only if certain conditions exist. For example, you have a table that records information such as the total number of orders and the largest order booked during the current month. Here's the table definition:

```
describe mtd_orders;
Name                                         Null?     Type
----------------------------------------- -------- ------------
TOT_ORDERS                                 NOT NULL NUMBER(7)
TOT_SALE_PRICE                             NOT NULL NUMBER(11,2)
MAX_SALE_PRICE                             NOT NULL NUMBER(9,2)
```

Each night, the table is updated with that day's order information. While most of the columns will be modified each night, the column for the largest order, which is called max_sale_price, will only change if one of the day's orders exceeds the current value of the column. The following PL/SQL block shows how this might be accomplished using a procedural language:

```
DECLARE
   tot_ord NUMBER;
   tot_price NUMBER;
   max_price NUMBER;
   prev_max_price NUMBER;
BEGIN
   SELECT COUNT(*), SUM(sale_price), MAX(sale_price)
   INTO tot_ord, tot_price, max_price
   FROM cust_order
   WHERE cancelled_dt IS NULL
     AND order_dt >= TRUNC(SYSDATE);

   UPDATE mtd_orders
   SET tot_orders = tot_orders + tot_ord,
      tot_sale_price = tot_sale_price + tot_price
   RETURNING max_sale_price INTO prev_max_price;

   IF max_price > prev_max_price THEN
      UPDATE mtd_orders
      SET max_sale_price = max_price;
   END IF;
END;
```

After calculating the total number of orders, the aggregate order price, and the maximum order price for the current day, the tot_orders and tot_sale_price columns of the mtd_orders table are modified with today's sales data. After the update is complete, the maximum sale price is returned from mtd_orders so that it can be compared with today's maximum sale price. If today's max_sale_price exceeds that stored in the mtd_orders table, a second UPDATE statement is executed to update the field.

Using DECODE or CASE, however, we can update the tot_orders and tot_sale_price columns *and* optionally update the max_sale_price column in the same UPDATE statement. Additionally, since we now have a single UPDATE statement, we can aggregate the data from the cust_order table within a subquery and eliminate the need for PL/SQL:

```
UPDATE mtd_orders mtdo
SET (mtdo.tot_orders, mtdo.tot_sale_price, mtdo.max_sale_price) =
 (SELECT mtdo.tot_orders + day_tot.tot_orders,
    mtdo.tot_sale_price + NVL(day_tot.tot_sale_price, 0),
    DECODE(GREATEST(mtdo.max_sale_price,
      NVL(day_tot.max_sale_price, 0)), mtdo.max_sale_price,
        mtdo.max_sale_price, day_tot.max_sale_price)
  FROM
   (SELECT COUNT(*) tot_orders, SUM(sale_price) tot_sale_price,
     MAX(sale_price) max_sale_price
   FROM cust_order
   WHERE cancelled_dt IS NULL
     AND order_dt >= TRUNC(SYSDATE)) day_tot);
```

In this statement, the max_sale_price column is set equal to itself unless the value returned from the subquery is greater than the current column value, in which case the column is set to the value returned from the subquery. The next statement uses CASE to perform the same optional update:

```
UPDATE mtd_orders mtdo
SET (mtdo.tot_orders, mtdo.tot_sale_price, mtdo.max_sale_price) =
 (SELECT mtdo.tot_orders + day_tot.tot_orders,
    mtdo.tot_sale_price + day_tot.tot_sale_price,
    CASE WHEN day_tot.max_sale_price > mtdo.max_sale_price
      THEN day_tot.max_sale_price
      ELSE mtdo.max_sale_price END
  FROM
   (SELECT COUNT(*) tot_orders, SUM(sale_price) tot_sale_price,
     MAX(sale_price) max_sale_price
   FROM cust_order
   WHERE cancelled_dt IS NULL
     AND order_dt >= TRUNC(SYSDATE)) day_tot);
```

One thing to keep in mind when using this approach is that setting a value equal to itself is still seen as a modification by the database and may trigger an audit record, a new value for the last_modified_date column, etc.

Selective Aggregation

To expand on the mtd_orders example in the previous section, imagine that you also want to store total sales for particular regions such as Europe and North America. You could modify the mtd_orders table to look as follows. Note the addition of three columns for European sales, and three columns for North American Sales.

```
Name                                      Null?    Type
----------------------------------------- -------- -----------
TOT_ORDERS                                NOT NULL NUMBER(7)
TOT_SALE_PRICE                            NOT NULL NUMBER(11,2)
MAX_SALE_PRICE                            NOT NULL NUMBER(9,2)
```

```
EUROPE_TOT_ORDERS                    NOT NULL NUMBER(7)
EUROPE_TOT_SALE_PRICE                NOT NULL NUMBER(11,2)
EUROPE_MAX_SALE_PRICE                NOT NULL NUMBER(9,2)
NORTHAMERICA_TOT_ORDERS              NOT NULL NUMBER(7)
NORTHAMERICA_TOT_SALE_PRICE          NOT NULL NUMBER(11,2)
NORTHAMERICA_MAX_SALE_PRICE          NOT NULL NUMBER(9,2)
```

For the new columns, individual orders will affect one set of columns or the other, but not both. An order will either be for a European or North American customer, but not for both at the same time. To populate these new columns, you could generate two more update statements, each targeted to a particular region, as in:

```
/* Europe buckets */
UPDATE mtd_orders mtdo
SET (mtdo.europe_tot_orders, mtdo.europe_tot_sale_price,
  mtdo.europe_max_sale_price) =
 (SELECT mtdo.europe_tot_orders + eur_day_tot.tot_orders,
    mtdo.europe_tot_sale_price + nvl(eur_day_tot.tot_sale_price, 0),
    CASE WHEN eur_day_tot.max_sale_price > mtdo.europe_max_sale_price
      THEN eur_day_tot.max_sale_price
      ELSE mtdo.europe_max_sale_price END
  FROM
   (SELECT COUNT(*) tot_orders, SUM(co.sale_price) tot_sale_price,
      MAX(co.sale_price) max_sale_price
    FROM cust_order co, customer c
    WHERE co.cancelled_dt IS NULL
      AND co.order_dt >= TRUNC(SYSDATE)
      AND co.cust_nbr = c.cust_nbr
      AND c.region_id IN
        (SELECT region_id FROM region
         START WITH name = 'Europe'
         CONNECT BY PRIOR region_id = super_region_id)) eur_day_tot);

/* North America buckets */
UPDATE mtd_orders mtdo
SET (mtdo.northamerica_tot_orders, mtdo. northamerica_tot_sale_price,
  mtdo.northamerica_max_sale_price) =
 (SELECT mtdo.northamerica_tot_orders + na_day_tot.tot_orders,
    mtdo.northamerica_tot_sale_price + nvl(na_day_tot.tot_sale_price, 0),
    CASE WHEN na_day_tot.max_sale_price > mtdo.northamerica_max_sale_price
      THEN na_day_tot.max_sale_price
      ELSE mtdo.northamerica_max_sale_price END
  FROM
   (SELECT COUNT(*) tot_orders, SUM(co.sale_price) tot_sale_price,
      MAX(co.sale_price) max_sale_price
    FROM cust_order co, customer c
    WHERE co.cancelled_dt IS NULL
      AND co.order_dt >= TRUNC(SYSDATE) - 60
      AND co.cust_nbr = c.cust_nbr
      AND c.region_id IN
        (SELECT region_id FROM region
         START WITH name = 'North America'
         CONNECT BY PRIOR region_id = super_region_id)) na_day_tot);
```

However, why not save yourself a trip through the cust_order table and aggregate the North American and European totals at the same time? The trick here is to put conditional logic within the aggregation functions so that only the appropriate rows influence each calculation. This approach is similar to the "Result Set Transformations" example earlier in the chapter, in that it selectively aggregates data based on data stored in the table:

```
UPDATE mtd_orders mtdo
SET (mtdo.northamerica_tot_orders, mtdo. northamerica_tot_sale_price,
  mtdo.northamerica_max_sale_price, mtdo.europe_tot_orders,
  mtdo.europe_tot_sale_price, mtdo.europe_max_sale_price) =
 (SELECT mtdo.northamerica_tot_orders + nvl(day_tot.na_tot_orders, 0),
   mtdo.northamerica_tot_sale_price + nvl(day_tot.na_tot_sale_price, 0),
   CASE WHEN day_tot.na_max_sale_price > mtdo.northamerica_max_sale_price
     THEN day_tot.na_max_sale_price
     ELSE mtdo.northamerica_max_sale_price END,
   mtdo.europe_tot_orders + nvl(day_tot.eur_tot_orders, 0),
   mtdo.europe_tot_sale_price + nvl(day_tot.eur_tot_sale_price, 0),
   CASE WHEN day_tot.eur_max_sale_price > mtdo.europe_max_sale_price
     THEN day_tot.eur_max_sale_price
     ELSE mtdo.europe_max_sale_price END
  FROM
  (SELECT SUM(CASE WHEN na_regions.region_id IS NOT NULL THEN 1
              ELSE 0 END) na_tot_orders,
    SUM(CASE WHEN na_regions.region_id IS NOT NULL THEN co.sale_price
        ELSE 0 END) na_tot_sale_price,
    MAX(CASE WHEN na_regions.region_id IS NOT NULL THEN co.sale_price
        ELSE 0 END) na_max_sale_price,
    SUM(CASE WHEN eur_regions.region_id IS NOT NULL THEN 1
              ELSE 0 END) eur_tot_orders,
    SUM(CASE WHEN eur_regions.region_id IS NOT NULL THEN co.sale_price
        ELSE 0 END) eur_tot_sale_price,
    MAX(CASE WHEN eur_regions.region_id IS NOT NULL THEN co.sale_price
        ELSE 0 END) eur_max_sale_price
  FROM cust_order co, customer c,
   (SELECT region_id FROM region
    START WITH name = 'North America'
    CONNECT BY PRIOR region_id = super_region_id) na_regions,
   (SELECT region_id FROM region
    START WITH name = 'Europe'
    CONNECT BY PRIOR region_id = super_region_id) eur_regions
  WHERE co.cancelled_dt IS NULL
    AND co.order_dt >= TRUNC(SYSDATE)
    AND co.cust_nbr = c.cust_nbr
    AND c.region_id = na_regions.region_id (+)
    AND c.region_id = eur_regions.region_id (+)) day_tot);
```

This is a fairly robust statement, so let's break it down. Within the day_tot inline view, you are joining the cust_order table to the customer table, and then outer-joining from customer.region_id to each of two inline views (na_regions and eur_regions) that perform hierarchical queries on the region table. Thus, orders from European customers will have a non-null value for eur_regions.region_id, since the outer join would find a matching row in the eur_regions inline view. Six aggregations are performed on this result set; three check for a join against the na_regions inline view (North American orders), and three check for a join against the eur_regions inline view (European orders). The six aggregations are then used to modify the six columns in mtd_orders.

This statement could (and should) be combined with the statement from the previous example (which updated the first three columns) to create an UPDATE statement that touches every column in the mtd_orders table via one pass through the cust_order table. For data warehouse applications, where large data sets must be manipulated each night within tight time constraints, such an approach can often make the difference between success and failure.

Division by Zero Errors

As a general rule, you should write your code so unexpected data values are handled gracefully. One of the more common arithmetic errors is ORA-01476: divisor is equal to zero. Whether the value is retrieved from a column, passed in via a bind variable, or returned by a function call, always wrap divisors with DECODE or CASE, as illustrated by the following example:

```
SELECT p.part_nbr, SYSDATE + (p.inventory_qty /
  DECODE(my_pkg.get_daily_part_usage(p.part_nbr), NULL, 1,
    0, 1, my_pkg.get_daily_part_usage(p.part_nbr))) anticipated_shortage_dt
FROM part p
WHERE p.inventory_qty > 0;
```

The DECODE function ensures that the divisor is something other than zero. Here is the CASE version of the statement:

```
SELECT p.part_nbr, SYSDATE + (p.inventory_qty /
  CASE WHEN my_pkg.get_daily_part_usage(p.part_nbr) > 0
    THEN my_pkg.get_daily_part_usage(p.part_nbr)
    ELSE 1 END) anticipated_shortage_dt
FROM part p
WHERE p.inventory_qty > 0;
```

Of course, if you are bothered by the fact that the get_daily_part_usage function is called a second time for each part that yields a positive response, simply wrap the function call in an inline view, as in:

```
SELECT parts.part_nbr, SYSDATE + (parts.inventory_qty /
  CASE WHEN parts.daily_part_usage > 0
    THEN parts.daily_part_usage
    ELSE 1 END) anticipated_shortage_dt
FROM
  (SELECT p.part_nbr part_nbr, p.inventory_qty inventory_qty,
    my_pkg.get_daily_part_usage(p.part_nbr) daily_part_usage
  FROM part p
  WHERE p.inventory_qty > 0) parts;
```

State Transitions

In certain cases, the order in which the values may be changed is constrained as well as the allowable values for a column. Consider the diagram shown in Figure 9-1, which shows the allowable state transitions for an order.

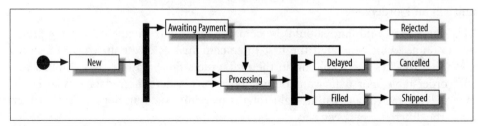

Figure 9-1. Order processing state transitions

As you can see, an order currently in the Processing state should only be allowed to move to either Delayed or Filled. Rather than allowing each application to implement logic to change the state of an order, write a user-defined function that returns the appropriate state depending on the current state of the order and the transition type. In this example, two transition types are defined: positive (POS) and negative (NEG). For example, an order in the Delayed state can make a positive transition to Processing or a negative transition to Cancelled. If an order is in one of the final states (Rejected, Cancelled, Shipped), the same state is returned. Here is the DECODE version of our PL/SQL function:

```
FUNCTION get_next_order_state(ord_nbr in NUMBER,
  trans_type in VARCHAR2 DEFAULT 'POS')
RETURN VARCHAR2 is
  next_state VARCHAR2(20) := 'UNKNOWN';
BEGIN
  SELECT DECODE(status,
    'REJECTED', status,
    'CANCELLED', status,
    'SHIPPED', status,
    'NEW', DECODE(trans_type, 'NEG', 'AWAIT_PAYMENT', 'PROCESSING'),
    'AWAIT_PAYMENT', DECODE(trans_type, 'NEG', 'REJECTED', 'PROCESSING'),
    'PROCESSING', DECODE(trans_type, 'NEG', 'DELAYED', 'FILLED'),
    'DELAYED', DECODE(trans_type, 'NEG', 'CANCELLED', 'PROCESSING'),
    'FILLED', DECODE(trans_type, 'POS', 'SHIPPED', 'UNKNOWN'),
    'UNKNOWN')
  INTO next_state
  FROM cust_order
  WHERE order_nbr = ord_nbr;

  RETURN next_state;
EXCEPTION
  WHEN NO_DATA_FOUND THEN
    RETURN next_state;
END get_next_order_state;
```

As of Oracle8*i* Version 8.1.7, the PL/SQL language does not include the CASE expression in its grammar, so you would need to be running Oracle9*i* to use the CASE version of the function:

```
FUNCTION get_next_order_state(ord_nbr in NUMBER,
  trans_type in VARCHAR2 DEFAULT 'POS')
RETURN VARCHAR2 is
  next_state VARCHAR2(20) := 'UNKNOWN';
BEGIN
  SELECT CASE
    WHEN status = 'REJECTED' THEN status
    WHEN status = 'CANCELLED' THEN status
    WHEN status = 'SHIPPED' THEN status
    WHEN status = 'NEW' AND trans_type = 'NEG' THEN 'AWAIT_PAYMENT'
    WHEN status = 'NEW' AND trans_type = 'POS' THEN 'PROCESSING'
    WHEN status = 'AWAIT_PAYMENT' AND trans_type = 'NEG' THEN 'REJECTED'
    WHEN status = 'AWAIT_PAYMENT' AND trans_type = 'POS' THEN 'PROCESSING'
    WHEN status = 'PROCESSING' AND trans_type = 'NEG' THEN 'DELAYED'
    WHEN status = 'PROCESSING' AND trans_type = 'POS' THEN 'FILLED'
    WHEN status = 'DELAYED' AND trans_type = 'NEG' THEN 'CANCELLED'
    WHEN status = 'DELAYED' AND trans_type = 'POS' THEN 'PROCESSING'
    WHEN status = 'FILLED' AND trans_type = 'POS' THEN 'SHIPPED'
    ELSE 'UNKNOWN'
  END
  INTO next_state
  FROM cust_order
  WHERE order_nbr = ord_nbr;

  RETURN next_state;
EXCEPTION
  WHEN NO_DATA_FOUND THEN
    RETURN next_state;
END get_next_order_state;
```

This example only handles the simple case where there are just two paths out of each state, but it does demonstrate one strategy for managing state transitions in your database. To demonstrate how the previous function could be used, here is the UPDATE statement used to change the status of an order once it has made a successful state transition:

```
UPDATE cust_order
SET status = my_pkg.get_next_order_state(order_nbr, 'POS')
WHERE order_nbr = 1107;
```

CHAPTER 10
Partitions, Objects, and Collections

Oracle8 introduced a host of new features to support large databases and object-relational constructs. The Oracle8*i* and Oracle9*i* releases further expanded and refined these areas. This chapter explores partitioning, which addresses the needs of large database implementations, and objects and collections, which facilitate the storage and propagation of complex datatypes.

Table Partitioning

Over the past 15 years, hard disk capacities have evolved from around 10 megabytes to over 100 gigabytes, and capacities are still growing. Disk arrays are fast approaching the 100 terabyte range. No matter how much storage is available, however, there is always a way to exhaust it. As databases grow in size, day-to-day operations become more and more challenging. For example, finding the time and resources to rebuild an index containing 100 million entries can prove quite demanding. Prior to Oracle8, database administrators would meet this challenge by manually breaking a large table into several smaller tables. Although the pieces could be hidden behind a special type of view (called a *partition view*) during a query, all DML statements had to be performed against the individual tables, thereby exposing the partitioning scheme to the database developers and users.

Starting with Version 8.0, Oracle provided a means for breaking a table into multiple pieces while preserving the look and feel of a single table. Each piece is called a *partition*, and, although every partition must share the same columns, constraints, indexes, and triggers, each partition can have its own unique storage parameters. While administrators generally deal with individual partitions when allocating storage and performing backups, developers may choose to deal with either the entire table or with individual partitions.

Partitioning Concepts

Database designers and administrators have been partitioning tables since long before Oracle8 hit the scene. In general, table partitioning within a single database is done to improve performance and simplify administration tasks, while table partitioning between databases is meant to facilitate data distribution. For example, sales data might be partitioned by region and each partition hosted in a database housed at its respective regional sales office. Whereas a central data warehouse might gather sales data from each office for reporting and decision-support queries, it might be perfectly reasonable for the operational sales data to be distributed across multiple sites.

Partitioning by sets of rows such as in the sales data example, in which the value of the sales office column determines where the data resides, is known as *horizontal partitioning*. Partitioning may also be accomplished by splitting up sets of columns, in which case it is called *vertical partitioning*. For example, sensitive data such as salary information and social security numbers may be split off from the employee table into a separate table with restricted access. When partitioning vertically, primary key columns must be included in the set of columns for every partition. Therefore, unlike horizontal partitioning, where each partition contains non-overlapping subsets of data, vertical partitioning mandates that some data be duplicated in each partition.

While both vertical and horizontal partitioning may be accomplished manually within and between Oracle databases, the Partitioning Option introduced in Oracle8 specifically deals with horizontal partitioning within a single database.

Partitioning Tables

When partitioning is employed, a table changes from a physical object to a virtual concept. There isn't really a table anymore, just a set of partitions. Since all of the partitions must share the same attribute and constraint definitions, however, it is possible to deal with the set of partitions as if they were a single table. The storage parameters, such as extent sizes and tablespace placement, are the only attributes that may differ among the partitions. This situation can facilitate some interesting storage scenarios, such as hosting infrequently accessed partitions on a CD jukebox while the heavily-hit data partitions reside on disk. You can also take advantage of Oracle's segmented buffer cache to keep the most active partitions in the keep buffer so they are always in memory, while the rest of the partitions can be targeted for the recycle or default buffers. Additionally, individual partitions may be taken offline without affecting the availability of the rest of the partitions, giving administrators a great deal of flexibility.

Depending on the partitioning scheme employed, you must choose one or more columns of a table to be the *partition key*. The values of the columns in the partition key determine the partition that hosts a particular row. Oracle also uses the partition key information in concert with your WHERE clause to determine which partitions to search during SELECT, UPDATE, and DELETE operations (see "Partition Pruning" later in the chapter for more information).

Partitioning Indexes

So what, you may wonder, happens to the indexes on partitioned tables? The answer is that you have to choose whether each index will stay intact (referred to as a *global index*), or be split into pieces corresponding to the table partitions (referred to as a *local index*). Furthermore, with global indexes, you can choose to partition the index in a different manner than the table was partitioned. When you throw the fact that you can partition both b-tree and bit-map indexes into the mix, things can become overwhelming. When you issue a SELECT, UPDATE, or DELETE statement against a partitioned table, the optimizer can take several routes to locate the target rows:

1. Use a global index, if one is available and its columns are referenced in the SQL statement, to find the target rows across one or more partitions.

2. Search a local index on every partition to identify whether any particular partition contains target rows.

3. Define a subset of the partitions that might contain target rows, and then access local indexes on those partitions.

While global indexes might seem to be the simplest solution, they can be problematic. Because global indexes span all of the partitions of a table, they are adversely affected by partition maintenance operations. For example, if a partition is split into multiple pieces, or if two partitions are merged into one, all global indexes on the partitioned table are marked as UNUSABLE and must be rebuilt before they can be used again. This is especially troubling when you consider that primary key constraints on partitioned tables utilize global indexes by default. Instead of global indexes, consider using local indexes. You may also want to explore the use of local unique indexes as the mechanism for maintaining integrity for your partitioned tables.*

Partitioning Methods

In order to horizontally partition a table (or index), you must specify a set of rules so that Oracle can determine in which partition a given row should reside. The following sections explore the four types of partitioning available in Oracle9i.

Range partitioning

The first partitioning scheme, introduced in Oracle8 and known as *range partitioning*, allows a table to be partitioned over ranges of values for one or more columns of the table. The simplest and most widely-implemented form of range partitioning is to partition using a single date column. Consider the following DDL statement:

```
CREATE TABLE cust_order (
  order_nbr NUMBER(7) NOT NULL,
```

---

* When creating a primary key constraint, you can name an existing index rather than have Oracle build a new global index.

```
    cust_nbr NUMBER(5) NOT NULL,
    order_dt DATE NOT NULL,
    sales_emp_id NUMBER(5) NOT NULL,
    sale_price NUMBER(9,2),
    expected_ship_dt DATE,
    cancelled_dt DATE,
    ship_dt DATE,
    status VARCHAR2(20))
    )
PARTITION BY RANGE (order_dt)
  (PARTITION orders_1999
    VALUES LESS THAN (TO_DATE('01-JAN-2000','DD-MON-YYYY'))
      TABLESPACE ord1,
  PARTITION orders_2000
    VALUES LESS THAN (TO_DATE('01-JAN-2001','DD-MON-YYYY'))
      TABLESPACE ord2,
  PARTITION orders_2001
    VALUES LESS THAN (TO_DATE('01-JAN-2002','DD-MON-YYYY'))
      TABLESPACE ord3);
```

Using this partitioning scheme, all orders prior to 2000 will reside in the orders_1999 partition; orders from 2000 will reside in the orders_2000 partition; and orders for the year 2001 will reside in the orders_2001 partition.

Hash partitioning

In some cases, you may wish to partition a large table, but there are no columns for which range partitioning is suitable. Available in Oracle8*i*, *hash partitioning* allows you to specify the number of partitions and the partition columns (the partition key), but leaves the allocation of rows to partition up to Oracle. As rows are inserted into the partitioned table, Oracle attempts to evenly spread the data across the partitions by applying a hashing function to the data in the partition key; the value returned by the hashing function determines the partition that hosts the row. If the partition columns are included in the WHERE clause of a SELECT, DELETE, or UPDATE statement, Oracle can apply the hash function to determine which partition to search. The following DDL statement demonstrates how the part table might be partitioned by hashing the part_nbr column:

```
CREATE TABLE part (
  part_nbr VARCHAR2(20) NOT NULL,
  name VARCHAR2(50) NOT NULL,
  supplier_id NUMBER(6) NOT NULL,
  inventory_qty NUMBER(6) NOT NULL,
  status VARCHAR2(10) NOT NULL,
  inventory_qty NUMBER(6),
  unit_cost NUMBER(8,2)
  resupply_date DATE)
PARTITION BY HASH (part_nbr)
  (PARTITION part1 TABLESPACE p1,
  PARTITION part2 TABLESPACE p2,
  PARTITION part3 TABLESPACE p3,
  PARTITION part4 TABLESPACE p4);
```

In order for the data to be evenly distributed across the partitions, it is important to choose columns with high cardinality as partition keys. A set of columns is said to have high cardinality if the number of distinct values is large compared to the size of the table.* Choosing a high cardinality column for your partition key ensures an even distribution across your partitions; otherwise, the partitions can become unbalanced, causing performance to be unpredictable and making administration more difficult.

Composite partitioning   *Range then Hash*

If you are torn between whether to apply range or hash partitioning to your table, you can do some of each. *Composite partitioning*, also unveiled with Oracle8i, allows you to create multiple range partitions, each of which contains two or more hash *subpartitions*. Composite partitioning is often useful when range partitioning is appropriate for the type of data stored in the table, but you want a finer granularity of partitioning than is practical using range partitioning alone. For example, it might make sense to partition your order table by year based on the types of queries against the table. If you want more than one partition per year, however, you could subpartition each year by hashing the customer number across four buckets. The following example expands on the range-partitioning example shown earler by generating subpartitions based on a hash of the customer number:

```
CREATE TABLE cust_order (
    order_nbr NUMBER(7) NOT NULL,
    cust_nbr NUMBER(5) NOT NULL,
    order_dt DATE NOT NULL,
    sales_emp_id NUMBER(5) NOT NULL,
    sale_price NUMBER(9,2),
    expected_ship_dt DATE,
    cancelled_dt DATE,
    ship_dt DATE,
    status VARCHAR2(20))
PARTITION BY RANGE (order_dt)
SUBPARTITION BY HASH (cust_nbr) SUBPARTITIONS 4
STORE IN (order_sub1, order_sub2, order_sub3, order_sub4)
 (PARTITION orders_1999
    VALUES LESS THAN (TO_DATE('01-JAN-2000','DD-MON-YYYY'))
      (SUBPARTITION orders_1999_s1 TABLESPACE order_sub1,
       SUBPARTITION orders_1999_s2 TABLESPACE order_sub2,
       SUBPARTITION orders_1999_s3 TABLESPACE order_sub3,
       SUBPARTITION orders_1999_s4 TABLESPACE order_sub4),
  PARTITION orders_2000
    VALUES LESS THAN (TO_DATE('01-JAN-2001','DD-MON-YYYY'))
      (SUBPARTITION orders_2000_s1 TABLESPACE order_sub1,
       SUBPARTITION orders_2000_s2 TABLESPACE order_sub2,
```

---

* A unique key has the highest cardinality, since every row in the table has a distinct value. An example of a low cardinality column might be the country column in a customer table with millions of entries.

```
        SUBPARTITION orders_2000_s3 TABLESPACE order_sub3,
        SUBPARTITION orders_2000_s4 TABLESPACE order_sub4),
    PARTITION orders_2001
      VALUES LESS THAN (TO_DATE('01-JAN-2002','DD-MON-YYYY'))
       (SUBPARTITION orders_2001_s1 TABLESPACE order_sub1,
        SUBPARTITION orders_2001_s2 TABLESPACE order_sub2,
        SUBPARTITION orders_2001_s3 TABLESPACE order_sub3,
        SUBPARTITION orders_2001_s4 TABLESPACE order_sub4));
```

Interestingly, when composite partitioning is used, all of the data is physically stored in the subpartitions, while the partitions, just like the table, become virtual.

List partitioning

Introduced in Oracle9i, *list partitioning* allows a table to be partitioned by one or more distinct values of a particular column. For example, a warehouse table containing sales summary data by product, state, and month/year could be partitioned into geographic regions, as in:

```
CREATE TABLE sales_fact (
    state_cd VARCHAR2(3) NOT NULL,
    month_cd NUMBER(2) NOT NULL,
    year_cd NUMBER(4) NOT NULL,
    product_cd VARCHAR2(10) NOT NULL,
    tot_sales NUMBER(9,2) NOT NULL)
PARTITION BY LIST (state_cd)
 (PARTITION sales_newengland VALUES ('CT','RI','MA','NH','ME','VT')
    TABLESPACE s1,
 PARTITION sales_northwest VALUES ('OR','WA','MT','ID','WY','AK')
    TABLESPACE s2,
 PARTITION sales_southwest VALUES ('NV','UT','AZ','NM','CO','HI')
    TABLESPACE s3,
 PARTITION sales_southeast VALUES ('FL','GA','AL','SC','NC','TN','WV')
    TABLESPACE s4,
 PARTITION sales_east VALUES ('PA','NY','NJ','MD','DE','VA','KY','OH')
    TABLESPACE s5,
 PARTITION sales_california VALUES ('CA')
    TABLESPACE s6,
 PARTITION sales_south VALUES ('TX','OK','LA','AR','MS')
    TABLESPACE s7,
 PARTITION sales_midwest VALUES ('ND','SD','NE','KS','MN','WI','IA',
    'IL','IN','MI','MO')
    TABLESPACE s8);
```

List partitioning is appropriate for low cardinality data in which the number of distinct values of a column is small relative to the number of rows. Unlike range and hash partitioning, where the partition key may contain several columns, list partitioning is limited to a single column. While it seems reasonable that composite partitioning could employ either range or list partitioning at the first level, only range/hash composite partitioning has been implemented by Oracle at this time.

Specifying Partitions

When you are writing SQL against partitioned tables, you have the option to treat the partitions as single, virtual tables, or to specify partition names within your SQL statements. If you write DML against a virtual table, the Oracle optimizer determines the partition or partitions that need to be involved. For an INSERT statement, the optimizer uses the values provided for the partition key to determine where to put each row. For UPDATE, DELETE, and SELECT statements, the optimizer uses the conditions from the WHERE clause along with information on local and global indexes to determine the partition or partitions that need to be searched.

If you know that your DML statement will utilize a single partition, and you know the name of the partition, you can use the PARTITION clause to tell the optimizer which partition to use. For example, if you want to summarize all orders for the year 2000, and you know that the cust_order table is range-partitioned by year, you could issue the following query:

```
SELECT COUNT(*) tot_orders, SUM(sale_price) tot_sales
FROM cust_order PARTITION (orders_2000)
WHERE cancelled_dt IS NULL;
```

Note that this query's WHERE clause doesn't specify a date range, even though the table contains data spanning multiple years. Because you specified the orders_2000 partition, you know that the query will only summarize orders from 2000, so there is no need to check each order's date.

If your table is composite-partitioned, you can use the SUBPARTITION clause to focus on a single subpartition of the table. For example, the following statement deletes all rows from the orders_2000_s1 subpartition of the composite-partitioned version of the cust_order table:

```
DELETE FROM cust_order SUBPARTITION (orders_2000_s1);
```

You can also use the PARTITION clause to delete the entire set of subpartitions that fall within a given partition:

```
DELETE FROM cust_order PARTITION (orders_2000);
```

This statement would delete all rows from the orders_2000_s1, orders_2000_s2, orders_2000_s3, and orders_2000_s4 subpartitions of the cust_order table.

Here are a few additional things to consider when working with partitioned tables:

- If the optimizer determines that two or more partitions are needed to satisfy the WHERE clause of a SELECT, UPDATE, or DELETE statement, the table and/or index partitions may be scanned in parallel. Therefore, depending on the system resources available to Oracle, scanning every partition of a partitioned table could be much faster than scanning an entire unpartitioned table.

- Because hash partitioning spreads data randomly across the partitions,[*] it is unclear why you would want to use the PARTITION clause for hash-partitioned tables or the SUBPARTITON clause for composite-partitioned tables, since you don't know what data you are working on. The only reasonable scenario that comes to mind might be when you want to modify every row in the table, but you don't have enough rollback available to modify every row in a single transaction. In this case, you can perform an UPDATE or DELETE on each partition or subpartition and issue a COMMIT after each statement completes.

- Partitions can be merged, split, or dropped at any time by the DBA. Therefore, use caution when explicitly naming partitions in your DML statements. Otherwise, you may find your statements failing, or worse, your statements might work on the wrong set of data because partitions have been merged or split without your knowledge. You may want to check with your DBA to determine her policy concerning naming partitions in your DML statements.

If you need to access a single partition or subpartition but don't like having partition names sprinkled throughout your code, consider creating views to hide the partition names, as in the following:

```
CREATE VIEW cust_order_2000 AS
SELECT *
FROM cust_order PARTITION (orders_2000);
```

You can then issue your SQL statements against the view:

```
SELECT order_nbr, cust_nbr, sale_price, order_dt
FROM cust_order_2000
WHERE quantity > 100;
```

Partition Pruning

Even when you don't name a specific partition in your SQL statement, the fact that a table is partitioned might still influence the manner in which you access the table. When an SQL statement accesses one or more partitioned tables, the Oracle optimizer attempts to use the information in the WHERE clause to eliminate some of the partitions from consideration during statement execution. This process, called *partition pruning*,[†] speeds statement execution by ignoring any partitions that cannot satisfy the statement's WHERE clause. To do so, the optimizer uses information from the table definition combined with information from the statement's WHERE clause. For example, given the following table definition:

```
CREATE TABLE tab1 (
    col1 NUMBER(5) NOT NULL,
    col2 DATE NOT NULL,
```

---

[*] It isn't actually random, but it will seem that way to you, since you don't have access to the hash function.

[†] Also known as *partition elimination*.

```
        col3 VARCHAR2(10) NOT NULL)
      PARTITION BY RANGE (col2)
       (PARTITION tab1_1998
          VALUES LESS THAN (TO_DATE('01-JAN-1999','DD-MON-YYYY'))
            TABLESPACE t1,
        PARTITION tab1_1999
          VALUES LESS THAN (TO_DATE('01-JAN-2000','DD-MON-YYYY'))
            TABLESPACE t1,
        PARTITION tab1_2000
          VALUES LESS THAN (TO_DATE('01-JAN-2001','DD-MON-YYYY'))
            TABLESPACE t3,
        PARTITION tab1_2001
          VALUES LESS THAN (TO_DATE('01-JAN-2002','DD-MON-YYYY'))
            TABLESPACE t4);
```

and the following query:

```
SELECT col1, col2, col3
FROM tab1
WHERE col2 > TO_DATE('01-OCT-2000','DD-MON-YYYY');
```

the optimizer would eliminate partitions tab1_1998 and tab1_1999 from consideration, since neither partition could contain rows with a value for col2 greater than October 1, 2000.

In order for the optimizer to make these types of decisions, the WHERE clause must reference at least one column from the set of columns that comprise the partition key. While this might seem fairly straightforward, not all queries against a partitioned table naturally include the partition key. If a unique index exists on the col1 column of the tab1 table from the previous example, for instance, the following query would generally offer the most efficient access:

```
SELECT col1, col2, col3
FROM tab1
WHERE col1 = 1578;
```

If the index on col1 had been defined as a local index, however, Oracle would need to visit each partition's local index to find the one that holds the value 1578. If you also have information about the partition key (col2 in this case), you might want to consider including it in the query so that the optimizer can eliminate partitions, as in the following:

```
SELECT col1, col2, col3
FROM tab1
WHERE col1 = 1578
  AND col2 > TO_DATE('01-JAN-2001','DD-MON-YYYY');
```

With the additional condition, the optimizer can now eliminate the tab1_1998, tab1_1999, and tab1_2000 partitions from consideration. Oracle will now search a single unique index on the tab1_2001 partition instead of searching a unique index on each of the four table partitions. Of course, you would need to know that data pertaining to the value 1578 also had a value for col2 greater then January 1, 2001. If you can reliably provide additional information regarding the partition keys, than you should do so; otherwise, you'll just have to let the optimizer do its best. Running EXPLAIN PLAN on your DML statements against partitioned tables will allow you to see which partitions the optimizer decided to utilize.

When checking the results of EXPLAIN PLAN, there are a couple of partition-specific columns that you should add to your query against plan_table in order to see which partitions are being considered by the optimizer. To demonstrate, we'll explain the following query against tab1:

```
EXPLAIN PLAN
SET STATEMENT_ID = 'qry1' FOR
SELECT col1, col2, col3
FROM tab1
WHERE col2 BETWEEN TO_DATE('01-JUL-1999','DD-MON-YYYY')
  AND TO_DATE('01-JUL-2000','DD-MON-YYYY');
```

When querying the plan_table table, you will include the partition_start and partition_end columns whenever the operation field starts with 'PARTITION':

```
SELECT lpad(' ',2 * level) || operation || ' ' ||
  options || ' ' || object_name ||
  DECODE(SUBSTR(operation, 1, 9), 'PARTITION',
    ' FROM ' || partition_start ||
    ' TO ' || partition_stop, ' ') "exec plan"
FROM plan_table
CONNECT BY PRIOR id = parent_id
START WITH id = 0 AND statement_id = 'qry1';

exec plan
-------------------------------------------------------
  SELECT STATEMENT
    PARTITION RANGE ITERATOR  FROM 2 TO 3
      TABLE ACCESS FULL TAB1
```

The value of PARTITION RANGE for the operator column along with the value of ITERATOR for the options column indicates that more than one partition will be involved in the execution plan.* The values of the partition_start and partition_end columns (2 and 3, respectively) indicate that the optimizer has decided to prune partitions 1 and 4, which correlate to the tab1_1998 and tab1_2001 partitions.† Given that our WHERE clause specifies a date range of July 1, 1999 to July 1, 2000, the optimizer has correctly pruned all partitions that cannot contribute to the result set.

---

* If the optimizer had pruned all but one partition, the options column would contain the value 'SINGLE'. If no partitions were pruned, the options column would contain the value 'ALL'.

† The number shown in the partition_start and partition_end columns correlates to the partition_position column in the user_tab_partitions table, so you can query this table to identify the names of the partitions that are included in the execution plan.

Objects and Collections

Beginning with Version 8.0, Oracle added object-oriented features to what was a purely relational database server. *Object types* and *collections* were introduced in Oracle8, and both have been sufficiently refined in Oracle8*i* and Oracle9*i* so that they may now be considered fully-functional.* Oracle now considers its database engine to be *object-relational*, in that a database may mix relational constructs such as tables and constraints with object-oriented constructs such as object types, collections, and references.

Object Types

An object type is a user-defined datatype that combines data and related methods in order to model complex entities. In this regard, they are similar to class definitions in an object-oriented language such as C++ or Java. Unlike Java and C++, however, Oracle object types have a built-in persistence mechanism, since a table can be defined to store an object type in the database. Thus, Oracle object types can be directly manipulated via SQL.

The best way to define the syntax and features of an object type is with an example. The following DDL statement creates an object type used to model an equity security such as a common stock:

```
CREATE TYPE equity AS OBJECT (
  issuer_id NUMBER,
  ticker VARCHAR2(6),
  outstanding_shares NUMBER,
  last_close_price NUMBER(9,2),
MEMBER PROCEDURE
  apply_split(split_ratio in VARCHAR2));
```

The equity object type has four data members and a single member procedure. The body of the apply_split procedure is defined within a CREATE TYPE BODY statement. The following example illustrates how the apply_split member procedure might be defined:

```
CREATE TYPE BODY equity AS
  MEMBER PROCEDURE apply_split(split_ratio in VARCHAR2) IS
    from_val NUMBER;
    to_val NUMBER;
  BEGIN
    /* parse the split ratio into its components */
    to_val := SUBSTR(split_ratio, 1, INSTR(split_ratio, ':') - 1);
    from_val := SUBSTR(split_ratio, INSTR(split_ratio, ':') + 1);
```

---

* In release 8.0, for example, object types didn't support inheritance, and collections could not be nested (i.e., an array of arrays), resulting in a fairly cool reception to Oracle's early attempts at object-orientation.

```
      /* apply the split ratio to the outstanding shares */
      SELF.outstanding_shares :=
        (SELF.outstanding_shares * to_val) / from_val;

      /* apply the split ratio to the last closing price */
      SELF.last_close_price :=
        (SELF.last_close_price * from_val) / to_val;
    END apply_split;
END;
```

In this example, the SELF keyword is used to identify the current instance of the equity object type. Although it is not required, we recommend using SELF in your code so that it is clear that you are referencing or modifying the current instance's data. We will explore how to call member functions and procedures a bit later in the chapter.

Instances of type equity are created using the default constructor, which has the same name as the object type and expects one parameter per attribute of the object type. As of Oracle9*i*, there is no way to generate your own constructors for your object types. The following PL/SQL block demonstrates how an instance of the equity object type can be created using the default constructor:

```
DECLARE
  eq equity := NULL;
BEGIN
  eq := equity(198, 'ACMW', 1000000, 13.97);
END;
```

Object type constructors may also be called from within DML statements. The next example queries the issuer table to find the issuer with the name 'ACME Wholesalers', and then uses the retrieved issuer_id field to construct an instance of the equity type:

```
DECLARE
  eq equity := NULL;
BEGIN
  SELECT equity(i.issuer_id, 'ACMW', 1000000, 13.97)
  INTO eq
  FROM issuer i
  WHERE i.name = 'ACME Wholesalers';
END;
```

The next three sections briefly describe some of the ways you can incorporate object types into your database and/or your database logic.

Object attributes

An object type may be used along with Oracle's built-in datatypes as an attribute of a table. The following table definition includes the equity object type as an attribute of the common_stock table:

```
CREATE TABLE common_stock (
  security_id NUMBER NOT NULL,
  security equity NOT NULL,
  issue_date DATE NOT NULL,
  currency_cd VARCHAR2(5) NOT NULL);
```

When adding records to the table, you must utilize the object type constructor, as illustrated by the following INSERT statement:

```
INSERT INTO common_stock (security_id, security, issue_date, currency_cd)
VALUES (1078, equity(198, 'ACMW', 1000000, 13.97), SYSDATE, 'USD');
```

In order to see the attributes of the equity object, you must provide an alias for the table and reference the alias, the name of the attribute containing the object type, and the object type's attribute. The next query retrieves the security_id, which is an attribute of the common_stock table, and the ticker, which is an attribute of the equity object within the common_stock table:

```
SELECT c.security_id security_id,
   c.security.ticker ticker
FROM common_stock c;

SECURITY_ID TICKER
----------- ------
       1078 ACMW
```

Object tables

In addition to embedding object types in tables alongside other attributes, you can also build a table specifically for holding instances of your object type. Known as an *object table*, these tables are created by referencing the object type in the CREATE TABLE statement using the OF keyword:

```
CREATE TABLE equities OF equity;
```

The equities table can be populated using the constructor for the equity object type, or it may be populated from existing instances of the equity object type. For example, the next statement populates the equities table using the security column of the common_stock table:

```
INSERT INTO equities
SELECT c.security FROM common_stock c;
```

When querying the equities table, you can reference the object type's attributes directly, just as you would an ordinary table:

```
SELECT issuer_id, ticker
FROM equities;

ISSUER_ID TICKER
--------- ------
      198 ACMW
```

If you want to retrieve the data in the equities table as an instance of an equity object rather than as a set of attributes, you can use the VALUE function to return an object. The following PL/SQL block retrieves the object having a ticker equal to 'ACMW' from the equities table:

```
DECLARE
  eq equity := NULL;
```

```
BEGIN
  SELECT VALUE(e)
  INTO eq
  FROM equities e
  WHERE ticker = 'ACMW';
END;
```

Thus, object tables represent the best of both worlds, in that you can treat them as either a relational table or as a set of objects.

 Note the use of a table alias with the VALUE function. Use of VALUE requires the use of tables aliases.

Now that you have an object stored in the database, you can explore how to call the apply_split member procedure defined earlier. Before you call the procedure, you need to find the target object in the table and then tell the object to run its apply_split procedure. The following PL/SQL block expands on the previous example, which finds the object in the equities table with a ticker of 'ACMW', by finding an equity object, invoking its apply_split method, and saving it back to the table again:

```
DECLARE
  eq equity := NULL;
BEGIN
  SELECT VALUE(e)
  INTO eq
  FROM equities e
  WHERE ticker = 'ACMW';

  /* apply a 2:1 stock split */
  eq.apply_split('2:1');

  /* store modified object */
  UPDATE equities e
  SET e = eq
  WHERE ticker = 'ACMW';
END;
```

It is important to realize that the apply_split procedure is not operating directly on the data in the equities table; rather, it is operating on a copy of the object held in memory. After the apply_split procedure has executed against the copy, the UPDATE statement overwrites the object in the equities table with the object referenced by the local variable eq, thus saving the modified version of the object.

Object parameters

Regardless of whether you decide to store object types persistently in the database, you can use them as vehicles for passing data within or between applications. Object types may be used as input parameters and return types for PL/SQL stored procedures and functions. Additionally, SELECT statements can instantiate and return object types even if none of the tables in the FROM clause contain object types. Therefore, object types may be used to graft an object-oriented veneer on top of a purely relational database design.

To illustrate how this might work, let's build an API for our example database that both accepts and returns object types in order to find and build customer orders. First, identify the necessary object types:

```
CREATE TYPE customer_obj AS OBJECT
 (cust_nbr NUMBER,
  name VARCHAR2(30));

CREATE TYPE employee_obj AS OBJECT
 (emp_id NUMBER,
  name VARCHAR2(50));

CREATE TYPE order_obj AS OBJECT
 (order_nbr NUMBER,
  customer customer_obj,
  salesperson employee_obj,
  order_dt DATE,
  price NUMBER,
  status VARCHAR2(20));

CREATE TYPE line_item_obj AS OBJECT (
  part_nbr VARCHAR2(20),
  quantity NUMBER(8,2));
```

Using these object definitions, you can now define a PL/SQL package containing procedures and functions that support the lifecycle of a customer order:

```
CREATE PACKAGE order_lifecycle AS
  FUNCTION create_order(v_cust_nbr IN NUMBER, v_emp_id IN NUMBER)
    RETURN order_obj;
  PROCEDURE cancel_order(v_order_nbr IN NUMBER);
  FUNCTION get_order(v_order_nbr IN NUMBER) RETURN order_obj;
  PROCEDURE add_line_item(v_order_nbr IN NUMBER,
    v_line_item IN line_item_obj);
END order_lifecycle;

CREATE PACKAGE BODY order_lifecycle AS
  FUNCTION create_order(v_cust_nbr IN NUMBER, v_emp_id IN NUMBER)
    RETURN order_obj IS
    ord_nbr NUMBER;
  BEGIN
    SELECT seq_order_nbr.NEXTVAL INTO ord_nbr FROM DUAL;

    INSERT INTO cust_order (order_nbr, cust_nbr, sales_emp_id,
      order_dt, expected_ship_dt, status)
    SELECT ord_nbr, c.cust_nbr, e.emp_id,
      SYSDATE, SYSDATE + 7, 'NEW'
    FROM customer c, employee e
    WHERE c.cust_nbr = v_cust_nbr
      AND e.emp_id = v_emp_id;
```

```
      RETURN order_lifecycle.get_order(ord_nbr);
  END create_order;

  PROCEDURE cancel_order(v_order_nbr IN NUMBER) IS
  BEGIN
    UPDATE cust_order SET cancelled_dt = SYSDATE,
      expected_ship_dt = NULL, status = 'CANCELED'
    WHERE order_nbr = v_order_nbr;
  END cancel_order;

  FUNCTION get_order(v_order_nbr IN NUMBER) RETURN order_obj IS
    ord order_obj := NULL;
  BEGIN
    SELECT order_obj(co.order_nbr,
      customer_obj(c.cust_nbr, c.name),
      employee_obj(e.emp_id, e.fname || ' ' || e.lname),
      co.order_dt, co.sale_price, co.status)
    INTO ord
    FROM cust_order co, customer c, employee e
    WHERE co.order_nbr = v_order_nbr
      AND co.cust_nbr = c.cust_nbr
      AND co.sales_emp_id = e.emp_id;

    RETURN ord;
  EXCEPTION
    WHEN NO_DATA_FOUND THEN
      RETURN ord;
  END get_order;

  PROCEDURE add_line_item(v_order_nbr IN NUMBER,
    V_line_item IN line_item_obj) IS
  BEGIN
    INSERT INTO line_item (order_nbr, part_nbr, qty)
    VALUES (v_order_nbr, v_line_item.part_nbr,
      v_line_item.quantity);
  END add_line_item;
END order_lifecycle;
```

From the API user's standpoint, objects are being stored and retrieved from the database, even though the database behind the API is purely relational. If you are squeamish about using object types in your database schema, this approach can be an attractive alternative to asking your Java coders to directly manipulate relational data.

Collection Types

During a traditional relational design process, one-to-many relationships, such as a department having many employees or an order consisting of many line items, are resolved as separate tables where the child table holds a foreign key to the parent table. In the example schema, each row in the line_item table knows which order it belongs to via a foreign key, but a row in the cust_order table does not directly know anything about line items. Beginning with Oracle8, such relationships can be internalized within the parent table using a *collection*. The two collection types available in Oracle8 and above are *variable arrays*, which are used for ordered, bounded sets of data, and *nested tables*, which are used for unordered, unbounded data sets.

Variable arrays

Variable arrays, also called *varrays*, are arrays stored within a table. Elements of a varray must be of the same datatype, are bounded by a maximum size, and are accessed positionally. Varrays may contain either a standard Oracle datatype, such as DATE or VARCHAR2, or a user-defined object type. The following example illustrates the creation of a varray and its use as a column of a table:

```
CREATE TYPE resupply_dates AS VARRAY(100) OF DATE;

CREATE TABLE part_c (
  part_nbr VARCHAR2(20) NOT NULL,
  name VARCHAR2(50) NOT NULL,
  supplier_id NUMBER(6),
  unit_cost NUMBER(8,2),
  inventory_qty NUMBER(6),
  restocks resupply_dates);
```

Along with descriptive information about the part, each row in the part_c table can hold up to 100 dates corresponding to when a shipment was received from the supplier.

Nested tables

Like varrays, nested table elements must be of the same datatype. Unlike varrays, however, nested tables do not have a maximum size and are not accessed positionally. Rows in the nested table can only have one column, which may be defined as a standard datatype or an object type. If an object type is used, the effect is the same as if the nested table were allowed to have multiple columns, since an object type may contain multiple attributes. The following example defines a nested table type containing an object type:

```
CREATE TYPE line_item_obj AS OBJECT (
  part_nbr VARCHAR2(20),
  quantity NUMBER(8,2));

CREATE TYPE line_item_tbl AS TABLE OF line_item_obj;
```

Now that you have created a nested table type for line_item objects, you can choose to embed it into our cust_order table, as in the following:

```
CREATE TABLE cust_order_c (
  order_nbr NUMBER(8) NOT NULL,
  cust_nbr NUMBER(6) NOT NULL,
  sales_emp_id NUMBER(6) NOT NULL,
  order_dt DATE NOT NULL,
  sale_price NUMBER(9,2),
  order_items line_item_tbl)
NESTED TABLE order_items STORE AS order_items_table;
```

Using a nested table, you have absorbed an order's line items into the cust_order table, eliminating the need for the line_item table. Later in the chapter, you'll see Oracle provides a way to detach the order_items collection when it is advantageous.

Collection Creation

While the table definitions in the previous section look fairly straightforward, it isn't immediately obvious how you might go about populating the resulting tables. Whenever you want to create an instance of a collection, you need to use its constructor, which is a system-generated function with the same name as the collection. The constructor accepts one or more elements; for varrays, the number of elements cannot exceed the maximum size of the varray. For example, adding a row to the part_c table, which contains a varray column, can be done as follows:

```
INSERT INTO part_c (part_nbr, name, supplier_id, unit_cost,
   inventory_qty, restocks)
VALUES ('GX5-2786-A2', 'Spacely Sprocket', 157, 75, 22,
   resupply_dates(TO_DATE('03-SEP-1999','DD-MON-YYYY'),
     TO_DATE('22-APR-2000','DD-MON-YYYY'),
     TO_DATE('21-MAR-2001','DD-MON-YYYY')));
```

In this example, the resupply_dates constructor is called with three parameters, one for each time a shipment of parts was received. If you are using a collection-savvy query tool such as Oracle's SQL*Plus, you can query the collection directly, and the tool will format the results:

```
SELECT part_nbr, restocks
FROM part_c
WHERE name = 'Spacely Sprocket';

PART_NBR        RESTOCKS
--------------  --------------------------------------------------------
GX5-2786-A2     RESUPPLY_DATES('03-SEP-99', '22-APR-00', '21-MAR-01')
```

You deal with nested tables in a manner similar to varrays. The next example demonstrates how you would insert a new row into the cust_order_c table, which contains a nested table column:

```
INSERT INTO cust_order_c (order_nbr, cust_nbr, sales_emp_id,
   order_dt, sale_price, order_items)
VALUES (1000, 9568, 275,
   TO_DATE('21-MAR-2001','DD-MON-YYYY'), 15753,
   line_item_tbl(
     line_item_obj('A675-015', 25),
     line_item_obj('GX5-2786-A2', 1),
     line_item_obj('X378-9JT-2', 3)));
```

If you look carefully, you will notice that there are actually two different constructors called: one to create the nested table line_item_tbl, and the other to create each of three instances of the line_item_obj object type. Remember, the nested table is a table of line_item_obj objects. The end result is a single row in cust_order_c containing a collection of three line items.

Collection Unnesting

Even if your developer community is comfortable manipulating collections within your database, it is often unrealistic to expect the various tools and applications accessing your data (data load and extraction utilities, reporting and ad-hoc query tools, etc.) to correctly handle them. Using a technique called *collection unnesting*, you can present the contents of the collection as if it were rows of an ordinary table. Using the TABLE expression, write a query which unnests the order_items nested table from the cust_order_c table, as in:

```
SELECT co.order_nbr, co.cust_nbr, co.order_dt, li.part_nbr, li.quantity
FROM cust_order_c co,
  TABLE(co.order_items) li;

ORDER_NBR   CUST_NBR ORDER_DT  PART_NBR              QUANTITY
----------  -------- --------- --------------------- ----------
      1000      9568 21-MAR-01 A675-015                    25
      1000      9568 21-MAR-01 GX5-2786-A2                   1
      1000      9568 21-MAR-01 X378-9JT-2                    3
```

Note that the two data sets do not need to be explicitly joined, since the collection members are already associated with a row in the cust_order_c table.

In order to make this unnested data set available to your users, you can wrap the previous query in a view:

```
CREATE VIEW cust_order_line_items AS
SELECT co.order_nbr, co.cust_nbr, co.order_dt, li.part_nbr, li.quantity
FROM cust_order_c co,
  TABLE(co.order_items) li;
```

Your users can now interact with the nested table via the view using standard SQL, as in the following:

```
SELECT *
FROM cust_order_line_items
WHERE part_nbr like 'X%';

ORDER_NBR   CUST_NBR ORDER_DT  PART_NBR              QUANTITY
----------  -------- --------- --------------------- ----------
      1000      9568 21-MAR-01 X378-9JT-2                    3
```

Querying Collections

Now that you know how to get data into a collection, you need a way to get it out. Oracle provides a special TABLE expression just for this purpose.[*] The TABLE expression can be used in the FROM, WHERE, and HAVING clauses of a query to allow a nested table or varray column to be referenced as if it were a separate table.

---

[*] Prior to release 8*i*, the TABLE expression was called THE. Only the TABLE expression is used here.

The following query extracts the resupply dates (from the restocks column) that were added previously to the part_c table:

```
SELECT *
FROM TABLE(SELECT restocks
  FROM part_c
  WHERE part_nbr = 'GX5-2786-A2');


COLUMN_VALU
-----------
03-SEP-1999
22-APR-2000
21-MAR-2001
```

To better illustrate the function of the TABLE expression, the next query retrieves the restocks varray directly from the part_c table:

```
SELECT restocks
FROM part_c
WHERE part_nbr = 'GX5-2786-A2'

RESTOCKS
--------------------------------------------------------
RESUPPLY_DATES('03-SEP-99', '22-APR-00', '21-MAR-01')
```

As you can see, the result set consists of a single row containing an array of dates, whereas the previous query unnests the varray so that each element is represented as a row with a single column.

Since the varray contains a built-in datatype rather than an object type, it is necessary to give it a name so that it may be explicitly referenced in SQL statements. Oracle assigns the varray's contents a default alias of 'column_value' for this purpose. The next example makes use of the column_value alias.

Let's say that you wanted to find all parts resupplied on a particular date. Using the TABLE expression, you can perform a correlated subquery against the restocks varray to see if the desired date is found in the set:

```
SELECT p1.part_nbr, p1.name
FROM part_c p1
WHERE TO_DATE('03-SEP-1999','DD-MON-YYYY') IN
  (SELECT column_value FROM TABLE(SELECT restocks FROM part_c p2
   WHERE p2.part_nbr = p1.part_nbr));

PART_NBR              NAME
-------------------- --------------------------------
GX5-2786-A2          Spacely Sprocket
```

Manipulating Collections

If you want to modify a collection's contents, you have two choices: replace the entire collection, or modify individual elements of the collection. If the collection is a varray, you will have no choice but to replace the entire collection. This can be accomplished by retrieving the contents of the varray, modifying the data, and then updating the table with the new varray. The following statement changes the restock dates for part number 'GX5-2786-A2'. Note that the varray is entirely recreated:

```
UPDATE part_c
SET restocks = resupply_dates(TO_DATE('03-SEP-1999','DD-MON-YYYY'),
    TO_DATE('25-APR-2000','DD-MON-YYYY'),
    TO_DATE('21-MAR-2001','DD-MON-YYYY'))
WHERE part_nbr = 'GX5-2786-A2';
```

If you are using nested tables, you can perform DML against individual elements of a collection. For example, the following statement adds an additional line item to your nested cust_order_c table for order number 1000:

```
INSERT INTO TABLE(SELECT order_items FROM cust_order_c
  WHERE order_nbr = 1000)
VALUES (line_item_obj('T25-ASM', 1));
```

To update data in the nested table, use the TABLE expression to create a data set consisting of part numbers from order number 1000, and then modify the element with a specified part number:

```
UPDATE TABLE(SELECT order_items FROM cust_order_c
  WHERE order_nbr = 1000) oi
SET oi.quantity = 2
WHERE oi.part_nbr = 'T25-ASM';
```

Similarly, you can use the same data set to remove elements from the collection:

```
DELETE FROM TABLE(SELECT order_items FROM cust_order_c
  WHERE order_nbr = 1000) oi
WHERE oi.part_nbr = 'T25-ASM';
```

CHAPTER 11

PL/SQL

There are many fine books on the market that cover the PL/SQL language in great detail.* Because this is a book about Oracle SQL, the focus of this chapter is the use of PL/SQL within SQL statements as well as the use of SQL within PL/SQL programs.

What Is PL/SQL?

PL/SQL is a procedural programming language from Oracle Corporation that combines the following elements:

- Logical constructs such as IF-THEN-ELSE and WHILE
- SQL DML statements, built-in functions, and operators
- Transaction control statements such as COMMIT and ROLLBACK
- Cursor control statements
- Object and collection manipulation statements

Despite its humble origins as a scripting language in Version 6.0, PL/SQL became an integral part of the Oracle server with release 7.0, which correlates to release 2.0 of PL/SQL. Because release 7.0 included the ability to compile and store PL/SQL programs within the server, Oracle began using the language to provide server functionality and to assist in database installation and configuration. When release 2.1 of PL/SQL was included with the 7.1 release of the server, Oracle added a new feature of particular use to SQL programmers: the ability to call PL/SQL stored functions from SQL statements (more on this later).

Along with the array of new features made available with each release of PL/SQL, Oracle began supplying prefabricated sets of PL/SQL functionality to allow programmers to tackle more sophisticated programming tasks and to help integrate with various

---

* For example, *Oracle PL/SQL Programming* by Steven Feuerstein (O'Reilly).

Oracle product offerings. These collections of stored procedures and functions, known as *Oracle Supplied Packages*, allow you to (among other things):

- Interface with and administer Oracle's Advanced Queueing option
- Schedule database tasks for periodic execution
- Manipulate Oracle large objects (LOBs)
- Read from and write to external files
- Interface with Oracle's Advanced Replication features
- Issue dynamic SQL statements
- Generate and parse XML files
- Issue LDAP commands

The ever-expanding feature set of the PL/SQL language combined with the wide array of supplied packages has yielded a powerful database programming environment. Whether you are generating reports, writing data loading scripts, or writing custom applications, there's probably a place for PL/SQL in your project.

Procedures, Functions, and Packages

Although PL/SQL can still be used to write scripts, also known as *anonymous blocks*, the focus of this chapter is PL/SQL routines stored in the Oracle server. PL/SQL routines stored in the database may be one of two types: *stored procedures* or *stored functions*.* Stored functions and procedures are essentially identical except for the following:

- Stored functions have a return type, whereas procedures do not.
- Because stored functions return a value, they can be used in expressions, whereas procedures cannot.

Stored functions and procedures may be compiled individually, or they may be grouped together into *packages*. Along with being a convenient way to group related functionality together, packages are important for the following reasons:

- Packages are loaded into memory as a whole, increasing the likelihood that a procedure or function will be resident in memory when called.
- Packages can include private elements, allowing logic to be hidden from view.
- Placing functions and procedures inside packages eliminates the need to recompile all functions and procedures that reference a newly-recompiled one.
- Function and procedure names may be overloaded within packages, whereas standalone functions and procedures cannot be overloaded.
- Functions and procedures inside packages can be checked for side effects at compile time rather than at execution time, which improves performance.

---

* Database triggers are another type of stored PL/SQL, but they are outside the scope of this discussion.

If these reasons haven't convinced you to place your stored functions and procedures inside packages, here's a bit of advice we can give after working with PL/SQL since Version 2.0: you will never be sorry that you bundled your PL/SQL code into packages, but you will eventually be sorry if you don't.

Packages consist of two distinct parts: the *package specification*, which defines the signatures of the package's public procedures and functions, and the *package body*, which contains the code for the public procedures and functions and may also contain code for any private functions and procedures not included in the package specification. To give you an idea of what a package looks like, here is a simple example of a package specification:

```
CREATE OR REPLACE PACKAGE my_pkg AS
  PROCEDURE my_proc(arg1 IN VARCHAR2);

  FUNCTION my_func(arg1 IN NUMBER) RETURN VARCHAR2;
END my_pkg;
```

and its matching package body:

```
CREATE OR REPLACE PACKAGE BODY my_pkg AS
  FUNCTION my_private_func(arg1 IN NUMBER) RETURN VARCHAR2 IS
    return_val VARCHAR2(20);
  BEGIN
    SELECT col1 INTO return_val
    FROM tab2
    WHERE col2 = arg1;

    RETURN return_val;
  EXCEPTION
    WHEN NO_DATA_FOUND THEN
      RETURN `NOT FOUND';
  END my_private_func;

  PROCEDURE my_proc(arg1 IN VARCHAR2) IS
  BEGIN
    UPDATE tab1 SET col1 = col1 + 1
    WHERE col2 = arg1;
  END my_proc;

  FUNCTION my_func(arg1 IN NUMBER) RETURN VARCHAR2 IS
  BEGIN
    RETURN my_private_func(arg1);
  END my_func;
END my_pkg;
```

As you can see, the my_pkg package includes one public procedure and one public function. The package specification includes the parameter names and types of the procedure and function, along with the return type of the function, but does not include any implementation code. The package body includes the implementation logic for the public function and procedure, and it also includes a private function (my_private_func) that is only accessible from inside the package body.

Calling Stored Functions from Queries

As mentioned earlier, stored functions may be called from within SQL statements. Since stored functions can in turn make calls to stored procedures, it can also be said that stored procedures may be called, albeit indirectly, from within SQL statements. Since stored functions may be used in expressions, they may be included wherever expressions are allowed in a query, including:

- The SELECT clause
- The WHERE clause
- The GROUP BY and HAVING clauses
- The ORDER BY clause
- The START WITH clause (for hierarchical queries)
- The FROM clause (indirectly by using inline views or TABLE statements)

One of the most common uses of stored functions is to isolate commonly-used functionality in order to facilitate code reuse and simplify maintenance. For example, imagine that you are working with a large team to build a custom N-tier application. In order to simplify integration efforts between the various layers, it has been decided that all dates will be passed back and forth as the number of milliseconds since January 1, 1970. You could include the conversion logic in all of your queries, as in:

```
SELECT co.order_nbr, co.cust_nbr, co.sale_price,
  ROUND((co.order_dt - TO_DATE('01011970','MMDDYYYY')) * 86400 * 1000)
FROM cust_order co
WHERE ship_dt = TRUNC(SYSDATE);
```

However, this could become somewhat tedious and prove problematic should you wish to modify your logic in the future. Instead, build a utility package that includes functions for translating between Oracle's internal date format and the desired format:

```
CREATE OR REPLACE PACKAGE BODY pkg_util AS
  FUNCTION translate_date(dt IN DATE) RETURN NUMBER IS
  BEGIN
    RETURN ROUND((dt - TO_DATE('01011970','MMDDYYYY')) * 86400 * 1000);
  END translate_date;

  FUNCTION translate_date(dt IN NUMBER) RETURN DATE IS
  BEGIN
    RETURN TO_DATE('01011970','MMDDYYYY') + (dt / (86400 * 1000));
  END translate_date;
END pkg_util;
```

Note that the package contains two identically-named functions; one requires a DATE parameter and returns a NUMBER, while the second requires a NUMBER parameter and returns a DATE. This strategy, called *overloading*, is only possible when your functions are contained in a package.

Your development team can now use these functions whenever they need to convert date formats, as in:

```
SELECT co.order_nbr, co.cust_nbr, co.sale_price,
  pkg_util.translate_date(co.order_dt) utc_order_dt
FROM cust_order co
WHERE co.ship_dt = TRUNC(SYSDATE);
```

Another common use of stored functions is to simplify and hide complex IF-THEN-ELSE logic from your SQL statements. Suppose you have to generate a report detailing all customer orders for the past month. You want to sort the orders using the ship_dt column if an order has been shipped, the expected_ship_dt column if a ship date has been assigned and is not in the past, the current day if the expected_ship_dt is in the past, or the order_dt column if the order hasn't been assigned a ship date. You could utilize a CASE statement in the ORDER BY clause:

```
SELECT co.order_nbr, co.cust_nbr, co.sale_price
FROM cust_order co
WHERE co.order_dt > TRUNC(SYSDATE, 'MONTH')
  AND co.cancelled_dt IS NULL
ORDER BY
  CASE
    WHEN co.ship_dt IS NOT NULL THEN co.ship_dt
    WHEN co.expected_ship_dt IS NOT NULL
      AND co.expected_ship_dt > SYSDATE
        THEN co.expected_ship_dt
    WHEN co.expected_ship_dt IS NOT NULL
      THEN GREATEST(SYSDATE, co.expected_ship_dt)
    ELSE co.order_dt
  END;
```

However, there are two problems with this approach:

1. The resulting ORDER BY clause is fairly complex.

2. You may wish to use this logic elsewhere, and duplicating it will create maintenance problems.

Instead, let's add a stored function to our pkg_util package that returns the appropriate date for a given order:

```
FUNCTION get_best_order_date(ord_dt IN DATE, exp_ship_dt IN DATE,
  ship_dt IN DATE) RETURN DATE IS
BEGIN
  IF ship_dt IS NOT NULL THEN
    RETURN ship_dt;
  ELSIF exp_ship_dt IS NOT NULL AND exp_ship_dt > SYSDATE THEN
    RETURN exp_ship_dt;
  ELSIF exp_ship_dt IS NOT NULL THEN
    RETURN SYSDATE;
  ELSE
    RETURN ord_dt;
  END IF;
END get_best_order_date;
```

You may then call this function from both the SELECT and ORDER BY clauses:

```
SELECT co.order_nbr, co.cust_nbr, co.sale_price,
  pkg_util.get_best_order_date(co.order_dt, co.expected_ship_dt,
    co.ship_dt) best_date
FROM cust_order co
WHERE co.order_dt > TRUNC(SYSDATE, 'MONTH')
  AND co.cancelled_dt IS NULL
ORDER BY pkg_util.get_best_order_date(co.order_dt, co.expected_ship_dt,
    co.ship_dt);
```

If you are bothered by the fact that the stored function is called twice per row with the same parameters, you can always retrieve the data within an inline view and sort the results afterward, as in:

```
SELECT orders.order_nbr, orders.cust_nbr,
  orders.sale_price, orders.best_date
FROM
  (SELECT co.order_nbr order_nbr, co.cust_nbr cust_nbr,
    co.sale_price sale_price,
    pkg_util.get_best_order_date(co.order_dt, co.expected_ship_dt,
    co.ship_dt) best_date
  FROM cust_order co
  WHERE co.order_dt > TRUNC(SYSDATE, 'MONTH')
    AND co.cancelled_dt IS NULL) orders
ORDER BY orders.best_date;
```

Stored Functions and Views

Since a view is nothing more than a stored query and stored functions can be called from the SELECT clause of a query, columns of a view can map to stored function calls. This is an excellent way to shield your user community from complexity, and it has another interesting benefit as well. Consider the following view definition, which includes calls to several different stored functions:

```
CREATE OR REPLACE VIEW vw_example
  (col1, col2, col3, col4, col5, col6, col7, col8)
AS SELECT t1.col1,
  t1.col2,
  t2.col3,
  t2.col4,
  pkg_example.func1(t1.col1, t2.col3),
  pkg_example.func2(t1.col2, t2.col4),
  pkg_example.func3(t1.col1, t2.col3),
  pkg_example.func4(t1.col2, t2.col4)
FROM tab1 t1, tab2 t2
WHERE t1.col1 = t2.col3;
```

While the first four columns of the view map to columns of the tab1 and tab2 tables, values for the remaining columns are generated by calling various functions in the pkg_example package. If one of your users executes the following query:

```
SELECT col2, col4, col7
FROM vw_example
WHERE col1 = 1001;
```

only one stored function (pkg_example.func3) is actually executed even though the view contains four columns that map to stored function calls. This is because when a query is executed against a view, the Oracle server constructs a new query by combining the original query and the view definition. In this case, the query that is actually executed looks as follows:

```
SELECT t1.col2,
    t2.col4,
    pkg_example.func3(t1.col1, t2.col3)
FROM tab1 t1, tab2 t2
WHERE t1.col1 = 1001 AND t1.col1 = t2.col3;
```

Therefore, your view could contain dozens of stored function calls, but only those that are explicitly referenced by queries will be executed.*

Avoiding Table Joins

Imagine that you have deployed a set of views for your users to generate reports and ad-hoc queries against, and one of your users asks that a new column be added to one of the views. The column is from a table not yet included in the FROM clause, and the column is only needed for a single report issued once a month. You could add the table to the FROM clause, add the column to the SELECT clause, and add the join conditions to the WHERE clause. However, every query issued against the view would include the new table, even though most queries don't reference the new column.

An alternative strategy is to write a stored function that queries the new table and returns the desired column. The stored function can then be added to the SELECT clause without the need to add the new table to the FROM clause. To illustrate, let's expand on the previous simple example. If the desired column is col6 in the tab3 table, you could add a new function to the pkg_example package such as:

```
FUNCTION func5(param1 IN NUMBER) RETURN VARCHAR2 IS
  ret_val VARCHAR2(20);
BEGIN
  SELECT col6 INTO ret_val
  FROM tab3
  WHERE col5 = param1;

  RETURN ret_val;
EXCEPTION
  WHEN NO_DATA_FOUND THEN
    RETURN null;
END func5;
```

---

* This is one reason why you should never use SELECT * when working with a view. Always explicitly name the columns that you need so that the server doesn't waste time generating data that you never reference.

You can now add a column to the view that maps to the new function, as in:

```
CREATE OR REPLACE VIEW vw_example
  (col1, col2, col3, col4, col5, col6, col7, col8, col9)
AS SELECT t1.col1,
  t1.col2,
  t2.col3,
  t2.col4,
  pkg_example.func1(t1.col1, t2.col3),
  pkg_example.func2(t1.col2, t2.col4),
  pkg_example.func3(t1.col1, t2.col3),
  pkg_example.func4(t1.col2, t2.col4),
  pkg_example.func5(t2.col3)
FROM tab1 t1, tab2 t2
WHERE t1.col1 = t2.col3;
```

Thus, you have provided your users access to column col6 of the tab3 table without adding the tab3 table to the view's FROM clause. Users who don't reference the new col9 column of the view will experience no changes to the performance of their queries against vw_example.

Even though the column was originally targeted for a single report, don't be surprised if other users decide to include the new column in their queries. As the column utilization increases, it may be advantageous to abandon the stored function strategy and include the tab3 table in the FROM clause. Since a view was employed, however, you would be able to make this change without the need for any of your users to modify their queries.

Restrictions on Calling PL/SQL from SQL

While calling stored functions from SQL is a powerful feature, it is important to understand how doing so might have unintended consequences. For example, imagine that one of your co-workers has written a stored function that, given a part number, returns the number of times that part is included in all open orders. The function is contained in a utilities package such as the following:

```
CREATE OR REPLACE PACKAGE pkg_util AS
  FUNCTION get_part_order_qty(pno IN VARCHAR2) RETURN NUMBER;
END pkg_util;
```

You have been tasked with generating a weekly inventory report, and you would like to make use of the function in one of your queries, as in:

```
SELECT p.part_nbr, p.name, s.name, p.inventory_qty,
  pkg_util.get_part_order_qty(p.part_nbr) open_order_qty
FROM part p, supplier s
WHERE p.supplier_id = s.supplier_id
ORDER BY s.name, p.part_nbr;
```

When you run the query, however, you are surprised to see the following error:

```
ORA-14551: cannot perform a DML operation inside a query
```

Upon checking the package body, you find that the get_part_order_qty function, along with calculating the number of times a part is included in all open orders, generates a request to restock the part by inserting a record into the part_order table if the calculated value exceeds the number in inventory. Had Oracle allowed your statement to be executed, your query would have resulted in changes to the database without your knowledge or consent.

Purity Level

In order to determine whether a stored function might have unintended consequences when called from an SQL statement, Oracle assigns a *purity level* to the function that answers the following four questions:

1. Does the function read from database tables?
2. Does the function reference any global package variables?
3. Does the function write to any database tables?
4. Does the function modify any global package variables?

For each negative response to these questions, a designation is added to the purity level, as shown in Table 11-1.

Table 11-1. Purity level designations

Question #	Designation	Description
1	RNDS	Reads no database state
2	RNPS	Reads no package state
3	WNDS	Writes no database state
4	WNPS	Writes no package state

Therefore, a function with a purity level of {WNPS, WNDS} is guaranteed not to write to the database or modify package variables, but it may reference package variables and/or read from database tables. In order for a function to be called from an SQL statement, its purity level must at a minimum include the WNDS designation.

When using packaged functions in Oracle versions prior to release 8.1, it was required that the purity level be specified prior to calling a function from an SQL statement. This is accomplished by adding a *pragma*, or compiler directive, to the package specification. The RESTRICT_REFERENCES pragma follows the function declaration in the package specification, as demonstrated here:

```
CREATE OR REPLACE PACKAGE my_pkg AS
  FUNCTION my_func(arg1 IN NUMBER) RETURN VARCHAR2;
  PRAGMA RESTRICT_REFERENCES(my_func, RNPS, WNPS, WNDS);
END my_pkg;
```

When the package body is compiled, the code is checked against the designations listed in the RESTRICT_REFERENCES pragma. If the code does not meet the purity level asserted in the pragma, compilation fails with the following error:

```
PLS-00452: Subprogram 'MY_FUNC' violates its associated pragma
```

Therefore, you tell the compiler what your function will and won't do via the RESTRICT_REFERENCES pragma, the compiler checks that you are telling it the truth, and you are then free to call the function in any way supported by the function's purity level without further intervention from Oracle. If, on the other hand, your function was not included in a package, the Oracle engine would have no way to check the function's purity level prior to it being called, and Oracle would be forced to check the function's logic for side effects every time it is called.

 The ability to assert a purity level is another reason to use packages for all your PL/SQL programming needs. Purity levels cannot be asserted for standalone procedures and functions.

Beginning with Oracle8i, you are no longer required to specify the purity level of functions in the package specification. If you choose not to, your functions will be checked each time they are called from SQL statements to ensure that they meet the minimum requirements. Whenever possible, however, you should include the pragma in your package specification so that the code can be examined at compile time rather than each time it is executed.

Trust Me...

One of the reasons Oracle has relaxed the requirement that the purity level be asserted at compile time is that PL/SQL can make calls to functions written in C and Java, which have no mechanisms similar to PL/SQL's PRAGMA for asserting purity. In order to allow functions written in different languages to call each other, Oracle introduced the TRUST keyword in Oracle8i. Adding TRUST to the RESTRICT_REF-ERENCES pragma for a function causes Oracle to:

1. Treat the function as if it satisfies the pragma without actually checking the code.
2. Treat any functions or procedures called from the function that have the TRUST keyword as if they satisfy the pragma as well.

Thus, a stored function whose RESTRICT_REFERENCES pragma includes WNDS and TRUST could make calls to other PL/SQL functions that do not specify RESTRICT_REFERENCES pragmas and/or external C and Java functions and still be callable from SQL statements. In the case of external C or Java calls, you will need to include the TRUST designation in your function's RESTRICT_REFERENCES pragma if you want to call the function from SQL, since the C or Java source code is not available to the server for inspection.

To use TRUST, simply append it to the end of the purity designation list, as in:

```
CREATE OR REPLACE PACKAGE my_pkg AS
  FUNCTION my_func(arg1 IN NUMBER) RETURN VARCHAR2;
  PRAGMA RESTRICT_REFERENCES(my_func, RNPS, WNPS, WNDS, TRUST);
END my_pkg;
```

While you may be tempted to always use TRUST when asserting the purity level of your functions, this is a feature that should be used sparingly. Once you add the TRUST designation to your pragma, future changes to your function or any downstream functions that violate WNDS will not be caught at either compilation or runtime, causing your queries to have unintended consequences.

Other Restrictions

In addition to the WNDS requirement, Oracle checks that each function invoked from an SQL statement abides by the following rules:

1. The function can't end the current transaction using COMMIT or ROLLBACK.

2. The function can't alter a transaction by creating savepoints or rolling back to a previously-defined savepoint.

3. The function can't issue an ALTER SYSTEM or ALTER SESSION statement.

4. All parameter types, including the return type, must be standard SQL types such as VARCHAR2, NUMBER, and DATE. PL/SQL types such as BOOLEAN and RECORD, collection types such as VARRAY, and object types are not allowed.

The first three restrictions are designed to protect against changes that could alter the operational environment of the parent query. The fourth restriction might be relaxed in a future release of the Oracle server, but it's a bit of a stretch to imagine how calling a function that returns a nested table of objects would add value to a SELECT statement.[*]

Consistency Issues

All of the restrictions detailed earlier must be met in order to call a stored function from a query. There is one additional topic, however, that is not so much a restriction as a pitfall: queries executed by stored functions will see the effects of transactions committed since the parent query began execution, while the parent query will not. Whether this is due to a design flaw is open to debate. Depending on the database environment and length of your queries, the impact could range from nonexistent to severe.

---

[*] Unless it is wrapped in a TABLE expression in the FROM clause.

For example, if you are running reports at 2 P.M. against a data-mart that is loaded between 2 and 4 A.M., your stored functions will see the same data as the parent query as long as the query finishes execution before the next data load. On the other hand, a long-running query executed against an OLTP database during peak activity might yield severe inconsistencies between the results returned by the parent query and those returned by the stored functions. Therefore, you should carefully consider your operating environment and the expected query runtimes before including stored function calls in your SQL statements.

Stored Functions in DML Statements

Stored functions may also be called from INSERT, UPDATE, and DELETE statements. While most of the restrictions outlined earlier apply equally to stored functions called from DML statements, there is one major difference: since the parent DML statement is changing the state of the database, stored functions invoked from DML statements do not need to abide by the WNDS restriction. However, such stored functions may not read or modify the same table as the parent DML statement.

Like queries, DML statements may call stored functions where expressions are allowed, including:

- The VALUES clause of an INSERT statement.
- The SET clause of an UPDATE statement.
- The WHERE clause of an INSERT, UPDATE, or DELETE statement.

Any subqueries called from a DML statement may also call stored functions as well under the same set of restrictions as the parent DML statement.

Often, sets of complimentary stored functions are called from both queries and DML statements. For example, we saw earlier how the pkg_util.translate_date function could be called from a query to translate from the Oracle date format stored in the database to the format needed by a Java client. Similarly, the overloaded pkg_util.translate_date function may be used within an update statement to perform the reverse translation, as in:

```
UPDATE cust_order
SET expected_ship_dt = pkg_util.translate_date(:1)
WHERE order_nbr = :2;
```

where :1 and :2 are placeholders for the UTC timedate and order number passed in by the Java client.

Stored functions may also be used in the WHERE clause in place of correlated subqueries, both to simplify the DML statement and to facilitate code reuse. For example, suppose you have been asked to push the expected ship date by five days for any order containing part number F34-17802. You could issue an UPDATE statement against the cust_order table using a correlated subquery, as in:

```
UPDATE cust_order co
SET co.expected_ship_dt = NVL(co.expected_ship_dt, SYSDATE) + 5
WHERE co.cancelled_dt IS NULL and co.ship_dt IS NULL
  AND EXISTS (SELECT 1 FROM line_item li
    WHERE li.order_nbr = co.order_nbr
      AND li.part_nbr = 'F34-17802');
```

After having written many subqueries against the line_item table, however, you feel it's time to write a multipurpose function and add it to the pkg_util package:

```
FUNCTION get_part_count(ordno IN NUMBER,
    partno IN VARCHAR2 DEFAULT NULL, max_cnt IN NUMBER DEFAULT 9999)
    RETURN NUMBER IS
    tot_cnt NUMBER(5) := 0;
    li_part_nbr VARCHAR2(20);
    CURSOR cur_li(c_ordno IN NUMBER) IS
      SELECT part_nbr
      FROM line_item
      WHERE order_nbr = c_ordno;
BEGIN
  OPEN cur_li(ordno);
  WHILE tot_cnt < max_cnt LOOP
    FETCH cur_li INTO li_part_nbr;
    EXIT WHEN cur_li%NOTFOUND;

    IF partno IS NULL OR
      (partno IS NOT NULL AND partno = li_part_nbr) THEN
      tot_cnt := tot_cnt + 1;
    END IF;
  END LOOP;
  CLOSE cur_li;

  RETURN tot_cnt;
END get_part_count;
```

The function may be used for multiple purposes, including:

1. To count the number of line items in a given order.

2. To count the number of line items in a given order containing a given part.

3. To determine whether the given order has at least X occurrences of a given part.

The UPDATE statement may now use the function to locate open orders that have at least one occurrence of part F34-17802:

```
UPDATE cust_order co
SET co.expected_ship_dt = NVL(co.expected_ship_dt, SYSDATE) + 5
WHERE co.cancelled_dt IS NULL and co.ship_dt IS NULL
  AND 1 = pkg_util.get_part_count(co.order_nbr, `F34-17802', 1);
```

The SQL Inside Your PL/SQL

Now that we've explored calling PL/SQL from SQL, let's turn the tables and explore the use of SQL inside your PL/SQL code. SQL is great at manipulating large sets of data, but there are situations where you need to work with data at the row level. PL/SQL, with its looping and cursor control capabilities, allows the flexibility to work at the set level using SQL or at the row level using cursors. However, many PL/SQL programmers forego the power of SQL and do everything at the row level, even when it is unnecessary and time-consuming to do so.

As an analogy, imagine that you are working at a warehouse, and a large shipment of parts arrives on the loading dock. Your job is to separate the shipment by part type and distribute the pieces to different areas of the warehouse. To make your job easier, the warehouse owner has procured the best forklift money can buy. There are two possible strategies to employ:

1. Pick up one box at a time, determine the type, and drive it to the appropriate destination.

2. Spend some time analyzing the situation, determine that every box on a pallet is of the same type, and drive entire pallets to the appropriate destination.

While this analogy might be overly simplistic, it does serve to illustrate the difference between set operations and row operations. Allowing the Oracle server to manipulate large sets in a single operation can often yield a performance improvement of several orders of magnitude over manipulating one row at a time, especially on systems with multiple CPUs.

When a procedural language is used for database access (whether it is PL/SQL, C with OCI calls, or Java using JDBC), there is a tendency to employ strategy #1. Perhaps programmers are accustomed to coding at a low level of granularity when using a procedural language and this spills over into their data access logic. This situation is especially prevalent in systems that need to process and load large amounts of data from external files, such as data warehouse load utilities.

Imagine that you are charged with building an infrastructure to accept files from multiple OLTP systems, perform various data cleaning operations, and aggregate the data into a data warehouse. Using PL/SQL (or C, Java, C++, Cobol, etc.), you could build functionality that:

1. Opens a given file.

2. Reads a line, verifies/cleans the data, and updates the appropriate row of the appropriate fact table in the data warehouse.

3. Repeats #2 until the file is exhausted.

4. Closes the file.

While this approach might work for small files, it is not uncommon for large warehouses to receive feeds containing hundreds of thousands or millions of items. Even if your code is extremely efficient, processing a million-line file would take several hours.

Here's an alternate strategy that employs the power of the Oracle server to make quick work of large data feeds:

1. Create a staging table for each unique data feed file format.

2. At the start of the load process, truncate the staging tables.

3. Use SQL*Loader with the direct path option to quickly load the data file into the appropriate staging table.

4. Update all rows of the staging table to clean, verify, and transform data, marking rows as invalid if they fail verification. Perform the operation in parallel if possible.

5. Update the appropriate fact table using a subquery against the staging table. Again, perform in parallel if possible.

In order for this strategy to succeed, you need to have adequate disk space and sufficiently large rollback and temporary tablespaces. With adequate resources and properly constructed SQL statements, however, this strategy can yield a 10X improvement over the previous strategy.

So what role should PL/SQL play in such a scenario? In this case, PL/SQL would be an excellent vehicle for executing steps 4 and 5 of the previous list. Although the stored procedures might contain only a single update statement, the SQL is likely to be complex and may contain optimizer hints and other advanced features. Therefore, it would be advisable to isolate the SQL from the rest of the application so that it may be independently monitored and tuned.

In general, when dealing with complex logic involving large data sets, it is advantageous to think in terms of data sets rather than programming steps. In other words, ask yourself where your data is, where it needs to move to, and what needs to happen to it during its journey instead of thinking in terms of what needs to happen with each piece of data to satisfy the business requirements. If you follow this strategy, you will find yourself writing substantial, efficient SQL statements that employ PL/SQL where appropriate, rather than writing complex PL/SQL routines that employ SQL when needed. In doing so, you will be providing the server with the opportunity to split large workloads into multiple pieces that run in parallel, which can greatly improve performance.

CHAPTER 12

Advanced Group Operations

Group operations aggregate data over multiple rows. We discussed the GROUP BY clause and basic group operations in Chapter 4. Decision support systems require more complex group operations. Data warehousing applications involve aggregation over multiple dimensions of data. To enable effective decision support, you need to summarize transaction data at various levels. We discuss advanced group operations used by decision support systems in this chapter.

Oracle8*i* introduced several handy extensions to SQL's ability to summarize data. These include the following:

* A ROLLUP function to insert totals and subtotals into summarized results.
* A CUBE function to generate subtotals for all possible combinations of grouped columns.
* A GROUPING function to help correctly interpret results generated using CUBE and ROLLUP.

In Oracle9*i*, yet another function was introduced to generate summary information at a specific level: the GROUPING SETS function.

ROLLUP

In Chapter 4, you saw how the GROUP BY clause, along with the aggregate functions, can be used to produce summary results. For example, if you want to print the monthly total sales for each region, you would probably execute the following query:

```
SELECT R.NAME REGION,
       TO_CHAR(TO_DATE(O.MONTH, 'MM'), 'Month') MONTH, SUM(O.TOT_SALES)
FROM ORDERS O, REGION R
WHERE R.REGION_ID = O.REGION_ID
GROUP BY R.NAME, O.MONTH;


REGION               MONTH     SUM(O.TOT_SALES)
-------------------- --------- ----------------
Mid-Atlantic         January             610697
Mid-Atlantic         February            428676
```

Mid-Atlantic	March	637031
Mid-Atlantic	April	541146
Mid-Atlantic	May	592935
Mid-Atlantic	June	501485
Mid-Atlantic	July	606914
Mid-Atlantic	August	460520
Mid-Atlantic	September	392898
Mid-Atlantic	October	510117
Mid-Atlantic	November	532889
Mid-Atlantic	December	492458
New England	January	509215
New England	February	615746
New England	March	566483
New England	April	597622
New England	May	566285
New England	June	503354
New England	July	559334
New England	August	547656
New England	September	575589
New England	October	549648
New England	November	461395
New England	December	533314
SouthEast US	January	379021
SouthEast US	February	618423
SouthEast US	March	655993
SouthEast US	April	610017
SouthEast US	May	661094
SouthEast US	June	568572
SouthEast US	July	556992
SouthEast US	August	478765
SouthEast US	September	635211
SouthEast US	October	536841
SouthEast US	November	553866
SouthEast US	December	613700

```
36 rows selected.
```

As expected, this report prints the total sales for each region and month combination. However, in a more complex application, you may also want to have the subtotal for each region over all months, along with the total for all regions, or you may want the subtotal for each month over all regions, along with the total for all months. In short, you may need to generate subtotals and totals at more than one level.

Using UNION (The Old Way)

In data warehouse applications, you frequently need to generate summary information over various dimensions, and subtotal and total across those dimensions. Generating and retrieving this type of summary information is a core goal of almost all data warehouse applications.

By this time, you have realized that a simple GROUP BY query is not sufficient to generate the subtotals and totals described in this section. In order to illustrate the complexity of the problem, let's attempt to write a query that would return the following in a single output:

- Sales for each month for every region
- Subtotals over all months for every region
- Total sales for all regions over all months

One way to generate multiple levels of summary (the only way prior to Oracle8*i*) is to write a UNION query. For example, the following UNION query will give us the desired three levels of subtotals:

```
SELECT R.NAME REGION,
       TO_CHAR(TO_DATE(O.MONTH, 'MM'), 'Month') MONTH, SUM(O.TOT_SALES)
FROM ORDERS O, REGION R
WHERE R.REGION_ID = O.REGION_ID
GROUP BY R.NAME, O.MONTH
UNION ALL
SELECT R.NAME REGION, NULL, SUM(O.TOT_SALES)
FROM ORDERS O, REGION R
WHERE R.REGION_ID = O.REGION_ID
GROUP BY R.NAME
UNION ALL
SELECT NULL, NULL, SUM(O.TOT_SALES)
FROM ORDERS O, REGION R
WHERE R.REGION_ID = O.REGION_ID;
```

```
REGION                MONTH     SUM(O.TOT_SALES)
--------------------  --------- ----------------
Mid-Atlantic          January             610697
Mid-Atlantic          February            428676
Mid-Atlantic          March               637031
Mid-Atlantic          April               541146
Mid-Atlantic          May                 592935
Mid-Atlantic          June                501485
Mid-Atlantic          July                606914
Mid-Atlantic          August              460520
Mid-Atlantic          September           392898
Mid-Atlantic          October             510117
Mid-Atlantic          November            532889
Mid-Atlantic          December            492458
New England           January             509215
New England           February            615746
New England           March               566483
New England           April               597622
New England           May                 566285
New England           June                503354
New England           July                559334
New England           August              547656
New England           September           575589
New England           October             549648
New England           November            461395
New England           December            533314
SouthEast US          January             379021
```

SouthEast US	February	618423
SouthEast US	March	655993
SouthEast US	April	610017
SouthEast US	May	661094
SouthEast US	June	568572
SouthEast US	July	556992
SouthEast US	August	478765
SouthEast US	September	635211
SouthEast US	October	536841
SouthEast US	November	553866
SouthEast US	December	613700
Mid-Atlantic		6307766
New England		6585641
SouthEast US		6868495
		19761902

40 rows selected.

This query produced 40 rows of output, 36 of which are the sales for each month for every region. The last 4 rows are the subtotals and the total. The three rows with region names and NULL values for the month are the subtotals for each region over all the months, and the last row with NULL values for both the region and month is the total sales for all the regions over all the months.

Now that you have the desired result, try to analyze the query a bit. You have a very small orders table with only 720 rows in this example. You wanted to have summary information over just two dimensions—region and month. You have 3 regions and 12 months. To get the desired summary information from this table, you have to write a query consisting of 3 SELECT statements combined together using UNION ALL. The EXPLAIN PLAN on this query is:

```
Query Plan
----------------------------------------
SELECT STATEMENT    Cost = 15
  UNION-ALL
    SORT GROUP BY
      HASH JOIN
        TABLE ACCESS FULL REGION
        TABLE ACCESS FULL ORDERS
    SORT GROUP BY
      HASH JOIN
        TABLE ACCESS FULL REGION
        TABLE ACCESS FULL ORDERS
    SORT AGGREGATE
      NESTED LOOPS
        TABLE ACCESS FULL ORDERS
        INDEX UNIQUE SCAN PK7
```

14 rows selected.

As indicated by the EXPLAIN PLAN output, Oracle needs to perform the following operations to get the results:

- Three FULL TABLE scans on ORDERS
- Two FULL TABLE scans on REGION
- One INDEX scan on PK7 (Primary key of table REGION)
- Two HASH JOINs
- One NESTED LOOP JOIN
- Two SORT GROUP BY operations
- One SORT AGGREGATE operation
- One UNION ALL

In any practical application the orders table will consist of hundreds of thousands of rows, and performing all these operations would be time-consuming. Even worse, if you have more dimensions for which to prepare summary information than the two shown in this example, you have to write an even more complex query. The bottom line is that such a query badly hurts performance.

Using ROLLUP (The New Way)

Oracle8*i* introduced several new features for generating multiple levels of summary information with one query. One such feature is a set of extensions to the GROUP BY clause. In Oracle8*i*, the GROUP BY clause comes with two extensions: ROLLUP and CUBE. Oracle9*i* introduces another extension: GROUPING SETS. We discuss ROLLUP in this section. CUBE and GROUPING SETS are discussed later in this chapter.

ROLLUP is an extension to the GROUP BY clause, and therefore can only appear in a query with a GROUP BY clause. The ROLLUP operation groups the selected rows based on the expressions in the GROUP BY clause, and prepares a summary row for each group. The syntax of ROLLUP is:

```
SELECT ...
FROM ...
GROUP BY ROLLUP (ordered list of grouping columns)
```

Using ROLLUP, you can generate the summary information discussed at the beginning of this section in a much easier way than in our UNION ALL query. For example:

```
SELECT R.NAME REGION,
       TO_CHAR(TO_DATE(O.MONTH, 'MM'), 'Month') MONTH, SUM(O.TOT_SALES)
FROM ORDERS O, REGION R
WHERE R.REGION_ID = O.REGION_ID
GROUP BY ROLLUP (R.NAME, O.MONTH);

REGION               MONTH     SUM(O.TOT_SALES)
-------------------- --------- ----------------
Mid-Atlantic         January             610697
Mid-Atlantic         February            428676
Mid-Atlantic         March               637031
Mid-Atlantic         April               541146
Mid-Atlantic         May                 592935
```

```
Mid-Atlantic        June               501485
Mid-Atlantic        July               606914
Mid-Atlantic        August             460520
Mid-Atlantic        September          392898
Mid-Atlantic        October            510117
Mid-Atlantic        November           532889
Mid-Atlantic        December           492458
Mid-Atlantic                          6307766
New England         January            509215
New England         February           615746
New England         March              566483
New England         April              597622
New England         May                566285
New England         June               503354
New England         July               559334
New England         August             547656
New England         September          575589
New England         October            549648
New England         November           461395
New England         December           533314
New England                           6585641
SouthEast US        January            379021
SouthEast US        February           618423
SouthEast US        March              655993
SouthEast US        April              610017
SouthEast US        May                661094
SouthEast US        June               568572
SouthEast US        July               556992
SouthEast US        August             478765
SouthEast US        September          635211
SouthEast US        October            536841
SouthEast US        November           553866
SouthEast US        December           613700
SouthEast US                          6868495
                                      19761902

40 rows selected.
```

As you can see in this output, the ROLLUP operation produced subtotals across the specified dimensions and a grand total. The argument to the ROLLUP operation is an ordered list of grouping columns. Since the ROLLUP operation is used in conjunction with the GROUP BY clause, it first generates aggregate values based on the GROUP BY operation on the ordered list of columns. Then it generates higher level subtotals and finally a grand total. ROLLUP not only simplifies the query, it results in more efficient execution. The explain plan for this ROLLUP query is as follows:

```
Query Plan
---------------------------------------
SELECT STATEMENT    Cost = 7
  SORT GROUP BY ROLLUP
    HASH JOIN
      TABLE ACCESS FULL REGION
      TABLE ACCESS FULL ORDERS
```

Rather than the multiple table scans, joins, and other operations required by the UNION version of the query, the ROLLUP query needs just one full table scan on REGION, one full table scan on ORDERS, and one join to generate the required output.

If you want to generate subtotals for each month instead of for each region, all you need to do is change the order of columns in the ROLLUP operation, as in the following example:

```
SELECT R.NAME REGION,
TO_CHAR(TO_DATE(O.MONTH, 'MM'), 'Month') MONTH, SUM(O.TOT_SALES)
FROM ORDERS O, REGION R
WHERE R.REGION_ID = O.REGION_ID
GROUP BY ROLLUP (O.MONTH, R.NAME);
```

REGION	MONTH	SUM(O.TOT_SALES)
Mid-Atlantic	January	610697
New England	January	509215
SouthEast US	January	379021
	January	1498933
Mid-Atlantic	February	428676
New England	February	615746
SouthEast US	February	618423
	February	1662845
Mid-Atlantic	March	637031
New England	March	566483
SouthEast US	March	655993
	March	1859507
Mid-Atlantic	April	541146
New England	April	597622
SouthEast US	April	610017
	April	1748785
Mid-Atlantic	May	592935
New England	May	566285
SouthEast US	May	661094
	May	1820314
Mid-Atlantic	June	501485
New England	June	503354
SouthEast US	June	568572
	June	1573411
Mid-Atlantic	July	606914
New England	July	559334
SouthEast US	July	556992
	July	1723240
Mid-Atlantic	August	460520
New England	August	547656
SouthEast US	August	478765
	August	1486941
Mid-Atlantic	September	392898
New England	September	575589
SouthEast US	September	635211
	September	1603698
Mid-Atlantic	October	510117
New England	October	549648

SouthEast US	October	536841	
	October	1596606	
Mid-Atlantic	November	532889	
New England	November	461395	
SouthEast US	November	553866	
	November	1548150	
Mid-Atlantic	December	492458	
New England	December	533314	
SouthEast US	December	613700	
	December	1639472	
		19761902	

49 rows selected.

Adding dimensions does not result in additional complexity. The following query rolls up subtotals for the region, the month, and the year for the first quarter:

```
SELECT O.YEAR, TO_CHAR(TO_DATE(O.MONTH, 'MM'), 'Month') MONTH,
R.NAME REGION, SUM(O.TOT_SALES)
FROM ORDERS O, REGION R
WHERE R.REGION_ID = O.REGION_ID
AND O.MONTH BETWEEN 1 AND 3
GROUP BY ROLLUP (O.YEAR, O.MONTH, R.NAME);
```

YEAR	MONTH	REGION	SUM(O.TOT_SALES)
2000	January	Mid-Atlantic	1221394
2000	January	New England	1018430
2000	January	SouthEast US	758042
2000	January		2997866
2000	February	Mid-Atlantic	857352
2000	February	New England	1231492
2000	February	SouthEast US	1236846
2000	February		3325690
2000	March	Mid-Atlantic	1274062
2000	March	New England	1132966
2000	March	SouthEast US	1311986
2000	March		3719014
2000			10042570
2001	January	Mid-Atlantic	610697
2001	January	New England	509215
2001	January	SouthEast US	379021
2001	January		1498933
2001	February	Mid-Atlantic	428676
2001	February	New England	615746
2001	February	SouthEast US	618423
2001	February		1662845
2001	March	Mid-Atlantic	637031
2001	March	New England	566483
2001	March	SouthEast US	655993
2001	March		1859507
2001			5021285
			15063855

27 rows selected.

Generating Partial ROLLUPs

In a ROLLUP query with N dimensions, the grand total is considered the top level. The various subtotal rows of N-1 dimensions constitute the next lower level, the subtotal rows of (N-2) dimensions constitute yet another level down, and so on. In the most recent example, you have three dimensions (year, month, and region), and the total row is the top level. The subtotal rows for the year represent the next lower level, because these rows are subtotals across two dimensions (month and region). The subtotal rows for the year and month combination are one level lower, because these rows are subtotals across one dimension (region). The rest of the rows are the result of the regular GROUP BY operation (without ROLLUP), and form the lowest level.

If you want to exclude some subtotals and totals from the ROLLUP output, you can only move top to bottom, i.e., exclude the top-level total first, then progressively go down to the next level subtotals, and so on. To do this, you have to take out one or more columns from the ROLLUP operation, and put them in the GROUP BY clause. This is called a *partial ROLLUP*.

As an example of a partial ROLLUP, let's see what happens when you take out the first column, which is O.YEAR, from the previous ROLLUP operation and move it into the GROUP BY clause.

```
SELECT O.YEAR, TO_CHAR(TO_DATE(O.MONTH, 'MM'), 'Month') MONTH,
R.NAME REGION, SUM(O.TOT_SALES)
FROM ORDERS O, REGION R
WHERE R.REGION_ID = O.REGION_ID
AND O.MONTH BETWEEN 1 AND 3
GROUP BY O.YEAR ROLLUP (O.MONTH, R.NAME);
```

YEAR	MONTH	REGION	SUM(O.TOT_SALES)
2000	January	Mid-Atlantic	1221394
2000	January	New England	1018430
2000	January	SouthEast US	758042
2000	January		2997866
2000	February	Mid-Atlantic	857352
2000	February	New England	1231492
2000	February	SouthEast US	1236846
2000	February		3325690
2000	March	Mid-Atlantic	1274062
2000	March	New England	1132966
2000	March	SouthEast US	1311986
2000	March		3719014
2000			10042570
2001	January	Mid-Atlantic	610697
2001	January	New England	509215
2001	January	SouthEast US	379021
2001	January		1498933
2001	February	Mid-Atlantic	428676
2001	February	New England	615746
2001	February	SouthEast US	618423

```
2001 February                                    1662845
2001 March       Mid-Atlantic                     637031
2001 March       New England                      566483
2001 March       SouthEast US                     655993
2001 March                                        1859507
2001                                              5021285
```

26 rows selected.

The query in this example excludes the grand-total row from the output. By taking out O.YEAR from the ROLLUP operation, you are asking the database not to roll up summary information over the years. Therefore, the database rolls up summary information on region and month. When you proceed to remove O.MONTH from the ROLLUP operation, the query will not generate the roll up summary for the month dimension, and only the region-level subtotals will be printed in the output. For example:

```
SELECT O.YEAR, TO_CHAR(TO_DATE(O.MONTH, 'MM'), 'Month') MONTH,
R.NAME REGION, SUM(O.TOT_SALES)
FROM ORDERS O, REGION R
WHERE R.REGION_ID = O.REGION_ID
AND O.MONTH BETWEEN 1 AND 3
GROUP BY O.YEAR, O.MONTH ROLLUP (R.NAME);
```

YEAR	MONTH	REGION	SUM(O.TOT_SALES)
2000	January	Mid-Atlantic	1221394
2000	January	New England	1018430
2000	January	SouthEast US	758042
2000	January		2997866
2000	February	Mid-Atlantic	857352
2000	February	New England	1231492
2000	February	SouthEast US	1236846
2000	February		3325690
2000	March	Mid-Atlantic	1274062
2000	March	New England	1132966
2000	March	SouthEast US	1311986
2000	March		3719014
2001	January	Mid-Atlantic	610697
2001	January	New England	509215
2001	January	SouthEast US	379021
2001	January		1498933
2001	February	Mid-Atlantic	428676
2001	February	New England	615746
2001	February	SouthEast US	618423
2001	February		1662845
2001	March	Mid-Atlantic	637031
2001	March	New England	566483
2001	March	SouthEast US	655993
2001	March		1859507

24 rows selected.

CUBE

The CUBE extension of the GROUP BY clause takes aggregation one step further than ROLLUP. The CUBE operation generates subtotals for all possible combinations of the grouping columns. Therefore, output of a CUBE operation will contain all subtotals produced by an equivalent ROLLUP operation and also some additional subtotals. For example, if you are performing ROLLUP on columns region and month, you will get subtotals for all months for each region, and a grand total. However, if you perform the corresponding CUBE, you will get:

- The regular rows produced by the GROUP BY clause
- Subtotals for all months on each region
- A subtotal for all regions on each month
- A grand total

Like ROLLUP, CUBE is an extension of the GROUP BY clause, and can appear in a query only along with a GROUP BY clause. The syntax of CUBE is:

```
SELECT ...
FROM ...
GROUP BY CUBE (list of grouping columns)
```

For example, the following query returns subtotals for all combinations of regions and months in the ORDER table:

```
SELECT R.NAME REGION, TO_CHAR(TO_DATE(O.MONTH, 'MM'), 'Month') MONTH,
SUM(O.TOT_SALES)
FROM ORDERS O, REGION R
WHERE R.REGION_ID = O.REGION_ID
GROUP BY CUBE(R.NAME, O.MONTH);
```

REGION	MONTH	SUM(O.TOT_SALES)
Mid-Atlantic	January	1832091
Mid-Atlantic	February	1286028
Mid-Atlantic	March	1911093
Mid-Atlantic	April	1623438
Mid-Atlantic	May	1778805
Mid-Atlantic	June	1504455
Mid-Atlantic	July	1820742
Mid-Atlantic	August	1381560
Mid-Atlantic	September	1178694
Mid-Atlantic	October	1530351
Mid-Atlantic	November	1598667
Mid-Atlantic	December	1477374
Mid-Atlantic		18923298
New England	January	1527645
New England	February	1847238
New England	March	1699449
New England	April	1792866
New England	May	1698855

New England	June	1510062
New England	July	1678002
New England	August	1642968
New England	September	1726767
New England	October	1648944
New England	November	1384185
New England	December	1599942
New England		19756923
SouthEast US	January	1137063
SouthEast US	February	1855269
SouthEast US	March	1967979
SouthEast US	April	1830051
SouthEast US	May	1983282
SouthEast US	June	1705716
SouthEast US	July	1670976
SouthEast US	August	1436295
SouthEast US	September	1905633
SouthEast US	October	1610523
SouthEast US	November	1661598
SouthEast US	December	1841100
SouthEast US		20605485
	January	4496799
	February	4988535
	March	5578521
	April	5246355
	May	5460942
	June	4720233
	July	5169720
	August	4460823
	September	4811094
	October	4789818
	November	4644450
	December	4918416
		59285706

52 rows selected.

Note that the output contains not only the subtotals for each region, but also the subtotals for each month. You can get the same result from a query without the CUBE operation. However, that query would be lengthy and complex and, of course, very inefficient. Such a query would look as follows:

```
SELECT R.NAME REGION, TO_CHAR(TO_DATE(O.MONTH, 'MM'), 'Month') MONTH,
SUM(O.TOT_SALES)
FROM ORDERS O, REGION R
WHERE R.REGION_ID = O.REGION_ID
GROUP BY R.NAME, O.MONTH
UNION ALL
SELECT R.NAME REGION, NULL, SUM(O.TOT_SALES)
FROM ORDERS O, REGION R
WHERE R.REGION_ID = O.REGION_ID
GROUP BY R.NAME
UNION ALL
```

```
SELECT NULL, TO_CHAR(TO_DATE(O.MONTH, 'MM'), 'Month') MONTH, SUM(O.TOT_SALES)
FROM ORDERS O, REGION R
WHERE R.REGION_ID = O.REGION_ID
GROUP BY O.MONTH
UNION ALL
SELECT NULL, NULL, SUM(O.TOT_SALES)
FROM ORDERS O, REGION R
WHERE R.REGION_ID = O.REGION_ID;
```

REGION	MONTH	SUM(O.TOT_SALES)
Mid-Atlantic	January	1832091
Mid-Atlantic	February	1286028
Mid-Atlantic	March	1911093
Mid-Atlantic	April	1623438
Mid-Atlantic	May	1778805
Mid-Atlantic	June	1504455
Mid-Atlantic	July	1820742
Mid-Atlantic	August	1381560
Mid-Atlantic	September	1178694
Mid-Atlantic	October	1530351
Mid-Atlantic	November	1598667
Mid-Atlantic	December	1477374
New England	January	1527645
New England	February	1847238
New England	March	1699449
New England	April	1792866
New England	May	1698855
New England	June	1510062
New England	July	1678002
New England	August	1642968
New England	September	1726767
New England	October	1648944
New England	November	1384185
New England	December	1599942
SouthEast US	January	1137063
SouthEast US	February	1855269
SouthEast US	March	1967979
SouthEast US	April	1830051
SouthEast US	May	1983282
SouthEast US	June	1705716
SouthEast US	July	1670976
SouthEast US	August	1436295
SouthEast US	September	1905633
SouthEast US	October	1610523
SouthEast US	November	1661598
SouthEast US	December	1841100
Mid-Atlantic		18923298
New England		19756923
SouthEast US		20605485
	January	4496799
	February	4988535
	March	5578521

```
                April            5246355
                May              5460942
                June             4720233
                July             5169720
                August           4460823
                September        4811094
                October          4789818
                November         4644450
                December         4918416
                                59285706
```

52 rows selected.

Since a CUBE produces aggregate results for all possible combinations of the grouping columns, the output of a query using CUBE is independent of the order of columns in the CUBE operation, if everything else remains the same. This is not the case with ROLLUP. If everything else in the query remains the same, ROLLUP(a,b) will produce a slightly different result set than ROLLUP(b,a). However, the result set of CUBE(a,b) will be the same as that of CUBE(b,a). The following example illustrates this by taking the example of the beginning of this section and reversing the order of columns in the CUBE operation.

```
SELECT R.NAME REGION, TO_CHAR(TO_DATE(O.MONTH, 'MM'), 'Month') MONTH,
SUM(O.TOT_SALES)
FROM ORDERS O, REGION R
WHERE R.REGION_ID = O.REGION_ID
GROUP BY CUBE(O.MONTH, R.NAME);
```

REGION	MONTH	SUM(O.TOT_SALES)
Mid-Atlantic	January	1832091
New England	January	1527645
SouthEast US	January	1137063
	January	4496799
Mid-Atlantic	February	1286028
New England	February	1847238
SouthEast US	February	1855269
	February	4988535
Mid-Atlantic	March	1911093
New England	March	1699449
SouthEast US	March	1967979
	March	5578521
Mid-Atlantic	April	1623438
New England	April	1792866
SouthEast US	April	1830051
	April	5246355
Mid-Atlantic	May	1778805
New England	May	1698855
SouthEast US	May	1983282
	May	5460942
Mid-Atlantic	June	1504455
New England	June	1510062
SouthEast US	June	1705716

	June	4720233
Mid-Atlantic	July	1820742
New England	July	1678002
SouthEast US	July	1670976
	July	5169720
Mid-Atlantic	August	1381560
New England	August	1642968
SouthEast US	August	1436295
	August	4460823
Mid-Atlantic	September	1178694
New England	September	1726767
SouthEast US	September	1905633
	September	4811094
Mid-Atlantic	October	1530351
New England	October	1648944
SouthEast US	October	1610523
	October	4789818
Mid-Atlantic	November	1598667
New England	November	1384185
SouthEast US	November	1661598
	November	4644450
Mid-Atlantic	December	1477374
New England	December	1599942
SouthEast US	December	1841100
	December	4918416
Mid-Atlantic		18923298
New England		19756923
SouthEast US		20605485
		59285706

```
52 rows selected.
```

This query produced the same results as the earlier query; only the order of the rows is different.

To exclude some subtotals from the output, you can do a *partial CUBE*, (similar to a partial ROLLUP) by taking out column(s) from the CUBE operation and putting them into the GROUP BY clause. Here's an example:

```
SELECT R.NAME REGION, TO_CHAR(TO_DATE(O.MONTH, 'MM'), 'Month') MONTH,
SUM(O.TOT_SALES)
FROM ORDERS O, REGION R
WHERE R.REGION_ID = O.REGION_ID
GROUP BY R.NAME CUBE(O.MONTH);

REGION               MONTH     SUM(O.TOT_SALES)
-------------------- --------- ----------------
Mid-Atlantic         January           1832091
Mid-Atlantic         February          1286028
Mid-Atlantic         March             1911093
Mid-Atlantic         April             1623438
Mid-Atlantic         May               1778805
Mid-Atlantic         June              1504455
Mid-Atlantic         July              1820742
```

Mid-Atlantic	August	1381560
Mid-Atlantic	September	1178694
Mid-Atlantic	October	1530351
Mid-Atlantic	November	1598667
Mid-Atlantic	December	1477374
Mid-Atlantic		18923298
New England	January	1527645
New England	February	1847238
New England	March	1699449
New England	April	1792866
New England	May	1698855
New England	June	1510062
New England	July	1678002
New England	August	1642968
New England	September	1726767
New England	October	1648944
New England	November	1384185
New England	December	1599942
New England		19756923
SouthEast US	January	1137063
SouthEast US	February	1855269
SouthEast US	March	1967979
SouthEast US	April	1830051
SouthEast US	May	1983282
SouthEast US	June	1705716
SouthEast US	July	1670976
SouthEast US	August	1436295
SouthEast US	September	1905633
SouthEast US	October	1610523
SouthEast US	November	1661598
SouthEast US	December	1841100
SouthEast US		20605485

39 rows selected.

If you compare the results of the partial CUBE operation with that of the full CUBE operation, discussed at the beginning of this section, you will notice that the partial CUBE has excluded the subtotals for each month and the grand total from the output. If you want to retain the subtotals for each month, but want to exclude the subtotals for each region, you can swap the position of R.NAME and O.MONTH in the GROUP BY...CUBE clause, as shown here:

```
SELECT R.NAME REGION, TO_CHAR(TO_DATE(O.MONTH, 'MM'), 'Month') MONTH,
SUM(O.TOT_SALES)
FROM ORDERS O, REGION R
WHERE R.REGION_ID = O.REGION_ID
GROUP BY O.MONTH CUBE(R.NAME);
```

One interesting thing to note is that if you have one column in the CUBE operation, it produces the same result as the ROLLUP operation. Therefore, the following two queries produce identical results:

```
SELECT R.NAME REGION, TO_CHAR(TO_DATE(O.MONTH, 'MM'), 'Month') MONTH,
SUM(O.TOT_SALES)
```

```
FROM ORDERS O, REGION R
WHERE R.REGION_ID = O.REGION_ID
GROUP BY R.NAME CUBE(O.MONTH);

SELECT R.NAME REGION, TO_CHAR(TO_DATE(O.MONTH, 'MM'), 'Month') MONTH,
SUM(O.TOT_SALES)
FROM ORDERS O, REGION R
WHERE R.REGION_ID = O.REGION_ID
GROUP BY R.NAME ROLLUP(O.MONTH);
```

The GROUPING Function

ROLLUP and CUBE produce extra rows in the output that contain subtotals and totals. These rows contain NULL values for one or more columns. An output containing NULLs and indicating subtotals doesn't make sense to an ordinary person who is unaware of the behavior of ROLLUP and CUBE operations. Does your VP care about whether you used ROLLUP or CUBE or any other operation to get him the monthly total sales for each region? Obviously, he doesn't. That's exactly why you are reading this page and not your VP.

If you know your way around the NVL function, you would probably attempt to translate each NULL value from CUBE and ROLLUP to some descriptive value, as in the following example:

```
SELECT NVL(TO_CHAR(O.YEAR), 'All Years') YEAR,
NVL(TO_CHAR(TO_DATE(O.MONTH, 'MM'), 'Month'), 'First Quarter') MONTH,
NVL(R.NAME, 'All Regions') REGION, SUM(O.TOT_SALES)
FROM ORDERS O, REGION R
WHERE R.REGION_ID = O.REGION_ID
AND O.MONTH BETWEEN 1 AND 3
GROUP BY ROLLUP (O.YEAR, O.MONTH, R.NAME);
```

YEAR	MONTH	REGION	SUM(O.TOT_SALES)
2000	January	Mid-Atlantic	1221394
2000	January	New England	1018430
2000	January	SouthEast US	758042
2000	January	All Regions	2997866
2000	February	Mid-Atlantic	857352
2000	February	New England	1231492
2000	February	SouthEast US	1236846
2000	February	All Regions	3325690
2000	March	Mid-Atlantic	1274062
2000	March	New England	1132966
2000	March	SouthEast US	1311986
2000	March	All Regions	3719014
2000	First Quarter	All Regions	10042570
2001	January	Mid-Atlantic	610697
2001	January	New England	509215
2001	January	SouthEast US	379021
2001	January	All Regions	1498933

```
2001          February       Mid-Atlantic       428676
2001          February       New England        615746
2001          February       SouthEast US       618423
2001          February       All Regions       1662845
2001          March          Mid-Atlantic       637031
2001          March          New England        566483
2001          March          SouthEast US       655993
2001          March          All Regions       1859507
2001          First Quarter All Regions        5021285
All Years     First Quarter All Regions       15063855

27 rows selected.
```

The NVL function works pretty well for this example. However, if the data itself contains some NULL values, it becomes impossible to distinguish whether a NULL value represents unavailable data or a subtotal row. The NVL function will cause a problem in such a case. The following data can be used to illustrate this problem:

```
SELECT * FROM CUST_ORDER;

ORDER_NBR CUST_NBR SALES_EMP_ID SALE_PRICE ORDER_DT  EXPECTED_ STATUS
--------- -------- ------------ ---------- --------- --------- ----------
     1001      231         7354         99 22-JUL-01 23-JUL-01 DELIVERED
     1000      201         7354            19-JUL-01 24-JUL-01
     1002      255         7368            12-JUL-01 25-JUL-01
     1003      264         7368         56 16-JUL-01 26-JUL-01 DELIVERED
     1004      244         7368         34 18-JUL-01 27-JUL-01 PENDING
     1005      288         7368         99 22-JUL-01 24-JUL-01 DELIVERED
     1006      231         7354            22-JUL-01 28-JUL-01
     1007      255         7368         25 20-JUL-01 22-JUL-01 PENDING
     1008      255         7368         25 21-JUL-01 23-JUL-01 PENDING
     1009      231         7354         56 18-JUL-01 22-JUL-01 DELIVERED
     1012      231         7354         99 22-JUL-01 23-JUL-01 DELIVERED
     1011      201         7354            19-JUL-01 24-JUL-01
     1015      255         7368            12-JUL-01 25-JUL-01
     1017      264         7368         56 16-JUL-01 26-JUL-01 DELIVERED
     1019      244         7368         34 18-JUL-01 27-JUL-01 PENDING
     1021      288         7368         99 22-JUL-01 24-JUL-01 DELIVERED
     1023      231         7354            22-JUL-01 28-JUL-01
     1025      255         7368         25 20-JUL-01 22-JUL-01 PENDING
     1027      255         7368         25 21-JUL-01 23-JUL-01 PENDING
     1029      231         7354         56 18-JUL-01 22-JUL-01 DELIVERED

20 rows selected.
```

Note that the column STATUS contains NULL values. If you want the summary status of orders for each customer, and you executed the following query (note the application of NVL to the STATUS column), the output might surprise you.

```
SELECT NVL(TO_CHAR(CUST_NBR), 'All Customers') CUSTOMER,
NVL(STATUS, 'All Status') STATUS,
COUNT(*) FROM CUST_ORDER
GROUP BY CUBE(CUST_NBR, STATUS);
```

```
CUSTOMER              STATUS                  COUNT(*)
-------------------   --------------------    ----------
201                   All Status                     2
201                   All Status                     2
231                   DELIVERED                      4
231                   All Status                     2
231                   All Status                     6
244                   PENDING                        2
244                   All Status                     2
255                   PENDING                        4
255                   All Status                     2
255                   All Status                     6
264                   DELIVERED                      2
264                   All Status                     2
288                   DELIVERED                      2
288                   All Status                     2
All Customers         DELIVERED                      8
All Customers         PENDING                        6
All Customers         All Status                     6
All Customers         All Status                    20

18 rows selected.
```

This output doesn't make any sense. You stand a good chance of losing your job if you send this output to your VP. The problem is that any time the STATUS column legitimately contains a NULL value, the NVL function returns the string "All Status". Obviously, NVL isn't useful in this situation. However, don't worry—Oracle8i provides a solution to this problem through the GROUPING function.

The GROUPING function is used only in conjunction with either a ROLLUP or a CUBE operation. The GROUPING function takes a grouping column name as input and returns either 1 or 0. A 1 is returned if the value is NULL as the result of aggregation (ROLLUP or CUBE); otherwise, 0 is returned. The general syntax of the GROUPING function is:

```
SELECT ... [GROUPING(grouping_column_name)] ...
FROM ...
GROUP BY ... {ROLLUP | CUBE} (grouping_column_name)
```

The following example illustrates the use of GROUPING function in a simple way by returning the GROUPING function results for the three columns passed to ROLLUP:

```
SELECT O.YEAR, TO_CHAR(TO_DATE(O.MONTH, 'MM'), 'Month') MONTH,
R.NAME REGION, SUM(O.TOT_SALES),
GROUPING(O.YEAR) Y, GROUPING(O.MONTH) M, GROUPING(R.NAME) R
FROM ORDERS O, REGION R
WHERE R.REGION_ID = O.REGION_ID
AND O.MONTH BETWEEN 1 AND 3
GROUP BY ROLLUP (O.YEAR, O.MONTH, R.NAME);
```

```
YEAR MONTH     REGION                  SUM(O.TOT_SALES)    Y    M    R
---------- ---------  --------------------    -----------------  ---- ---- ----
2000 January  Mid-Atlantic                     1221394    0    0    0
2000 January  New England                      1018430    0    0    0
```

2000	January	SouthEast US	758042	0	0	0
2000	January		2997866	0	0	1
2000	February	Mid-Atlantic	857352	0	0	0
2000	February	New England	1231492	0	0	0
2000	February	SouthEast US	1236846	0	0	0
2000	February		3325690	0	0	1
2000	March	Mid-Atlantic	1274062	0	0	0
2000	March	New England	1132966	0	0	0
2000	March	SouthEast US	1311986	0	0	0
2000	March		3719014	0	0	1
2000			10042570	0	1	1
2001	January	Mid-Atlantic	610697	0	0	0
2001	January	New England	509215	0	0	0
2001	January	SouthEast US	379021	0	0	0
2001	January		1498933	0	0	1
2001	February	Mid-Atlantic	428676	0	0	0
2001	February	New England	615746	0	0	0
2001	February	SouthEast US	618423	0	0	0
2001	February		1662845	0	0	1
2001	March	Mid-Atlantic	637031	0	0	0
2001	March	New England	566483	0	0	0
2001	March	SouthEast US	655993	0	0	0
2001	March		1859507	0	0	1
2001			5021285	0	1	1
			15063855	1	1	1

27 rows selected.

Look at the Y, M, and R columns in this output. Row 4 is a region-level subtotal for a particular month and year, and therefore, the GROUPING function results in a value of 1 for the region and a value 0 for the month and year. Row 26 (the second to last) is a subtotal for all regions and months for a particular year, and therefore, the GROUPING function prints 1 for the month and the region and 0 for the year. Row 27 (the grand total) contains 1 for all the GROUPING columns.

With a combination of GROUPING and DECODE, you can produce more readable query output when using CUBE and ROLLUP, as in the following example:

```
SELECT DECODE(GROUPING(O.YEAR), 1, 'All Years', O.YEAR) Year,
DECODE(GROUPING(O.MONTH), 1, 'All Months',
TO_CHAR(TO_DATE(O.MONTH, 'MM'), 'Month')) Month,
DECODE(GROUPING(R.NAME), 1, 'All Regions', R.NAME) Region, SUM(O.TOT_SALES)
FROM ORDERS O, REGION R
WHERE R.REGION_ID = O.REGION_ID
AND O.MONTH BETWEEN 1 AND 3
GROUP BY ROLLUP (O.YEAR, O.MONTH, R.NAME);
```

YEAR	MONTH	REGION	SUM(O.TOT_SALES)
2000	January	Mid-Atlantic	1221394
2000	January	New England	1018430
2000	January	SouthEast US	758042
2000	January	All Regions	2997866

2000	February	Mid-Atlantic	857352
2000	February	New England	1231492
2000	February	SouthEast US	1236846
2000	February	All Regions	3325690
2000	March	Mid-Atlantic	1274062
2000	March	New England	1132966
2000	March	SouthEast US	1311986
2000	March	All Regions	3719014
2000	All Months	All Regions	10042570
2001	January	Mid-Atlantic	610697
2001	January	New England	509215
2001	January	SouthEast US	379021
2001	January	All Regions	1498933
2001	February	Mid-Atlantic	428676
2001	February	New England	615746
2001	February	SouthEast US	618423
2001	February	All Regions	1662845
2001	March	Mid-Atlantic	637031
2001	March	New England	566483
2001	March	SouthEast US	655993
2001	March	All Regions	1859507
2001	All Months	All Regions	5021285
All Years	All Months	All Regions	15063855

```
27 rows selected.
```

By using DECODE with GROUPING, you produced the same result that was produced by using NVL at the beginning of the section. However, the risk of mistreating a NULL data value as a summary row is eliminated by using GROUPING and DECODE. You will notice this in the following example, in which NULL data values in subtotal and total rows are treated differently by the GROUPING function than the NULL values in the summary rows.

```
SELECT DECODE(GROUPING(CUST_NBR), 1, 'All Customers', CUST_NBR) CUSTOMER,
DECODE(GROUPING(STATUS), 1, 'All Status', STATUS) STATUS, COUNT(*)
FROM CUST_ORDER
GROUP BY CUBE(CUST_NBR, STATUS);
```

CUSTOMER	STATUS	COUNT(*)
201		2
201	All Status	2
231	DELIVERED	4
231		2
231	All Status	6
244	PENDING	2
244	All Status	2
255	PENDING	4
255		2
255	All Status	6
264	DELIVERED	2
264	All Status	2
288	DELIVERED	2

```
288                          All Status              2
All Customers                DELIVERED               8
All Customers                PENDING                 6
All Customers                                        6
All Customers                All Status             20
```

18 rows selected.

 Oracle9*i* introduced two new functions that are related to GROUP-
ING: GROUPING_ID and GROUP_ID, discussed later in the section
titled "Oracle 9*i* Grouping Features." They are worth knowing about
if you are using Oracle9*i*.

GROUPING SETS

Earlier in this chapter, you saw how to generate summary information using ROL-
LUP and CUBE. However, the output of ROLLUP and CUBE include the rows produced by the regular GROUP BY operation along with the summary rows. Oracle9*i*
introduces another extension to the GROUP BY clause called GROUPING SETS that
you can use to generate summary information at the level you choose without
including all the rows produced by the regular GROUP BY operation.

Like ROLLUP and CUBE, GROUPING SETS is also an extension of the GROUP BY
clause, and can appear in a query only along with a GROUP BY clause. The syntax of
GROUPING SETS is:

```
SELECT ...
FROM ...
GROUP BY GROUPING SETS (list of grouping columns)
```

Let's take an example to understand the GROUPING SETS operation further.

```
SELECT O.YEAR, TO_CHAR(TO_DATE(O.MONTH, 'MM'), 'Month') MONTH,
R.NAME REGION, SUM(O.TOT_SALES)
FROM ORDERS O, REGION R
WHERE R.REGION_ID = O.REGION_ID
AND O.MONTH BETWEEN 1 AND 3
GROUP BY GROUPING SETS (O.YEAR, O.MONTH, R.NAME);
```

```
    YEAR MONTH     REGION                 SUM(O.TOT_SALES)
---------- --------- -------------------- ----------------
    2000                                          10042570
    2001                                           5021285
         January                                   4496799
         February                                  4988535
         March                                     5578521
                   Mid-Atlantic                    5029212
                   New England                     5074332
                   SouthEast US                    4960311
```

8 rows selected.

Note that the output contains only the subtotals at the region, month, and year levels, but that none of the normal, more detailed, GROUP BY data is included. The order of columns in the GROUPING SETS operation is not critical. The operation produces the same output regardless of the order of the columns, except that the sequence of the rows in the output will be as per the sequence of the columns in the GROUPING operation. For example, if you alter the order of the columns from (O.YEAR, O.MONTH, R.NAME) to (O.MONTH, R.NAME, O.YEAR), the summary rows for the month will be displayed first, followed by the summary rows for the region, and then the summary rows for the year. For example:

```
SELECT O.YEAR, TO_CHAR(TO_DATE(O.MONTH, 'MM'), 'Month') MONTH,
R.NAME REGION, SUM(O.TOT_SALES)
FROM ORDERS O, REGION R
WHERE R.REGION_ID = O.REGION_ID
AND O.MONTH BETWEEN 1 AND 3
GROUP BY GROUPING SETS (O.MONTH, R.NAME, O.YEAR);
```

YEAR	MONTH	REGION	SUM(O.TOT_SALES)
	January		4496799
	February		4988535
	March		5578521
		Mid-Atlantic	5029212
		New England	5074332
		SouthEast US	4960311
2000			10042570
2001			5021285

```
8 rows selected.
```

Oracle9i Grouping Features

The grouping examples you have seen so far represent simple ways of aggregating data using the extensions of the GROUP BY clause. Oracle9i provides ways to aggregate data for more complex requirements. The next sections discuss these features in detail:

- Repeating column names in the GROUP BY clause
- Grouping on composite columns
- Concatenated groupings
- The GROUPING_ID and GROUP_ID functions

Repeating Column Names in the GROUP BY Clause

In Oracle8i, repeating column names are not allowed in a GROUP BY clause. If the GROUP BY clause contains an extension (i.e., ROLLUP or CUBE), you cannot use the same column inside the extension as well as outside the extension. The following SQL will be invalid in Oracle8*i* and throw an error:

```
SELECT O.YEAR, TO_CHAR(TO_DATE(O.MONTH, 'MM'), 'Month') MONTH,
R.NAME REGION, SUM(O.TOT_SALES) Total
FROM ORDERS O, REGION R
WHERE R.REGION_ID = O.REGION_ID
AND O.MONTH BETWEEN 1 AND 3
GROUP BY O.YEAR, ROLLUP (O.YEAR, O.MONTH, R.NAME);
GROUP BY O.YEAR, ROLLUP (O.YEAR, O.MONTH, R.NAME)
                        *
ERROR at line 6:
ORA-30490: Ambiguous expression in GROUP BY ROLLUP or CUBE list
```

However, the same query works in Oracle9*i*:

```
SELECT O.YEAR, TO_CHAR(TO_DATE(O.MONTH, 'MM'), 'Month') MONTH,
R.NAME REGION, SUM(O.TOT_SALES) TOTAL
FROM ORDERS O, REGION R
WHERE R.REGION_ID = O.REGION_ID
AND O.MONTH BETWEEN 1 AND 3
GROUP BY O.YEAR, ROLLUP (O.YEAR, O.MONTH, R.NAME);
```

```
     YEAR MONTH     REGION                    TOTAL
---------- --------- --------------------- ----------
     2000 January   Mid-Atlantic            1221394
     2000 January   New England             1018430
     2000 January   SouthEast US             758042
     2000 January                           2997866
     2000 February  Mid-Atlantic             857352
     2000 February  New England             1231492
     2000 February  SouthEast US            1236846
     2000 February                          3325690
     2000 March     Mid-Atlantic            1274062
     2000 March     New England             1132966
     2000 March     SouthEast US            1311986
     2000 March                             3719014
     2001 January   Mid-Atlantic             610697
     2001 January   New England              509215
     2001 January   SouthEast US             379021
     2001 January                           1498933
     2001 February  Mid-Atlantic             428676
     2001 February  New England              615746
     2001 February  SouthEast US             618423
     2001 February                          1662845
     2001 March     Mid-Atlantic             637031
     2001 March     New England              566483
     2001 March     SouthEast US             655993
     2001 March                             1859507
     2000                                   10042570
     2001                                    5021285
     2000                                   10042570
     2001                                    5021285

28 rows selected.
```

Repetition of O.YEAR in the GROUP BY clause as well as in the ROLLUP operation repeats the summary rows of each year in the output and suppresses the grand total. Repetition of column names in a GROUP BY clause isn't very useful, but it's worth knowing that such constructs are allowed in Oracle9i.

Grouping on Composite Columns

Oracle8i supports grouping on individual columns only. Oracle9i extends the grouping operations to include grouping on composite columns. A *composite column* is a collection of two or more columns, but their values are treated as one for the grouping computation. Oracle8i allows group operations of the form ROLLUP (a,b,c), whereas, Oracle9i allows group operations of the form ROLLUP (a,(b,c)) as well. In this case, (b,c) is treated as one column for the purpose of the grouping computation. For example:

```
SELECT O.YEAR, TO_CHAR(TO_DATE(O.MONTH, 'MM'), 'Month') MONTH,
R.NAME REGION, SUM(O.TOT_SALES) Total
FROM ORDERS O, REGION R
WHERE R.REGION_ID = O.REGION_ID
AND O.MONTH BETWEEN 1 AND 3
GROUP BY ROLLUP ((O.YEAR, O.MONTH),R.NAME);
```

YEAR	MONTH	REGION	TOTAL
2000	January	Mid-Atlantic	1221394
2000	January	New England	1018430
2000	January	SouthEast US	758042
2000	January		2997866
2000	February	Mid-Atlantic	857352
2000	February	New England	1231492
2000	February	SouthEast US	1236846
2000	February		3325690
2000	March	Mid-Atlantic	1274062
2000	March	New England	1132966
2000	March	SouthEast US	1311986
2000	March		3719014
2001	January	Mid-Atlantic	610697
2001	January	New England	509215
2001	January	SouthEast US	379021
2001	January		1498933
2001	February	Mid-Atlantic	428676
2001	February	New England	615746
2001	February	SouthEast US	618423
2001	February		1662845
2001	March	Mid-Atlantic	637031
2001	March	New England	566483
2001	March	SouthEast US	655993
2001	March		1859507
			15063855

```
25 rows selected.
```

In this example, two columns (O.YEAR, O.MONTH) are treated as one composite column. This causes Oracle to treat the combination of year and month as one dimension, and the summary rows are computed accordingly. Note that while this query is not allowed in Oracle8i, you can fake composite column groupings in Oracle8i by using the concatenation operator (||) to combine two columns and treat the result as one composite column. Oracle8i can then produce the same result as the previous query in Oracle 9i. For example:

```
SELECT TO_CHAR(O.YEAR)||' '||TO_CHAR(TO_DATE(O.MONTH,'MM'),'Month')
       Year_Month,
       R.NAME REGION, SUM(O.TOT_SALES)
FROM ORDERS O, REGION R
WHERE R.REGION_ID = O.REGION_ID
AND O.MONTH BETWEEN 1 AND 3
GROUP BY
ROLLUP (TO_CHAR(O.YEAR)||' '||TO_CHAR(TO_DATE(O.MONTH,'MM'),'Month'), R.NAME);
```

YEAR_MONTH	REGION	SUM(O.TOT_SALES)
2000 February	Mid-Atlantic	857352
2000 February	New England	1231492
2000 February	SouthEast US	1236846
2000 February		3325690
2000 January	Mid-Atlantic	1221394
2000 January	New England	1018430
2000 January	SouthEast US	758042
2000 January		2997866
2000 March	Mid-Atlantic	1274062
2000 March	New England	1132966
2000 March	SouthEast US	1311986
2000 March		3719014
2001 February	Mid-Atlantic	428676
2001 February	New England	615746
2001 February	SouthEast US	618423
2001 February		1662845
2001 January	Mid-Atlantic	610697
2001 January	New England	509215
2001 January	SouthEast US	379021
2001 January		1498933
2001 March	Mid-Atlantic	637031
2001 March	New England	566483
2001 March	SouthEast US	655993
2001 March		1859507
		15063855

25 rows selected.

This query converts the numeric month into the string expression of the name of the month and concatenates it with the string representation of the year. The same expression has to be used in the SELECT list and the ROLLUP clause. The expression TO_CHAR(O.YEAR)||' '||TO_CHAR(TO_DATE(O.MONTH,'MM'),'Month') is treated as one composite column.

Concatenated Groupings

With Oracle9i, you can have multiple ROLLUP, CUBE, or GROUPING SETS operations, or a combination of these under the GROUP BY clause in a query. This is not allowed in Oracle8i. You will get an error message if you attempt the following query in Oracle8i:

```
SELECT O.YEAR, TO_CHAR(TO_DATE(O.MONTH, 'MM'), 'Month') MONTH,
R.NAME REGION, SUM(O.TOT_SALES) Total
FROM ORDERS O, REGION R
WHERE R.REGION_ID = O.REGION_ID
AND O.MONTH BETWEEN 1 AND 3
GROUP BY ROLLUP (O.YEAR, O.MONTH), ROLLUP(R.NAME);
GROUP BY ROLLUP (O.YEAR, O.MONTH), ROLLUP(R.NAME)
                            *
ERROR at line 6:
ORA-30489: Cannot have more than one rollup/cube expression list
```

However, the same query works in Oracle9i:

```
SELECT O.YEAR, TO_CHAR(TO_DATE(O.MONTH, 'MM'), 'Month') MONTH,
R.NAME REGION, SUM(O.TOT_SALES) Total
FROM ORDERS O, REGION R
WHERE R.REGION_ID = O.REGION_ID
AND O.MONTH BETWEEN 1 AND 3
GROUP BY ROLLUP (O.YEAR, O.MONTH), ROLLUP(R.NAME);
```

YEAR	MONTH	REGION	TOTAL
2000	January	Mid-Atlantic	1221394
2000	January	New England	1018430
2000	January	SouthEast US	758042
2000	January		2997866
2000	February	Mid-Atlantic	857352
2000	February	New England	1231492
2000	February	SouthEast US	1236846
2000	February		3325690
2000	March	Mid-Atlantic	1274062
2000	March	New England	1132966
2000	March	SouthEast US	1311986
2000	March		3719014
2000		Mid-Atlantic	3352808
2000		New England	3382888
2000		SouthEast US	3306874
2000			10042570
2001	January	Mid-Atlantic	610697
2001	January	New England	509215
2001	January	SouthEast US	379021
2001	January		1498933
2001	February	Mid-Atlantic	428676
2001	February	New England	615746
2001	February	SouthEast US	618423
2001	February		1662845
2001	March	Mid-Atlantic	637031

```
2001 March     New England                   566483
2001 March     SouthEast US                  655993
2001 March                                  1859507
2001           Mid-Atlantic                 1676404
2001           New England                  1691444
2001           SouthEast US                 1653437
2001                                        5021285
               Mid-Atlantic                 5029212
               New England                  5074332
               SouthEast US                 4960311
                                           15063855
```

36 rows selected.

When you have multiple grouping operations (ROLLUP, CUBE, or GROUPING SETS) in a GROUP BY clause, what you have is called a *concatenated grouping*. The result of the concatenated grouping is to produce a cross-product of groupings from each grouping operation. Therefore, the query:

```
SELECT O.YEAR, TO_CHAR(TO_DATE(O.MONTH, 'MM'), 'Month') MONTH,
R.NAME REGION, SUM(O.TOT_SALES) Total
FROM ORDERS O, REGION R
WHERE R.REGION_ID = O.REGION_ID
AND O.MONTH BETWEEN 1 AND 3
GROUP BY ROLLUP(O.YEAR),  ROLLUP (O.MONTH), ROLLUP (R.NAME);
```

behaves as a CUBE and produces the same result as the query:

```
SELECT O.YEAR, TO_CHAR(TO_DATE(O.MONTH, 'MM'), 'Month') MONTH,
R.NAME REGION, SUM(O.TOT_SALES) Total
FROM ORDERS O, REGION R
WHERE R.REGION_ID = O.REGION_ID
AND O.MONTH BETWEEN 1 AND 3
GROUP BY CUBE (O.YEAR, O.MONTH, R.NAME);
```

Since a CUBE contains aggregates for all possible combinations of the grouping columns, the concatenated grouping of CUBES is no different from a regular CUBE, and all the following queries return the same result as the query shown previously.

```
SELECT O.YEAR, TO_CHAR(TO_DATE(O.MONTH, 'MM'), 'Month') MONTH,
R.NAME REGION, SUM(O.TOT_SALES) Total
FROM ORDERS O, REGION R
WHERE R.REGION_ID = O.REGION_ID
AND O.MONTH BETWEEN 1 AND 3
GROUP BY CUBE (O.YEAR, O.MONTH), CUBE (R.NAME);
```

```
SELECT O.YEAR, TO_CHAR(TO_DATE(O.MONTH, 'MM'), 'Month') MONTH,
R.NAME REGION, SUM(O.TOT_SALES) Total
FROM ORDERS O, REGION R
WHERE R.REGION_ID = O.REGION_ID
AND O.MONTH BETWEEN 1 AND 3
GROUP BY CUBE (O.YEAR), CUBE (O.MONTH, R.NAME);
```

```
SELECT O.YEAR, TO_CHAR(TO_DATE(O.MONTH, 'MM'), 'Month') MONTH,
R.NAME REGION, SUM(O.TOT_SALES) Total
```

```
FROM ORDERS O, REGION R
WHERE R.REGION_ID = O.REGION_ID
AND O.MONTH BETWEEN 1 AND 3
GROUP BY CUBE (O.YEAR, O.MONTH), CUBE (O.YEAR, R.NAME);
```

Concatenated groupings with GROUPING SETS

Concatenated groupings come in handy while using GROUPING SETS. Since GROUPING SETS produces only the subtotal rows, you can specify just the aggregation levels you want in your output by using a concatenated grouping of GROUPING SETS. The concatenated grouping of GROUPING SETS (a,b) and GROUPING SETS (c,d) will produce aggregate rows for the aggregation levels (a,c), (a,d), (b,c), and (b,d). The concatenated grouping of GROUPING SETS (a,b) and GROUPING SETS (c) will produce aggregate rows for the aggregation levels (a,c) and (b,c). For example:

```
SELECT O.YEAR, TO_CHAR(TO_DATE(O.MONTH, 'MM'), 'Month') MONTH,
R.NAME REGION, SUM(O.TOT_SALES) Total
FROM ORDERS O, REGION R
WHERE R.REGION_ID = O.REGION_ID
AND O.MONTH BETWEEN 1 AND 3
GROUP BY GROUPING SETS (O.YEAR, O.MONTH), GROUPING SETS (R.NAME);
```

```
YEAR MONTH     REGION                    TOTAL
---------- --------- -------------------- ----------
      2000           Mid-Atlantic          3352808
      2000           New England           3382888
      2000           SouthEast US          3306874
      2001           Mid-Atlantic          1676404
      2001           New England           1691444
      2001           SouthEast US          1653437
           January   Mid-Atlantic          1832091
           January   New England           1527645
           January   SouthEast US          1137063
           February  Mid-Atlantic          1286028
           February  New England           1847238
           February  SouthEast US          1855269
           March     Mid-Atlantic          1911093
           March     New England           1699449
           March     SouthEast US          1967979
```

```
15 rows selected.
```

The concatenated grouping GROUP BY GROUPING SETS (O.YEAR, O.MONTH), GROUPING SETS (R.NAME) in this example produces rows for aggregate levels (O.YEAR, R.NAME) and (O.MONTH, R.NAME). Therefore, you see aggregate rows for (Year, Region) and (Month, Region) combinations in the output. The following example extends the previous query:

```
SELECT O.YEAR, TO_CHAR(TO_DATE(O.MONTH, 'MM'), 'Month') MONTH,
R.NAME REGION, SUM(O.TOT_SALES) Total
FROM ORDERS O, REGION R
```

```
WHERE R.REGION_ID = O.REGION_ID
AND O.MONTH BETWEEN 1 AND 3
GROUP BY GROUPING SETS (O.YEAR, O.MONTH), GROUPING SETS (O.YEAR, R.NAME);
```

```
 1:     YEAR MONTH     REGION                    TOTAL
 2:  ---------- --------- -------------------- ----------
 3:     2000                                    10042570
 4:     2001                                     5021285
 5:     2000 January                             2997866
 6:     2000 February                            3325690
 7:     2000 March                               3719014
 8:     2001 January                             1498933
 9:     2001 February                            1662845
10:     2001 March                               1859507
11:     2000          Mid-Atlantic              3352808
12:     2000          New England               3382888
13:     2000          SouthEast US              3306874
14:     2001          Mid-Atlantic              1676404
15:     2001          New England               1691444
16:     2001          SouthEast US              1653437
17:          January  Mid-Atlantic              1832091
18:          January  New England               1527645
19:          January  SouthEast US              1137063
20:          February Mid-Atlantic              1286028
21:          February New England               1847238
22:          February SouthEast US              1855269
23:          March    Mid-Atlantic              1911093
24:          March    New England               1699449
25:          March    SouthEast US              1967979
```

```
23 rows selected.
```

This example produces four grouping combinations. Table 12-1 describes the various grouping combinations produced by this query and references their corresponding row numbers in the output.

Table 12-1. Grouping combinations

Grouping combination	Corresponding rows
(O.YEAR, O.YEAR)	3–4
(O.YEAR, R.NAME)	11–16
(O.MONTH, O.YEAR)	5–10
(O.MONTH, R.NAME)	17–25

The GROUPING SETS operation is independent of the order of columns. Therefore, the following two queries will produce the same results as shown previously:

```
SELECT O.YEAR, TO_CHAR(TO_DATE(O.MONTH, 'MM'), 'Month') MONTH,
R.NAME REGION, SUM(O.TOT_SALES) Total
FROM ORDERS O, REGION R
WHERE R.REGION_ID = O.REGION_ID
```

```
AND O.MONTH BETWEEN 1 AND 3
GROUP BY GROUPING SETS (O.YEAR, R.NAME), GROUPING SETS (O.YEAR, O.MONTH);

SELECT O.YEAR, TO_CHAR(TO_DATE(O.MONTH, 'MM'), 'Month') MONTH,
R.NAME REGION, SUM(O.TOT_SALES) Total
FROM ORDERS O, REGION R
WHERE R.REGION_ID = O.REGION_ID
AND O.MONTH BETWEEN 1 AND 3
GROUP BY GROUPING SETS (O.MONTH, O.YEAR), GROUPING SETS (R.NAME, O.YEAR);
```

It is permissible to have a combination of ROLLUP, CUBE, and GROUPING SETS in a single GROUP BY clause, as in the following example:

```
SELECT O.YEAR, TO_CHAR(TO_DATE(O.MONTH, 'MM'), 'Month') MONTH,
R.NAME REGION, SUM(O.TOT_SALES) Total
FROM ORDERS O, REGION R
WHERE R.REGION_ID = O.REGION_ID
AND O.MONTH BETWEEN 1 AND 3
GROUP BY GROUPING SETS (O.MONTH, O.YEAR), ROLLUP(R.NAME), CUBE (O.YEAR);
```

However, the output from such queries seldom makes any sense. You should carefully evaluate the need for such queries when you intend to write one.

ROLLUP and CUBE as arguments to GROUPING SETS

Unlike the ROLLUP and CUBE operations, the GROUPING SETS operation can take a ROLLUP or a CUBE as its argument. As you have seen earlier, GROUPING SETS produces only subtotal rows. However, there are times when you may need to print the grand total along with the subtotals. In such situations, you can perform the GROUPING SETS operation on ROLLUP operations, as in the following example.

```
SELECT O.YEAR, TO_CHAR(TO_DATE(O.MONTH, 'MM'), 'Month') MONTH,
       R.NAME REGION, SUM(O.TOT_SALES) Total
FROM ORDERS O, REGION R
WHERE R.REGION_ID = O.REGION_ID
AND O.MONTH BETWEEN 1 AND 3
GROUP BY GROUPING SETS (ROLLUP (O.YEAR), ROLLUP (O.MONTH), ROLLUP(R.NAME));
```

YEAR	MONTH	REGION	TOTAL
2000			10042570
2001			5021285
	January		4496799
	February		4988535
	March		5578521
		Mid-Atlantic	5029212
		New England	5074332
		SouthEast US	4960311
			15063855
			15063855
			15063855

```
11 rows selected.
```

Notice that this example produces the subtotals for each dimension, as expected from the regular GROUPING SETS operations. Also, it produces the grand total across all the dimensions. However, you get three identical grand-total rows. The grand-total rows are repeated because they are produced by each ROLLUP operation inside the GROUPING SETS. If you insist on only one grand-total row, you may use the DISTINCT keyword in the SELECT clause:

```
SELECT DISTINCT O.YEAR, TO_CHAR(TO_DATE(O.MONTH, 'MM'), 'Month') MONTH,
R.NAME REGION, SUM(O.TOT_SALES) Total
FROM ORDERS O, REGION R
WHERE R.REGION_ID = O.REGION_ID
AND O.MONTH BETWEEN 1 AND 3
GROUP BY GROUPING SETS (ROLLUP (O.YEAR), ROLLUP (O.MONTH), ROLLUP(R.NAME));
```

YEAR	MONTH	REGION	TOTAL
2000			10042570
2001			5021285
	February		4988535
	January		4496799
	March		5578521
		Mid-Atlantic	5029212
		New England	5074332
		SouthEast US	4960311
			15063855

```
9 rows selected.
```

Note that the DISTINCT keyword eliminated the duplicate grand-total rows. You can also eliminate duplicate rows by using the GROUP_ID function, as discussed in later in this chapter.

If you are interested in subtotals and totals on composite dimensions, you can use composite or concatenated ROLLUP operations within GROUPING SETS, as in the following example:

```
SELECT O.YEAR, TO_CHAR(TO_DATE(O.MONTH, 'MM'), 'Month') MONTH,
R.NAME REGION, SUM(O.TOT_SALES) Total
FROM ORDERS O, REGION R
WHERE R.REGION_ID = O.REGION_ID
AND O.MONTH BETWEEN 1 AND 3
GROUP BY GROUPING SETS (ROLLUP (O.YEAR, O.MONTH), ROLLUP(R.NAME));
```

YEAR	MONTH	REGION	TOTAL
2000	January		2997866
2000	February		3325690
2000	March		3719014
2000			10042570
2001	January		1498933
2001	February		1662845
2001	March		1859507
2001			5021285

```
                Mid-Atlantic              5029212
                New England               5074332
                SouthEast US              4960311
                                         15063855
                                         15063855
```

```
13 rows selected.
```

This query generates subtotals for (YEAR, MONTH) combinations, subtotals for the REGION, subtotals for the YEAR, and the grand total. Note that there are duplicate grand-total rows because of the multiple ROLLUP operations within the GROUP-ING SETS operation.

The GROUPING_ID and GROUP_ID Functions

·Earlier in this chapter, you saw how to use the GROUPING function to distinguish between the regular GROUP BY rows and the summary rows produced by the GROUP BY extensions. Oracle9*i* extends the concept of the GROUPING function and introduces two new functions that you can use with a GROUP BY clause:

- GROUPING_ID
- GROUP_ID

These functions can only be used with a GROUP BY clause. However, unlike the GROUPING function that can only be used with a GROUP BY extension, the GROUPING_ID and GROUP_ID functions can be used in a query, even without a GROUP BY extension.

 Although it is legal to use these two functions without a GROUP BY extension, using GROUPING_ID and GROUP_ID without ROLLUP, CUBE, or GROUPING SETS doesn't produce any meaningful output, because GROUPING_ID and GROUP_ID are 0 for all regular GROUP BY rows.

The following sections discuss these two functions in detail.

GROUPING_ID

The syntax of the GROUPING_ID function is as follows:

```
SELECT ... , GROUPING_ID(ordered_list_of_grouping_columns)
FROM ...
GROUP BY ...
```

The GROUPING_ID function takes an ordered list of grouping columns as input, and computes the output by working through the following steps:

1. First, it generates the results of the GROUPING function as applied to each of the individual columns in the list. The result of this step is a set of ones and zeros.

2. It puts these ones and zeros in the same order as the order of the columns in its argument list to produce a bit vector.

3. Treating this bit vector (a series of ones and zeros) as a binary number, it converts the bit vector into a decimal (base 10) number.

4. The decimal number computed in Step 3 is returned as the GROUPING_ID function's output.

The following example illustrates this process and compares the results from GROUPING_ID with those from GROUPING:

```
SELECT O.YEAR, TO_CHAR(TO_DATE(O.MONTH, 'MM'), 'Month') MONTH,
R.NAME REGION, SUM(O.TOT_SALES) Total,
GROUPING(O.YEAR) Y, GROUPING(O.MONTH) M, GROUPING(R.NAME) R,
GROUPING_ID (O.YEAR, O.MONTH, R.NAME) GID
FROM ORDERS O, REGION R
WHERE R.REGION_ID = O.REGION_ID
AND O.MONTH BETWEEN 1 AND 3
GROUP BY CUBE (O.YEAR, O.MONTH, R.NAME);
```

YEAR	MONTH	REGION	TOTAL	Y	M	R	GID
2000	January	Mid-Atlantic	1221394	0	0	0	0
2000	January	New England	1018430	0	0	0	0
2000	January	SouthEast US	758042	0	0	0	0
2000	January		2997866	0	0	1	1
2000	February	Mid-Atlantic	857352	0	0	0	0
2000	February	New England	1231492	0	0	0.	0
2000	February	SouthEast US	1236846	0	0	0	0
2000	February		3325690	0	0	1	1
2000	March	Mid-Atlantic	1274062	0	0	0	0
2000	March	New England	1132966	0	0	0	0
2000	March	SouthEast US	1311986	0	0	0	0
2000	March		3719014	0	0	1	1
2000		Mid-Atlantic	3352808	0	1	0	2
2000		New England	3382888	0	1	0	2
2000		SouthEast US	3306874	0	1	0	2
2000			10042570	0	1	1	3
2001	January	Mid-Atlantic	610697	0	0	0	0
2001	January	New England	509215	0	0	0	0
2001	January	SouthEast US	379021	0	0	0	0
2001	January		1498933	0	0	1	1
2001	February	Mid-Atlantic	428676	0	0	0	0
2001	February	New England	615746	0	0	0	0
2001	February	SouthEast US	618423	0	0	0	0
2001	February		1662845	0	0	1	1
2001	March	Mid-Atlantic	637031	0	0	0	0
2001	March	New England	566483	0	0	0	0
2001	March	SouthEast US	655993	0	0	0	0
2001	March		1859507	0	0	1	1
2001		Mid-Atlantic	1676404	0	1	0	2
2001		New England	1691444	0	1	0	2
2001		SouthEast US	1653437	0	1	0	2
2001			5021285	0	1	1	3

```
January    Mid-Atlantic    1832091    1    0    0    4
January    New England     1527645    1    0    0    4
January    SouthEast US    1137063    1    0    0    4
January                    4496799    1    0    1    5
February   Mid-Atlantic    1286028    1    0    0    4
February   New England     1847238    1    0    0    4
February   SouthEast US    1855269    1    0.   0    4
February                   4988535    1    0    1    5
March      Mid-Atlantic    1911093    1    0    0    4
March      New England     1699449    1    0    0    4
March      SouthEast US    1967979    1    0    0    4
March                      5578521    1    0    1    5
           Mid-Atlantic    5029212    1    1    0    6
           New England     5074332    1    1    0    6
           SouthEast US    4960311    1    1    0    6
                           15063855   1    1    1    7
```

48 rows selected.

Note that the GROUPING_ID is the decimal equivalent of the bit vector generated by the individual GROUPING functions. In this output, the GROUPING_ID has values 0, 1, 2, 3, 4, 5, 6, and 7. Table 12-2 describes these aggregation levels.

Table 12-2. Result of GROUPING_ID(O.YEAR, O.MONTH, R.NAME)

Aggregation level	Bit vector	GROUPING_ID
Regular GROUP BY rows	000	0
Subtotal for Year-Month, aggregated at (Region)	001	1
Subtotal for Year-Region, aggregated at (Month)	010	2
Subtotal for Year, aggregated at (Month, Region)	011	3
Subtotal for Month-Region, aggregated at (Year)	100	4
Subtotal for Month, aggregated at (Year, Region)	101	5
Subtotal for Region, aggregated at (Year, Month)	110	6
Grand total for all levels, aggregated at (Year, Month, Region)	111	7

The GROUPING_ID function can be used effectively in a query to filter rows according to your requirement. Let's say you want only the summary rows to be displayed in the output, and not the regular GROUP BY rows. You can use the GROUPING_ID function in the HAVING clause to do this by restricting output to only those rows that contain totals and subtotals (i.e., for which GROUPING_ID > 0):

```
SELECT O.YEAR, TO_CHAR(TO_DATE(O.MONTH, 'MM'), 'Month') MONTH,
R.NAME REGION, SUM(O.TOT_SALES) Total
FROM ORDERS O, REGION R
WHERE R.REGION_ID = O.REGION_ID
AND O.MONTH BETWEEN 1 AND 3
GROUP BY CUBE (O.YEAR, O.MONTH, R.NAME)
HAVING GROUPING_ID (O.YEAR, O.MONTH, R.NAME) > 0;
```

```
YEAR MONTH     REGION                    TOTAL
---------- --------- -------------------- ----------
     2000 January                         2997866
     2000 February                        3325690
     2000 March                           3719014
     2000           Mid-Atlantic          3352808
     2000           New England           3382888
     2000           SouthEast US          3306874
     2000                                10042570
     2001 January                         1498933
     2001 February                        1662845
     2001 March                           1859507
     2001           Mid-Atlantic          1676404
     2001           New England           1691444
     2001           SouthEast US          1653437
     2001                                 5021285
          January   Mid-Atlantic          1832091
          January   New England           1527645
          January   SouthEast US          1137063
          January                         4496799
          February  Mid-Atlantic          1286028
          February  New England           1847238
          February  SouthEast US          1855269
          February                        4988535
          March     Mid-Atlantic          1911093
          March     New England           1699449
          March     SouthEast US          1967979
          March                           5578521
                    Mid-Atlantic          5029212
                    New England           5074332
                    SouthEast US          4960311
                                         15063855

30 rows selected.
```

As you can see, GROUPING_ID makes it easier to filter the output of aggregation operations. Without the GROUPING_ID function, you have to write a more complex query using the GROUPING function to achieve the same result. For example, the following query uses GROUPING rather than GROUPING_ID to display only totals and subtotals. Note the added complexity in the HAVING clause.

```
SELECT O.YEAR, TO_CHAR(TO_DATE(O.MONTH, 'MM'), 'Month') MONTH,
R.NAME REGION, SUM(O.TOT_SALES) Total
FROM ORDERS O, REGION R
WHERE R.REGION_ID = O.REGION_ID
AND O.MONTH BETWEEN 1 AND 3
GROUP BY CUBE (O.YEAR, O.MONTH, R.NAME)
HAVING GROUPING(O.YEAR) > 0
OR GROUPING(O.MONTH) > 0
OR GROUPING(R.NAME) > 0;

YEAR MONTH     REGION                    TOTAL
---------- --------- -------------------- ----------
     2000 January                         2997866
     2000 February                        3325690
```

2000	March		3719014
2000		Mid-Atlantic	3352808
2000		New England	3382888
2000		SouthEast US	3306874
2000			10042570
2001	January		1498933
2001	February		1662845
2001	March		1859507
2001		Mid-Atlantic	1676404
2001		New England	1691444
2001		SouthEast US	1653437
2001			5021285
	January	Mid-Atlantic	1832091
	January	New England	1527645
	January	SouthEast US	1137063
	January		4496799
	February	Mid-Atlantic	1286028
	February	New England	1847238
	February	SouthEast US	1855269
	February		4988535
	March	Mid-Atlantic	1911093
	March	New England	1699449
	March	SouthEast US	1967979
	March		5578521
		Mid-Atlantic	5029212
		New England	5074332
		SouthEast US	4960311
			15063855

```
30 rows selected.
```

GROUP_ID

As you saw in previous sections, Oracle9*i* allows you to have repeating grouping columns and multiple grouping operations in a GROUP BY clause. Some combinations could result in duplicate rows in the output. The GROUP_ID distinguishes between otherwise duplicate result rows.

The syntax of the GROUP_ID function is:

```
SELECT ... , GROUP_ID( )
FROM ...
GROUP BY ...
```

The GROUP_ID function takes no argument, and returns 0 through n − 1, where n is the occurrence count for duplicates. The first occurrence of a given row in the output of a query will have a GROUP_ID of 0, the second occurrence of a given row will have a GROUP_ID of 1, and so forth. The following example illustrates the use of the GROUP_ID function:

```
SELECT O.YEAR, TO_CHAR(TO_DATE(O.MONTH, 'MM'), 'Month') MONTH,
R.NAME REGION, SUM(O.TOT_SALES) Total, GROUP_ID( )
FROM ORDERS O, REGION R
```

```
WHERE R.REGION_ID = O.REGION_ID
AND O.MONTH BETWEEN 1 AND 3
GROUP BY O.YEAR, ROLLUP (O.YEAR, O.MONTH, R.NAME);
```

YEAR	MONTH	REGION	TOTAL	GROUP_ID()
2000	January	Mid-Atlantic	1221394	0
2000	January	New England	1018430	0
2000	January	SouthEast US	758042	0
2000	January		2997866	0
2000	February	Mid-Atlantic	857352	0
2000	February	New England	1231492	0
2000	February	SouthEast US	1236846	0
2000	February		3325690	0
2000	March	Mid-Atlantic	1274062	0
2000	March	New England	1132966	0
2000	March	SouthEast US	1311986	0
2000	March		3719014	0
2001	January	Mid-Atlantic	610697	0
2001	January	New England	509215	0
2001	January	SouthEast US	379021	0
2001	January		1498933	0
2001	February	Mid-Atlantic	428676	0
2001	February	New England	615746	0
2001	February	SouthEast US	618423	0
2001	February		1662845	0
2001	March	Mid-Atlantic	637031	0
2001	March	New England	566483	0
2001	March	SouthEast US	655993	0
2001	March		1859507	0
2000			10042570	0
2001			5021285	0
2000			10042570	1
2001			5021285	1

```
28 rows selected.
```

Note the value 1 returned by the GROUP_ID function for the last two rows. These rows are indeed duplicates of the previous two rows. If you don't want to see the duplicates in your result set, restrict your query's results to GROUP_ID 0:

```
SELECT O.YEAR, TO_CHAR(TO_DATE(O.MONTH, 'MM'), 'Month') MONTH,
R.NAME REGION, SUM(O.TOT_SALES) Total, GROUP_ID()
FROM ORDERS O, REGION R
WHERE R.REGION_ID = O.REGION_ID
AND O.MONTH BETWEEN 1 AND 3
GROUP BY O.YEAR, ROLLUP (O.YEAR, O.MONTH, R.NAME)
HAVING GROUP_ID() = 0;
```

YEAR	MONTH	REGION	TOTAL	GROUP_ID()
2000	January	Mid-Atlantic	1221394	0
2000	January	New England	1018430	0
2000	January	SouthEast US	758042	0

2000	January		2997866	0
2000	February	Mid-Atlantic	857352	0
2000	February	New England	1231492	0
2000	February	SouthEast US	1236846	0
2000	February		3325690	0
2000	March	Mid-Atlantic	1274062	0
2000	March	New England	1132966	0
2000	March	SouthEast US	1311986	0
2000	March		3719014	0
2001	January	Mid-Atlantic	610697	0
2001	January	New England	509215	0
2001	January	SouthEast US	379021	0
2001	January		1498933	0
2001	February	Mid-Atlantic	428676	0
2001	February	New England	615746	0
2001	February	SouthEast US	618423	0
2001	February		1662845	0
2001	March	Mid-Atlantic	637031	0
2001	March	New England	566483	0
2001	March	SouthEast US	655993	0
2001	March		1859507	0
2000			10042570	0
2001			5021285	0

```
26 rows selected.
```

This version of the query uses HAVING GROUP_ID = 0 to eliminate the two dupli-cate totals from the result set. GROUP_ID is only meaningful in the HAVING clause, because it applies to summarized data. You can't use GROUP_ID in a WHERE clause, and it wouldn't make sense to try.

CHAPTER 13

Advanced Analytic SQL

For years, SQL has been criticized for its inability to handle routine decision support queries. With the host of new analytic functions introduced in Oracle8*i* and Oracle9*i*, Oracle has taken giant strides towards eliminating this deficiency. In doing so, Oracle has further blurred the distinction between its multipurpose relational database server and other, special-purpose data warehouse and statistical analysis servers.

Analytic SQL Overview

The types of queries issued by Decision Support Systems (DSS) differ from those issued against OLTP systems. Consider the following business queries:

- Find the top ten salespeople in each sales district last year.
- Find all customers whose total orders last year exceeded 20% of the aggregate sales for their geographic region.
- Identify the region that suffered the worst quarter-to-quarter sales decline last year.
- Find the best and worst selling menu items by state for each quarter last year.

Queries such as these are staples of DSS, and are used by managers, analysts, marketing executives, etc. to spot trends, identify outliers, uncover business opportunities, and predict future business performance. DSS systems typically sit atop data warehouses, in which large quantities of scrubbed, aggregated data provide fertile grounds for researching and formulating business decisions.

While all of the previous queries can be easily expressed in English, they have historically been difficult to formulate using SQL for the following reasons:

- They may require different levels of aggregation of the same data.
- They may involve intra-table comparisons (comparing one or more rows in a table with other rows in the same table).
- They may require an extra filtering step after the result set has been sorted (i.e., finding the top ten and bottom ten salespeople last month).

While it is possible to generate the desired results using such SQL features as self joins, inline views, and user-defined functions, the resulting queries can be difficult to understand and might yield unacceptably long execution times. To illustrate the difficulty in formulating such queries, we will walk through the construction of this query: "Find all customers whose total orders last year exceeded 20% of the aggregate sales for their geographic region."

For this and other examples in this chapter, we use a simple star schema consisting of a single fact table (called "orders") containing aggregated sales information across the following dimensions: region, salesperson, customer, and month. There are two main facets to this query, each requiring a different level of aggregation of the same data:

1. Sum all sales per region last year.

2. Sum all sales per customer last year.

After these two intermediate result sets have been constructed, we need to compare each customer's total to the total for their region and see if it exceeds 20%. The final result set will show the customer names along with their total sales, region name, and the percentage of their region's sales.

The query to aggregate sales by region looks as follows:

```
SELECT o.region_id region_id, SUM(o.tot_sales) tot_sales
FROM orders o
WHERE o.year = 2001
GROUP BY o.region_id;

REGION_ID  TOT_SALES
---------- ----------
        5    6585641
        6    6307766
        7    6868495
        8    6853015
        9    6739374
       10    6238901
```

The query to aggregate sales by customer would be:

```
SELECT o.cust_nbr cust_nbr, o.region_id region_id,
    SUM(o.tot_sales) tot_sales
FROM orders o
WHERE o.year = 2001
GROUP BY o.cust_nbr, o.region_id;

CUST_NBR  REGION_ID  TOT_SALES
--------- ---------- ----------
        1          5    1151162
        2          5    1224992
        3          5    1161286
        4          5    1878275
        5          5    1169926
        6          6    1788836
```

7	6	971585
8	6	1141638
9	6	1208959
10	6	1196748
11	7	1190421
12	7	1182275
13	7	1310434
14	7	1929774
15	7	1255591
16	8	1068467
17	8	1944281
18	8	1253840
19	8	1174421
20	8	1412006
21	9	1020541
22	9	1036146
23	9	1224992
24	9	1224992
25	9	2232703
26	10	1808949
27	10	1322747
28	10	986964
29	10	903383
30	10	1216858

By placing each of the two queries in an inline view and joining them on region_id, we can locate those customers whose total sales exceeds 20% of their region, as in:

```
SELECT cust_sales.cust_nbr cust_nbr, cust_sales.region_id region_id,
  cust_sales.tot_sales cust_sales, region_sales.tot_sales region_sales
FROM
  (SELECT o.region_id region_id, SUM(o.tot_sales) tot_sales
   FROM orders o
   WHERE o.year = 2001
   GROUP BY o.region_id) region_sales,
  (SELECT o.cust_nbr cust_nbr, o.region_id region_id,
     SUM(o.tot_sales) tot_sales
   FROM orders o
   WHERE o.year = 2001
   GROUP BY o.cust_nbr, o.region_id) cust_sales
WHERE cust_sales.region_id = region_sales.region_id
  AND cust_sales.tot_sales > (region_sales.tot_sales * .2);
```

```
CUST_NBR  REGION_ID CUST_SALES REGION_SALES
--------- --------- ---------- ------------
        4         5    1878275      6585641
        6         6    1788836      6307766
       14         7    1929774      6868495
       17         8    1944281      6853015
       20         8    1412006      6853015
       25         9    2232703      6739374
       26        10    1808949      6238901
       27        10    1322747      6238901
```

The final step is to join the region and customer dimensions in order to include the customer and region names in the result set:

```
SELECT c.name cust_name,
   big_custs.cust_sales cust_sales, r.name region_name,
   100 * ROUND(big_custs.cust_sales /
   big_custs.region_sales, 2)  percent_of_region
FROM region r, customer c,
  (SELECT cust_sales.cust_nbr cust_nbr, cust_sales.region_id region_id,
     cust_sales.tot_sales cust_sales,
     region_sales.tot_sales region_sales
   FROM
    (SELECT o.region_id region_id, SUM(o.tot_sales) tot_sales
     FROM orders o
     WHERE o.year = 2001
     GROUP BY o.region_id) region_sales,
    (SELECT o.cust_nbr cust_nbr, o.region_id region_id,
       SUM(o.tot_sales) tot_sales
     FROM orders o
     WHERE o.year = 2001
     GROUP BY o.cust_nbr, o.region_id) cust_sales
   WHERE cust_sales.region_id = region_sales.region_id
     AND cust_sales.tot_sales > (region_sales.tot_sales * .2)) big_custs
WHERE big_custs.cust_nbr = c.cust_nbr
   AND big_custs.region_id = r.region_id;
```

CUST_NAME	CUST_SALES	REGION_NAME	PERCENT_OF_REGION
Flowtech Inc.	1878275	New England	29
Spartan Industries	1788836	Mid-Atlantic	28
Madden Industries	1929774	SouthEast US	28
Evans Supply Corp.	1944281	SouthWest US	28
Malden Labs	1412006	SouthWest US	21
Worcester Technologies	2232703	NorthWest US	33
Alpha Technologies	1808949	Central US	29
Phillips Labs	1322747	Central US	21

Using nothing more exotic than inline views, we can construct a single query that generates the desired results. The solution, however, has the following shortcomings:

- The query is fairly complex.
- Two passes through the same rows of the orders table are required to generate the different aggregation levels needed by the query.

Let's see how we can both simplify the query and perform the same work in a single pass through the orders table using one of the new analytic functions. Rather than issuing two separate queries to aggregate sales per region and per customer, we will create a single query that aggregates sales over both region and customer. We can then call an analytic function that performs a second level of aggregation to generate total sales per region:

```
1  SELECT o.region_id region_id, o.cust_nbr cust_nbr,
2    SUM(o.tot_sales) tot_sales,
```

```
3   SUM(SUM(o.tot_sales)) OVER (PARTITION BY o.region_id) region_sales
4   FROM orders o
5   WHERE o.year = 2001
6   GROUP BY o.region_id, o.cust_nbr;
```

REGION_ID	CUST_NBR	TOT_SALES	REGION_SALES
5	1	1151162	6584167
5	2	1223518	6584167
5	3	1161286	6584167
5	4	1878275	6584167
5	5	1169926	6584167
6	6	1788836	6307766
6	7	971585	6307766
6	8	1141638	6307766
6	9	1208959	6307766
6	10	1196748	6307766
7	11	1190421	6868495
7	12	1182275	6868495
7	13	1310434	6868495
7	14	1929774	6868495
7	15	1255591	6868495
8	16	1068467	6853015
8	17	1944281	6853015
8	18	1253840	6853015
8	19	1174421	6853015
8	20	1412006	6853015
9	21	1020541	6726929
9	22	1036146	6726929
9	23	1212547	6726929
9	24	1224992	6726929
9	25	2232703	6726929
10	26	1808949	6238901
10	27	1322747	6238901
10	28	986964	6238901
10	29	903383	6238901
10	30	1216858	6238901

The analytic function can be found in line 3 of the previous query and the result has the alias *region_sales*. The aggregate function (SUM(o.tot_sales)) in line 2 generates the total sales per customer and region as directed by the GROUP BY clause, and the analytic function in line 3 aggregates these sums for each region, thereby computing the aggregate sales per region. The value for the region_sales column is identical for all customers within the same region and is equal to the sum of all customer sales within that region. We can then wrap the query in an inline view,* filter out those customers with less than 20% of their region's total sales, and join the region and customer tables to generate the desired result set:

```
SELECT c.name cust_name,
    cust_sales.tot_sales cust_sales, r.name region_name,
```

---

* Using an inline view will save us from having to join the region and customer tables to the orders table; otherwise, we would have to include columns from the region and customer tables in the GROUP BY clause.

```
    100 * ROUND(cust_sales.tot_sales /
      cust_sales.region_sales, 2)  percent_of_region
  FROM region r, customer c,
   (SELECT o.region_id region_id, o.cust_nbr cust_nbr,
      SUM(o.tot_sales) tot_sales,
      SUM(SUM(o.tot_sales)) OVER (PARTITION BY o.region_id) region_sales
    FROM orders o
    WHERE o.year = 2001
    GROUP BY o.region_id, o.cust_nbr) cust_sales
  WHERE cust_sales.tot_sales > (cust_sales.region_sales * .2)
    AND cust_sales.region_id = r.region_id
    AND cust_sales.cust_nbr = c.cust_nbr;
```

CUST_NAME	CUST_SALES	REGION_NAME	PERCENT_OF_REGION
Flowtech Inc.	1878275	New England	29
Spartan Industries	1788836	Mid-Atlantic	28
Madden Industries	1929774	SouthEast US	28
Evans Supply Corp.	1944281	SouthWest US	28
Malden Labs	1412006	SouthWest US	21
Worcester Technologies	2232703	NorthWest US	33
Alpha Technologies	1808949	Central US	29
Phillips Labs	1322747	Central US	21

Without getting into the details of how the SUM...OVER function works (we will discuss it later in this chapter under "Reporting Functions"), we can see that Oracle is performing an aggregation of an aggregation rather than revisiting the detail rows twice. Thus, the query runs faster and should also prove easier to understand and maintain once the syntax is familiar.

Unlike built-in functions such as DECODE, GREATEST, and SUBSTR, Oracle's suite of analytic functions can only be used in the SELECT clause of a query. This is because analytic functions are only executed *after* the FROM, WHERE, GROUP BY, and HAVING clauses have been evaluated. After the analytic functions have executed, the query's ORDER BY clause is evaluated in order to sort the final result set, and the ORDER BY clause is allowed to reference columns in the SELECT clause generated via analytic functions.

The remainder of the chapter introduces the Oracle8*i* and Oracle9*i* analytic functions, grouped by functionality.

Ranking Functions

Determining the performance of a particular business entity compared to its peers is central to a wide variety of business decisions. Examples include:

- Identifying assets with the highest utilization.
- Determining the worst-selling products by region.
- Finding the best-performing salespeople.

Prior to the release of Oracle8*i*, programmers could use the ORDER BY clause to sort a result set on one or more columns, but any further processing to calculate rankings or percentiles had to be performed using a procedural language. Beginning with Oracle8*i*, however, developers can take advantage of several new functions to either generate rankings for each row in a result set or to group rows into buckets for percentile calculations.

RANK, DENSE_RANK, and ROW_NUMBER

The RANK, DENSE_RANK, and ROW_NUMBER functions generate an integer value from 1 to N for each row, where N is less than or equal to the number of rows in the result set. The differences in the values returned by these functions revolves around how each one handles ties:

- ROW_NUMBER returns a unique number for each row starting with 1. For rows that have duplicate values, numbers are arbitrarily assigned.
- DENSE_RANK assigns a unique number for each row starting with 1, except for rows that have duplicate values, in which case the same ranking is assigned.
- RANK assigns a unique number for each row starting with 1, except for rows that have duplicate values, in which case the same ranking is assigned and a gap appears in the sequence for each duplicate ranking.

To illustrate the differences, we generate rankings for each customer according to their total yearly sales. Here is the query to generate the sales data for the year 2001:

```
SELECT region_id, cust_nbr, SUM(tot_sales) cust_sales
FROM orders
WHERE year = 2001
GROUP BY region_id, cust_nbr
ORDER BY region_id, cust_nbr;

REGION_ID   CUST_NBR CUST_SALES
---------- ---------- ----------
        5          1    1151162
        5          2    1224992
        5          3    1161286
        5          4    1878275
        5          5    1169926
        6          6    1788836
        6          7     971585
        6          8    1141638
        6          9    1208959
        6         10    1196748
        7         11    1190421
        7         12    1182275
        7         13    1310434
        7         14    1929774
        7         15    1255591
        8         16    1068467
```

8	17	1944281
8	18	1253840
8	19	1174421
8	20	1412006
9	21	1020541
9	22	1036146
9	23	**1224992**
9	24	**1224992**
9	25	2232703
10	26	1808949
10	27	1322747
10	28	986964
10	29	903383
10	30	1216858

Notice that three of the customers (2, 23, and 24) have the same value for total sales ($1,224,992). In the next query, we will add three function calls to generate rankings for each customer across all regions, and we will order the result set by the ROW_NUMBER function to make the difference in rankings easier to observe:

```
SELECT region_id, cust_nbr,
  SUM(tot_sales) cust_sales,
  RANK( ) OVER (ORDER BY SUM(tot_sales) DESC) sales_rank,
  DENSE_RANK( ) OVER (ORDER BY SUM(tot_sales) DESC) sales_dense_rank,
  ROW_NUMBER( ) OVER (ORDER BY SUM(tot_sales) DESC) sales_number
FROM orders
WHERE year = 2001
GROUP BY region_id, cust_nbr
ORDER BY 6;
```

REGION_ID	CUST_NBR	CUST_SALES	SALES_RANK	SALES_DENSE_RANK	SALES_NUMBER
9	25	2232703	1	1	1
8	17	1944281	2	2	2
7	14	1929774	3	3	3
5	4	1878275	4	4	4
10	26	1808949	5	5	5
6	6	1788836	6	6	6
8	20	1412006	7	7	7
10	27	1322747	8	8	8
7	13	1310434	9	9	9
7	15	1255591	10	10	10
8	18	1253840	11	11	11
5	2	**1224992**	**12**	**12**	**12**
9	23	**1224992**	**12**	**12**	**13**
9	24	**1224992**	**12**	**12**	**14**
10	30	1216858	**15**	**13**	**15**
6	9	1208959	16	14	16
6	10	1196748	17	15	17
7	11	1190421	18	16	18
7	12	1182275	19	17	19
8	19	1174421	20	18	20
5	5	1169926	21	19	21

5	3	1161286	22	20	22
5	1	1151162	23	21	23
6	8	1141638	24	22	24
8	16	1068467	25	23	25
9	22	1036146	26	24	26
9	21	1020541	27	25	27
10	28	986964	28	26	28
6	7	971585	29	27	29
10	29	903383	30	28	30

Don't be confused by the ORDER BY clause at the end of the query and the ORDER BY clauses within each function call; the functions use their ORDER BY clause internally to sort the results for the purpose of applying a ranking. Thus, each of the three functions applies its ranking algorithm to the sum of each customer's sales in descending order. The final ORDER BY clause specifies the results of the ROW_NUMBER function as the sort key for the final result set, but we could have picked any of the six columns as our sort key.

Both the RANK and DENSE_RANK functions assign the rank of 12 to the 3 rows with total sales of $1,224,992, while the ROW_NUMBER function assigns the ranks 12, 13, and 14 to the same rows. The difference between the RANK and DENSE_RANK functions manifests itself in the ranking assigned to the next-lowest sales total; the RANK function leaves a gap in the ranking sequence and assigns a rank of 15 to customer number 30, while the DENSE_RANK function continues the sequence with a ranking of 13.

Deciding which of the three functions to use depends on the desired outcome. If we want to identify the top 13 customers from this result set, we would use:

- ROW_NUMBER if we want exactly 13 rows without regard to ties. In this case, one of the customers who might otherwise be included in the list will be excluded from the final set.

- RANK if we want at least 13 rows but don't want to include rows that would have been excluded had there been no ties. In this case, we would retrieve 14 rows.

- DENSE_RANK if we want all customers with a ranking of 13 or less, including all duplicates. In this case, we would retrieve 15 rows.

While the previous query generates rankings across the entire result set, it is also possible to generate independent sets of rankings across multiple partitions of the result set. The following query generates rankings for customer sales within each region rather than across all regions. Note the addition of the PARTITION BY clause:

```
SELECT region_id, cust_nbr, SUM(tot_sales) cust_sales,
  RANK( ) OVER (PARTITION BY region_id
    ORDER BY SUM(tot_sales) DESC) sales_rank,
  DENSE_RANK( ) OVER (PARTITION BY region_id
    ORDER BY SUM(tot_sales) DESC) sales_dense_rank,
  ROW_NUMBER( ) OVER (PARTITION BY region_id
    ORDER BY SUM(tot_sales) DESC) sales_number
```

```
FROM orders
WHERE year = 2001
GROUP BY region_id, cust_nbr
ORDER BY 1,6;
```

REGION_ID	CUST_NBR	CUST_SALES	SALES_RANK	SALES_DENSE_RANK	SALES_NUMBER
5	4	1878275	1	1	1
5	2	1224992	2	2	2
5	5	1169926	3	3	3
5	3	1161286	4	4	4
5	1	1151162	5	5	5
6	6	1788836	1	1	1
6	9	1208959	2	2	2
6	10	1196748	3	3	3
6	8	1141638	4	4	4
6	7	971585	5	5	5
7	14	1929774	1	1	1
7	13	1310434	2	2	2
7	15	1255591	3	3	3
7	11	1190421	4	4	4
7	12	1182275	5	5	5
8	17	1944281	1	1	1
8	20	1412006	2	2	2
8	18	1253840	3	3	3
8	19	1174421	4	4	4
8	16	1068467	5	5	5
9	25	2232703	1	1	1
9	23	1224992	2	2	2
9	24	1224992	2	2	3
9	22	1036146	4	3	4
9	21	1020541	5	4	5
10	26	1808949	1	1	1
10	27	1322747	2	2	2
10	30	1216858	3	3	3
10	28	986964	4	4	4
10	29	903383	5	5	5

Each customer receives a ranking between one and five depending on their relation to other customers in the same region. Of the three customers with duplicate total sales, two of them are in region 9; as before, the RANK and DENSE_RANK functions generate identical rankings for both customers.

The PARTITION BY clause used in ranking functions is used to divide a result set into pieces so that rankings can be applied within each subset. This is completely different from the PARTITION BY RANGE/HASH/LIST clauses introduced in Chapter 10 for breaking a table or index into multiple pieces.

Handling NULLs

All ranking functions allow the caller to specify where in the ranking order NULL values should appear. This is accomplished by appending either NULLS FIRST or NULLS LAST after the ORDER BY clause of the function, as in:

```
SELECT region_id, cust_nbr, SUM(tot_sales) cust_sales,
  RANK( ) OVER (ORDER BY SUM(tot_sales) DESC NULLS LAST) sales_rank
FROM orders
WHERE year = 2001
GROUP BY region_id, cust_nbr;
```

If omitted, NULL values will either appear last in ascending rankings or first in descending rankings.

Top/Bottom-N queries

One of the most common uses of a ranked data set is to identify the top-N or bottom-N performers. Since we can't call analytic functions from the WHERE or HAVING clauses, we are forced to generate the rankings for all the rows and then use an outer query to filter out the unwanted rankings. For example, the following query uses an inline view to identify the top-5 salespersons for 2001:

```
SELECT s.name, sp.sp_sales total_sales
FROM salesperson s,
  (SELECT salesperson_id, SUM(tot_sales) sp_sales,
     RANK( ) OVER (ORDER BY SUM(tot_sales) DESC) sales_rank
   FROM orders
   WHERE year = 2001
   GROUP BY salesperson_id) sp
WHERE sp.sales_rank <= 5
  AND sp.salesperson_id = s.salesperson_id
ORDER BY sp.sales_rank;
```

```
NAME                                             TOTAL_SALES
------------------------------------------------ -----------
Jeff Blake                                           1927580
Sam Houseman                                         1814327
Mark Russell                                         1784596
John Boorman                                         1768813
Carl Isaacs                                          1761814
```

FIRST/LAST

While there is no function for returning only the top or bottom-N from a ranked result set, Oracle provides functionality for identifying the first (top 1) or last (bottom 1) records in a ranked set. This is useful for queries such as the following: "Find the regions with the best and worst total sales last year." Unlike the top-5 salespeople example from the previous section, this query needs an additional piece of information—the size of the result set—in order to answer the question.

Oracle 9*i* provides the ability to answer such queries efficiently using functions that rank the result set based on a specified ordering, identify the row with the top or bottom ranking, and report on any column available in the result set. These functions are composed of three parts:

1. An ORDER BY clause that specifies how to rank the result set.
2. The keywords FIRST and LAST to specify whether to use the top or bottom-ranked row.
3. An aggregate function (i.e., MIN, MAX, AVG, COUNT) used as a tiebreaker in case more than one row of the result set tie for the FIRST or LAST spot in the ranking.

The following query uses the MIN aggregate function to find the regions that rank FIRST and LAST by total sales:

```
SELECT
  MIN(region_id)
    KEEP (DENSE_RANK FIRST ORDER BY SUM(tot_sales) DESC) best_region,
  MIN(region_id)
    KEEP (DENSE_RANK LAST ORDER BY SUM(tot_sales) DESC) worst_region
FROM orders
WHERE year = 2001
GROUP BY region_id;


BEST_REGION WORST_REGION
----------- ------------
          7           10
```

The use of the MIN function in the previous query is a bit confusing: it is only used if more than one region ties for either first or last place in the ranking. If there were a tie, the row with the minimum value for region_id would be chosen. To find out if a tie actually exists, we could call each function twice using MIN for the first and MAX for the second, and see if they return the same results:

```
SELECT
  MIN(region_id)
    KEEP (DENSE_RANK FIRST ORDER BY SUM(tot_sales) DESC) min_best_region,
  MAX(region_id)
    KEEP (DENSE_RANK FIRST ORDER BY SUM(tot_sales) DESC) max_best_region,
  MIN(region_id)
    KEEP (DENSE_RANK LAST ORDER BY SUM(tot_sales) DESC) min_worst_region,
  MAX(region_id)
    KEEP (DENSE_RANK LAST ORDER BY SUM(tot_sales) DESC) max_worst_region
FROM orders
WHERE year = 2001
GROUP BY region_id;


MIN_BEST_REGION MAX_BEST_REGION MIN_WORST_REGION MAX_WORST_REGION
--------------- --------------- ---------------- ----------------
              7               7               10               10
```

In this case, there are no ties for either first or last place. Depending on the type of data you are working with, using an aggregate function as a tiebreaker can be somewhat arbitrary.

NTILE

Another way rankings are commonly used is to generate buckets into which sets of rankings are grouped. For example, we may want to find those customers whose total sales ranked in the top 25%. The following query uses the NTILE function to group the customers into four buckets (or quartiles):

```
SELECT region_id, cust_nbr, SUM(tot_sales) cust_sales,
  NTILE(4) OVER (ORDER BY SUM(tot_sales) DESC) sales_quartile
FROM orders
WHERE year = 2001
GROUP BY region_id, cust_nbr
ORDER BY 4,3 DESC;
```

REGION_ID	CUST_NBR	CUST_SALES	SALES_QUARTILE
9	25	2232703	1
8	17	1944281	1
7	14	1929774	1
5	4	1878275	1
10	26	1808949	1
6	6	1788836	1
8	20	1412006	1
10	27	1322747	1
7	13	1310434	2
7	15	1255591	2
8	18	1253840	2
5	2	1224992	2
9	23	1224992	2
9	24	1224992	2
10	30	1216858	2
6	9	1208959	2
6	10	1196748	3
7	11	1190421	3
7	12	1182275	3
8	19	1174421	3
5	5	1169926	3
5	3	1161286	3
5	1	1151162	3
6	8	1141638	4
8	16	1068467	4
9	22	1036146	4
9	21	1020541	4
10	28	986964	4
6	7	971585	4
10	29	903383	4

The sales_quartile column in this query specifies NTILE(4) in order to create four buckets. The NTILE function finds each row's place in the ranking, and then assigns each row to a bucket such that every bucket contains the same number of rows. If the number of rows is not evenly divisible by the number of buckets, then the extra rows are distributed so that the number of rows per bucket differs by one at most. In the previous example, there are four buckets allocated for 30 rows, with buckets one and two containg eight rows each, and buckets three and four containing seven rows each. This approach is referred to as *equiheight buckets* because each bucket contains (optimally) the same number of rows.

Just like in the top-N query discussed earlier, we will need to wrap the query in an inline view if we want to filter on the NTILE result:

```
SELECT r.name region, c.name customer, cs.cust_sales
FROM customer c, region r,
 (SELECT region_id, cust_nbr, SUM(tot_sales) cust_sales,
    NTILE(4) OVER (ORDER BY SUM(tot_sales) DESC) sales_quartile
  FROM orders
  WHERE year = 2001
  GROUP BY region_id, cust_nbr) cs
WHERE cs.sales_quartile = 1
  AND cs.cust_nbr = c.cust_nbr
  AND cs.region_id = r.region_id
ORDER BY cs.cust_sales DESC;
```

REGION	CUSTOMER	CUST_SALES
NorthWest US	Worcester Technologies	2232703
SouthWest US	Evans Supply Corp.	1944281
SouthEast US	Madden Industries	1929774
New England	Flowtech Inc.	1878275
Central US	Alpha Technologies	1808949
Mid-Atlantic	Spartan Industries	1788836
SouthWest US	Malden Labs	1412006
Central US	Phillips Labs	1322747

The outer query filters on sales_quartile = 1, which removes all rows not in the top 25% of sales, and then joins the region and customer dimensions to generate the final results.

WIDTH_BUCKET

Similar to the NTILE function, the WIDTH_BUCKET function groups rows of the result set into buckets. Unlike NTILE, however, the WIDTH_BUCKET function attempts to create *equiwidth buckets*, meaning that the range of values is evenly distributed across the buckets. If your data were distributed across a bell curve, therefore, you could expect the buckets representing the low and high ranges of the bell curve to contain few records, whereas the buckets representing the middle ranges would contain many records.

New in Oracle9*i*, WIDTH_BUCKET can operate on numeric or date types, and takes the following four parameters:

1. The expression that generates the buckets.
2. The value used as the start of the range for bucket #1.
3. The value used as the end of the range for bucket #N.
4. The number of buckets to create (N).

WIDTH_BUCKET uses the values of the second, third, and fourth parameters to generate N buckets containing comparable ranges. If the expression yields values that fall outside the range specified by the second and third parameters, the WIDTH_BUCKET function will generate two additional buckets, numbered 0 and N+1, into which the outliers are placed. If we want to work with the entire result set, we need to make sure our values for the second and third parameters completely enclose the range of values in the result set. However, if we only wish to work with a subset of the data, we can specify values for the second and third parameters that enclose the desired range, and any rows falling outside the range will be placeds into buckets 0 and N+1.

To illustrate, we will use the NTILE example from earlier to generate three buckets for the total sales per customer:

```
SELECT region_id, cust_nbr,
  SUM(tot_sales) cust_sales,
  WIDTH_BUCKET(SUM(tot_sales), 1, 3000000, 3) sales_buckets
FROM orders
WHERE year = 2001
GROUP BY region_id, cust_nbr
ORDER BY 3;
```

REGION_ID	CUST_NBR	CUST_SALES	SALES_BUCKETS
10	29	903383	1
6	7	971585	1
10	28	986964	1
9	21	1020541	2
9	22	1036146	2
8	16	1068467	2
6	8	1141638	2
5	1	1151162	2
5	3	1161286	2
5	5	1169926	2
8	19	1174421	2
7	12	1182275	2
7	11	1190421	2
6	10	1196748	2
6	9	1208959	2
10	30	1216858	2
5	2	1224992	2
9	24	1224992	2
9	23	1224992	2

8	18	1253840	2
7	15	1255591	2
7	13	1310434	2
10	27	1322747	2
8	20	1412006	2
6	6	1788836	2
10	26	1808949	2
5	4	1878275	2
7	14	1929774	2
8	17	1944281	2
9	25	2232703	3

Based on these parameters, the WIDTH_BUCKET function generates three buckets; the first bucket starts at 1, and the third bucket has an upper range of 3,000,000. Since there are three buckets, the ranges for each bucket will be 1 to 1,000,000, 1,000,0001 to 2,000,000, and 2,000,0001 to 3,000,000. When the rows are placed in the appropriate bucket, we find that three rows fall into bucket #1, a single row falls in bucket #3, and the remaining 26 rows fall into the second bucket.

The values 1 and 3,000,000 were chosen to guarantee that all rows in the result set would be placed into one of the three buckets. If we want to generate buckets only for rows that have aggregate sales between $1,000,000 and $2,000,000, the WIDTH_BUCKET function will place the remaining rows in the 0th and 4th buckets:

```
SELECT region_id, cust_nbr,
  SUM(tot_sales) cust_sales,
   WIDTH_BUCKET(SUM(tot_sales), 1000000, 2000000, 3) sales_buckets
FROM orders
WHERE year = 2001
GROUP BY region_id, cust_nbr
ORDER BY 3;

REGION_ID   CUST_NBR CUST_SALES SALES_BUCKETS
---------- ---------- ---------- -------------
        10         29     903383             0
         6          7     971585             0
        10         28     986964             0
         9         21    1020541             1
         9         22    1036146             1
         8         16    1068467             1
         6          8    1141638             1
         5          1    1151162             1
         5          3    1161286             1
         5          5    1169926             1
         8         19    1174421             1
         7         12    1182275             1
         7         11    1190421             1
         6         10    1196748             1
         6          9    1208959             1
        10         30    1216858             1
         5          2    1224992             1
         9         24    1224992             1
         9         23    1224992             1
```

8	18	1253840	1
7	15	1255591	1
7	13	1310434	1
10	27	1322747	1
8	20	1412006	2
6	6	1788836	3
10	26	1808949	3
5	4	1878275	3
7	14	1929774	3
8	17	1944281	3
9	25	2232703	4

Keep in mind that the WIDTH_BUCKET function does not remove rows from the result set that do not lie within the specified range; rather, they are placed into special buckets that your query can either utilize or ignore as needed.

CUME_DIST and PERCENT_RANK

The final two ranking functions, CUME_DIST and PERCENT_RANK, use the rank of a particular row to calculate additional information. The CUME_DIST function (short for Cumulative Distribution) calculates the ratio of the number of rows that have a lesser or equal ranking to the total number of rows in the partition. The PERCENT_RANK function calculates the ratio of a row's ranking to the number of rows in the partition using the formula:

$$(RRP - 1) / (NRP - 1)$$

where:

RRP
    Stands for "rank of row in partition."

NRP
    Stands for "number of rows in partition."

Both calculations utilize DENSE_RANK for their rankings and can be specified to be in ascending or descending order. The following query demonstrates the use of these two functions (both specifying descending order) with our customer yearly sales query:

```
SELECT region_id, cust_nbr,
  SUM(tot_sales) cust_sales,
  CUME_DIST( ) OVER (ORDER BY SUM(tot_sales) DESC) sales_cume_dist,
  PERCENT_RANK( ) OVER (ORDER BY SUM(tot_sales) DESC) sales_percent_rank
FROM orders
WHERE year = 2001
GROUP BY region_id, cust_nbr
ORDER BY 3 DESC;
```

REGION_ID	CUST_NBR	CUST_SALES	SALES_CUME_DIST	SALES_PERCENT_RANK
9	25	2232703	.033333333	0
8	17	1944281	.066666667	.034482759
7	14	1929774	.1	.068965517

5	4	1878275	.133333333	.103448276
10	26	1808949	.166666667	.137931034
6	6	1788836	.2	.172413793
8	20	1412006	.233333333	.206896552
10	27	1322747	.266666667	.24137931
7	13	1310434	.3	.275862069
7	15	1255591	.333333333	.310344828
8	18	1253840	.366666667	.344827586
5	2	1224992	**.466666667**	**.379310345**
9	23	1224992	**.466666667**	**.379310345**
9	24	1224992	**.466666667**	**.379310345**
10	30	1216858	.5	.482758621
6	9	1208959	.533333333	.517241379
6	10	1196748	.566666667	.551724138
7	11	1190421	.6	.586206897
7	12	1182275	.633333333	.620689655
8	19	1174421	.666666667	.655172414
5	5	1169926	.7	.689655172
5	3	1161286	.733333333	.724137931
5	1	1151162	.766666667	.75862069
6	8	1141638	.8	.793103448
8	16	1068467	.833333333	.827586207
9	22	1036146	.866666667	.862068966
9	21	1020541	.9	.896551724
10	28	986964	.933333333	.931034483
6	7	971585	.966666667	.965517241
10	29	903383	1	1

Let's walk through a couple of calculations for customer number 1 in the previous result set. With total sales of $1,151,162, customer number 1 ranks 23rd in the set of 30 customers in descending order of sales. Since there are a total of 30 rows, the CUME_DIST is equal to 23/30, or .766666667. The PERCENT_RANK function yields (23 – 1) / (30 – 1) = .75862069. It should come as no surprise that both functions return identical values for the rows that have identical sales totals, since the calculations are based on rank, which is identical for all three rows.

Hypothetical Functions

For some types of analysis, determining what *might* have happened is more revealing than knowing what really happened. With the Oracle9i release, Oracle provides special versions of RANK, DENSE_RANK, CUME_DIST, and PERCENT_RANK that allow rankings and distributions to be calculated for hypothetical data, allowing the user to see what would have happened if a specific value (or set of values) was included in a data set.

In order to illustrate this concept, we will first rank our customers by total sales for 2001, and then we will see where a hypothetical sales figure would fall in the ranking. Here is the query that generates the rankings and distributions:

```
SELECT cust_nbr, SUM(tot_sales) cust_sales,
  RANK( ) OVER (ORDER BY SUM(tot_sales) DESC) rank,
  DENSE_RANK( ) OVER (ORDER BY SUM(tot_sales) DESC) dense_rank,
```

```
  CUME_DIST( ) OVER (ORDER BY SUM(tot_sales) DESC) cume_dist,
  PERCENT_RANK( ) OVER (ORDER BY SUM(tot_sales) DESC) percent_rank
FROM orders
WHERE year = 2001
GROUP BY cust_nbr
ORDER BY 3;
```

CUST_NBR	CUST_SALES	RANK	DENSE_RANK	CUME_DIST	PERCENT_RANK
25	2232703	1	1	.033333333	0
17	1944281	2	2	.066666667	.034482759
14	1929774	3	3	.1	.068965517
4	1878275	4	4	.133333333	.103448276
26	1808949	5	5	.166666667	.137931034
6	1788836	6	6	.2	.172413793
20	1412006	7	7	.233333333	.206896552
27	1322747	8	8	.266666667	.24137931
13	1310434	9	9	.3	.275862069
15	1255591	10	10	.333333333	.310344828
18	1253840	11	11	.366666667	.344827586
2	1224992	12	12	.466666667	.379310345
23	1224992	12	12	.466666667	.379310345
24	1224992	12	12	.466666667	.379310345
30	1216858	15	13	.5	.482758621
9	1208959	16	14	.533333333	.517241379
10	1196748	17	15	.566666667	.551724138
11	1190421	18	16	.6	.586206897
12	1182275	19	17	.633333333	.620689655
19	1174421	20	18	.666666667	.655172414
5	1169926	21	19	.7	.689655172
3	1161286	22	20	.733333333	.724137931
1	1151162	23	21	.766666667	.75862069
8	1141638	24	22	.8	.793103448
16	1068467	25	23	.833333333	.827586207
22	1036146	26	24	.866666667	.862068966
21	1020541	27	25	.9	.896551724
28	986964	28	26	.933333333	.931034483
7	971585	29	27	.966666667	.965517241
29	903383	30	28	1	1

Now let's see where a customer with an even million dollars of sales would have
ranked:

```
SELECT
  RANK(1000000) WITHIN GROUP
    (ORDER BY SUM(tot_sales) DESC) hyp_rank,
  DENSE_RANK(1000000) WITHIN GROUP
    (ORDER BY SUM(tot_sales) DESC) hyp_dense_rank,
  CUME_DIST(1000000) WITHIN GROUP
    (ORDER BY SUM(tot_sales) DESC) hyp_cume_dist,
  PERCENT_RANK(1000000) WITHIN GROUP
    (ORDER BY SUM(tot_sales) DESC) hyp_percent_rank
FROM orders
WHERE year = 2001
GROUP BY cust_nbr;
```

```
HYP_RANK HYP_DENSE_RANK HYP_CUME_DIST HYP_PERCENT_RANK
---------- -------------- -------------- ----------------
        28             26    .903225806               .9
```

The WITHIN GROUP clause has the effect of injecting a fictitious row into the result set before determining the rankings. One possible use of this functionality would be to see how actual sales compare to sales targets.

Windowing Functions

The ranking functions described thus far are quite useful when comparing items within a fixed window of time, such as "last year" or "second quarter." But what if we want to perform computations using a window that slides as we progress through the data set? Oracle's windowing functions allow aggregates to be calculated for each row in a result set based on a specified window. The aggregation window can be defined in one of three ways:

- By specifying a set of rows: "From the current row to the end of the partition."
- By specifying a time interval: "For the 30 days preceeding the transaction date."
- By specifying a range of values: "All rows having a transaction amount within 5% of the current row's transaction amount."

To get started, we generate a window that fills the entire partition, and then we see how the window can be detached from one or both ends of the partition so that it floats with the current row. All of the examples will be based on the following query, which calculates total monthly sales for the Mid-Atlantic region:

```
SELECT month, SUM(tot_sales) monthly_sales
FROM orders
WHERE year = 2001
  AND region_id = 6
GROUP BY month
ORDER BY 1month;

    MONTH MONTHLY_SALES
---------- -------------
        1        610697
        2        428676
        3        637031
        4        541146
        5        592935
        6        501485
        7        606914
        8        460520
        9        392898
       10        510117
       11        532889
       12        492458
```

First, we will sum the monthly sales for the entire result set by specifying an "unbounded" window. Note the ROWS BETWEEN clause in the following example:

```
SELECT month, SUM(tot_sales) monthly_sales,
  SUM(SUM(tot_sales)) OVER (ORDER BY month
    ROWS BETWEEN UNBOUNDED PRECEDING AND UNBOUNDED FOLLOWING) total_sales
FROM orders
WHERE year = 2001
  AND region_id = 6
GROUP BY month
ORDER BY month;
```

MONTH	MONTHLY_SALES	TOTAL_SALES
1	610697	6307766
2	428676	6307766
3	637031	6307766
4	541146	6307766
5	592935	6307766
6	501485	6307766
7	606914	6307766
8	460520	6307766
9	392898	6307766
10	510117	6307766
11	532889	6307766
12	492458	6307766

Each time the function executes, it sums the monthly sales from months 1 through 12; thus, the same calculation is being performed 12 times. This is a rather inefficient way to generate the yearly sales total (see "Reporting Functions" later in this chapter for a better method), but it should give you an idea of the syntax for building an aggregation window. In the next query, we will create a window that spans from the top of the partition to the current row. The function identifies the month that has the maximum sales, up to and including the current month:

```
SELECT month, SUM(tot_sales) monthly_sales,
  MAX(SUM(tot_sales)) OVER (ORDER BY month
    ROWS BETWEEN UNBOUNDED PRECEDING AND CURRENT ROW) max_preceeding
FROM orders
WHERE year = 2001
  AND region_id = 6
GROUP BY month
ORDER BY month;
```

MONTH	MONTHLY_SALES	MAX_PRECEEDING
1	610697	610697
2	428676	610697
3	637031	637031
4	541146	637031
5	592935	637031
6	501485	637031
7	606914	637031

8	460520	637031
9	392898	637031
10	510117	637031
11	532889	637031
12	492458	637031

Unlike the first query, which has a window size fixed at 12 rows, this query's aggregation window grows from a single row for month 1 to 12 rows for month 12. The keywords CURRENT ROW are used to indicate that the window should end at the current row being inspected by the function. If we replace MAX in the previous query with SUM, we can calculate a running total:

```
SELECT month, SUM(tot_sales) monthly_sales,
  SUM(SUM(tot_sales)) OVER (ORDER BY month
    ROWS BETWEEN UNBOUNDED PRECEDING AND CURRENT ROW) max_preceeding
FROM orders
WHERE year = 2001
  AND region_id = 6
GROUP BY month
ORDER BY month;
```

```
MONTH MONTHLY_SALES MAX_PRECEEDING
---------- -------------- --------------
       1        610697         610697
       2        428676        1039373
       3        637031        1676404
       4        541146        2217550
       5        592935        2810485
       6        501485        3311970
       7        606914        3918884
       8        460520        4379404
       9        392898        4772302
      10        510117        5282419
      11        532889        5815308
      12        492458        6307766
```

We have now seen examples using windows that are fixed at one or both ends. In the next query, we will define a window that floats freely with each row:

```
SELECT month, SUM(tot_sales) monthly_sales,
  AVG(SUM(tot_sales)) OVER (ORDER BY month
    ROWS BETWEEN 1 PRECEDING AND 1 FOLLOWING) rolling_avg
FROM orders
WHERE year = 2001
  AND region_id = 6
GROUP BY month
ORDER BY month;
```

```
MONTH MONTHLY_SALES ROLLING_AVG
---------- -------------- ------------
       1        610697     519686.5
       2        428676    558801.333
       3        637031    535617.667
       4        541146    590370.667
```

5	592935	545188.667
6	501485	567111.333
7	606914	522973
8	460520	486777.333
9	392898	454511.667
10	510117	478634.667
11	532889	511821.333
12	492458	512673.5

For each of the 12 rows, the function calculates the average sales of the current month, the previous month, and the following month. The value of the ROLLING_AVG column is therefore the average sales within a three month floating window centered on the current month.*

FIRST_VALUE and LAST_VALUE

Oracle provides two additional aggregate functions, called FIRST_VALUE and LAST_VALUE, that can be used with windowing functions to identify the values of the first and last values in the window. In the case of the 3-month rolling average query shown previously, we could display the values of all three months along with the average of the three, as in:

```
SELECT month,
   FIRST_VALUE(SUM(tot_sales)) OVER (ORDER BY month
      ROWS BETWEEN 1 PRECEDING AND 1 FOLLOWING) prev_month,
   SUM(tot_sales) monthly_sales,
   LAST_VALUE(SUM(tot_sales)) OVER (ORDER BY month
      ROWS BETWEEN 1 PRECEDING AND 1 FOLLOWING) next_month,
   AVG(SUM(tot_sales)) OVER (ORDER BY month
      ROWS BETWEEN 1 PRECEDING AND 1 FOLLOWING) rolling_avg
FROM orders
WHERE year = 2001
   AND region_id = 6
GROUP BY month
ORDER BY month;
```

MONTH	PREV_MONTH	MONTHLY_SALES	NEXT_MONTH	ROLLING_AVG
1	610697	610697	428676	519686.5
2	610697	428676	637031	558801.333
3	428676	637031	541146	535617.667
4	637031	541146	592935	590370.667
5	541146	592935	501485	545188.667
6	592935	501485	606914	567111.333
7	501485	606914	460520	522973
8	606914	460520	392898	486777.333
9	460520	392898	510117	454511.667

---

* Months 1 and 12 are calculated using a 2-month window, since there is no previous month for month 1 or following month for month 12.

10	392898	510117	532889	478634.667
11	510117	532889	492458	511821.333
12	532889	492458	492458	512673.5

These functions are useful for queries that compare each value to the first or last value in the period, such as: "How did each month's sales compare to the first month?"

LAG/LEAD Functions

While not technically windowing functions, the LAG and LEAD functions are included here because they allow rows to be referenced by their position relative to the current row, much like the PRECEDING and FOLLOWING clauses within windowing functions. LAG and LEAD are useful for comparing one row of a result set with another row of the same result set. For example, the query "Compute the total sales per month for the Mid-Atlantic region, including the percent change from the previous month" requires data from both the current and preceding rows in order to calculate the answer. This is, in effect, a two row window, but the offset from the current row can be specified as one or more rows, making LAG and LEAD act like specialized windowing functions where only the outer edges of the window are utilized.

Here is the SQL that uses the LAG function to generate the data needed to answer the question posed in the previous paragraph:

```
SELECT month, SUM(tot_sales) monthly_sales,
  LAG(SUM(tot_sales), 1) OVER (ORDER BY month) prev_month_sales
FROM orders
WHERE year = 2001
  AND region_id = 6
GROUP BY month
ORDER BY month;
```

MONTH	MONTHLY_SALES	PREV_MONTH_SALES
1	610697	
2	428676	610697
3	637031	428676
4	541146	637031
5	592935	541146
6	501485	592935
7	606914	501485
8	460520	606914
9	392898	460520
10	510117	392898
11	532889	510117
12	492458	532889

As we might expect, the LAG value for month 1 is NULL, since there is no preceding month. This would also be the case for the LEAD value for month 12. Take this into account when performing calculations that utilize the results of the LAG or LEAD functions.

The next query utilizes the output from the previous query to generate the percentage difference from month to month. Note how the prev_month_sales column is wrapped in the NVL function so that month 1 won't generate a NULL value for the percentage change:

```
SELECT months.month month, months.monthly_sales monthly_sales,
  ROUND((months.monthly_sales - NVL(months.prev_month_sales,
    months.monthly_sales)) /
    NVL(months.prev_month_sales, months.monthly_sales),
    3) * 100 percent_change
FROM
  (SELECT month, SUM(tot_sales) monthly_sales,
    LAG(SUM(tot_sales), 1) OVER (ORDER BY month) prev_month_sales
  FROM orders
  WHERE year = 2001
    AND region_id = 6
  GROUP BY month) months
ORDER BY month;
```

MONTH	MONTHLY_SALES	PERCENT_CHANGE
1	610697	0
2	428676	-29.8
3	637031	48.6
4	541146	-15.1
5	592935	9.6
6	501485	-15.4
7	606914	21
8	460520	-24.1
9	392898	-14.7
10	510117	29.8
11	532889	4.5
12	492458	-7.6

Reporting Functions

Similar to the windowing functions described earlier, reporting functions allow the execution of various aggregate functions (MIN, MAX, SUM, COUNT, AVG, etc.) against a result set. Unlike windowing functions, however, the reporting functions cannot specify localized windows and thus generate the same result for the entire partition (or the entire result set, if no partitions are specified). Therefore, anything that can be accomplished using a reporting function could also be accomplished using a windowing function with an unbounded window, although it would generally be more efficient to use the reporting function.

Earlier in the chapter, we used a windowing function with an unbounded reporting window to generate the total sales for the 12 months of 2001:

```
SELECT month,
  SUM(tot_sales) monthly_sales,
  SUM(SUM(tot_sales)) OVER (ORDER BY month
```

```
      ROWS BETWEEN UNBOUNDED PRECEDING AND UNBOUNDED FOLLOWING) total_sales
FROM orders
WHERE year = 2001
  AND region_id = 6
GROUP BY month
ORDER BY month;

    MONTH MONTHLY_SALES TOTAL_SALES
---------- ------------- -----------
         1        610697     6307766
         2        428676     6307766
         3        637031     6307766
         4        541146     6307766
         5        592935     6307766
         6        501485     6307766
         7        606914     6307766
         8        460520     6307766
         9        392898     6307766
        10        510117     6307766
        11        532889     6307766
        12        492458     6307766
```

The next query adds a reporting function to generate the same results:

```
SELECT month,
  SUM(tot_sales) monthly_sales,
  SUM(SUM(tot_sales)) OVER (ORDER BY month
    ROWS BETWEEN UNBOUNDED PRECEDING AND UNBOUNDED FOLLOWING) window_sales,
  SUM(SUM(tot_sales)) OVER () reporting_sales
FROM orders
WHERE year = 2001
  AND region_id = 6
GROUP BY month
ORDER BY month;

    MONTH MONTHLY_SALES WINDOW_SALES REPORTING_SALES
---------- ------------- ------------ ---------------
         1        610697      6307766         6307766
         2        428676      6307766         6307766
         3        637031      6307766         6307766
         4        541146      6307766         6307766
         5        592935      6307766         6307766
         6        501485      6307766         6307766
         7        606914      6307766         6307766
         8        460520      6307766         6307766
         9        392898      6307766         6307766
        10        510117      6307766         6307766
        11        532889      6307766         6307766
        12        492458      6307766         6307766
```

The empty parentheses after the OVER clause in the reporting_sales column indicates that the entire result set should be included in the sum, which has the same effect as using an unbounded window function. Hopefully, you will agree that the reporting function is easier to understand than the unbounded window function.

Reporting functions are useful when we need both detail and aggregate data (or different aggregation levels) to answer a business query. For example, the query "Show the monthly sales totals for 2001 along with each month's percentage of yearly sales" requires the detail rows to be aggregated first to the month level, and then to the year level in order to answer the question. Rather than computing both aggregations from the detail rows, we can use the SUM function with a GROUP BY clause to aggregate to the month level, and then use a reporting function to aggregate the monthly totals, as in:

```
SELECT month,
  SUM(tot_sales) monthly_sales,
  SUM(SUM(tot_sales)) OVER () yearly_sales
FROM orders
WHERE year = 2001
GROUP BY month
ORDER BY month;
```

MONTH	MONTHLY_SALES	YEARLY_SALES
1	3028325	39593192
2	3289336	39593192
3	3411024	39593192
4	3436482	39593192
5	3749264	39593192
6	3204730	39593192
7	3233532	39593192
8	3081290	39593192
9	3388292	39593192
10	3279637	39593192
11	3167858	39593192
12	3323422	39593192

We would then simply divide MONTHLY_SALES by YEARLY_SALES to compute the requested percentage (see the section "RATIO_TO_REPORT" later in the chapter).

Report Partitions

Like ranking functions, reporting functions can include PARTITION BY clauses to split the result set into multiple pieces, allowing multiple aggregations to be computed across different subsets of the result set. The following query generates total sales per salesperson per region along with the total regional sales for comparison:

```
SELECT region_id, salesperson_id,
  SUM(tot_sales) sp_sales,
  SUM(SUM(tot_sales)) OVER (PARTITION BY region_id) region_sales
FROM orders
WHERE year = 2001
GROUP BY region_id, salesperson_id
ORDER BY region_id, salesperson_id;
```

REGION_ID	SALESPERSON_ID	SP_SALES	REGION_SALES
5	1	1927580	6585641
5	2	1461898	6585641

5	3	1501039	6585641
5	4	1695124	6585641
6	5	1688252	6307766
6	6	1392648	6307766
6	7	1458053	6307766
6	8	1768813	6307766
7	9	1735575	6868495
7	10	1723305	6868495
7	11	1737093	6868495
7	12	1672522	6868495
8	13	1516776	6853015
8	14	1814327	6853015
8	15	1760098	6853015
8	16	1761814	6853015
9	17	1710831	6739374
9	18	1625456	6739374
9	19	1645204	6739374
9	20	1757883	6739374
10	21	1542152	6238901
10	22	1468316	6238901
10	23	1443837	6238901
10	24	1784596	6238901

The value for the REGION_SALES column is the same for all salespeople in the same region. In the next section, we will see two different approaches for using this information to generate percentage calculations.

RATIO_TO_REPORT

One of the more common uses of reporting functions is to generate the value of the denominator for performance calculations. With the query from the previous section, for example, the next logical step would be to divide each salesperson's total sales (SP_SALES) by the total region sales (REGION_SALES) to determine what ratio of the total region sales can be attributed to each salesperson. One option is to use the reporting function as the denominator in the percentage calculation, as in:

```
SELECT region_id, salesperson_id,
  SUM(tot_sales) sp_sales,
  ROUND(SUM(tot_sales) /
    SUM(SUM(tot_sales)) OVER (PARTITION BY region_id),
    2) percent_of_region
FROM orders
WHERE year = 2001
GROUP BY region_id, salesperson_id
ORDER BY region_id, salesperson_id1,2;

REGION_ID  SALESPERSON_ID   SP_SALES PERCENT_OF_REGION
---------- --------------- ---------- ------------------
        5               1    1927580               .29
        5               2    1461898               .22
        5               3    1501039               .23
        5               4    1695124               .26
        6               5    1688252               .27
```

6	6	1392648	.22
6	7	1458053	.23
6	8	1768813	.28
7	9	1735575	.25
7	10	1723305	.25
7	11	1737093	.25
7	12	1672522	.24
8	13	1516776	.22
8	14	1814327	.26
8	15	1760098	.26
8	16	1761814	.26
9	17	1710831	.25
9	18	1625456	.24
9	19	1645204	.24
9	20	1757883	.26
10	21	1542152	.25
10	22	1468316	.24
10	23	1443837	.23
10	24	1784596	.29

Because this is such a common operation, however, Oracle has spared us the trouble by including the RATIO_TO_REPORT function. The RATIO_TO_REPORT function allows us to calculate each row's contribution to either the entire result set, or some subset of the result set if the PARTITION BY clause is included. The next query uses RATIO_TO_REPORT to generate the percentage contribution of each salesperson to her region's total sales:

```
SELECT region_id, salesperson_id,
  SUM(tot_sales) sp_sales,
  ROUND(RATIO_TO_REPORT(SUM(tot_sales))
    OVER (PARTITION BY region_id), 2) sp_ratio
FROM orders
WHERE year = 2001
GROUP BY region_id, salesperson_id
ORDER BY 1,2;
```

REGION_ID	SALESPERSON_ID	SP_SALES	SP_RATIO
5	1	1927580	.29
5	2	1461898	.22
5	3	1501039	.23
5	4	1695124	.26
6	5	1688252	.27
6	6	1392648	.22
6	7	1458053	.23
6	8	1768813	.28
7	9	1735575	.25
7	10	1723305	.25
7	11	1737093	.25
7	12	1672522	.24
8	13	1516776	.22
8	14	1814327	.26
8	15	1760098	.26

8	16	1761814	.26
9	17	1710831	.25
9	18	1625456	.24
9	19	1645204	.24
9	20	1757883	.26
10	21	1542152	.25
10	22	1468316	.24
10	23	1443837	.23
10	24	1784596	.29

Summary

We have covered a lot of ground in this chapter, so don't feel bad if it takes a couple of passes to get a feel for all of the different analytic functions and how they can be applied. While there are many different functions, it is easier to digest if you concentrate on one category at a time (Ranking, Windowing, Reporting). Those who have worked with Oracle for many years are probably chomping at the bit to give these functions a try. Along with being compact and efficient, Oracle's analytic functions keep analytical calculations where they belong—in the database server—instead of relying on procedural languages or spreadsheet macros to finish the job.

CHAPTER 14

SQL Best Practices

Writing efficient SQL statements requires experience. You can write a SQL query in many different ways, each giving the same result, but one may be a hundred times slower than another. In this chapter, we discuss some tips and techniques that will help you write efficient SQL statements.

Know When to Use Specific Constructs

Depending on the circumstances, certain SQL constructs are preferable to others. For example, use of the EXISTS predicate is often preferable to IN. The same is not true for NOT EXISTS versus NOT IN. The next sections discuss the usage of such constructs.

EXISTS Is Preferable to DISTINCT

The DISTINCT keyword used in a SELECT clause eliminates duplicate rows in the result set. To eliminate those duplicates, Oracle performs a sort, and that sort requires time and disk space. Therefore, avoid using DISTINCT if you can tolerate having duplicate rows returned by a query. If you can't tolerate the duplicate rows, or your application can't handle them, use EXISTS in place of DISTINCT.

For example, assume you are trying to find the names of customers who have orders. Your query has to be based on two tables: CUSTOMER and CUST_ORDER. Using DISTINCT, your query would be written as follows:

```
SELECT DISTINCT C.CUST_NBR, C.NAME
FROM CUSTOMER C, CUST_ORDER O
WHERE C.CUST_NBR = O.CUST_NBR;
```

The corresponding execution plan for this query is as follows. Note the SORT operation, which is a result of DISTINCT being used.

```
Query Plan
------------------------------------------
SELECT STATEMENT    Cost = 3056
  SORT UNIQUE
```

```
MERGE JOIN
    INDEX FULL SCAN IND_ORD_CUST_NBR
    SORT JOIN
        TABLE ACCESS FULL CUSTOMER
```

To use EXISTS, the query needs to be rewritten as follows:

```
SELECT C.CUST_NBR, C.NAME
FROM CUSTOMER C
WHERE EXISTS (SELECT 1 FROM CUST_ORDER O WHERE C.CUST_NBR = O.CUST_NBR);
```

Here is the execution plan for the EXISTS version of the query. Look at the cost of this query versus the earlier DISTINCT query, and notice the performance improvement.

```
Query Plan
----------------------------------------
SELECT STATEMENT    Cost = 320
    FILTER
        TABLE ACCESS FULL CUSTOMER
        INDEX RANGE SCAN IND_ORD_CUST_NBR
```

The version of the query using EXISTS is less than one-ninth as costly as the version using DISTINCT. This is because the sort has been avoided.

EXISTS Versus IN

Many SQL books discuss the fact that NOT EXISTS performs better than NOT IN. We have found that with Oracle8i, the EXPLAIN PLAN generated by NOT EXISTS is exactly the same as that generated by NOT IN, and the performance for the two predicates is the same.

However, the comparison between EXISTS and IN is a different story. We've found that EXISTS often performs better than IN. Let's look at an example that demonstrates this. The following query uses IN to delete the orders for customers in region 5:

```
DELETE FROM CUST_ORDER
WHERE CUST_NBR IN
(SELECT CUST_NBR FROM CUSTOMER
WHERE REGION_ID = 5);
```

The execution plan for this query is as follows:

```
Query Plan
------------------------------------
DELETE STATEMENT    Cost = 3
    DELETE  CUST_ORDER
        HASH JOIN
            TABLE ACCESS FULL CUST_ORDER
            TABLE ACCESS FULL CUSTOMER
```

Now, let's look at that same query, written using EXISTS:

```
DELETE FROM CUST_ORDER
WHERE EXISTS
(SELECT CUST_NBR FROM CUSTOMER
WHERE CUST_ORDER.CUST_NBR = CUSTOMER.CUST_NBR
AND REGION_ID = 5);
```

The execution plan for the EXISTS version of the query is:

```
Query Plan
---------------------------------------------
DELETE STATEMENT    Cost = 1
  DELETE  CUST_ORDER
    FILTER
       TABLE ACCESS FULL CUST_ORDER
       TABLE ACCESS BY INDEX ROWID CUSTOMER
         INDEX UNIQUE SCAN CUSTOMER_PK
```

Notice the cost difference between the two queries. The IN version of the query has a cost of 3, while the EXISTS version of the query has a cost of only 1. When the EXISTS clause is used, the execution plan is driven by the outer table, whereas when the IN clause is used, the execution plan is driven by the table in the subquery. The EXISTS query will almost always be faster than the IN query, except for cases when the table in the subquery has very few rows as compared to the outer table.

WHERE Versus HAVING

We discussed the GROUP BY and HAVING clauses in Chapter 4. Sometimes, when writing a GROUP BY query, you have a condition that you can specify in either the WHERE clause or the HAVING clause. In situations where you have a choice, you'll always get better performance if you specify the condition in the WHERE clause. The reason is that it's less expensive to eliminate rows before they are summarized than it is to eliminate results after summarization.

Let's look at an example illustrating the advantage of WHERE over HAVING. Here's a query with the HAVING clause that reports the number of orders in the year 2000:

```
SELECT YEAR, COUNT(*)
FROM ORDERS
GROUP BY YEAR
HAVING YEAR = 2000;

    YEAR    COUNT(*)
---------- ----------
    2000        720
```

The execution plan for this query is as follows:

```
Query Plan
---------------------------------------------
SELECT STATEMENT    Cost = 6
  FILTER
    SORT GROUP BY
      INDEX FAST FULL SCAN ORDERS_PK
```

Now, look at that same query, but with the year restriction in the WHERE clause:

```
SELECT YEAR, COUNT(*)
FROM ORDERS
WHERE YEAR = 2000
GROUP BY YEAR;
```

```
YEAR    COUNT(*)
---------- ----------
    2000        720
```

The execution plan for this version of the query is:

```
Query Plan
-------------------------------------
SELECT STATEMENT    Cost = 2
  SORT GROUP BY NOSORT
    INDEX FAST FULL SCAN ORDERS_PK
```

With the HAVING clause, the query performs the group operation first, and then filters the groups for the condition specified. The WHERE clause version of the query filters the rows *before* performing the group operation. The result of filtering with the WHERE clause is that there are fewer rows to summarize, and consequently the query performs better.

However, you should note that not all types of filtering can be achieved using the WHERE clause. Sometimes, you may need to summarize the data first, and then filter the summarized data based upon the summarized values. In such situations, you have to filter using the HAVING clause, because only the HAVING clause can "see" summarized values. Moreover, there are situations when you may need to use the WHERE clause and the HAVING clause together in a query to filter the results the way you want. For details, see Chapter 4.

UNION Versus UNION ALL

We discussed UNION and UNION ALL in Chapter 6. UNION ALL combines the results of two SELECT statements. UNION combines the results of two SELECT statements, and then returns only distinct rows from the combination; duplicates are eliminated. It is, therefore, obvious that to remove the duplicates, UNION performs one extra step than UNION ALL. This extra step is a sort, which is costly in terms of performance. Therefore, whenever your application can handle duplicates or you are certain that no duplicates will result, consider using UNION ALL instead of UNION.

Let's look an example to understand this issue better. The following query uses UNION to return a list of orders where the sale price exceeds $50.00 or where the customer is located in region 5:

```
SELECT ORDER_NBR, CUST_NBR FROM CUST_ORDER WHERE SALE_PRICE > 50
UNION
SELECT ORDER_NBR, CUST_NBR FROM CUST_ORDER
WHERE CUST_NBR IN
(SELECT CUST_NBR FROM CUSTOMER WHERE REGION_ID = 5);


ORDER_NBR   CUST_NBR
---------- ----------
     1000          1
     1001          1
     1002          5
     1003          4
```

```
1004           4
1005           8
1006           1
1007           5
1008           5
1009           1
1011           1
1012           1
1015           5
1017           4
1019           4
1021           8
1023           1
1025           5
1027           5
1029           1
```

```
20 rows selected.
```

The execution plan for this UNION query is:

```
Query Plan
-------------------------------------------------------------------------------
SELECT STATEMENT    Cost = 8
  SORT UNIQUE
    UNION-ALL
      TABLE ACCESS FULL CUST_ORDER
      HASH JOIN
        TABLE ACCESS FULL CUSTOMER
        TABLE ACCESS FULL CUST_ORDER
```

The following query uses UNION ALL instead of UNION to get the same information:

```
SELECT ORDER_NBR, CUST_NBR FROM CUST_ORDER WHERE SALE_PRICE > 50
UNION ALL
SELECT ORDER_NBR, CUST_NBR FROM CUST_ORDER
WHERE CUST_NBR IN
(SELECT CUST_NBR FROM CUSTOMER WHERE REGION_ID = 5);
```

```
ORDER_NBR    CUST_NBR
----------   ----------
     1001           1
     1003           4
     1005           8
     1009           1
     1012           1
     1017           4
     1021           8
     1029           1
     1001           1
     1000           1
     1002           5
     1003           4
     1004           4
     1006           1
```

```
1007       5
1008       5
1009       1
1012       1
1011       1
1015       5
1017       4
1019       4
1023       1
1025       5
1027       5
1029       1
```

```
26 rows selected.
```

Note the duplicate rows in the output. However, note also that UNION ALL performs better than UNION, as you can see from the following execution plan:

```
Query Plan
-------------------------------------------------------------------------------
SELECT STATEMENT    Cost = 4
   UNION-ALL
      TABLE ACCESS FULL CUST_ORDER
      HASH JOIN
         TABLE ACCESS FULL CUSTOMER
         TABLE ACCESS FULL CUST_ORDER
```

Compare this execution plan with its cost of 4 with the previous plan and its cost of 8. You can see that the extra operation (SORT UNIQUE) in the UNION makes it run slower than UNION ALL.

Avoid Unnecessary Parsing

Before your SQL can be executed by Oracle, it needs to be parsed. The importance of parsing when it comes to tuning SQL lies in the fact that no matter how many times a given SQL statement is executed, it needs to be parsed only once. During parsing, the following steps are performed (not necessarily in the sequence shown):

- The syntax of the SQL statement is verified.
- The data dictionary is searched to verify table and column definitions.
- The data dictionary is searched to verify security privileges on relevant objects.
- Parse locks are acquired on the relevant objects.
- The optimal execution plan is determined.
- The statement is loaded into the shared SQL area (also known as the library cache) in the shared pool of the system global area (SGA). The execution plan and parse information are saved here in case the same statement is executed once again.

If a SQL statement involves any remote objects (e.g., database links) then these steps are repeated for the remote objects. As you can see, lots of work is performed during the parsing of a SQL statement. However, a statement is parsed only if Oracle doesn't find an identical SQL statement already in the shared SQL area (library cache) of the SGA.

Before parsing a SQL statement, Oracle searches the library cache for an identical SQL statement. If Oracle finds an exact match, there is no need to parse the statement again. However, if an identical SQL statement is not found, Oracle goes through all the aforementioned steps to parse the statement.

The most important keyword in the previous paragraph is "identical." To share the same SQL area, two statements need to be truly identical. Two statements that look similar, or that return the same result, need not be identical. To be truly identical, the statements must:

- Have the same uppercase and lowercase characters.
- Have the same whitespace and newline characters.
- Reference the same objects using the same names, which must in turn have the same owners.

If there is a possibility that your application executes the same (or similar) SQL statements multiple times, by all means try to avoid unnecessary parsing. This will improve the overall performance of your applications. The following techniques can help you reduce SQL parsing:

- Use bind variables.
- Use table aliases.

Using Bind Variables

When multiple users use an application, they actually execute the same set of SQL statements over and over, but with different data values. For example, one customer service representative may be executing the following statement:

```
SELECT * FROM CUSTOMER WHERE CUST_NBR = 121;
```

while another customer service representative will be executing:

```
SELECT * FROM CUSTOMER WHERE CUST_NBR = 328;
```

These two statements are similar, but not "identical"—the customer ID numbers are different, therefore Oracle has to parse twice.

Because the only difference between these statements is the value used for the customer number, this application could be rewritten to use bind variables. In that case, the SQL statement in question could be as follows:

```
SELECT * FROM CUSTOMER WHERE CUST_NBR = :X;
```

Oracle needs to parse this statement only once. The actual customer numbers would be supplied after parsing for each execution of the statement. Multiple, concurrently executing programs could share the same copy of this SQL statement while at the same time supplying different customer number values.

In a multi-user application, situations such as the one described here are very common, and overall performance can be significantly improved by using bind variables, thereby reducing unnecessary parsing.

Using Table Aliases

The use of table aliases can help to improve the performance of your SQL statements. Before getting into the performance aspects of table aliases, let's quickly review what table aliases are and how they are used.

When you select data from two or more tables, you should specify which table each column belongs to. Otherwise, if the two tables have columns with the same name, you will end up with an error:

```
SELECT CUST_NBR, NAME, ORDER_NBR
FROM CUSTOMER, CUST_ORDER;
SELECT CUST_NBR, NAME, ORDER_NBR
       *
ERROR at line 1:
ORA-00918: column ambiguously defined
```

The error in this case occurs because both the CUSTOMER and CUST_ORDER tables have columns named CUST_NBR. Oracle can't tell which CUST_NBR column you are referring to. To fix this problem, you could rewrite this statement as follows:

```
SELECT CUSTOMER.CUST_NBR, CUSTOMER.NAME, CUST_ORDER.ORDER_NBR
FROM CUSTOMER, CUST_ORDER
WHERE CUSTOMER.CUST_NBR = CUST_ORDER.CUST_NBR;
```

```
CUST_NBR NAME                                ORDER_NBR
-------- ----------------------------------- ----------
       1 Cooper Industries                        1001
       1 Cooper Industries                        1000
       5 Gentech Industries                       1002
       4 Flowtech Inc.                            1003
       4 Flowtech Inc.                            1004
       8 Zantech Inc.                             1005
       1 Cooper Industries                        1006
       5 Gentech Industries                       1007
       5 Gentech Industries                       1008
       1 Cooper Industries                        1009
       1 Cooper Industries                        1012
       1 Cooper Industries                        1011
       5 Gentech Industries                       1015
       4 Flowtech Inc.                            1017
       4 Flowtech Inc.                            1019
```

```
   8 Zantech Inc.                          1021
   1 Cooper Industries                     1023
   5 Gentech Industries                    1025
   5 Gentech Industries                    1027
   1 Cooper Industries                     1029
```

20 rows selected.

Note the use of the table name to qualify each column name. This eliminates any ambiguity as to which CUST_NBR column the query is referring to.

Instead of qualifying column names with full table names, you can use table aliases, as in the following example:

```
SELECT C.CUST_NBR, C.NAME, O.ORDER_NBR
FROM CUSTOMER C, CUST_ORDER O
WHERE C.CUST_NBR = O.CUST_NBR;
```

```
CUST_NBR NAME                                    ORDER_NBR
-------- --------------------------------        ---------
       1 Cooper Industries                            1001
       1 Cooper Industries                            1000
       5 Gentech Industries                           1002
       4 Flowtech Inc.                                1003
       4 Flowtech Inc.                                1004
       8 Zantech Inc.                                 1005
       1 Cooper Industries                            1006
       5 Gentech Industries                           1007
       5 Gentech Industries                           1008
       1 Cooper Industries                            1009
       1 Cooper Industries                            1012
       1 Cooper Industries                            1011
       5 Gentech Industries                           1015
       4 Flowtech Inc.                                1017
       4 Flowtech Inc.                                1019
       8 Zantech Inc.                                 1021
       1 Cooper Industries                            1023
       5 Gentech Industries                           1025
       5 Gentech Industries                           1027
       1 Cooper Industries                            1029
```

20 rows selected.

The letters "C" and "O" in this example are table aliases. You can specify these aliases following their respective table names in the FROM clause, and they can be used everywhere else in the query in place of the table name. Table aliases provide a convenient shorthand notation, allowing your queries to be more readable and concise.

 Table aliases are not limited to one character in length. Table aliases can be up to 30 characters in length.

An important thing to remember while using table aliases is that if you define aliases in the FROM clause, you must use only those aliases, and not the actual table names, in the rest of the query. If you alias a table, and then use the actual table name in a query, you will encounter errors. For example:

```
SELECT C.CUST_NBR, C.NAME, O.ORDER_NBR
FROM CUSTOMER C, CUST_ORDER O
WHERE CUSTOMER.CUST_NBR = CUST_ORDER.CUST_NBR;
WHERE CUSTOMER.CUST_NBR = CUST_ORDER.CUST_NBR
                         *
ERROR at line 3:
ORA-00904: invalid column name
```

The column CUST_NBR appears in both the CUSTOMER and CUST_ORDER tables. Without proper qualification, this column is said to be "ambiguously defined" in the query. Therefore, you must qualify the CUST_NBR column with a table alias (or a full table name, if your are not using aliases). However, the other two columns used in the query are not ambiguous. Therefore, the following statement, which only qualifies the CUST_NBR column, is valid:

```
SELECT C.CUST_NBR, NAME, ORDER_NBR
FROM CUSTOMER C, CUST_ORDER O
WHERE C.CUST_NBR = O.CUST_NBR;
```

```
CUST_NBR NAME                                    ORDER_NBR
-------- ------------------------------------    ----------
       1 Cooper Industries                             1001
       1 Cooper Industries                             1000
       5 Gentech Industries                            1002
       4 Flowtech Inc.                                 1003
       4 Flowtech Inc.                                 1004
       8 Zantech Inc.                                  1005
       1 Cooper Industries                             1006
       5 Gentech Industries                            1007
       5 Gentech Industries                            1008
       1 Cooper Industries                             1009
       1 Cooper Industries                             1012
       1 Cooper Industries                             1011
       5 Gentech Industries                            1015
       4 Flowtech Inc.                                 1017
       4 Flowtech Inc.                                 1019
       8 Zantech Inc.                                  1021
       1 Cooper Industries                             1023
       5 Gentech Industries                            1025
       5 Gentech Industries                            1027
       1 Cooper Industries                             1029

20 rows selected.
```

This is where the performance aspect of using table aliases comes into play. Since the query doesn't qualify the columns NAME and ORDER_NBR, Oracle has to search both the CUSTOMER and CUST_ORDER tables while parsing this statement to find which table each of these columns belongs to. The time required for this search may be negligible for one query, but it does add up if you have a number of such queries to parse. It's good programming practice to qualify *all* columns in a query with table aliases, even those that are not ambiguous, so that Oracle can avoid this extra search when parsing the statement.

Consider Literal SQL for Decision Support Systems

We discussed the benefits of using bind variables previously. The use of bind variables is often beneficial in terms of performance. However, there is a downside to consider. Bind variables hide actual values from the optimizer. This hiding of actual values can have negative performance implications, especially in decision support systems. For example, consider the following statement:

```
SELECT * FROM CUSTOMER WHERE REGION_ID = :X
```

The optimizer can parse this statement, but it won't be able to take into account the specific region being selected. If 90% of your customers were in region 5, then a full table scan would likely be the most efficient approach when selecting those customers. An index scan would probably be more efficient when selecting customers in other regions. When you hardcode values into your SQL statements, the cost-based optimizer (CBO) can look at histograms (a type of statistic) and generate an execution plan that takes into account the specific values you are supplying. When you use bind variables, however, the optimizer generates an execution plan without having a complete picture of the SQL statement. Such an execution plan may or may not be the most efficient.

In Decision Support Systems (DSS), it is very rare that multiple users use the same query over and over. More typically, a handful of users execute complex, different queries against a large database. Since it is very rare that the SQL statements will be repetitive, the parsing time saved by using bind variables will be negligible. At the same time, since DSS applications run complex queries against large databases, the time required to fetch the resulting data can be significant. Therefore, it is important that the optimizer generate the most efficient execution plan for the query. To help the optimizer generate the best possible plan, provide the optimizer as much information as you can, including the actual values of the columns or variables. Therefore, in DSS applications, use literal SQL statements with hardcoded values instead of bind variables.

Our earlier advice about using bind variables in Online Transaction Processing (OLTP) applications is still valid. In OLTP systems, multiple users all use the same programs, and thus issue the same queries. The amount of data returned per query is typically small. Thus, parse time is a more significant performance factor than in DSS systems. When developing OLTP applications, save parsing time and space in the shared SQL area by using bind variables.

Index

We'd like to hear your suggestions for improving our indexes. Send email to *index@oreilly.com*.

conditions *(continued)*
    equality/inequality, 19
    inner joins, 28
        equi-joins compared to
            non-equi-joins, 29
    joins, new syntax and, 51
    matching, 21
    membership, 20
    pattern-matching, 21
    precedence, 24
    range, 20
    union compatibility, 144
    WHERE clause, 15
CONNECT BY clause, hierarchical
    queries, 84
constants, GROUP BY clause, 60
containing statements, 68
Coordinated Universal Time (UTC), 125
correlated subqueries, 69, 75–77
CREATE TABLE statement, object
    tables, 204
CREATE TYPE BODY statement, 202
CUBE keyword
    group operations, 238–243
    partial, 242
CUME_DIST analytic function, 283
CURRENT ROW keywords
    windowing functions, 288
CURRENT_DATE function, 137
CURRENT_TIMESTAMP function, 137
customer table, SELECT statement
    example, 6

D

Data Definition Language (DDL), 1
data dictionary, views, USER_UPDATABLE_
    COLUMNS, 48
Data Manipulation Language (see DML)
data warehouse applications, group
    operations and, 229
datatypes
    DATE
        converting, 96
        default format, 97
        internal storage format, 95
        NULL values and, 152
        specifying format, 98
    join conditions, 29
    object types, 202
        attributes, 203
        parameters, 205
        tables, 204

DATE datatype
    converting, 96
        errors, 98
    default format, 97
    format, specifying, 98
    internal storage format, 95
    NULL values and, 152
dates
    arithmetic
        addition, 111
        overview, 111
        subtraction, 113
    format codes, 101–104
    formatting, 101
        case-sensitivity, 105
    functions, 135–143
    interval data, 130
        INTERVAL DAY TO SECOND
            datatype, 131
        INTERVAL YEAR TO MONTH
            datatype, 130
    ISO standards
        overview, 109
        weeks, 109
        years, 110
    literals, 108
    pivot tables, creating, 121
    ranges, SELECT statement, 120
    rounding/truncating, 116–119
    RTRIM function, 123
    summarizing by, 123
    time zones
        database, 125
        overview, 125
        session, 126
    working days, calculating, 123
    years
        AD/BC indicators, 104
        two-digit, 107
DATETIME functions, 135–143
days (working), calculating, 123
DBA_UPDATABLE_COLUMNS data
    dictionary view, 48
DBTIMEZONE function, 136
DBTIMEZONE keyword, 126
DDL (Data Definition Language), 1
Decision Support Systems (see DSS)
DECODE function
    divide by zero errors, 189
    errors, 176
    optional updates, 185
    result sets, transforming, 181

hierarchical trees, traversing, 163
horizontal partitioning, 193
hypothetical analytic functions, 284

I

if-then-else functionality, 179
implicit type conversions, DATE
    datatype, 98
IN operator, 20
    compared to EXISTS, 298
    multiple-row subqueries, 72
    outer joins, 33
indexes
    function-based, 121
    partitions, 194
inequality conditions, 19
inequality operator (!=), 19
inline views, 77
    aggregate queries, overcoming limitations
        of, 85
    columns, hiding with WITH CHECK
        OPTION, 88
    creating data sets, 80–83
    DML statements, 86
    errors, 87, 88
    execution, 78
    hierarchical queries, overcoming
        limitations of, 83
    mimicking analytic queries with, 269
    outer joins, 33
    overview, 77
    selective aggregation, 188
inner joins, 26, 30
    Cartesian products, 27
    conditions, 28
    equi-joins compared to
        non-equi-joins, 29
INSERT statement, 11
    DML (Data Manipulation Language), 1
    join views, 46
    partitions, specifying, 198
    strings, converting to default date
        format, 97
INTERSECT set operator, 145, 147
interval data (date and time), 130
    INTERVAL DAY TO SECOND
        datatype, 131
    INTERVAL YEAR TO MONTH
        datatype, 130
INTERVAL DAY TO SECOND
    datatype, 131
INTERVAL functions, 135–143

INTERVAL YEAR TO MONTH
    datatype, 130
ISO standards, dates
    overview, 109
    weeks, 109
    years, 110

J

JOIN keyword, 49
join views, 46
    DELETE statements, 46
    errors, 48
    INSERT statements, 46
    UPDATE statements, 47
joins, 26, 50
    ANSI syntax, 49
        advantages, 54
    anti-joins, 73
    conditions
        new syntax and, 51
        WHERE clause, 7, 24
    hierarchical queries, 174
    inner, 26
        Cartesian products, 27
        conditions, 28
        equi-joins compared to
            non-equi-joins, 29
    mimicking analytic queries with, 269
    outer, 30–32
        ANSI syntax, 51–54
        full, 34–37
        restrictions, 32
    self, 37
        non-equi, 39–42
        outer, 38
    semi-joins, 76
    stored functions, avoiding, 219
    subqueries, 42
    USING clause, 50
    vertical, 144
    views
        DML statements and, 43–49
        key-preserved tables, 43

K

key-preserved tables, join views, 43
keys
    foreign
        join conditions, 28
        relationships and, 4
    key-preserved tables, join views, 43

NOT operator
  pattern-matching and, 21
  WHERE clause, 18
NTILE analytic function, 279
NULL expression, 22–24
NULL values, 63
  aggregate functions, 57
  analytic ranking functions, 277
  compound queries, 151
  GROUP BY clause, 63
  NVL function compared to GROUPING
      function, 244–246
  testing for, 177
numbers, converting to dates, 97, 98
NUMTODSINTERVAL function, 141
NUMTOYMINTERVAL function, 141
NVL function, 23
  averages, 57
  NULL values, compared to GROUPING
      function, 244–246
  syntax, 175, 177
NVL2 function, syntax, 175, 177

O

object types, 202
  attributes, 203
  parameters, 205
  tables, 204
operators
  AND, 17
  BETWEEN, 20
  conditions, 18
  equality (=), 19
  EXISTS
    compared to DISTINCT keyword, 297
    compared to IN operator, 298
    correlated subqueries, 75
  greater than (>), 21
    self non-equi-joins, 41
  greater than or equal to (>=), 21
  IN, 20
    multiple-row subqueries, 72
    outer joins, 33
  inequality (!=), 19
  join conditions, 29
  less than (<), 21
    self non-equi-joins, 41
  less than or equal to (<=), 21
  LIKE, 21
  logical, WHERE clause, 16
  multiple-row subqueries, 71

NOT, 18
  pattern-matching and, 21
NOT BETWEEN, 21
NOT IN, 20
  multiple-row subqueries, 73
OR, 17
  efficiency considerations, 25
  outer joins, 34
outer join (+), 31
  self outer joins, 39
precedence, 24
PRIOR, hierarchical queries, 164
scalar subqueries, 69
set, 145
  INTERSECT, 145, 147
  MINUS, 145, 148, 149
  UNION, 145, 146
  UNION ALL, 145, 146, 149
subtraction (-), dates, 113
optimizer
  anti-joins, 73
  evaluating conditions, 15
  partition keys and, 200
  partition pruning, 199
  semi-joins, 76
  specifying partitions, 198
OR operator
  efficiency considerations, 25
  outer joins, 34
  WHERE clause, 17
ORA-00904 error, 88
ORA-00932 error, 176
ORA-01402 error, 89
ORA-01427 error, 72
ORA-01468 error, 32
ORA-01476 error, 189
ORA-01733 error, 48
ORA-01779 error, 87
ORA-01790 error, 152
ORA-01861 error, 99
Oracle Supplied Packages (PL/SQL), 214
Oracle9i, ANSI join syntax, 49
  advantages, 54
ORDER BY clause, 9, 174
  analytic ranking functions, 275
  set operations, 154
  stored functions, calling from, 218
outer join operator (+), 31
  self outer join operator, 39
outer joins, 26, 30–32
  ANSI syntax, 51–54
  errors, 32

restrictions, 32
self, 38
OUTER keyword, ANSI join syntax, 52
overloading functions, 216

P

package body, 215
package specification, 215
packages (stored procedures and
        functions), 214
parameters, object types, 205
parentheses ( )
    operator/condition precedence, 24
    subqueries, 68
parents
    hierarchical queries, 159
    root nodes, finding, 160
parsing, avoiding unnecessary, 302
PARTITION BY clause, analytic ranking
        functions, 276
PARTITION clause, 198
partition key, 193
    hash partitioning, 195
    optimizer and, 200
partitions
    composite, 196
    hash, 195
    horizontal, 193
    indexes, 194
    list, 197
    naming considerations, 199
    pruning, 199–201
    range, 194
    reporting functions, 293
    specifying, 198
    storage considerations, 193
    tables, overview, 192
    vertical, 193
    views, 199
pattern-matching
    built-in functions, 21
    conditions, 21
percent sign (%), pattern-matching
        character, 21
PERCENT_RANK analytic function, 283
performance
    OR operator, efficiency
            considerations, 25
    partitioning and, 192
    selective function execution, 183
pivot tables, dates, creating, 121

PL/SQL
    CASE expressions and, 179
    date pivot tables, 121
    including SQL, 226
    overview, 213
    stored functions compared to stored
            procedures, 214
    variables, converting to DATE
            datatype, 96
P.M. indicator (time format), 105
precedence, operator/condition, 24
primary keys
    comparing tables, 151
    join conditions, 29
PRIOR operator, hierarchical queries, 164
procedures, stored, compared to stored
        functions, 214
programming languages, nonprocedural, 1
programming, style issues, 24
pruning partitions, 199–201
pseudocolumns, LROWID, 8
purity levels, 221
    stored functions, 221

R

range conditions, 20
range partitions, 194
ranges
    dates, returning, 120
    eliminating gaps, 81
RANK analytic function, 92, 273–279
ranking analytic functions
    DENSE_RANK, 273–279
    overview, 272
    RANK, 273–279
    ROW_NUMBER, 273–279
RATIO_TO_REPORT analytic function, 294
records, listing in hierarchical
        order, 168–170
recursive relationships, traversing, 83
relationships, 4
    collection types, 207
        creating, 209
        nested tables, 208
        unnesting, 210
        variable arrays, 208
    correlated subqueries, 75
    hierarchical data
            representations, 157–159
    key-preserved tables, 45
    recursive, traversing, 83
    self-referential integrity constraints, 158

tables *(continued)*
  comparing, set operations, 149–151
  customer, SELECT statement example, 6
  entities, 4
  equi-joins compared to
    non-equi-joins, 29
  inner joins, 26
  joins, subqueries, 42
  key-preserved, join views and, 43
  modifying
    UPDATE statement, 16
    without WHERE clause, 14
  NOT NULL columns, INSERT statement
    and, 11
  object type, 204
  outer joins, 30–32
    full, 34–37
    restrictions, 32
  partitioning, overview, 192
  self joins, 37
    non-equi, 39–42
    outer, 38
  self-referential integrity constraints, 158
terminology, 3
  hierarchical queries, 159
text, date formatting, case-sensitivity
    rules, 106
time
  A.M./P.M. indicators, 105
  fractional seconds
    overview, 126
    TIMESTAMP datatype, 126
    TIMESTAMP WITH LOCAL TIME
      ZONE datatype, 129
    TIMESTAMP WITH TIME ZONE
      datatype, 127
  functions, 135–143
  rounding and truncating dates, 117
time zones
  database, 125
  default, 125
  NEW_TIME function, 119
  overview, 125
  session, 126
TIMESTAMP datatype, 126
TIMESTAMP WITH LOCAL TIME ZONE
    datatype, 129
TIMESTAMP WITH TIME ZONE
    datatype, 127
TO_CHAR function, 96
  combining with TO_DATE function, 100
  overview, 100

TO_DATE function, 96
  combining with TO_CHAR function, 100
  default date format, 97
  overview, 96
  specifying format, 98
TO_DSINTERVAL function, 142
top-n/bottom-n queries (analytic ranking
    functions), 277
TO_TIMESTAMP function, 138
TO_TIMESTAMP_TZ function, 139
TO_YMINTERVAL function, 142
traversing hierarchical trees, 163
TRUNC function, 116
  date pivot tables, 121
  date ranges and, 121
truncating dates, 116–119
TRUST keyword, stored procedures, 222
two-digit years, 107
TZ_OFFSET function, 143

U

underscore (_), pattern-matching
    character, 21
UNION ALL set operator, 145, 146
  comparing tables, 149
UNION clause, data sets, creating
    custom, 80
union compatibility conditions, 144
UNION operation compared to UNION
    ALL, 300
UNION queries, 230
  ANSI join syntax and, 54
  full outer joins, 36
UNION set operator, 145, 146
UPDATE statement, 12
  CASE expression, 184
  collections and, 211
  DECODE function, 184
  DML (Data Manipulation Language), 1
  inline views, 86
  join views, 47
  multiple-column subqueries, 74
  optional updates, 185
  selective aggregation, 186–189
  WHERE clause and, 16
USER_UPDATABLE_COLUMNS data
    dictionary view, 48
USING clause, 50
UTC (Coordinated Universal Time), 125

V

VALUE function, returning objects, 204
VARCHAR2 datatype, TO_DATE
        datatype, 96
variable arrays, 208
variables, blind, 303
varrays, 208
vertical joins, 144
vertical partitioning, 193
viewing all in schema, 48
views
    data dictionary, USER_UPDATABLE_
        COLUMNS, 48
    hierarchical queries, 174
    inline, 77
        aggregate queries, overcoming
           limitations of, 85
        creating data sets, 80–83
        DML statements, 86
        execution, 78
        hiding columns with WITH CHECK
           OPTION, 88
        hierarchical queries, overcoming
           limitations of, 83
        overview, 77
        selective aggregation, 188
    joins, DML statements and, 43–49
    outer joins, 33
    partitions, 199
    stored functions, 218

W

weekends, date math and, 123
weeks
    date math, 112
    ISO standard, 109
WHERE clause, 64
    capabilities of, 15
    columns, restricting access, 88

compared to HAVING clause, 299
conditions, 15
    components of, 18
    equality/inequality, 19
    matching, 21
    membership, 20
    range, 20
evaluation, 16–18
    conditions, 15
GROUP BY clause, 64
HAVING clause and, 66
hierarchical queries, filtering, 168
join conditions, 24, 28
logical operators, 16
new join syntax and, 49
noncorrelated subqueries, 70
NULL expression, 22–24
outer join operator (+), 31
partition pruning, 199
subqueries, 69
tips for using, 24
UPDATE statement and, 16
value of, 14
WHERE clause (SELECT statements), 6
WIDTH_BUCKET analytic function, 280
windowing analytic functions, 286–289
WITH CHECK OPTION clause, 46
WITH CHECK OPTION, hiding
        columns, 88
working days, calculating, 123
WW (ISO week) indicator, 109

Y

years
    A.D./B.C. indicators, 104
    finding number between dates, 115
    ISO standard, 110
    two-digit, 107
YY (year) indicator, 107

About the Authors

Sanjay Mishra is a certified Oracle database administrator with more than ten years of IT experience. He has been involved in the design, architecture, and implementation of many mission-critical and decision support databases. He has worked extensively in database architecture, database management, backup/recovery, performance tuning, Oracle Parallel Server, and parallel execution. He has a Bachelor of Science degree in Electrical Engineering and a Master of Engineering degree in Systems Science and Automation. He is the coauthor of *Oracle Parallel Processing* and *Oracle SQL Loader: The Definitive Guide* (both published by O'Reilly). Presently, he works as a database architect at Dallas-based i2 Technologies, and can be reached at *Sanjay_Mishra@i2.com*.

Alan Beaulieu has been designing, building, and implementing custom database applications for over 13 years. He currently runs his own consulting company that specializes in designing Oracle databases and supporting services in the fields of financial services and telecommunications. In building large databases for both OLTP and OLAP environments, Alan utilizes such Oracle features as Parallel Query, Partitioning, and Parallel Server. Alan has a Bachelor of Science degree in Operations Research from the Cornell University School of Engineering. He lives in Massachusetts with his wife and two daughters and can be reached at *albeau_mosql@yahoo.com*.

Colophon

Our look is the result of reader comments, our own experimentation, and feedback from distribution channels. Distinctive covers complement our distinctive approach to technical topics, breathing personality and life into potentially dry subjects.

The insect on the cover of *Mastering Oracle SQL* is a lantern fly. The lantern fly is mostly tropical, with a wingspan of up to six inches. The lantern fly's elongated head is an evolutionary adaptation called automimicry, in which parts of the body are disguised or artifically shifted to other areas to confuse predators: the lantern fly's head looks like a tail, and its tail looks like a head. On the rear it has artificial eyes and antennae.

Colleen Gorman was the production editor and copyeditor for *Mastering Oracle SQL*. Sheryl Avruch and Ann Schirmer provided quality control. Tom Dinse wrote the index.

Ellie Volckhausen and Emma Colby designed the cover of this book, based on a series design by Edie Freedman. The cover image is a 19th-century engraving from Johnson's *Natural History*. Emma Colby produced the cover layout with Quark-XPress 4.1 using Adobe's ITC Garamond font.

David Futato designed the interior layout. Neil Walls converted the files from Microsoft Word to FrameMaker 5.5.6 using tools written in Perl by Erik Ray, Jason McIntosh, and Neil Walls, as well as tools written by Mike Sierra. The text font is Linotype Birka; the heading font is Adobe Myriad Condensed; and the code font is LucasFont's TheSans Mono Condensed. The illustrations that appear in the book were produced by Robert Romano and Jessamyn Read using Macromedia FreeHand 9 and Adobe Photoshop 6. The tip and warning icons were drawn by Christopher Bing. This colophon was written by Colleen Gorman.